Acknowledgements

Many people have helped with information for this book, starting with the ministers who have so obligingly opened their chapels for me to view and the owners of converted chapels who have talked so knowledgeably about the history of their homes. Across the county numerous representatives of local history societies and local museums, as well as individuals, have supplied me with invaluable data, particularly the following: Richard Adams, Angela Armstrong of Bourne Valley Historical Society, Michael Asbury, Nick Baxter, Carolyn Birch of Redlynch and District Local History Society, Sue Boddington, David Broome, Allie Burchill of North Wiltshire Methodist Circuit, Neil Burton, David Chandler, Alan Clarke of Salisbury Museum, Sara Crabb, Pam Debenham of Cricklade Museum, Nick Fogg, Bruce Fox, Richard Giles, John Hacker, Lyn Hartman, Judith Hassey of Tisbury History Society, Rosalind Johnson, Elaine Jones, Rev. Ward Jones, Gordon Lewis, Peter Maslen of Melksham Historical Association, Roger Mawby, the late Roger Newman, Ruth Newman, Nikki Ritson of Trowbridge Museum, Peter Roberts, Michael Rumsey, Peter Saunders, Jane Schon of Wiltshire Museum, Christopher Sloane, Roger Smith of Wootton Bassett Museum, Mary Spender, Christina Staff,

Monkton Hill Wesleyan, Chippenham: the dentilled lunette windows echo the organ arch; choir stalls and pulpit combined below create a single focus.

The ceremonial opening of Froxfield Primitive Methodist in 1909.
Photograph courtesy of Tim Allen.

Mike Stone, Christine Suter of Highworth Historical Society, Sally Thomson and Bea Tilbrook.

The story of nonconformity in Swindon is a particularly complicated one to unravel and here I have been greatly helped by the substantial work undertaken by Clive Carter, Hilary Dunscombe and Tom Smith, as well as by Katherine Cole of Swindon libraries and Paul Williams of the Swindon Society.

Lastly I would like again to thank Pam Slocombe and Dorothy Treasure of the Wiltshire Buildings Record for their continuing advice and support, Julian Orbach for kindly giving me access to his notes and draft text for the new Wiltshire 'Buildings of England', John Chandler for his many helpful comments as well as his work as Hobnob Press in producing this book, and the ever-helpful staff of the Wiltshire and Swindon History Centre.

WILTSHIRE NONCONFORMIST CHAPELS
AND MEETING HOUSES

Horningsham Congregational, interior

*This book has been generously grant aided
by the Marc Fitch Fund*

Wiltshire Nonconformist Chapels and Meeting Houses

a Guide and Gazetteer

James Holden

HOBNOB PRESS

for the

WILTSHIRE BUILDINGS RECORD

First published in the United Kingdom in 2022
on behalf of the Wiltshire Buildings Record
by The Hobnob Press, 8 Lock Warehouse, Severn Road, Gloucester GL1 2GA.
        www.hobnobpress.co.uk

British Library Cataloguing in Publication Data
A catalogue record for this book is available from the British Library.

ISBN 978-1-914407-28-4

Typeset in 10/12 pt Scala. Typesetting and origination by John Chandler

The Wiltshire Buildings Record is a voluntary society and educational charity, with members in historic Wiltshire and beyond. The archive of the Record, gathered together since 1979 from fieldwork and from a variety of sources, covers over 18,500 sites representing buildings of all dates and types. The collection is housed at the Wiltshire & Swindon History Centre, Cocklebury Road, Chippenham, Wiltshire SN15 3QN, telephone 01249 705508, www.wiltshirebuildingsrecord.org.uk. It is open to the public on Tuesdays, 9 a.m. to 5 p.m. or by arrangement.

Also available from Wiltshire Buildings Record:

Wiltshire Farmhouses and Cottages 1500-1850	£6
Medieval Houses of Wiltshire	£6
Wiltshire Town Houses 1500-1900	£6
Architects and Building Craftsmen with Work in Wiltshire (Part 1)	£5
Architects and Craftsmen with Work in Wiltshire (Part 2)	£5
Wiltshire Village Reading Rooms (Ivor Slocombe)	£8
Wiltshire Gate Lodges (James Holden)	£8

        All plus £1.50 per copy post and packing.

The Dovecotes and Pigeon Lofts of Wiltshire (J & P McCann)	reduced to £5
Wiltshire Almshouses and their Founders (Sally Thomson)	£10.50

        Both plus £2.50 per copy post and packing

You can help the Record by allowing us to copy photographs, drawings and any other information, structural or historical you may have about Wiltshire buildings. Please join the Record and help to record buildings in your locality or assist us by drawing our attention to threatened buildings which may be worth recording.

Contents

All photographs are by the author except where otherwise indicated

Front cover illustration: Zion Baptist Chapel, Lea (Lea & Cleverton)
Back cover illustration: Chippenham, Monkton Hill Wesleyan Methodist

1. Introduction

Nonconformist chapels and meeting houses derive ultimately from the Protestant Reformation but much more directly from the English Civil War, which left those who opposed the trappings, ritual and hierarchy of the established church in a strong position. Indeed, for a while the old church was just one amongst a number of Protestant sects alongside Presbyterians, Independents, Baptists, Quakers and others.

But King Charles the Second, restored to the throne in 1660, promptly set the clock back as if the events of the preceding 20 years had not taken place. The Puritans were no longer to be tolerated; they were dissenters from the established church and must be suppressed. There was a brief period of relaxation following his Declaration of Indulgence in 1672 but a growing fear of 'Popish plots' soon ended even that limited tolerance. Only in 1689, with the Act of Toleration, was the often-fierce persecution of those years eased and it was from that date that the nonconformists were able to worship in relative peace in the chapels they were at last able to build.

A few brave communities had built chapels in the brief intervals after 1660 in which it appeared there might be more tolerance, but by 1689 there were still almost none in Wiltshire, or any other county. The Wesleyan revival contributed to growth through the eighteenth century but by 1800 there were still only around 100 chapels here,[1] though many more people were meeting for worship in houses and other buildings. The period of major growth was the first half of the nineteenth century: by 1850 a combination of evangelism and a rapidly growing population had increased the Wiltshire total to around 400, and these were no longer concentrated in the towns but spread out across more and more communities. By 1900 the number had increased further to around 550.

This growth has left us with very many interesting buildings, all with a story to tell and many of real architectural interest. The purpose of this book is to describe these buildings, and those added to the total in the twentieth century.

If the rate of growth was fast, so has been the decline. There are still about 480 chapels standing but only 180 of those are in use: the remainder have been converted for other purposes, usually as houses, or are derelict. Since 1900 about 150 chapels have been demolished.

This history of expansion and decline is illustrated in the buildings which remain. Chapel builders were persecuted in the early days and often opposed well into the nineteenth century; their buildings were consequently simple, small and often hidden away. By the mid nineteenth century those times had largely passed and most village chapels assumed that simple dignity of design which is so characteristic. In towns, the astonishing growth in congregations led to ever bigger buildings, holding sometimes over 1,000 people, and with a far more assertive presence. Towards the end of the century that growing confidence meant that worshippers no longer defined themselves with respect to the Anglican church as 'nonconformists', but instead as members of fully independent Free Churches, willing and able to build highly decorated chapels in a variety of styles.

There are numerous Edwardian chapels but attendances declined rapidly following the First World War and chapel building almost ceased. There are a few from the 1930s and a number of post-war chapels, particularly those serving new housing areas, but far fewer than in the previous century.

Though chapels are designed in a wide range of styles, all are characterised by the sense that they derive from the commitment of a community of worshippers, that they are the work of the people rather than built at the behest of the wealthy as was so often the case with Anglican churches. There is integrity in the design of these buildings: appealing simplicity, sometimes eccentricity and always a rootedness reflecting their central role in the communities they served. And when we reach the large town chapels of the nineteenth century there are splendours as well.

Attendance at chapel has been in decline for over a hundred years and, while many of those remaining will surely continue to prosper, there are others where the congregation is now small and elderly. Chapels are still closing: several have done so even during the period of research for this book. Most of those which close will become houses and, though residential conversions are nowadays generally far more sensitive to the building's original purpose than in the past, nevertheless a converted chapel is inevitably in some way diminished. This book is thus both a celebration of the delights of so much chapel design and a record against the likelihood that further buildings will be lost in the years ahead.

In the book I set out to describe all the chapels and former chapels still standing in Wiltshire, including the Borough of Swindon, with enough description of the past history and of previous buildings to give adequate context. To be fully comprehensive and accurate is an aim not easily achieved but I hope that, through my own research and through the information given me by many contacts across the county, it will not fall far short of the target.

There are many different nonconformist churches and this book concentrates on the main groups, namely the Independents/Congregationalists, Quakers, Baptists, Methodists, Brethren, Moravians and the Salvation Army. Other groups are also mentioned but Christian Scientists, Jehovah's Witnesses and Mormons, all of which might be viewed as not adhering to the central tenets of Protestant religion, are not included; nor are chapels associated with cemeteries, workhouses and other private institutions. Schoolrooms, so frequently found, are often an integral part of the chapel building so are described, but manses and chapel graveyards are usually not.

This introduction is followed by a short history of nonconformity in Wiltshire, tracing the development of the different denominations and intended to help understanding of the background to the chapels detailed later. A further introductory chapter then describes the development of chapel design, from the simplest early buildings to the large town churches of later times, looking not only at the external appearance but also how the interior layout reflected the nature of nonconformist worship.

Then comes the main part of the book, the gazetteer, describing chapels place by place. Village chapels are considered first, then those in the smaller towns where the history of chapel development is often more complicated. Finally the four largest urban areas – Chippenham, Salisbury, Swindon and Trowbridge – are treated separately: chapels here are present in large numbers, particularly in Salisbury and Swindon, and the history has to be untangled to appreciate the place of each building.

It may seem disrespectful to make aesthetic judgements about the appearance of religious buildings but it would be misleading to pretend that all chapels are equal. Judgements are made, therefore, and what I consider the more interesting ones are highlighted with a star; those of exceptional interest or importance are given two stars. There are plenty amongst these which are worth going out of one's way to see. Exteriors are generally visible, though the privacy of people living in converted chapels should of course be respected. Some interiors of those in use are particularly interesting and, though few are left open nowadays, contact with the minister will often produce the opportunity to see inside.

The book ends with an assessment of the role of different architects in chapel design and a list of those known to have been involved in Wiltshire.

There are two halves to the chapel story. One is about the people, whose faith and persistence created so many of these buildings: their story is not told here but is related in the many chapel histories available online or in the Wiltshire and Swindon History Centre and other archives and libraries. The second half is about the buildings themselves, and I hope that this book will provide a useful guide to these, in all their variety.

A note on terminology

Early nonconformist buildings were often called meeting houses, and some denominations, notably the Quakers, still use that name. The term 'chapel' was in general use right through to the late nineteenth century; thereafter the buildings were often called churches. In a similar way the term 'nonconformist' tended to be replaced around that time by 'free church', and both of these changes reflected the increased self-confidence of congregations which no longer defined themselves solely by reference to the Anglican church. In this book I have generally used the words 'chapel' or 'meeting house' for the building and 'church' for the body of people worshipping there.

The denomination using a particular chapel has sometimes changed during its life and the denominations themselves have changed names over the last hundred years: Congregational chapels are now mostly United Reformed; General, Strict and Particular Baptists are mostly known just as Baptist; and Wesleyan, Primitive and other groups of Methodists are combined as Methodists. I have generally used the name of the owning denomination as it was known for the major period of the chapel's life.

2. *Nonconformity in Wiltshire*[2]

The range of nonconformist chapels is vast, from the early vernacular building scarcely distinguishable from a cottage to the Victorian Gothic town church of almost cathedral-like proportions. Each is what it is and where it is because of the local history of that denomination, the strength of its congregation and its ministers, and the often complicated relationships between different branches of the same church. These individual histories are indicated in the gazetteer to give a context for each building, while this chapter provides an introduction to the wider background of nonconformist development in Wiltshire.

Early Dissent

In the sixteenth century all English Protestants objected to the practices of the Roman Catholic church but, when a reformed Protestant church was established by Queen Elizabeth after the violent swings in the short reigns of Edward and Mary, it became clear that many objected to that as well, chiefly on the grounds that it was insufficiently distanced from Catholic ritual. These were the Protestant dissenters and they believed that the Protestant Reformation was as yet incomplete. They wished to strip away church ceremony and formulaic prayers, instead seeking God by reading the Bible, praying in groups and listening to the evangelical sermons of learned and zealous ministers.

There are some records of religious dissent in Wiltshire from that time, but it was in the following century, culminating in the Civil War, that dissent gained rapidly in strength. By that time four groups were active, though definitions of each remained fluid for a considerable time. The Presbyterians, governed by representative assemblies of elders, came to the fore during the Commonwealth period. Independents or Congregationalists believed in the autonomy of the single congregation: in later years almost all became known as Congregationalist. Baptists developed slightly later than these and were characterised by a belief in the necessity for adult baptism of believers. Quakers, more correctly known as the Society of Friends, believed in direct experience of Christ without the aid of clergy and came to prominence nationally from the 1650s.

Three parts of the county appear to have been early breeding grounds for dissent from the beginning of the seventeenth century. The first was the Box/Castle Combe area, the second was the cloth-working district stretching from Bradford on Avon down to Warminster, and the third was Salisbury. By mid-century there was a strong body of Puritan clergy in the county, mostly Presbyterian or Independent. Other more radical groups were developing, including Baptists at Salisbury, Calne and Southwick, the last-named the start of a Baptist community which remained prominent for long afterwards. Quakers were later arriving but by the end of the Commonwealth period there were meetings in the Marlborough and Devizes/Lavington areas and also in Calne, Chippenham and elsewhere.

The Restoration Period

Under the Commonwealth, with the oversight of bishops removed, there was a relatively relaxed attitude to experimentation in church services, but any hope that the Restoration of Charles II in 1660 might see a continuation of such tolerance was soon dashed. Instead, he restored the Church of England to its previous position. The Act of Uniformity of 1662 required ministers to accept everything in the book of common prayer and led to the ejection of 2000 nationally from their livings. 60 of these were in Wiltshire, though some had been removed even before the passing of the Act.

Further repressive Acts followed, including the Conventicle Act of 1664 which made it illegal for five persons, in addition to the occupiers of a house, to assemble for religious worship; the 1665 Five Mile Act which forbade nonconforming ministers from coming within five miles of any place where they had previously officiated; and the 1673 Test Act which excluded nonconformists and Roman Catholics from civil offices and military commands.

During this period dissenters were hounded and many Quakers, regarded as the most subversive of the dissenting sects, were imprisoned, usually for their refusal to pay tithes for the support of the established church. But this by no means suppressed dissenting worship. In Wiltshire, though the Church of England was fierce in opposition, many magistrates were lenient towards dissent and by 1669 there were over 60 clandestine meetings taking place in the county. A few worshipped openly, for example at Warminster, and many more met in secluded spots, often outdoors and sometimes near the county boundary so that they could if necessary flee into another magistrate's jurisdiction.

Many Independent meetings in towns - for example Calne, Malmesbury, Marlborough, Salisbury and Westbury - were formed in this same period. The Quakers expanded rapidly in the 1660s and by 1678 there were meetings in eighteen places, but at the same time continued persecution meant that some from Wiltshire were amongst those choosing to emigrate to America.

Few Baptist ministers had taken church livings during the Commonwealth period so the 1662 Act had relatively less effect on them. Most of their early churches were formed in villages, particularly on the Wiltshire/Somerset border and in the river valleys converging on Salisbury. Southwick Baptist already had 200 to 300 members by 1669 and was 'planting' churches in other communities, including by tradition Bradford on Avon.

Unsurprisingly, purpose-built meeting houses were rare but two from this period do still exist, both built by Quakers. That at Slaughterford (Biddestone), of c1670, is now a ruin on a remote hillside while the Monks Chapel at Corsham, of 1662 and later to become Congregational, is still in use and contains a truly remarkable interior. Both of these provided well-hidden retreats for worshippers, as did another example, the Quakers' meeting house at Cumberwell on the outskirts of Bradford on Avon.

The 1689 Act and After

Though it was the arrival of William and Mary in the 'Glorious Revolution' of 1688 which brought about the beginnings of religious tolerance, the feeling had been growing for some years under both Charles II and James II that acceptance of nonconformity would not be such a threat to the state as had been feared in the past. The result, under William and Mary, was the 1689 Act of Toleration.

This gave freedom of worship to most nonconformists but not to Unitarians (those who denied the Holy Trinity) and Roman Catholics. This freedom, combined with growing support from more affluent members of the community – clothiers, farmers and country gentry – meant that more chapels were built, to supplement the meetings in houses and barns. The Quakers had already been building in anticipation and in 1690 made an application to register 22 premises as Quaker meeting houses, 17 in the north of the county where Quaker presence was strongest and five in the south.[3] Only 10 of these were purpose-built, the remainder being rooms set aside in people's houses, and in this early period this was very much the pattern. Registration was a requirement of the 1689 Act and the records show that before 1700 newly built chapels were a small minority of those registered, with houses and barns much the majority.[4] These various buildings, under the provisions of the Act, were not to be locked, barred or bolted during meetings, for fear of conspiracies.

Examples still standing from this early period include Grittleton Baptist of c1720, Tisbury Independent of 1726, Avebury Congregational of 1707, Bradford on Avon Grove Presbyterian of 1698, the Quaker meeting house of 1704 in Devizes and the Presbyterian of 1704 in Warminster. Horningsham Congregational, which proclaims the remarkably early date of 1566 on its gable, is believed actually to have been built in this period, c1700.

These were the buildings of the 'Old Dissent' – Presbyterians, Independents/Congregationalists, Quakers and Baptists – and in the period of roughly 50 years from 1689 many more such were built. Much of this was consolidation, the replacement of barn or house meetings by chapels, and there was actually little expansion amongst Baptists and Independents. The Presbyterians and Quakers had already started to contract.

The strictly enforced dogma of the established church had discouraged dissent but once groups had successfully broken away the seed was sown and it was not surprising that there were further splits. The cause of one such, and a part explanation of the decline in Presbyterian congregations, was the conflict between Unitarian and Trinitarian belief which flared up during this period. The Grove meeting house in Bradford on Avon, for example, was moving towards Unitarianism in the 1730s, provoking a group to secede and form the Morgan's Hill Congregational chapel.

Baptists split over the same issue, but the earlier and perhaps more fundamental split was between Particular Baptists, who believed in the Calvinist teaching that God had predestined only certain people for salvation and that everyone else was doomed however good a life they led, and the General Baptists who believed that everyone had the opportunity to secure personal salvation, part of the so-called Arminian doctrine. Later, many General Baptists became Unitarian

Bratton Baptist Chapel

Bradford on Avon, Old Baptist Chapel

and a third grouping, called Strict Baptists, formed. The Strict Baptists believed that only those who had had full immersion baptism as adults should have access to communion: most but not all were also Particular.

This pattern of splits was to be repeated in the century ahead, with many variations in belief. Only the Congregationalists were largely immune to it.

Wesley and the Religious Revival

The second half of the eighteenth century was an era of great preachers and evangelists. The spark to light this flame came from the Methodists but Independents and Baptists benefited from the new religious enthusiasm and even the Presbyterians and Quakers gained some improvement in their fortunes. The expansion was also caused in part by disillusionment at Anglicanism's lack of emotional and social engagement and with the authoritarianism and social exclusivity of its clergy.

The term Methodist came from the supposedly methodical way of life undertaken by a group of Oxford dons and students in the 1730s, of whom John Wesley and his brother Charles were two, but it was after 1738 that John Wesley turned away from securing his personal salvation and towards bringing salvation to others. Always loyal to the Church of England, he nevertheless soon created friction with his inspirational preaching. Thus he came to Bradford on Avon from his base in Bristol in 1739, was coldly received by the parish priest and the minister of the Grove chapel, so then preached in a nearby field where he attracted an audience of 1000.

Wesley always considered himself an Anglican: he did not preach at the same time as Anglican services and resisted the creation of separate chapels, though he did encourage the provision of meeting rooms which soon became preaching rooms in practice. But the 'enthusiasm' shown by him and George Whitefield, another member of the Oxford group who can lay perhaps equal claim to the founding of Methodism, caused resentment, as did the fact that their preaching emptied nearby Anglican churches. The result was that Methodism began to be established as an independent denomination, not an offshoot of the Church of England, and with that chapels began to be founded in Wiltshire as elsewhere. Early Methodist centres were in the larger towns where there were already dissenting bodies, mainly Bradford on Avon, Devizes, Salisbury and Trowbridge. Others were in the countryside, including the 1775 chapel in Seend which was opened by Wesley himself.

Early in his career Wesley had come under the influence of the Moravians, of a church originally founded in Bohemia in the 15th century, whose communal living and quiet spirituality had a profound effect on him. One of these, John Cennick, who had split with Wesley on theological grounds in 1740, founded the East Tytherton (Bremhill) Moravian settlement in 1742.

George Whitefield was a Calvinist, believing in Calvin's doctrine that God had predestined the majority of mankind to eternal damnation but a few to salvation through Jesus Christ. Wesley rejected this view and held the Arminian belief that personal salvation was possible for all. They split around 1751, whereafter Wesley 'constructed' Wesleyan Methodism and continued his peripatetic preaching until his death in 1791. Whitefield spent substantial periods in North America and died there in 1770.

In 1748 Whitefield had become chaplain to Selina, Countess of Huntingdon, a fellow Calvinist. A rich widow, she established the Countess of Huntingdon's Connexion, following his advice to erect chapels, engage ministers and found a training college. The Connexion of that period can be considered a subset of Methodism for 'polite society', though since then most of its churches have become Congregational. In Wiltshire the Bearfield chapel in Bradford on Avon became a Connexion church for a period from c1816 and the Union chapel at Kington Langley was built in 1835 for the Connexion but with joint use by Independents and Baptists. These are thought to be the only examples in the county.

The Wesleyan revival sparked growth also in other nonconformist denominations. As examples, Congregational churches at Chippenham, Corsham, Lacock and several other places are all supposed to have been inspired directly by the revival.[5] Registrations under the 1689 Act show the growth of nonconformity in Wiltshire in the late eighteenth century from an average four a year in the 1770s to six a year in the 1780s and 16 in the 1790s, with 45 buildings registered in 1798 alone.[6] Preaching was often carried out by lay people – 50 to 60 are said to have streamed out from Salisbury each Sunday in the 1790s[7] – and often took place outdoors. Tracts were distributed to the literate minority in the hope that they might read to others.

The surge of registrations at the end of the century seems to have been due firstly to people being led towards religion by the hardship caused by poor harvests and the wars with France. New enthusiasm for foreign missionary work seems also to have provoked the view that there were still many 'heathens' at home to be converted and hence a need for renewed missionary efforts. The combined effect of these was to alarm the established church which, already frightened at the possibility of a French-style revolution, responded with a barrage of pamphlets. These in turn provoked a fear amongst nonconformists that there might be new restrictions and so further increased the pace of registration.[8]

The newly registered buildings were much more likely to be houses or barns than purpose-built chapels: throughout the late 18th century well over half of all registrations in Wiltshire were for houses or barns and in the peak year of 1798 all but one were. This trend was obviously accentuated by the urgency of the times but remained typical. Groups newly formed would usually meet first in a house before undertaking the substantial commitment of funding and building a chapel. Some groups never reached the chapel-building stage and either continued worshipping in a room in a house for the long term or else faded away. Hence, in the gazetteers which follow, the absence of a recorded chapel for a particular denomination in any place does not necessarily imply that that denomination was absent from there.

Apart from Methodists, Congregationalists/Independents and Baptists were the main beneficiaries of this growth. Congregational chapels of the 1790s include those at Corsham, Westbury (the Upper Meeting) and Wilton, and in villages such as Atworth and Winterbourne Dauntsey. Baptist building at the same time included chapels at Bradford, Westbury Leigh and Chapmanslade. Somewhat earlier were St Mary's, Devizes, the Providence Chapel, Bradenstoke (Lyneham) and Old Broughton Road, Melksham.

Although their meeting house in Melksham was rebuilt in this same period, this should not mask the long-term decline of the Quakers, which continued through into the next century. The same can be said of Presbyterianism, which had almost disappeared before 1900. Indeed, the overall growth of nonconformity in the eighteenth century should not be exaggerated: Church of England priests making their returns for the bishop's visitation of 1783 claimed that 158 parishes in the county had no dissenters in them at all.⁹ The Anglican clergy are unlikely to have been objective reporters about something they opposed but nevertheless this does illustrate just how much growth was still to come.

If the expansion of nonconformity should not be exaggerated, so the continued opposition to it should not be under-estimated. As one example amongst many, the influential preacher Rowland Hill visited Devizes twice in 1771 and preached in the open air. The second meeting was broken up by a mob instigated by Edward Innes, the assistant curate who some years before had stirred up opposition to Wesley himself.¹⁰ Even early in the next century, when the Primitive Methodists began to be active in Highworth, it was reported that the members were driven from 'cottage to cottage and so violently opposed by earth and hell that they could not for weeks together hold a meeting in peace'.¹¹ They eventually managed to build a chapel in 1838.

As if to rub salt into the wounds of such mistreatment, nonconformists in the eighteenth century, and for many years to come, still had to pay tithes. These payments, in kind until turned into money payments by the Tithe Commutation Act of 1836, were for the upkeep of the established church and its clergy and hence the cause of much resentment.

The Nineteenth Century

The greatest expansion of the Baptists in Wiltshire came between 1800 and 1850. This was driven particularly by a zeal for village preaching, with 'village stations' starting as cottage meetings but often ending in the provision of small chapels. There were 16 Baptist churches in the county in 1798 but 31 in 1827 and 77 in 1889, with 23 village stations in addition. Trowbridge Back Street Baptist, for example, produced village stations at Lower Westwood, Upper Studley and Yarnbrook. This support of smaller chapels by larger continued over a long period: as late as 1900 the rebuilding of the Bodenham (Odstock) Baptist was part-funded by Brown Street in Salisbury.

Baptists also expanded with the growing towns in places like Warminster, Westbury, Trowbridge, Chippenham and particularly Swindon, with its rapid growth following the arrival of the railway works. Not all chapel construction was purely down to growth, however, for splits developed not only between Particular and General Baptists but also between these and the Strict Baptists. There were other splinter groups also, as well as numerous personality clashes, often with a new preacher, which led to congregations splitting into two and new chapels being built. One example is in Trowbridge, where by 1830 there were five Baptist chapels: Little Bethel broke from Zion, which with Bethesda had broken from Back Street, which itself had broken from the original Baptist meeting at Conigre which by then had become Unitarian.

Each Congregationalist church was fully independent from external control but despite this there remained a remarkable uniformity of faith and practices. Not so with the Methodists, who split at least as much as the Baptists. Wesleyan Methodism remained the biggest grouping but before the century was far advanced there were also Primitive Methodists, the Methodist New Connexion, Bible Christians and others.

The Primitive Methodists were the most numerous of these breakaway sects, formed at the start of the century by a group which thought the Wesleyans were becoming too 'respectable' and moving too far from the 'primitive' roots of their faith. A dispute over the holding of camp meetings led to their foundation in 1810, whereafter the main body began to call themselves Wesleyan Methodists. Primitive Methodism was often seen as more working class than Wesleyan, although this generalisation may hide significant variation from place to place. The impact of the Primitive Methodists was considerable: as one admittedly partisan figure claimed, 'In the days of the foxhunting parson they were almost alone in caring for the souls of the villagers.'[12]

The vigorous growth of Congregationalism, so evident in the later eighteenth century, continued but with gradually slackening force. The largest expansion in the new century came from Methodism, though from the 1830s the more radical Primitive Methodists were more active than the Wesleyans, focussing on places neglected by them. Thus Samuel Heath, who began the Primitive Methodist mission to Wiltshire, established his first base at Brinkworth in 1824 and in the next couple of years claimed to have created missions in eight towns from Malmesbury down to Devizes. Brinkworth then, for the next twenty years and more, became a major centre for the expansion of Primitive Methodism, initiating circuits of meetings in areas as far afield as Bristol, Cirencester and Cheltenham: an astonishing achievement for such a tiny community.[13]

Countywide, the Methodists had only 13 meeting houses in 1802 but nearly 300 by 1935, of which the great majority were built before 1900. Managing such a rapidly expanding network was a challenge. The Methodists had from early on worked in local circuits, with ministers preaching at all the chapels in the circuit in turn in a carefully laid out circuit plan; amongst other benefits this ensured that less well supported meetings still received visits from all the ministers. They, like other denominations, also relied heavily on local preachers: in the Brinkworth circuit in 1907 there were 22 Primitive Methodist meetings served by only four ministers, two of them 'superannuated', but they had 57 local preachers and 74 Sunday school teachers to help them.[14]

The Brethren, sometimes known as Plymouth Brethren because their first centre in England was in that city, were formed in Dublin in the 1820s but active in England from 1831. They believed in the Bible as the sole source of authority, hence had no ministers but held services led by elders. They established themselves in Wiltshire from mid century, initially in smaller towns such as Calne, Corsham, Marlborough and Mere. The group split in 1848 into two main strands, the Exclusive and the Open Brethren, and there have been other splits since then.

A much smaller group was the Catholic Apostolic Church, developing in London from the 1830s and started by ministers whose evangelism and belief in prophecy led them to be rejected by the established church. To that degree they were nonconformist but they never considered themselves such and indeed their use of a hierarchy of bishops, priests and deacons as well as their churches provided with altars marked them apart from all other nonconformist denominations. They never had many churches in England: the maximum was around 110 at the start of the 20th century and there is now only one, in London.

Over a hundred years after the Act of Toleration there was still widespread opposition to nonconformity. For example, Methodists attending the St Edmund's Church Street chapel in Salisbury early in the century were taunted by mobs who 'would follow them up from Harnham with tin pots, kettles and frying pans..... and no one to interfere, no policeman, no order, no nothing.'[15] The Congregationalists opened their new chapel in Highworth in 1825 and found their services disrupted by invaders who talked loudly, laughed and played tin whistles or fiddles.[16] When Wesleyans were negotiating with the Great Western Railway for a new site for a chapel in Swindon in the 1860s, the objection of the Bishop of Bristol and Gloucester that a proposed site was too close to the Anglican church was enough to prevent the sale.[17]

Building a chapel gave ample opportunity for disruptive opposition and there are many examples in Wiltshire. The opposition when Congregationalists in Tisbury built their first chapel in the High Street in 1726 was so severe that it had to be built at night by quarrymen, their wives and daughters guarding it during the daytime. More than a hundred years later, in 1840, Primitive Methodists in Hindon obtained a plot of land for a chapel, but there was so much objection that they also had to build at night, over a stile because the farmer had locked the gate into the field. In Sutton Veny in 1793 there was opposition to the building of the Independent chapel and one farmer threatened to pull down the walls as they were being erected: it is said that he died in mysterious circumstances the night before he intended to do so.[18] As a final example from late on, when Primitive Methodists came to build their chapel at Lydiard Green in 1863 the local brickmaker refused to sell them bricks, no doubt fearing the anger of the lord of the manor who was also the village parson. They procured their bricks from further afield and built their chapel, whereupon the lord of the manor attempted to claim the land upon which the chapel was built as his; the claim failed.[19]

Even when there was little or no opposition the effort involved in building for a poor community was great. At Derry Hill, Lord Lansdowne leased a site for the Little Zoar chapel early in the century and local farmers lent men and horses; but even so the women had to dig out stone from the quarry during the day and their husbands move it to the site in the evenings.[20] Despite these difficulties, many early chapels were built with impressive speed: the 1815 Southwick Old Baptist, a substantial building, had its foundation stone laid in May and opened on 1st November.[21] Even more remarkably, the foundation stone of the Primitive Methodist in Lower Stratton was laid on May 31st 1830 and it was opened on 27th June: they might not have applied every last coat of varnish by this date but this was nevertheless quite a feat.[22] Matching Southwick for speed and size was the Penknap Baptist at Dilton Marsh, whose opening service was held 17 weeks after the foundation stone was laid, although it was noted that such finishing touches as adding window glass had not been completed at that time.[23]

The opening of any chapel was celebrated with several services, speeches and usually a tea, often in a tent or barn because the number attending would far exceed the capacity of the chapel: the tiny Witcha Farm Primitive Methodist in the wilds north east of Ramsbury attracted a crowd of 180 to its opening in 1859,[24] and the Sandridge Lane (Melksham Without) non-sectarian chapel, seating 100, opened in 1882 with a crowd of 800 people.[25]

In 1851 a census of religious worship in England and Wales was carried out, prompted by a fear that church attendance overall was falling. This showed

402 nonconformist chapels in the county, including 76 Independent/ Congregationalist, 101 Baptist and 192 Methodist, against 352 Anglican. Anglican churches, on average larger, contained approximately 60% of total sittings and still attracted more worshippers though not many more: 63,726 at the best-attended service on Sunday 30th March against 57,519 at Protestant nonconformist services on the same day. These totals hide a marked contrast between the west of the county, where only a quarter to a third of worshippers were Anglican, and the chalk-land districts where two thirds were. Concern at the growth of nonconformity, along with the mismatch of existing parish churches to the urban growth of the Industrial Revolution, had been behind the Church Building Acts of 1818 and 1824 which funded the provision of more Anglican churches, and the findings of the 1851 census could only underline this concern.

Nonconformity reached throughout the county: only 42 out of the 312 ancient parishes had no chapel registered at all[26] and most of those were tiny. Furthermore, as noted above, the absence of a chapel for a particular denomination in a particular place did not necessarily indicate the lack of a presence there: often a group would meet to worship in a house but never graduate to building a chapel. There were large numbers of such houses registered for worship, some no doubt having a very short life: in the decade from 1840, for example, there were still around twice as many Wiltshire registrations for dwelling houses as for chapels. Cottage meetings were always regarded as second best, and it was claimed that a meeting was much more likely to fail without the anchor of its own building,[27] but finding a site for a new chapel could be extremely difficult in the face of opposition from parson and squire.

Chapels in the nineteenth century were not only built but rebuilt, larger. The growth of congregations, linked to but not fully correlated with the growth in population, led to existing chapels being repeatedly extended or replaced with larger versions. Amongst very many examples, the Congregational chapel in Mere, founded in 1795 and enlarged in both the 1830s and the 1840s, proved still too small and was replaced by a new building in 1852. This lasted a mere 16 years before it was in turn replaced by the present building in 1868. On the census Sunday in 1851 315 people attended the evening service here, a large total but one exceeded at many other town chapels, like the Endless Street Congregational in Salisbury which attracted 600. It is interesting to note, however, that this growth in capacity did not continue indefinitely: the Endless Street chapel had seating for 800 but the replacement Fisherton Street chapel of 1879 had seating only for a more modest 650, still a large number.

Village chapel attendances were also high, though not uniformly so. Semley Baptist had 200 at its evening service on census day while the nearby Birdbush chapel at Donhead St Mary attracted 160, but Teffont Magna Primitive Methodist attracted only 80 and the Baptist at Ridge, Chilmark, had a congregation of only 38. The reasons for these variations are beyond the scope of this book but the general point, that chapel attendances were at levels hard to credit nowadays, remains true.

The 1864 Bishop's Visitation Queries provide an excellent snapshot of the extent of Anglican nervousness about the strength of nonconformity at this period. In advance of the periodic round of visits from the Bishop of Salisbury, incumbents had to answer a long series of questions about the state of their parishes, and two in particular, about the numbers of nonconformists and their meeting houses and about things which might 'specially impede' the Anglican ministry, gave opportunities for expression of sometimes surprisingly intemperate feelings. Primitive Methodists were often dismissed as 'Ranters,' a reference back two centuries, and Baptists seemed to incur particular dislike, referred to as 'Anabaptists' in similarly anachronistic fashion and described as 'very ignorant and bigoted' (Studley) or representing the 'most malignant' form of dissent (Charlton South). A large number of priests mentioned 'dissent' as a significant problem and many reported half or more of parishioners as attending nonconformist chapels in preference to the parish church, though a perhaps surprising number reported people attending both, as at Allington: 'nearly all the parish at times go to the meeting house, at times to the church.'

Others looked for people to blame, like at Monkton Deverill where it was stated that 'most of the lower orders go (to chapel) occasionally because the preacher is a grocer and they are all in his debt', or at Charlton All Saints (Downton) and Enford where Lord Folkestone and Sir Edward Antrobus respectively were accused, implicitly, of betraying their class interests by providing funding for chapels. Perhaps worse still, in the parsons' eyes, was the wealthy Charles Jupe of Mere, a large employer, who was blamed both at that place and at East Knoyle for spending large amounts in support of Congregationalists. Finally, some took comfort where they could find it, such as the incumbent of Imber who noted that 'a great proportion of the humbler class' attended the 'Anabaptist' there but 'none of the upper class', and the priest at Teffont Evias who remarked of nonconformists 'none, I am thankful to say,' which was possibly true of his own small parish but ignored the presence of the Primitive Methodist chapel in Teffont Magna barely half a mile from his rectory.

Even if nonconformity was in the ascendant, money for building chapels was often raised with great difficulty, and it was a proud boast when a congregation could say that it had managed to pay off the building loan over a short period. At Seend Cleeve, for example, the Primitive Methodist of 1841 cost £82 of which £24 had been raised by the time of opening: some free labour and materials seem to have kept down the total cost.[28] The Stockley (Calne Without) Primitive Methodist of the same year cost £76 of which £33 was raised by the time of opening, with the trustees taking out a loan for a further £40.[29]

Supportive and more affluent locals sometimes made loans, though this could be a mixed blessing. The Landford Primitive Methodist of 1866, for example, cost £166, paid for by a loan from a Dorset farmer which was not fully repaid until 1906.[30] In Trowbridge the Zion Baptist of 1817 benefited from loans of £500 from one person and £100 each from two others, but the interest rate was 5% and the congregation here did not manage to pay them off until 1841.[31]

Loans from the central organisations of the churches were another source of funds. The Baptist Building Loan Society, for example, was set up in 1824 and initially gave grants for chapel building but from 1846 moved over to making loans:[32] they contributed £100 towards the £400 cost of the Westwood Baptist in 1865, the remainder having been raised locally, and £100 towards the £440 cost of Marden Baptist in 1899. Other denominations had similar arrangements, the Methodists' Connexional Chapel Fund ultimately loaning the difference between the £1,200 cost of the 1897 Methodist in Box and the £500 the local community had managed to raise.[33]

Occasionally a local supporter paid for the chapel outright. The outstanding example in Wiltshire is Charles Jupe, already mentioned, who was a silk manufacturer in Mere. After his marriage into a strongly Congregationalist family he left the Church of England in 1829, expanded his business and in the 1850s and 1860s paid part or all of the cost of Congregational chapels in Crockerton, East Knoyle, Malmesbury, Mere, Swindon, Wylye and Zeals, as well as paying for the new manse at Horningsham.[34]

If a chapel had a particularly effective preacher, or one with strong links elsewhere, he was sometimes sent off on a preaching tour to raise funds. Thus Mr Macfarlane, minister of the new Bethesda chapel in Trowbridge in 1823, preached in Scotland and raised £53 towards the £2100 cost of the chapel, £1200 of which had been paid off soon after opening.[35] The slightly earlier Zion chapel in the same town, which incidentally seated 750 and had a Sunday attendance of 700 at the time of the 1851 census, cost £1232 and here again the minister, 'travelling and preaching, laboured to pay off the debt'.[36] Richard Parsons, minister of Whitbourne (Corsley) Baptist, raised £150 towards the cost of that chapel in the early nineteenth century on a preaching tour to Bristol, London and other places during which he is said to have walked an average 40 miles a day.[37]

Another source of funds sometimes used to help pay off building debts was to sell pews in the new chapel for exclusive use. In the Old Meeting in Warminster, for example, a number of the pews were sold in this way, the owners being able then to pass them on by gift or will at their own discretion.[38]

Most new congregations, on building their first chapel, would set themselves up as a charitable trust to ensure the proper future management of their various assets. Doing so would guard against many problems but not against the issues which could arise if the chapel was not owned or was on leased land. Such circumstances sometimes gave opportunities for opponents, usually the Anglican church, to cause harm, as in East Knoyle in 1849 when the lady who had paid for the new Congregational chapel was persuaded by a new rector to sell it to him, or in Great Cheverell in 1907 when the lease of the Baptist chapel was put up for sale and the parish priest outbid the Baptists in an attempt to stamp out nonconformity in the village. In neither case was the attempt at suppression successful: the East Knoyle Congregationalists had indeed to wait until 1854 before they could build another chapel but in Great Cheverell the new Baptist chapel was erected in the same year.

Less drastic than selling pews was to rent them, and this was a very commonly used source of continuing income. Members of the chapel could secure their own pew for a modest payment, a system which was also used in Anglican churches and which endured over a long period before eventual replacement in the early twentieth century with plate collections and systems of voluntary regular giving: pew rents at Old Broughton Road Baptist, Melksham, for example, lasted until 1931,[39] while those at Bearfield, Bradford on Avon lasted right through until 1948.[40] Some seats were retained for those who could not afford to pay rentals and the proportions varied: Mere Congregational had 180 free seats out of 380 in 1851 whereas the Endless Street Congregational in Salisbury had only 150 free out of a total 800.[41] Rents could be an important source of income: at Zion Baptist in Trowbridge, pew rents brought in £150 in 1870 against chapel running costs of £155 that year of which £80 was the minister's salary; collections brought in

Dilton Marsh: Penknap Providence Particular Baptist Chapel

Tisbury, Zion Hill Congregational Chapel

only £15.[42] The chapel had 200 free seats against 550 rented in 1851, with typical congregations of around 700.

In village chapels there was often a higher proportion of free seats: Teffont Magna Primitive Methodist had 60 free out of 100 while at Ridge, Chilmark, all the seats in the Baptist chapel were free. Seating in galleries was generally less favoured so was often free, and where these seats were rented it may have been at a lesser amount: the rents in the Old Baptist in Bradford on Avon, for example, were raised in 1887 to 2/- a quarter downstairs and 1/6d in the gallery.[43] There were other disadvantages in occupying the free seats, as for example at the Planks Wesleyan in Swindon in the first half of the nineteenth century where those who rented pews sat in families in the central block while the free seats were in the side aisles with the women segregated to one side and the men to the other.[44] Galleries were often used to accommodate children, a group which would not be expected to pay: in one example, the Broad Town Primitive Methodist added a gallery in 1858 specifically for the use of children attending Sunday services.[45]

It would be wrong to think of nonconformity as focussed solely on worship. Almost all chapels played an active part in the community and in the later nineteenth century, particularly, the range of meetings, classes and events associated with them helped to form the substance of social life for many. The various roles available gave opportunities for leadership and personal development much like those provided later by the trade unions, and a number gained the confidence to become lay preachers.

Some ventured into the provision of day schools – usually categorised as British schools in contrast to the Anglicans' National schools and outside the scope of this book – but almost all provided Sunday schools. Attendances at Sunday school were as remarkable as the attendances at chapel noted above. Often quite small communities had Sunday school rolls of over 100 and at the other end of the scale, the Brown Street Baptist in Salisbury, a large urban chapel, in 1882 had no less than 24 rooms available for Sunday school with 400 pupils on the roll.[46] The Back Street Baptist in Trowbridge could beat even that: by 1890 it had 87 Sunday school superintendents and teachers and 588 pupils.[47] Sunday schools at this period were concerned with literacy, particularly to enable children to read the Bible, and so taught reading and writing, not just Bible stories.

By the end of the nineteenth century nonconformist worship was close to its peak. The last restrictions had been removed - though it was 1871 before nonconformists were admitted to all universities - and they could now consider themselves as in all senses equal to the Anglicans. They continued to expand, particularly into the growing suburbs of places like Swindon but also back into town centres where mission chapels and central halls attempted to make contact with the urban poor, most notably in Wiltshire through the Methodist Central Hall in Swindon, built just after the turn of the century. Perhaps most successful in this, and reaching out to the poorest, were the Salvation Army, formed by William and Catherine Booth in London in 1865 and coming to Chippenham, Devizes, Salisbury, Swindon and Trowbridge in 1880/81 and to other Wiltshire towns not long afterwards.

Although still a minority, the nonconformist influence both locally and nationally was increasingly strong. At the start of the century they were still resented and opposed; by the end of it they were truly in a position to consider themselves not as nonconforming to the established church but as members of their own Free Churches. As the minister said at the opening of the Wingfield Baptist in 1896: 'We are not discontents or dissenters, we are Free Churchmen'.[48]

The Twentieth Century

Nonconformity was at its strongest in the Edwardian period, both in its influence and in the numbers in its congregations. But in the last third of the previous century its growth nationally had failed to keep pace with the growth of population, perhaps an early sign of the decline which was soon to follow. The decline of course affected all organised religion and its causes are to be found in accelerating changes in society as well as the profound shock delivered by the First World War. By the 1920s the fall in congregations was under way and it was to accelerate during the rest of the century.

One response to decline was amalgamation. General and Particular Baptists had combined into the Baptist Union in the early 1890s, though some Strict Baptists stayed out, and three strands of Methodism combined into the United Methodist Church in 1907, joining the main bodies of Wesleyan and Primitive Methodists in 1932 as the Methodist Church. Later in the century, the United Reformed Church was formed in 1972 by the union of the Presbyterian with most Congregational churches.

New groupings also emerged, notably the Federation of Independent Evangelical Churches, established in 1922 to provide support for independent churches which may have begun to struggle in more difficult times: around 15 Wiltshire churches are currently members of this organisation.[49]

Amalgamation gave opportunities for consolidation: in one example amongst many, the Primitive and Wesleyan Methodist chapels in Highworth were both closed in 1964 when the congregations joined in a new building. But much more common, with examples too numerous to cite here, was the complete closure of a chapel. Some had closed by the beginning of the century but the trend to closure, noticeable between the two wars, only accelerated thereafter. In another example the minister of the Avon Valley Methodist churches of Chisenbury, Figheldean, Netheravon and Upavon was proposing their amalgamation in Upavon in 1975, though the ultimate solution here was different.[50]

Chapels were still built in new housing areas - like the Methodist of 1932 on Roman Road, Bemerton, Salisbury - but in much smaller numbers than in the past. In Swindon, whose housing expanded far more than that of any other place in the county, there are examples up to the 1950s and later, though even some of those have now closed.

Nor has the decline been uniform, for some newer denominations, particularly the Christian Scientists, the Mormons and Jehovah's Witnesses, have expanded in the county, sometimes taking over buildings abandoned by the older denominations. Also increasingly prominent have been new Pentecostal groups, again sometimes taking over older chapels but often adapting other halls or building anew. The West Wilts Vineyard Church, for example, has taken over the Back Street Baptist in Trowbridge and the Emmanuel Free Church has taken over the Wilton Road Wesleyan in Salisbury. Finally the Brethren, who have had recent success in attracting large congregations, have built a number of very large warehouse-like chapels in places including Salisbury and Kington Langley.

Around 150 Wiltshire chapels have been demolished since 1900. More encouragingly, about 230 have been saved from probable demolition by conversion into houses and a further 70 either stand empty or are in commercial use. This leaves about 180 still in use for worship, though not always by the original denomination. 480 chapel buildings are still standing.

The larger towns have fared relatively well, losing just under half of their chapels to conversion or demolition during this period. In the smaller towns this figure rises to 60% and in the villages to 83%. This underlines just how severe the decline has been in the county's rural areas: three quarters of all the chapel buildings still standing in the villages are now used as houses.

Whatever happens in the future – whether this decline continues or whether nonconformist churches find new success – their impressive history will remain, as will the remarkable set of buildings they have created. The next chapter shifts the focus to the chapels themselves.

3. Chapel Design[51]

The main period of chapel building lasted for just over 200 years, from the late seventeenth to the early twentieth centuries. From the start of that time is the Monks Lane chapel in Corsham, of 1662, the interior mainly 1690, a small and plain vernacular design in stone. Towards the end is the Fisherton

Monks Lane Congregational, Corsham

Street Congregational in Salisbury, in vast Victorian Gothic. The difference between these two chapels is immense, as is that between for example the disciplined classicism of the 1838 Salem Baptist in Devizes and the lively but very typical country facade of the 1877 Wesleyan at Semley.

The shared purpose of facilitating a particular form of worship creates great similarities of interior design in these buildings despite their differences of scale: this chapter attempts to define those. The other task here is to explain why there is such a remarkably wide range of external appearance. The story of why the Salem Baptist is so different from Fisherton Street Congregational, and the Semley Wesleyan so different from Monks Lane Congregational, brings in many factors from oppression to affluence and from quiet country worship to displays of urban self-confidence. Understanding these helps one to understand why chapels look as they do.

Semley Wesleyan

Salem Baptist in Devizes

Horningsham Congregational

Fisherton Street, Salisbury
Congregational of 1879

The First Chapels

It is not surprising that dissenters during the Restoration period made themselves as unobtrusive as possible. Most meetings were in houses or other adapted buildings and those few brave enough to build chapels kept them inconspicuous and out of the way. So the Monks Lane Quaker meeting house, the only one of this period in the county still complete, is tucked away down a country lane and looked like any other small vernacular building – the distinctive eyebrow window above the door came later.

Even after the 1689 Act there was still strong and active opposition to nonconformity and, though some began to build more openly, many were still in hidden places or set back out of sight behind other buildings. The Horningsham chapel of c1700 was one such, and like Monks Lane presented an entirely vernacular appearance even down to the thatched roof, with nothing externally to show it was a chapel. As with Monks, the features which might give it away, in this case the tall windows on the west gable, are part of a later alteration.

Simplicity was not just a means to unobtrusiveness: the nonconformists wanted no ornament on their buildings – it smacked too much of the decoration and ritual which they found so offensive in the established church – and they seldom had the money to pay for it in any case. That a building was a chapel later became more obvious from its external appearance but the emphasis for many years was on simple dignity of design with almost no ornament.

This commitment to simplicity was expressed at least as strongly inside the buildings, matched with that desire for order and balance which led to an insistence on symmetry, an insistence which persisted despite the intrusion of a few very asymmetrical Gothic town churches in the later nineteenth century. A major element here was the central position of the pulpit: 'The pulpit is the kernel around which the chapel is merely an elaborate shell'.[52] People went to chapel not for ritual but to hear the word of the Lord spoken from the pulpit, so it had to be both central and visible to all. Again, this feature lasted through the succeeding centuries and chapel architects went to great lengths to ensure all could see clearly; only a few of those same late Victorian town chapels broke the rule by moving the pulpit to the side.

Horningsham Congregational – note the curved ceiling and crude bench seating in the gallery

Horningsham, though altered later, well illustrates the point. The pulpit on the west wall is raised high so that the preacher can see and be seen by those in the three-sided gallery which faces it. Below were box pews, now replaced by benches: Monks Lane chapel retains original box pews of around 1690. The interiors of these early chapels are compelling, and Horningsham in particular illustrates aspects of design which continued to feature for the next two centuries. As one example, a row of hat pegs marks the north gallery, where the men sat apart from the women, a segregation which was commonplace well into the nineteenth century, as at the Bath Road Wesleyan in Swindon where in 1853 women occupied the free seats on one side and men the other.[53]

Horningsham Congregational, the rear gallery – clock faces the preacher; singing stand behind

In the gallery facing the pulpit the pews have sloping front shelves and a raised stand to hold the music used by the small choir which was positioned there. Many early nonconformists were opposed to any form of singing, seen as an element of ritual, but it became accepted and choirs were formed. There was equally opposition to the use of accompanying instruments but again this was gradually overcome. The Stratton Green Baptist in the 1830s had a band consisting of flute, clarinet, bass and harmonium,[54] while the Planks Wesleyan in Swindon in 1853 had a choir in the gallery with a bass viol and a 'small fiddle'.[55] Although harmoniums were compact and relatively cheap, organs were bulky and expensive and so generally appeared quite late. When they did arrive, they were usually in the gallery opposite the pulpit or else above and behind it, forming an imposing end to the chapel: the Trowbridge Back Street Baptist provides one of many town church examples of this. At Horningsham, where space was so limited, the later organ is squeezed in rather awkwardly to the left of the pulpit.

Two other features are worth mentioning. The first is more evident at the Monks Lane chapel where the interior is all of c1690, and it is that the box pews below are smartly panelled whereas in the gallery are to be found crude benches with almost non-existent backs. This disparity is to be found in chapel after chapel. Sitting downstairs meant higher status, a feature perhaps surprising in what might be believed to be a more egalitarian congregation than that found in the Anglican church but one underlined by the system of pew rents described previously.

The last feature to note at Horningsham is the large clock perched on the gallery front opposite the preacher where it could be seen by him but not by most of the congregation: the preacher needed to know how long the sermon was lasting; the congregation should have their minds on higher things. The clock at Horningsham is probably a century or more later than the chapel but this feature, again, is to be found in many chapels up and down the county.

Both these chapels were Congregational by the end of the seventeenth century but the same basic internal layout was to be found in chapels of all the main denominations bar one. The Baptists were only partly an exception: their requirements for adult baptism were met originally in a local river or by the construction of an external baptistery as at Crockerton Green (Longbridge Deverill) and Whitbourne (Corsley), but it eventually became the practice to construct a baptistery within the body of the chapel. This was often located in a covered tank under the communion table so that the usual appearance of the interior was identical to that of a Congregational or Methodist chapel.

The true exception was the Quaker meeting house, which in conformity to their more simple form of worship usually just had benches round three sides of a room with a further bench behind a table on the fourth. Sometimes the women's

The external baptistery at Whitbourne Baptist; schoolrooms at rear of chapel behind

meeting room was separated from the main room only by hinged shutters, allowing the two spaces to be combined on occasion, and the meeting house in Devizes had shutters on a landing overlooking the main room for a similar purpose. There are no Quaker meeting houses of original form left in Wiltshire.

The Brethren, in whose worships individuals were free to contribute as they felt moved, also did without raised seating or a pulpit, and their varied forms of worship meant that from an early date they preferred the flexibility of individual chairs rather than fixed pews.[56]

This similarity of internal layout goes some way to explain why it was found so straightforward for one denomination to take over a chapel built for another, something that happened at numerous places and times as the gazetteer illustrates. One of the more extreme examples was the late 17th century Presbyterian chapel in Back Road, Calne, which became Unitarian by the early 19th century, was used by Primitive Methodists for two periods between the 1830s and the 1880s, and was finally taken over by the Salvation Army, the Primitives meanwhile taking over a former Wesleyan chapel nearby.

Horningsham chapel faces west and Monks Lane north: neither follows the Anglican convention in which churches face east. This flexibility in orientation remained and meant that it was much easier to find sites for chapels than if all had been required to face east, something that was particularly helpful when squeezing a chapel into the built environment of a town.

The Eighteenth Century

The interior design of early chapels thus set a pattern which was to be followed generally thereafter, though later chapels became very much larger. Not so the exterior appearance, which became both more varied and more assertive in the course of the eighteenth century, reflecting growing self-confidence and larger congregations.

Many chapels of this date were of the 'long-wall' type, where a longer wall faced the street. One example is the North Row Presbyterian of 1704 in Warminster, but perhaps most typical is the Grove meeting house of 1698 in Bradford on Avon. Here a south wall looks out from the hillside above the town, with a door at each end and four bays between, the whole in far from reticent ashlar. Inside, the pulpit would originally have been on the north wall with galleries round the other three. The chapel was joined at the west end to a terrace of houses but the roof at the other end was hipped.

Grove meeting house, Bradford on Avon – the 'long wall' containing the original entrances

There are variants, but the combination of a long-wall entrance and hipped roof was commonly found at this time. Eventually, though, the advantages of the 'short-wall' alternative became apparent, particularly in towns where street frontage was at a premium. There were perceived also to be advantages to the 'lecture hall' internal layout produced by the short-wall pattern and soon this became almost universal. Many long-wall chapels later had the interior layout turned at right angles, as happened at Grittleton where the Baptist of c1720 was first laid out in long-wall style facing the original access, with the pulpit facing the door, but later altered so that the pulpit is now on one of the short walls. The Grove at Bradford on Avon was similarly turned, but perhaps as late as 1873 when it was converted into a Sunday school.

Village chapels

Very few chapels survive in anything like unaltered form from the eighteenth century. Town chapels were often replaced by larger versions, or altered and extended out of recognition. In villages, where chapels were built by poor communities against the opposition of the village hierarchy, the result was often flimsy and impermanent, and anyway few were built – only about 40 across the county by 1800. Nearly all of these latter would have been in vernacular style – there was not the money to do otherwise – and nearly all have gone. One example was the 1798 Wesleyan at Hodson (Chiseldon), made of wattle and daub under a thatched roof; another was the first Congregational at Christian Malford, of the early eighteenth century, half-timbered

under a chaotically thatched roof; a third was the tiny hipped-roofed Baptist at Rushall of 1760 which remained until as recently as 1982. An almost unique survival is the

Christian Malford Congregational – the original chapel, demolished for the present building in 1836. Drawing courtesy of Wiltshire Buildings Record

Independent, later Methodist, at Winterbourne Dauntsey, of c1799, made of cob on brick footings under thatch and solidly vernacular. It lost a previous front door and window when the new chapel was built alongside in 1980.

Surviving village chapels of this period are characterised by unpretentious solidity. The Independent at Atworth, of c1790 and with a hipped roof, has a short wall facing the

Winterbourne Dauntsey Methodist – page 176 has a photograph of the original chapel before alteration

street with just a central door and window over, but it does run to pointed windows and ashlar quoins. Seend Wesleyan of 1775, similar in look but of brick not stone, has a surprisingly grand pedimented doorway and windows whose Gothic arches might have been added later. The Providence Baptist at Bradenstoke (Lyneham) is of 1777 and a degree more imposing with large windows either side of a later porch and an attic window above that, the whole topped by a half-hipped roof with a cupola on top. As well as a clock, the facade carries a stone plaque with the date of construction, a feature which became almost universal on the fronts of smaller chapels and is very useful, although occasionally misleading, in dating them.

The Bratton Baptist of 1734 and East Tytherton (Bremhill) Moravian of

1792, the former much altered, share the 'door plus windows either side' pattern which was to become so dominant for smaller chapels. Both soon had buildings attached at each end and both might appear to be of the long-wall type. In fact the Moravian has the pulpit on the wall to the left of the entrance, not on the opposite wall where it might be expected, and the interior space of the Bratton Baptist is almost square. This

Seend Wesleyan

might reflect a fashion of around that time for square chapels, following a literal interpretation of Revelations 21, 16: 'And the city lieth foursquare, and the length is as large as the breadth....'.[57] The East Tytherton Moravian shows also the particular characteristic of this denomination, namely their desire to build a community of the faithful, demonstrated in the self-contained group of buildings of which the chapel is the centre.

It is notable that almost all these survivors are from late in the century, underlining the fragility of much early chapel building. Earlier fabric does survive in other chapels, as in the 1716 Quaker meeting house in Market Lavington, later sold to Congregationalists: the ghost of the original meeting house faces the road, with

East Tytherton Moravian

the 1809 extension by the Congregationalists under the raised roofline to the right.

The Market Lavington meeting house illustrates also the need felt by

Market Lavington Quaker meeting house, later Congregational – the window facing the street was central in the original wall

many in the early days to keep their chapels out of the way and inconspicuous in design so as to avoid trouble, something the Quakers experienced particularly. The difficulty of finding a site may have played a part but it is noticeable that this one is located on the edge of the village a long way from the centre and the parish church; the Baptist of 1832, by contrast, was right in the centre. Similar positioning on the outskirts is to be found in many other villages, including for example chapels of 1796 and 1831 in Shrewton and that of 1838 in Upavon.

It is worth noting that chapels did not usually stand alone. Schoolrooms have been mentioned, and there was often a minister's house or manse adjacent or at least nearby. Burial grounds were common, at least until the introduction of municipal cemeteries in the mid nineteenth century, and there were also occasionally stables provided, for the use of those coming from further afield. At the Providence Baptist in Bradenstoke (Lyneham) there used to be a stables in front of the chapel, and at the first Congregational chapel in Market Lavington the stables, perhaps of early nineteenth century date, were behind the chapel and the burial ground and were later converted into a cottage.

Town Chapels

Eighteenth century town chapels followed a generally similar style to that of the larger village chapels, not emphatically Classical but with attention to that symmetry and proportion which were so important to nonconformists. Two of the most interesting surviving examples, at Devizes and Melksham, are hard to see but worth seeking out nonetheless. The Devizes Northgate Street Congregational is hidden behind the later lecture hall and schoolroom opposite Wadworth's brewery and was itself much extended, but the hipped roof and two tiers of Y-traceried windows indicate its age. Built in 1776, it has a self-confident assertiveness which would not have been possible earlier.

Devizes Northgate Street Congregational of 1776

Melksham Old Broughton Road of 1776-7

The Melksham example, the Old Broughton Road Baptist, of the same date and similarly placed behind later ancillary rooms, is easier to see if more crude in execution. There are the same two tiers of windows, this time round-arched above and flat below, under a dramatically tall hipped roof. The interior is essentially of the late nineteenth century, with galleries on three sides, the one opposite the pulpit containing the organ. It illustrates another characteristic feature, that the presence of two tiers of windows, particularly in the end containing the door, almost always reveals the presence of galleries.

Layouts like that of Old Broughton Road became normal for larger town chapels. Inside a rectangular box, pews are set out with side aisles but no centre aisle – processions up a centre aisle were no part of nonconformist worship – a pattern which was near universal in chapels right up to the late nineteenth century. Three galleries are carried on columns, usually of iron but timber in some earlier chapels. The pulpit is placed centrally and high so that the preacher can command the galleries, often originally with a sounding board above although these rarely survive.

Such buildings look very different from the typical medieval Anglican church with its side aisles and long chancel separated from the nave, but are much less different from the Anglican churches being built in the seventeenth and eighteenth centuries which themselves reflected the rites of the reformed Protestant church. Wren, rebuilding after the Great Fire of London, accepted the need for galleries to bring the congregation closer, avoided long chancels as being unnecessary, did without choir stalls and placed the organ, where there was one at all, in the west gallery. This set a precedent, for the next 100 years and more, for a style of Anglican church which differed not so much

Westbury Upper Congregational of 1763

as may at first appear from the larger nonconformist chapels.[58]

It is interesting to note in passing that both the Melksham and Devizes chapels were set well back from the road, the Devizes one on the edge of the town centre but the Melksham one well away from it. There may have been other reasons for the choices of location but the need to be away from potential trouble was probably still one: both extended forwards towards the road in later years. Salisbury offers another and even later example of this in the Fisherton Street Primitive Methodist of 1826 which was hidden away down an alleyway: its successor of 1869 was built right on the street.

At Westbury the Upper Congregational of 1763 is big and plain, again with two tiers of windows, and the first in this series to have the un-hipped gable end which became so nearly universal in the following century, though the rear remained hipped. Finally in this group is the Crow Lane Congregational in Wilton, from 1791, in very much the same style with two tiers of windows and a tall hipped roof. As ever, changes have to some extent hidden the appearance, for the stone plinth, the string course and the heavy stone window detailing are late nineteenth

Wilton Crow Lane Congregational of 1791 – the paler brick shows where the Sunday school building was previously attached

century additions.

All four of these examples were of substantial size. There were smaller town chapels in this century but the evidence for their appearance is limited. Probably nearly all followed the general patterns displayed by those town and village chapels of that period which we still have.

The Nineteenth Century

Chapel design at the end of the eighteenth century comprised a mix of small vernacular buildings and larger, designed constructions, confident but restrained. The century which followed brought some continuity but much more change. Village chapels developed into the gable-fronted pattern which is many people's image of what a nonconformist chapel looks like, with increasingly elaborate decorative additions as the century progressed. Town chapels blossomed into a full Classicism which lasted the century. Gothic Revival architecture, at first much opposed, established itself and by late on was producing chapels which, in external appearance, were little different from contemporary Anglican churches.

Early chapels were simple buildings, designed by their builders with no doubt some input from the minister and congregation: architects were rarely if ever used. Thomas Angell of Highworth was one of many examples: he designed the Zion chapel there in 1825 but there is no suggestion that he had any training in architecture; he was a builder and surveyor. This blurring of the lines between builders, surveyors and architects continued well into the nineteenth century, particularly for village chapels, with Thomas Hardick of Warminster a good example. He designed several chapels but he was also a carpenter, a builder, worked for Brunel on the Great Western Railway and was for more than 30 years manager of the Salisbury Gas Company.[59] Such Victorian versatility by enterprising people meant that trained architects were often little missed.

By late in the century, however, it was more rare for a chapel to be built without the services of an architect. Many were the work of 'jobbing' architects but a few specialised in chapel design, of whom the most prolific was William Jervis Stent of Warminster, who built or altered 15 chapels in Wiltshire between 1852 and 1881, mostly Congregational but also Baptist and Wesleyan. There is more about him, and the role of architects, in Chapter 10.

Village Chapels

The new century brought no immediate change to the appearance of chapels. The Little Zoar Baptist at Derry Hill (Calne Without) of 1814, for example, remained entirely vernacular, distinguishable from other buildings in the area of similar date only by its larger windows. The Staverton Wesleyan of 1824, a notably pure design, retained a hipped roof. The Southwick Old Baptist of 1815, of a much greater status than its village location might suggest, with its two tiers of windows and hipped roof could easily have been a town chapel of the previous century.

Staverton Wesleyan

Southwick Old Baptist

Upavon, Cave of Adullam Baptist

Union Chapel, Kington Langley

Southwick has segmental-arched windows in contrast to the pointed arches of Staverton which reflect the growing influence of the Gothic Revival, but to claim the pared-back design of Staverton as genuinely Gothic is a step too far. 'Gothic' in a village chapel usually meant simply the choice of pointed arches over round and it was left to larger town chapels later in the century to introduce more intense decoration and detail in greater sympathy with the mainstream Revival.

Nonconformists, seeing dedication of chapels to saints as idolatrous, instead searched for names from the bible, hence Bethel, Ebenezer, Zion and others through to the almost unpronounceable Pethahiah Primitive Methodist in Cricklade. The Cave of Adullam Baptist at Upavon is named for the place to which David escaped from the king of Gath: once there, he was joined by other discontented people (1 Samuel 22, 1-2) so the name serves as a metaphor for nonconformity. It was built as late as 1838 and still had a long-wall layout, if that expression is appropriate for such a tiny chapel, before a door was inserted in the street end later in the century. Its cheap construction underlines the difficulties of funding. The Minety Baptist of two years later had the same problems of cheap construction and was described thus: 'roof of straw, the floor of stones of every shape except square, the seats were benches without backs, whilst the pulpit consisted of rough boards painted with lime wash.'[60]

The gable-ended design was present from early in the century and soon became dominant. The Fovant Congregational of 1820, for example, with its single lunette window above the doorway, is almost identical to the Atworth Independent of 1790 save that it has a gable end rather than the hipped roof of the former. Soon there were examples across the county, including the Union chapel at Kington Langley of 1835, with its charmingly mis-spaced inscription, and the rather more grand Congregational of 1824 at Colerne. This has an ashlar front and a pedimental gable, and illustrates another very common characteristic in using rubble-stone for the side walls. Chapels were far from the only buildings to use cheaper materials away from the 'show' front, but it is particularly prevalent amongst them.

Building materials almost always followed the local norm, with stone dominant in the west and north and brick in the chalk-lands, with some flint also

Coulston Baptist – note also the roof ventilator, though with later flue behind

in that part of the county. Ashlar stone was always expensive, in almost all cases used only for the front facade in the stone districts and scarcely used at all except for detailing outside those areas. Other stone, however, came in varied shapes and sizes from the roughest rubble to crudely shaped blocks more or less held together in courses, to neat blockwork, the latter sometimes near smooth and occasionally dramatically rock-faced. Slate and tile were in common use as roofing materials across the county, though often an earlier roof in other material may have been replaced by tile. Stone slates were confined to the west and north and thatch is now very rare, the Winterbourne Dauntsey example already quoted, along with Horningsham and a very few others, being the only surviving examples.

Round-arched windows were the dominant type for village chapels in this century, though flat- heads were much used for subsidiary windows and schoolrooms. Pointed arch windows, some with stone tracery, were as noted above found occasionally in chapels which were not overtly Gothic, but segmental-arched windows, and curved window heads with four centres, were more complex and hence most often found in larger town chapels. Chapels often set windows in sets of three in the gable end, as for example in the High Street Wesleyan in Wroughton or the little Baptist in Coulston, a practice which it has been suggested might have been intended to represent the Holy Trinity.[61] There were, however, plenty of exceptions to the general patterns and the variety of different window treatments provides one of the pleasures of looking at chapels.

Many chapels were built with no porch or just a small hood above the door, and it was common for a more commodious porch to be added later in a building's life. Indeed, for any small chapel with a porch, it is more likely than not that the porch is of a later date than the main building. Later in the century, porches were sometimes expanded to provide ancillary rooms as well, like the Baptist at Bodenham (Odstock), whose porch was turned into a triple gabled affair.

The austerity of early in the century was gradually replaced by more decorative

Bodenham (Odstock) Baptist

treatments. The use of contrasting colours of brick was particularly common, from the tiny Wesleyan at Barkers Hill (Sedgehill and Semley) of 1877 with its pale brick detailing for windows and quoins, to the Primitive Methodist of 1882 at Chittoe Heath (Bromham) with its raised quoins in pale brick, exuberantly detailed pediment with large plaque at its centre and schoolroom to the rear a miniature version of

the same. Schoolrooms like this one, added in 1914 but carefully matched to the chapel, are more common than those built concurrently. Often there were not the funds to build both chapel and schoolroom at the same time, but a very high proportion of chapels acquired a schoolroom at some point. Sometimes the former chapel became

Chittoe Heath (Bromham) Primitive Methodist

Bradenstoke (Lyneham) Primitive Methodist

the schoolroom when the replacement chapel was built, as at the Bower Chalke Baptist.

By the end of the century some were even more decorated than this, like the Bradenstoke (Lyneham) Primitive Methodist of 1887, its facade containing almost more added stonework than the brick of its construction, or the Bishopstone North Primitive Methodist, built a year earlier with corner pilasters and a star window. Here, though, they economised on the sides which remain entirely undecorated. Elsewhere other local materials were used to add interest, like the Wylye Congregational of 1860 with its mix of stone and flint typical of the area.

The gable end chapel with central door and a symmetrical combination of windows alongside and above, usually with a date plaque at top centre, was dominant but far from universal. At Coulston, for example, the Baptist of 1872 has its door on the side for no apparent reason, as well as markedly overhanging eaves which were not a common feature. It also displays a large roof ventilator at the mid point of the ridge, something that is often found, though more generally on larger chapels than small. Smaller chapels tend to have a modest ventilator at the gable head, usually a pierced iron grill in a circular or trefoil surround, as noted below.

Others were more adventurous. In Downton the remarkable South Lane Baptist of 1857, admittedly really more of a town than a village church, has a strong protruding centre to the front gable, heavily overhanging eaves and a large

Wylye Congregational   *Downton South Lane Baptist*

and ornate stone pedestal above. At Purton, the Hoggs Lane Primitive Methodist of 1893 is the single pile remainder of what used to be a double pile building, lengthways to the road with large windows below subsidiary gables and a single-storey porch with service rooms either side. If this looks back towards mid-century, the Hilperton Wesleyan of 1891 is certainly looking forward, with elements of almost modernist style in its immensely tall end gable.

Finally, Holt provides an example of full-blooded Gothic, rare in village chapels. The 1880 Congregational, complete with clock tower, transept and apse, has abandoned nonconformist symmetry in favour of something

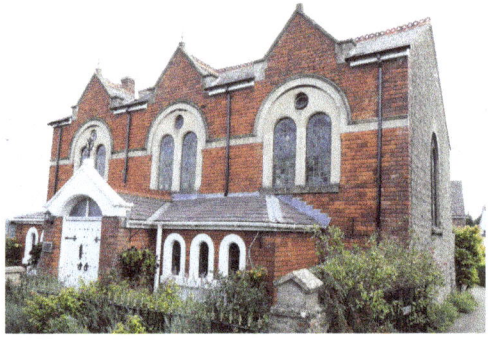

Holt Congregational of 1880   *Purton, Hoggs Lane Primitive Methodist*

which could as easily be an Anglican church. Inside, the problem of producing a symmetrical worship space inside an asymmetrical exterior is solved by placing the organ in the transept, adding a very non Anglican-Gothic rear gallery and putting the pulpit and communion table in the apse. It works, and the numbered and asymmetrically divided pews are a delight. This asymmetrical splitting, by the way, is encountered frequently in larger chapels, for example at the Zion Baptist in Trowbridge. It may have been a way of improving the stability of the wide central rows of pews but was more likely used to delineate the sections of pew rented by different families. Numbering the pews helped to identify which was whose, as did the name-card holders which can still sometimes be found attached at their ends. By this date box pews were largely a thing of the past, replaced even in older

chapels by bench pews which gave more capacity and more focus on the preacher. Bench pews also, as pointed out by William Doel in his famous treatise 'Twenty Golden Candlesticks', gave the occupants less opportunity to fall asleep unseen during services.

Braydon Primitive Methodist

Corrugated Iron Chapels

From late in the century manufacturers began to offer prefabricated corrugated iron buildings for use as chapels, the so-called 'Tin Tabernacles'. Most were small, easy to erect though not necessarily so much cheaper than those of conventional construction as might have been expected: by 1896, when prices had fallen from an initially much higher level, they cost typically £1 per sitting, with perhaps £70

Unitarian Free Christian Chapel, Regent Street, Swindon. Photograph courtesy of Local Studies, Swindon Libraries

extra for foundations, heating and lighting for a chapel seating 200.[62] They were usually timber-lined and of conventional appearance with a door in the end gable and rectangular windows; ornament was restricted to the use of wavy barge-boards, roof finials and sometimes porches. No doubt many were intended only as stop gaps but they have in fact been remarkably long-lived. Several survive as stores and the like and at least three, at Braydon, Luckington and Winterslow, are in good condition and still in use.

Larger ones were built as well, including the Wesleyan mission halls in Ludgershall, though these were added well into the twentieth century. Nor were they confined to villages: perhaps most remarkable of all was the 1861 Free Christian Unitarian chapel in Swindon which had a segmental curved roof and a capacity of 500: it closed in 1874 but was then moved to Stratton where it survived into the early twentieth century. The Free Christians, it might be noted in passing, were a group emerging from the work of James Martineau in the later nineteenth century; while basically Unitarian they emphasised inclusivity.[63]

Town Chapels

Unsurprisingly, the same continuity from the last century was to be found in town chapels as in village ones. The 1828 Ebenezer Baptist in Corsham, for example, with its dignified two-tiered ashlar front and hipped roof, could well have been a product of the previous century. The 1810 Ebenezer Baptist in Warminster has even more of an eighteenth century feel if one discounts the later window tracery.

Corsham Ebenezer Baptist, Priory Street

But the most notable characteristic of the new century was the gradual increase in size of town chapels until we reach the monsters seating 1000 plus. Gothic design played its part later but the dominant style for larger chapels was Classical, gradually increasing in size and in decoration. The taste for Classical had much to do with distaste for the Gothic Revival, which was associated with High Anglicanism and Roman Catholicism, and this distaste was only partly overcome towards the century's end.

Mere Primitive Methodist, North Street *Chippenham Station Hill Baptist*

The development of the Classical chapel can be traced through a series of buildings, not in date order, starting with the Mere Primitive Methodist in North Street, of 1846. This, in remarkable rock-faced stone, has a coped gable and corner buttressing but is otherwise a clear relative of the dozens of gable-ended chapels of all sizes appearing across the county.

The Station Hill Baptist in Chippenham, of 1854, has by relatively minor changes turned this into a full Classical facade: an added entablature creates a pedimented apex and below that a series of gently protruding pilasters underlines the point. Earlier, the 1829 Brown Street Baptist in Salisbury had used the same devices, though also following the then-fashionable 'Egyptian' fashion by the use of trapezoid window and door framing. We have only a drawing of this as it was later altered out of recognition.

The Classical style persisted, with the Melksham High Street Wesleyan of 1872 a good later example. In this showy building the pilasters have become full columns, the pediment is brought forward as if emulating the entrance to some country house, and at the top corners the architect has added urns and balustrades. The vast Monkton Hill Methodist in Chippenham, of just after the end of the century, shows the echoes of the style hanging on. A Classical pediment occupies only the central part of the facade and is hemmed in by bulky corner towers; the visible side could almost be that of a factory. The Monkton Hill chapel, incidentally, illustrates how congregations were still growing so late on: the demand was said to be such that the predecessor Causeway chapel could not provide enough seats and some were forced to worship elsewhere.

Melksham Wesleyan, High Street *Chippenham, Monkton Hill Wesleyan*

Swindon Baptist Tabernacle. Photograph courtesy of Local Studies, Swindon Libraries

The apotheosis of the Classical chapel, now lost, was the Swindon Baptist Tabernacle on Regent Street. This very large building, 74ft by 48ft with a schoolroom 67ft by 30ft behind, was fronted by a Greek temple portico on six Tuscan columns. But in case such purity of design should be thought normal, there were plenty of others whose adherence to Classical rules was far more lax. One impressive if ill-disciplined example is the 1896 Methodist Reformed in Milford Street, Salisbury, whose mix of Italianate skyline with Gothic detailing is at least exuberant.

Gothic Revival design was nearly all-conquering for Anglican churches for much of the century, but far less so for nonconformists for the reason already stated. The ones that were built could be modest: the Pickwick Road Methodist in Corsham, for example, of just after the century's end in 1904, manages to be both Gothic and politely symmetrical. More typical is the Calne Free Church of 1868, which was founded by dissenting members of the parish church, so making

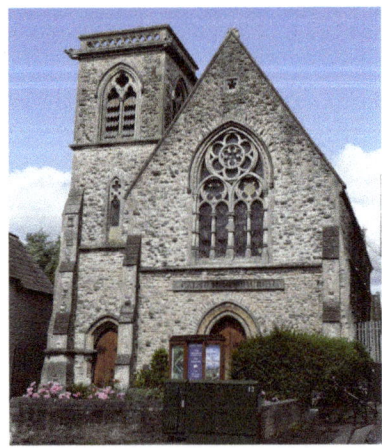

above: Salisbury, Methodist Reformed, Milford Street; right: Calne Free Church

the choice of Gothic unsurprising. It is rock-faced, in early French Gothic with a particularly ornate west window, and has a flat-topped bell tower alongside.

Mere Congregational of 1868

By the same architect, W J Stent, and of the same year, is the Congregational in Mere, making the most of its side-on position to the road with entrance tower, side aisle and transept, all much detailed and buttressed. The whole, in Early Gothic, conveys a French rather than an English feel. Stent was at least striving for some sort of architectural purity here and in Calne but, as with the Classical examples, there were plenty of architects willing to interpret the underlying disciplines more freely. The Trinity Presbyterian in Swindon of 1899 is attractively idiosyncratic in brick and the Bath Road Wesleyan, in the same town and built in 1880, is almost hubristically assertive in stone. This, not much more than nominally Gothic, has curved staircase towers

Swindon Bath Road Wesleyan

each capped with a clerestory either side of tall pillars which themselves provide punctuation for the front facade. This is a very long way from the simplicity of early nonconformist worship.

Enthusiasm for Gothic varied between the denominations. Almost all Congregational town churches of the later Victorian period in Wiltshire are

Trowbridge Back Street Baptist

Gothic, whereas the reverse is true for the Baptists, who clung to Classical design throughout the century. Primitive Methodists may have shown less enthusiasm for Gothic nationally but in Wiltshire towns they built very much the same number of Gothic as Classical churches, a pattern matched by the Wesleyans.

Many village chapels had a rear gallery and larger ones sometimes added side galleries to that. In larger town chapels a full set of galleries was common, some providing capacity for several hundred people and accessed by stairways symmetrically placed in the corners nearest to the street. In the most extreme cases two tiers of galleries were built: the Bethesda Baptist in Trowbridge, for example, by this means managed to fit 840 people into quite a modest space. Galleries were far from universal though and the Swindon Bath Road Methodist and Melksham High Street Methodist are two amongst numerous examples of large churches without a full set. Gothic chapels, because of their internal arches, found it harder to accommodate galleries: the Mere Congregational manages three by placing the side gallery fronts awkwardly immediately behind the pillars but the Salisbury Fisherton Street Congregational had none.

The biggest chapels often carried the gallery round all four sides, the fourth containing the organ either above the pulpit or above the doors. There are a number of interesting examples of this in the county but perhaps the finest is the Back Street Baptist in Trowbridge, now the West Wilts Vineyard Church. The original fabric is eighteenth century but the interior is pure nineteenth, probably only reaching its final form c1900. The four-sided gallery is carried on iron columns with a barley sugar twist and the gallery fronts are of ornately pierced metalwork, a common replacement for the wood panelling of earlier times. The organ is set back in an alcove above the very broad pulpit which, approached by steps on both sides, is a long way from the austere preaching stand of the earliest chapels.

Being able to see the preacher remained a major criterion for the internal design of chapels and most remained successful in this, in contrast to many

Westbury Old Congregational

Anglican churches of the Victorian age. The deep galleries of the Trowbridge Back Street Baptist must have caused some to strain their necks but perhaps more successful in this respect is the smaller Westbury Old Congregational whose three galleries retain the more old-fashioned wood-panelled fronts. This has the archetypal layout of an organ in an alcove behind the pulpit, which itself stands behind the communion table.

Rarely, the conventional gallery arrangement was abandoned and the rear gallery was brought forward to create a horseshoe shape akin to the 'circle' of a theatre. The Methodist Reform in Milford Street, Salisbury has such a gallery, of considerable capacity; it has raked seating as do the 'stalls' below it. Despite its current use as a nightclub it retains the organ in an alcove behind the pulpit and many of the pews. This is a chapel designed for listening, not for participating, and many were concerned that buildings of this type turned church services into mere spectacle: 'Formerly the preacher had stood up like the father of the family, with the rest all gathered round him because the old (style of) building reflected Calvin's belief that the communion was a supper round a table. Now the preacher is like a school master facing a class and the minister and the people are separated in a way against which the Puritans had protested.'[64]

The increasing size and number of schoolrooms has already been remarked upon. In larger chapels the accommodation for Sunday schools became increasingly complex and a common pattern, found at Back Street Baptist in Trowbridge, Penknap Baptist at Dilton Marsh and several others, was to have a large central hall where all the children could congregate at once, with a series of smaller rooms adjacent for class teaching.

There was increasing concern about the failure to reach the urban poor, particularly in central areas, and this produced a number of central halls, designed to look as secular as possible and incorporating rooms for lectures and concerts as

Salisbury, Methodist Reformed, Milford Street

Trowbridge Back Street Baptist – note the smaller rooms for class teaching off the central hall

well as the space for worship. Swindon's Methodist central hall on Clarence Street was a good example, from just into the new century in 1907. Now demolished, it had seating for 1,000 beneath an octagonal roof and, on the street, a tower with its own small dome.

Swindon Wesleyan Central Hall, Clarence Street. Photograph thanks to Paul Williams, custodian and copyright owner of images from the William Hooper collection

These are the large urban chapels but, in town as in country, many were of much more modest size. Sometimes this was simply because the congregation did not increase in the way found elsewhere, as for example in the Old Baptist in Chippenham which, though built in 1810, was increased in size only modestly and still retains an intimate, almost eighteenth century, interior with wood-panelled galleries on three sides and a high pulpit. Others were newly created in locations at the edge of town where there was never likely to be a large congregation, like the Primitive Methodist of 1845 and the Providence Baptist of 1858, both in Bradford on Avon. The former is of conventional gable end appearance whereas the Providence was converted from terraced houses by removing a floor and inserting tall windows, a procedure which was reversed when it became two houses again c1990.

Providence Baptist, Bradford on Avon
left: reconverted to residential use and looking, apart from the round window-heads, probably much as it did originally;
right: in use as a chapel. Photograph courtesy of Wiltshire Buildings Record

Smaller chapels are also to be found in the expanding suburbs and Swindon, whose expansion was incomparably greater than that of any other town, provides the best examples. Gorse Hill, just north of the railway and expanding from the 1870s, attracted a Wesleyan mission hall and a Primitive Methodist chapel in 1871 and a Baptist chapel in 1883; by 1898 the Salvation Army had joined them.

These small chapels were usually entirely conventional in appearance. The Butterworth Street Primitive Methodist of 1893, also in Swindon, provides one example amongst many: it is of gable-end design with an accretion of stone banding typical of its date, and is attached directly to the adjacent terrace, symbolic of its integration with the community it serves. The Salvation Army's citadels tended towards a fortress-like appearance, the best Wiltshire example being their former building in Chippenham.

left: Swindon, Butterworth Street Primitive Methodist
right: Chippenham, former Salvation Army Citadel

In the same way that the exteriors of late nineteenth century chapels became more decorative, so the long embargo on the use of stained glass in windows was finally raised. Nonconformists objected to stained glass as part of the decoration and ritual which they found so repugnant, and the great majority of chapels to this day have entirely clear glass. Towards the end of the nineteenth century, however, some chapels began to use patterns of coloured squares in leaded glass, as for example at the Hoggs Lane Primitive Methodist in Purton of 1893, the Barford

left: Floral pattern stained glass in Morgan's Hill Congregational, Bradford on Avon
right: Figures began to be represented late on, as in this at Back Street Baptist, Trowbridge

St Martin Primitive Methodist of 1902, and the Marden Baptist of 1899, the last-named paid for separately by a member of the congregation.

Elsewhere, small patterns were set into much larger plain glass windows as in the Holt Congregational of 1880 where figurative elements are introduced, or the Marlborough New Road Wesleyan of 1910 which uses only pattern. The Zion Congregational in Highworth has prominent biblical images in windows on the pulpit wall, perhaps introduced in alterations made in 1888, but this and the other examples remain exceptions to the more general pattern: indeed the strong objection to religious imagery explains also why the painted wall decoration of scrolls and texts, which became so popular during the Victorian period, did not include images of Biblical figures. There does seem to have been at least one much earlier exception to this rule, however, in the Manvers Street Wesleyan in Trowbridge which had a stained glass window representing Jesus blessing bread as early as 1836.[65]

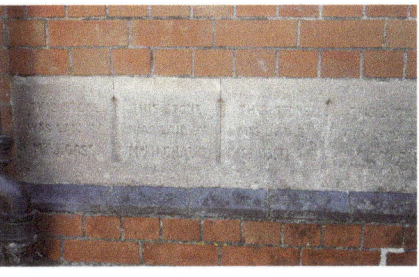

More common than coloured glass are stone plaques commemorating foundation-stone ceremonies and those who had donated to the building of a chapel. These are usually set low in the front wall and were sometimes moved to the new building when one chapel was replaced by another: the set in the 1907 Wesleyan at Burbage is a good example, as is that at the Barford St Martin Primitive Methodist.

Part of a set of 12 foundation stones at Barford St Martin Primitive Methodist

The comfort of worshippers gradually improved: the spacious interior of a late Victorian town chapel, with its gas lighting, piped heating and comfortable pews, was a very different proposition from the cold, dark and draughty inside of an early chapel. Lighting by candle, as at Horningsham and elsewhere, was replaced by oil,

Overthrow light at Broughton Gifford Baptist – the lantern sat in the square frame at top centre

then by gas in urban areas and finally by electricity. Devizes New Baptist replaced oil by gas in 1901, and in 1927 converted to electricity; Melksham Old Broughton Road Baptist followed a very similar timescale, converting to gas in 1907 and electricity in 1925. Most chapels seem to have converted to electricity between the wars but there are exceptions: the Spirthill Wesleyan was not connected to electricity until 1961 and the Braydon Primitive Methodist, out in the wilds, as late as 1968.

Lighting was not confined to the chapel interior: the overthrow light, supported on a metal frame above the entrance to the chapel path from the road, was a common feature still frequently seen: one example is at the Zion Baptist in Highworth. The lights would have been fuelled by oil for much of their life.

Most chapels were not heated at all until probably well into the nineteenth century. There

were exceptions – Monks Lane in Corsham had an open fireplace, used to heat
the chapel and also for members of the congregation to warm a midday meal, but
generally if a fireplace was provided at all it was in the vestry as at Hullavington
Newtown Baptist and Grittleton Baptist, and for the use mainly of the minister,
though the vestry was often used also for smaller meetings on church business.
The lack of heating may not have been too much of a privation given the large
numbers of people in their outdoor clothes crowding into small buildings, but
equally on winter evenings it could have been a considerable penance.

Stoves burning coal or coke began to appear in the early nineteenth century
and indeed Monks Lane had one for a time in the middle of the floor in front of the
pulpit. The tortoise type – 'slow but sure' –, developed in the 1830s, was common
and amongst many users of this contrivance were Boyton Corton Baptist, where
the stove was behind the pulpit, and Hay Lane Primitive Methodist in Lydiard
Tregoze. South Marston Wesleyan had one in the middle of the floor with the flue
travelling horizontally to exit through a wall: on one celebrated occasion here, with
the preacher in stormy voice and repeatedly stamping his feet, the pipe joints burst
and, the flue not having been swept for many years, the congregation was covered
with soot.[66]

Probably more or less coincident with the introduction of stoves and gas
lighting was the addition of ventilators to remove the worst of the fumes. The most

common type was a metal grille in
some sort of decorative surround
placed high up on a gable wall,
but more imposing were the large
chimney-type ventilators attached
to the roofline in buildings like the
1904 Primitive Methodist at Forest
in Melksham. More unusual were

Melksham Forest Primitive Methodist of 1904

wall ventilators like those found at Penknap
Providence Baptist (Dilton Marsh), which have
an opening to the outside disguised by a wall-
mounted box and controlled by an internal flap.
Ventilation was certainly needed: a comment
added to an 1853 plan of the Planks Wesleyan
in Swindon remarks ruefully that the stove was
'noted for smoking the chapel well.'[67]

The next development, much more
disruptive to the fabric of the chapel, was the
introduction of piped hot water circulating from
a central coal or coke boiler. There are plentiful
examples of these, including the new heating
system in Purton Upper Square Primitive

Wall ventilator at Penknap
Providence Baptist, Dilton Marsh

Methodist in 1911 and that in the Old Baptist in Bradford on Avon in 1914. Because of the disruption, new heating was often installed at the same time as other work was being carried out.

The system fitted in Swindon's Presbyterian Church of England when it was built in 1899 was fuelled by gas from the start but the change to a more domestic type of gas-fired central heating, as was done at the Salisbury Congregational in Fisherton Street in 1978, was late and infrequent; as

An equally imposing roof ventilator at the Free United Methodist, East Grimstead, now lost. Photograph courtesy of Salisbury Museum

likely to be introduced were energy-saving measures like the false ceiling installed in the Warminster George Street Wesleyan Methodist in 1976.

Another aspect of comfort was draught-proofing. It has been noted already that many early chapels were built without porches, the porch now so common on smaller buildings being often a later addition. Equally, most earlier chapels, from Grittleton Baptist in the early eighteenth century to Hawkeridge (Heywood) Congregational in the mid nineteenth, were built with the doors opening straight into the worship space. With no porch, such an arrangement was guaranteed to freeze the congregation on winter Sundays. It is not surprising, therefore, that later buildings included an internal porch, that at Monkton Hill Methodist in Chippenham being one amongst many. Equally often the screening off of an internal porch is a later alteration, as with the example at Bradford on Avon Old Baptist.

Later rear screen at Bradford on Avon Old Baptist. Note the staircases, almost always a symmetrical pair in chapels with 3 or 4 galleries

The Twentieth Century

Relatively few chapels were built in the twentieth century, probably no more than around 80 in total in Wiltshire. A large majority either replaced earlier buildings or were built in newly expanding housing areas, with Swindon again prominent for the latter. Most of those from the Edwardian period followed the design conventions of the late nineteenth century, with gable-end chapels more exuberantly decorated than would have been seen earlier. Between the wars a more angular design reflected the styles of the time, sometimes with notable results. After the second war chapels became increasingly anonymous: many could have served equally well as village halls or primary schools though again a few exceptions stand out.

The 1906 Cheney Manor Road Primitive Methodist, later Baptist, in Swindon provides a typical example of end-of-century design, with plenty of decorative stonework offsetting the brick including both an inscription in very large text and a bizarre broken-pediment doorway. More unusual is the Congregational at Durrington, its long brick facade with doors either end seeming to revert back to the long-wall type of two centuries previously. The Winsley Congregational of 1903, constrained by its site, has a conventional but convincing Gothic exterior and a well-preserved interior making much use of both angled wood panelling and metal tracery. Perhaps most remarkable of the chapels of this period is the Wesleyan at Littleton Panell (Market Lavington), now Roman Catholic, of 1900. This is hard

Former Wesleyan at Littleton Pannell (West Lavington), the door bricked in when Roman Catholics took over the church

Swindon Evangelical Church, Devizes Road   *Salisbury Bemerton Methodist*

to see but offers a stimulating mix of flattened brick arches with a gable-end window which looks like the truncated top section of one from a medieval cathedral, the whole with more than a whiff of the Art Nouveau.

Four examples will illustrate the variety beginning to

Westbury Station Road Methodist

be seen in the period between the wars. The Evangelical Church in Devizes Road, Swindon, built in 1923 but re-faced in 1935, is at one level an entirely typical gable-end chapel with small windows either side of a large central door, yet the intense brick detailing and the blind arcade stepping its way up the gable would surely not

Bethesda Baptist, Gloucester Road, Trowbridge

have been found in an earlier building. More uncomfortable is the Bemerton Methodist in Salisbury of 1932. Here the echoes of Gothic in the windows pull against both a brick stepped gable of almost Art Deco appearance and an ashlar porch with echoes of Lutyens.

The 1926 Station Road Methodist in Westbury, though rather hidden by its large new porch, has a basilica-like shape with a clerestory formed by rows of Diocletian windows; the use of concrete allows a barrel-vaulted ceiling and an uncluttered interior space. In Trowbridge the second Bethesda Baptist of

1931 interprets the same basic concept in Renaissance style with round-headed windows below a line of small oblongs. The porch, almost like a Roman gatehouse, is integrated more successfully into the overall design that that at Westbury and, but for the decision to make the side windows at either end smaller than the rest, this would be a remarkably successful conception. Its interior is light and open with just a rear gallery.

The Ladyfield Evangelical in Chippenham, of 1996 and 2009, can be taken as typical of postwar chapels. Long and low in brick and tile, its monotony is almost unbroken by detail. Earlier and more successful is the North Bradley Baptist of 1961. Though of brick like the Chippenham chapel it uses ashlar stone uprights alongside tall glass to make a statement of the entrance and behind that an angled clerestory convincingly ties the porch into the main hall behind.

Swindon St Andrew's Methodist

Swindon has its share of dull post-war chapels but St Andrew's Methodist in Moredon Road is not one of them. Here a big bowed front window crisply defined in concrete is set against a squat tower with a spirelet to create an entirely harmonious whole. In complete contrast are the buildings of the Brethren, found in various places across the county. Always gated and anonymous, their newest buildings are also vast, as for example that of 2015 at Kington Langley which with its blank walls and curved roof looks like a warehouse, even down to the roof extension to one side as if to cover a loading bay. Their buildings are characteristically built without windows, symbolising a withdrawal from the world, and this feature was there from the start: 'After sufficient space to accommodate the people, there is nothing worth spending a shilling upon in churches.'[68] Time spent beautifying buildings instead of preaching the gospel was viewed as time wasted.

Brethren, Kington Langley

Modernisation

Not many chapels were built in the last century but plenty were modernised in the interests of making them more welcoming and more flexible and reducing running costs. Most of these changes took place well into the post-war period.

Modernised chapels show few external changes, the most obvious being the introduction of glass entrance doors often coupled with larger porches, as at both Castle Street Baptist and Silver Street Methodist in Calne. Internally, however, the alterations are more significant.

In the same way that bench pews replaced box pews, so these in turn have been replaced in many if not most chapels by single chairs, their great advantage being the flexibility they offer in allowing seating layouts to be reconfigured for different types and sizes of meeting. They also present a more modern appearance,

top left: Porton (Idmiston) Baptist before redecoration of the interior. Photograph courtesy of Porton Baptist Church; top right: Original pews and pulpit in Devizes Old Baptist but the walls painted in neutral colour; bottom left: St Edmund's Church Street Wesleyan, Salisbury, the line of the former galleries still marked on the walls and the worship space turned at right angles; bottom right: Closing off the gallery at Highworth Zion Congregational creates a new first floor room.

and this has been coupled with attempts to make interiors less 'fusty' by removing clutter, lowering the heights of pulpits and painting walls all white where in the nineteenth century they had often been covered with Biblical texts. At Porton (Idmiston), for example, the Baptist until quite recently had painted scrolls behind the pulpit exhorting the congregation to 'Sing unto the Lord' and 'Praise ye the Lord'. As late as 1925, the interior of Westbury West End Baptist was redecorated

Downton South Lane Baptist after insertion of a floor

to celebrate its centenary with green walls and a text above the pulpit reading 'We Preach Christ Crucified'.[69] Changing from such highly decorative schemes to plain white can make a chapel interior seem bland, though it should be noted that just as many chapel interiors were probably the 'dreary brown' complained of at the Lydiard Millicent Primitive Methodist in the 1930s.[70] There is undoubtedly some loss of original character but, for congregations struggling to maintain their chapel's relevance in difficult times, making the interior more welcoming and flexible must seem an obvious step.

The same arguments apply to moves to economise on running costs. In larger chapels the galleries on three or four sides can add greatly to their character, yet their capacity is seldom needed now and often they become merely resting homes for old junk: the Mere Congregational even had a large shed erected in one of its galleries, used until recently to store records. The considerable maintenance liability of these unused spaces is avoided by removing them and this has been done in a number of places, including at the St Edmund's Church Street Wesleyan in Salisbury where a line of panelling has been left on the walls to mark where the galleries once were.

To reduce heating costs and allow more flexible use of space, many chapels have partitioned off parts of the interior. A common device in those with a rear gallery is to build a partition wall up from the gallery front to make a separate first floor room: the Highworth Zion Congregational is one of numerous examples. Most dramatic is the insertion of a floor across the whole interior, leaving a truncated upper floor for worship and the lower for meeting rooms. Downton South Lane Baptist is one example of this, Salisbury Brown Street Baptist another. The result can be decidedly strange, though the Downton chapel is perhaps saved by its splendid hammer-beam roof; the spaces for worship thereby created are certainly more intimate.

Chapel Conversions

When a chapel is converted to other use an essential part of its character is lost. One view of this transition was expressed in an article about the converted Shrewton Zion Baptist, saying 'it has the introverted, shifty look of a public building converted into a private residence.' Perhaps this does not capture everything about the loss of character but it is certainly an interesting take.[71]

The converted Shrewton Zion Baptist, a victim of the early 2000s fashion for grey window framing

However, conversions can be more or less successful in preserving character, and it is worth considering what works and what does not. A few, like the Primitive Methodist in Kingsbury Square, Wilton, are converted for offices or other purposes but the great majority become houses, currently around 230 across the county.

There is a broad correlation between the date a chapel was converted and its new appearance. Early conversions can end up hiding all traces of the chapel:

Easton Wesleyan, left after conversion; right: before conversion. Photograph courtesy of the owner

Redlynch Chapel Lane Wesleyan, left: after conversion; right: before conversion.
Photograph courtesy of Carolyn Birch

the Wesleyan in Potterne, for example, converted some time after 1938, is so much altered that only the end gable gives a small clue to its previous life. The Wesleyan at Easton, converted in 1965, retains its chapel porch but otherwise looks like any other vernacular cottage, and the Bishopstone (South) Primitive Methodist, converted as late as 1979, is again betrayed only by the gable end.

The latter date corresponded with the popularity of 'picture windows' for houses and a number of chapel conversions replaced the original windows by these. The results were utterly out of sympathy with the proportions of a gable-end chapel as the Wesleyan on Chapel Lane Redlynch and the Hilperton Baptist show.

More recent conversions have generally been in sympathy with the original building, usually leaving door and window shapes unaltered. Sometimes the main body of the chapel is left open as a main living space, with the rear gallery re-formed as bedrooms: as these are the interiors of people's homes it would be inappropriate to give examples. Often a full floor is inserted, creating

left: Hullavington Mount Zion Baptist – the chapel originally had rectangular
windows set high; right: Easterton Wesleyan – the conversion is faithful to the original
window shapes but at the cost of heavy window framing

the problem of what to do with the windows which are usually tall and hence stretching across two floors. Sometimes there is a clumsy division of the tall window into two with some sort of panelling in between, as at the Easterton Wesleyan or the Mount Zion Baptist in Hullavington. At the extreme, one half of the tall windows is blocked entirely as at the Winterbourne Bassett Primitive Methodist converted c1960.

Elsewhere, complex window framing is used to disguise the floor with varying degrees of success, as at the Primitive Methodist in Purton Stoke, the Primitive Methodist at Lydiard Green (Lydiard Millicent) and the Wesleyan at Easterton. But perhaps most successful are those conversions where the inserted floor is inset slightly so that the original windows can be retained. Amongst many examples are the High Street Primitive Methodist in Bishopstone (North) and the Staverton Wesleyan. At Spirthill (Bremhill) Wesleyan the inserted floor has been obscured by a panel of darker glass across the window.

Bishopstone (N) High Street Primitive Methodist – inserted floor inset so that the window framing can remain unaltered

The Gazetteers

These introductory chapters have discussed the history and design of chapels countywide. The gazetteers which follow detail this place by place. The history of urban chapels is often both more complex and more inter-related than that of those in the villages and for that reason they are separated in the gazetteers: Chapter 4 covers the villages, Chapter 5 the smaller towns and Chapters 6 to 9 the largest urban areas of Chippenham, Salisbury, Swindon and Trowbridge.

The village gazetteer is given in order of parish name: settlements which are not parishes are cross-referenced. The use of bold text indicates a chapel which is no longer standing; bold italic text shows where the building still exists, whether in use, empty or converted. Chapels with interesting features or an interesting history are highlighted with a star; the most important ones have two.

4. The Villages

Aldbourne

Independents are believed to have had a meeting house in the village in the mid eighteenth century; it burned down later in the century and was not replaced.[72] **Baptists** converted cottages in Back Lane into a chapel in c1841; this was replaced by a new chapel there in 1868 which in turn was demolished some time after 1931. The graveyard remained in place and its railings were still there in 2019.[73] **Wesleyan Methodists** built a chapel in 1807, probably on the site in Lottage Road of a later chapel said to have been built in 1844. This in turn was replaced on the same site by the:

New Methodist Church of 1968, Lottage Road, a large plain brick hall under a slate roof with commemorative stones from the earlier building inset to the brickwork. In use in 2019.[74]

Wesleyan Methodists also built a chapel at Woodsend in around 1845, north of the Ogbourne road and immediately west of the road junction. The chapel closed in 1906 or 1907, the proceeds going towards the purchase of a chapel at Ogbourne St George, and it was demolished soon afterwards.[75]

Primitive Methodists converted cottages in West Street into a chapel in around 1840. It became unsafe and was replaced by a new building on the same site in 1856 and this in turn was replaced by a new chapel in Gothic style in 1906. The new chapel was extended in 1936 and at that stage was a substantial building of five bays, side on to the road, in brick with ashlar dressings. The porch had crenellations with dates 1936 and 1906 on piers either side. It was demolished in the early 1980s after the Methodist churches combined in the new hall in Lottage Road and was replaced by two new cottages carrying a plaque, 'Chapel Cottages 1986'.[76]

Alderbury

Wesleyan Methodists built a chapel at the north end of Folly Lane in 1825, adjacent to what is now Old Chapel Close. It was rebuilt in 1839 and a Sunday school room was added in 1912. The chapel was closed in 1970 and demolished in 1977.[77]

Whaddon Primitive Methodist Chapel, * in use by Roman Catholics. This was built at the south end of Whaddon in 1884, in red brick with round-arched windows, corner pilasters and plentiful pale brick dressings in typical late 19th century style, with a small and probably later schoolroom behind. The original impact of these multiple arches with their prominent keystones – the door, windows either side, an arch over the large square date plaque for 1884, the three bays on the return – would have been

Alderbury, Whaddon Primitive Methodist

considerable but the later porch and postwar addition to the left hand side have reduced the effect. It was sold to the Roman Catholics in 1990 and they have used it as the Holy Family church since, combining the whole interior into a single space. Further to the rear is what may have been the manse, now sold off as a separate house.[78]

All Cannings

Allington Bethel Baptist, All Cannings

Bethel Baptist Chapel, Allington. * Built in the centre of Allington in 1829, it closed for a period between the two world wars but now remains open for a weekly service. Grade 2 listed, of brick under a hipped slate roof, the appealing early facade seems full of windows, five in all in two tiers, one blind and all with stone Y-tracery. The porch is of wood and is later with a stone above dated 1829. There are two taller Y-tracery windows to the rear and small brick pavilions either side, presumably schoolroom and vestry and perhaps mid 19th century. It has a gallery.[79]

All Cannings Wesleyan Methodist, now a house. Opened in 1889 in The Street and designed by John Ashley Randell of Devizes. The facade facing the road was originally of plain brick with stone dressings; windowless, it had a small porch with a cusped doorway and a broad inscription above. It was closed in the late 1950s and then converted into a house, rendered, the porch removed and four unhappy windows inserted, one of them initially a garage door. It is now called Chapel House but otherwise only recognisable by trefoil decoration at the gable head and a retained roof ventilator.[80]

Allington

Primitive Methodist Chapel, * now a private house, east of village street. It is the central one of a block of three houses and perhaps originally 18th century but converted to a very small chapel in 1843 and reconverted c2002. It is probably of cob construction, originally thatched but now tiled. A porch at the north end, added after 1911, carries the inscription 'Primitive Methodist Chapel' which was previously placed on the wall behind. Before conversion there was a single large window to the right but there are now two pairs of smaller windows. A window above the porch lit the gallery.[81]

left: Allington Primitive Methodist, converted back to a house
right: Allington Primitive Methodist in use c1900, the central building of three. Photograph courtesy of Bourne Valley Historical Society

Allington – see also All Cannings

Alton

In the early 20th century **Wesleyan Methodists** built a small chapel south east of Alton Priors Manor. It was in use until c1947, later used as a garage, then demolished and replaced by a house called Chapel Cottage.[82]

Alvediston

Primitive Methodist Chapel, east of centre and south of road to Berwick St John, now derelict. Built in 1894 for £200, it is of red brick with pale brick bands under a slate roof. The gable facing the road has a small porch, wavy barge-boards and a now-illegible inscription at the gable head. It was closed by 1951 and in 2019 the windows were blocked and the whole heavily overgrown.[83]

Ansty

No chapels recorded.[84]

Ashton Keynes

Baptists held meetings in a house, The Grove, 8 and 9 High Road, from c1874 to c1891. The house, Grade 2 listed, still stands.[85]

Bethesda Congregational Chapel, now a house, Grade 2 listed. It and its adjacent handsome manse were erected in Fore Street in 1838. The chapel is of gable-end design but with unusually elaborate ashlar window dressings on a facade of squared stone blocks. The windows are round-arched, one either side and two above the porch, and there is a date plaque for 1838. The sides are of rubble-stone and the roof of slate. It closed in 1970 and was converted to a house.[86]

Primitive Methodist Chapel, towards east end of Gosditch. This was constructed in 1839-40 at a cost of £220 and renovated inside with the addition of a gallery in 1862. It was one of the weakest meetings in the Brinkworth circuit by the turn of the century and closed in 1933 to become a bakery complete with large 'Hovis' sign. Later converted to a private house now called 'The Old Bakery,' it is of squared stone block to the front, rubble-stone to the sides, with a slate roof and brick dressings to round-arched windows. The simple gable facing the road has a small porch, two tall windows placed unusually high above and a plaque, now illegible. .[87]

Atworth

Independent Chapel, * of 1790-92, by the junction of Bradford Road and the A365, in use. A simple early chapel in coursed rubble-stone with ashlar dressings and a hipped roof formerly of slate but now tiled. The plain front has an arched doorway and matching stone hood with a pointed lunette above; each side has four arched windows. There is a rear gallery and wall panelling has been retained though the interior is otherwise plain. Despite its apparently modest size it was said to have had capacity for 400 in 1851.[88]

Atworth Independent

Ebenezer Baptist, at east end of village by turn to Purlpit; closed 1979 and a private house since 1981. Of gable-end design in plain coursed stone block under slate with ashlar dressings and large rectangular windows to front and sides. The door has a small flat hood; the gable plaque above dates it to 1860 though it did not open until 1864. There is a substantial modern side extension to the rear dated 1981.[89]

There was a short-lived **Primitive Methodist** chapel in the village: this opened in 1843, was still in existence in 1864 but probably closed soon thereafter.[90]

A *Free Church* was formed in the *Workmen's Hall*, now 37a Bath Road, in 1882: those involved had fallen out with a new minister at the Baptist chapel. The Workmen's Hall itself was built c1876 in coursed shaped rubble-stone with ashlar dressings under a roof of graduated stone slates. The gable to the road has centrally-placed sash windows above and below, though the lower one may have been a door originally, and there is a blank plaque above. The hall was never used exclusively by the Free Church, which is believed to have closed in the early 1950s, and the building has subsequently been converted into a house.[91]

Avebury

Avebury Congregational

*Congregational Chapel,*** within the stone circle, in the ownership of the National Trust since 2017. An important early chapel with a complex history. Dissenting ministers from Marlborough, Devizes and Calne met in Avebury from c1670 as a convenient centre outside the restrictions of the 1665 Five Mile Act. A chapel was opened at around that date in cottages opposite the present one, which itself opened in 1707. Originally square under a double gable roof, it was built of sarsen blocks with one square window each side. It was extended 10ft towards the road (north) in the mid 18th century in similar materials, with one small window each side to illuminate the new gallery, then again in brick in two bays to the south c1830 to provide a schoolroom. Finally in the late 19th century the north front was remodelled with a pointed-arch doorway, Y-tracery arched windows to either side and a single similar window above. The main chapel roof is now of tile, the schoolroom roof of slate; the schoolroom rear gable is of rubble-stone with brick dressings for three stepped lancet windows and the chapel gable shows by its upper courses of brick where the roof was raised to accommodate the gallery. Inside, the gallery retains its benches and the chapel its 19th century pews, with the pulpit placed in the arch separating chapel from schoolroom.[92]

Baptists worshipped in a cob-walled building from c1826 and a new **Providence Strict Baptist chapel** was built north of the High Street in 1873, opposite what is now the village shop. It closed c1953, was sold to the National Trust and later demolished to form part of a car park.[93]

Barford St Martin

*Primitive Methodist Chapel, West Street,** now a house. A good example of turn of the century style, in brick with plentiful ashlar dressings on the gable facing the road, including prominent pilasters at the corners with pyramidal heads. The porch has doors on the angle either side and a double round-arched window between with a small circular light above. There are tall round-arched windows either side of the

Exuberant stained glass from 1902 in the Barford Primitive Methodist, retained after conversion and insertion of floor. Note the panelled ceiling and ornate stops to window mouldings

porch and, above, a large stepped three-light round-arched window of patterned stained glass with the inscription 'Primitive 1902 Methodist' in large lettering. The sides, largely unornamented, are of three bays. A meeting started here c1830 and a first chapel was built, on this site, c1843: the earlier chapel was smaller and with 'mud' walls. The chapel closed and was unobtrusively converted in the 1980s, retaining stained glass in the front and side windows together with ceiling and some wall panelling.[94]

Photograph also on page 47.

Baydon

The **Providence Particular Baptist Chapel** was built on the east side of Aldbourne Road in 1806 and went out of use probably around 1910, at which date it was offered to the Wesleyan Methodists. It has since been demolished and 'Old Chapel House' now occupies the site.[95]

The first *Wesleyan Methodist Chapel,* now a house, was built south of Ermin Street at the east end of the village in 1823. Now called Chapel Cottage, it is rendered under slate, much extended and almost unrecognisable, although it carries a date of 1946 where there might have been an original gable plaque.[96]

The second *Methodist Chapel,* now a house, was built west of Aldbourne Road in 1939 to replace that on Ermin Street. It is of brick under tile in an idiosyncratic mixture of styles. The porch carries a balcony above; the door surround is in ashlar and dated 1939 with blind cusped lancets either side. There is a Venetian window above the balcony and the sides have conventional flat-headed windows. It closed in 1985.[97]

Beanacre – see Melksham Without

Beechingstoke

No chapels recorded.[98]

Berwick Bassett

No chapels recorded.[99]

Berwick St James

No chapels recorded.[100]

Berwick St John

Ebenezer Particular Baptist Chapel, south side of Luke Street, Grade 2 listed, now part of Chapel House. This is dated 1828, with a three-bay manse attached to the east end. It is of ashlar under slate; the gable has a small Tudor-arched porch door, two pointed windows above and a date plaque. The sides each have two large pointed windows and there was formerly a panelled gallery over the entrance. The chapel closed in 1984.[101]

Wesleyan Methodist Chapel, south of Alvediston Road by village crossroads, derelict in 2019. This was built in 1875, closed by 1964 and is now boarded up though the grounds are maintained. The gable facing the road is in ashlar with a round-arched door and tall round-arched windows either side. Above the door is a plaque 'Memorial Stone laid by T F Grove MP July 14 1873.' The sides and rear are of brick and flint bands with ashlar dressings and each side has three round-arched windows. The roof is of clay tiles.[102]

Berwick St Leonard

No chapels recorded.[103]

Biddestone

Ruins of Friends' Meeting House, Slaughterford, * in woods behind 'Rock Cottage', east of Germains Lane. George Fox attended meetings here in the late 1650s and it is possible that this small and very early chapel was built some time before c1670, the date usually given for its construction by the Friends. It was in use by them until c1776 but

Friends' Meeting House at Slaughterford (Biddestone) – it is now wholly ruinous and surrounded by trees. Photograph courtesy of Wiltshire Museum, Devizes

attendances fell and, discouraged, they sold it to the Congregationalists in 1806 for £20. The Congregationalists thrived for some time but by 1913, when they offered it back to the Quakers, it had not been in regular use for many years. The Quakers refused it and it became derelict, collapsing in the 1960s though the ruins and some gravestones are still there and perhaps worth a pilgrimage. The chapel was of simple design in rubble-stone with a roof of graduated stone slates. A door to the front gable with a plain hood and a square-headed window above can still be made out but the sides, that to the left containing a small transomed window, are mostly gone. The hillside, now densely wooded, was previously almost clear of vegetation.[104]

Ebenezer Particular Baptist Chapel, west of Cuttle Lane just north of village centre; Grade 2 listed; now 'Yew Bank House'. It is of rubble-stone with ashlar dressings under a hipped slate roof. The plain porch in ashlar is later and above it is a plaque, 'Ebenezer Chapel 1832' and a small circular window in a square surround with spandrels. There are two shallow-pointed side windows, a narrow extension to the rear in rubble-stone with ashlar dressings - the school room of 1928 - and a modern lean-to extension to the side of that. The chapel closed in 2003 and was converted in 2011.[105]

Primitive Methodist Chapel, of 1884, west of Cuttle Lane at north end of village; now a house. It is of coursed rubble-stone with ashlar dressings under slate; the plain gable facing the road has a more recent stone block porch and a plaque above now illegible; the sides are of two bays with round-arched windows. It closed in 1979.[106]

Bishops Cannings

A **Friends' Meeting House** and burial ground of 1689 is mentioned but no further references to it have been found.[107]

General Baptist Chapel, Coate, * east of Fieldside, now a house. This was built in 1848 by a philanthropic Devizes tobacco manufacturer as a chapel and day school: the day school closed in 1876 when the National school in the village opened but the chapel continued in use until 1973. It was converted to a house in 1976 and has had further alterations since. The layout of the building is now most apparent from above, with a hipped slate roof in a U shape with uneven arms. The two bays to the rendered front on the left were the chapel and schoolroom, originally with a pair of doors in a small pointed porch at the centre and flat-headed windows either side. A plaque, 'Coate School 1848,' remains and there are two pairs of new windows in two tiers. The right hand bay, stretching back three bays on the return, was the minister's house, again much altered. The chapel interior was basic, with simple benches.[108]

Providence Particular Baptist Chapel, attached at the rear of the house called Meadow View at the south end of The Street and now forming part of it. The chapel was probably built in the 1870s, at the same time as the house to which it is attached. The different sized windows suggest it might not have been intended

Coate Baptist, Bishops Cannings, the minister's house to the right larger than the chapel. Photograph courtesy of Penny Cann.

originally as a chapel but it was in use as such by the 1880s and remained in use until the 1930s. It is small, single-storey, in painted brick under tile with a central doorway and windows either side, all probably in their original positions.[109]

Horton Wesleyan Methodist Chapel, south of road at west end of village, now a house. This was built in 1831 on a piece of land 27ft square bought for £5; it closed in 1984 and was then used as a workshop before conversion to a house. The chapel is of brick under a hipped slate roof raised on conversion to accommodate the insertion of a first floor. The original windows in the entrance front have been replaced lower down the facade by similar paired lights under pointed arches either side of a new porch; a double-headed arched window to the side is in the original position.[110]

Bishopstone North

A **Wesleyan Methodist Chapel** was built in Little Hinton by 1851 but its location is unknown and it probably did not survive long after 1864.[111]

Primitive Methodist Chapel, Mount Pleasant. Built in 1833 for £65 and seating 100, this is a low thatched building in rubble-stone with brick corners, now painted white. In 2019 it was used for storage and heavily overgrown with ivy on the street side. Symmetrically placed doors on the opposite side, with a window between, hint at its possible original appearance. It was replaced by the High Street chapel in 1886 and used for a period after closure for cheese processing.[112]

Primitive Methodist Chapel, High Street. At south end of street; now a house.

1886 Primitive Methodist, Bishopstone (N)

Made of brick under slate with profuse stone dressings in late 19th century style, the gable facing the road has two tall round-arched windows with iron lattice glazing bars either side of a protruding porch which has a double round-arched window to the front. Above is a star window in a roundel with inscription: 'Primitive Methodist 1886' and there are prominent corner pilasters with pyramidal tops. The sides are more plain, with three bays of round-arched windows. The chapel closed c1966.[113]

Hinton Parva Mission Hall, south side of lane running north west from church, empty but well maintained in 2019. Built in 1911 with funds from the County Towns Mission, it continued in use until 2006. It is small, of brick under tile, and the gable facing the road has pointed windows either side of an altered porch. Above are a gable plaque 'Mission Hall 1911', and plain barge-boards replacing previous decorative ones. The sides each have two pointed windows and there is a circular window in the rear gable above the pulpit. It has had various non-domestic uses since being sold.[114]

Bishopstone South

*Primitive Methodist Chapel, Croucheston,** now a private house called The Old Chapel, north of Chapel Lane. This was registered in 1833 but may be earlier. The building is an L shape of substantial size, the left wing being an earlier and much altered house. The chapel itself, of brick under tile, originally had two tall round-arched windows on the long side, each with two pointed-arch lights. These have been bricked in on conversion and replaced by three smaller pairs in two tiers but the end gable remains largely unaltered. This is pedimented but austere with just one small circular window, for the former gallery, above a round-arched doorway with a flat hood. The chapel closed in 1978 and was converted in 1979: only the end gable gives its former use away.[115]

Croucheston Primitive Methodist, Bishopstone (S) after conversion, original entrance gable to right

The same during conversion showing original chapel windows.

Bishopstrow

No chapels recorded.[116]

Blunsdon St Andrew

Strict Baptist Chapel, Blunsdon Hill, in use. This is pebble-dashed, probably over original brick; the roof is slate, half-hipped; the wall facing the road is blank but for pointed-arch windows, previously square-headed, on the porch and the lean-to rear extension. The opposite side has two mullioned windows with drip mouldings, these having external shutters previously. The chapel was built for Independents c1808 and the Baptist church was formed in 1834.[117]

Wesleyan Methodist Chapel, north of High Street, Broad Blunsdon, closed 2020 and for sale in 2021. This is of coursed stone blocks with ashlar dressings and pointed-arch windows under slate. The sides are of four bays and the gable facing the road has tall windows either side of the porch and, above, an unusual clock at the centre of a circular window with surrounding inscription 'Wesley Chapel 1881'. There is a 1950s extension to the rear.[118]

Primitive Methodist Chapel, Chapel Hill, Broad Blunsdon, now a house. The original chapel of 1837, in rough stone with brick dressings under slate, was rebuilt with a Classical brick facade, some ashlar dressings and perhaps a raised roof in 1864. The gable facing the road has a round-arched door and similar tall windows either side; there is a plaque above stating 'Primitive Methodist Chapel 1837 rebuilt 1864', pilasters and a pediment. The rear has two round-arched windows with a ventilator at the gable head; the north wall is now blank. It was still open in 1939 but may have closed and combined with the High Street Wesleyan not long after that. It was then used for a time as a store before conversion to a house.[119]

Bodenham – see Odstock

Bottlesford – see Manningford

Bower Chalke

General Baptist Chapel, Church Street, in use. The original chapel of 1863-4 is to the right, its gable facing the road in random stone block with some flint interspersed above. The door has a pointed head and there is a similar window with Y-tracery above; the roof is of slate and there is a crude lean-to extension to the right. On the left is the new chapel built in 1897 whereupon the original became the schoolroom. The new chapel is in brick under slate with tall rectangular windows with small leaded panes, two to the front and three to the left side. There are string courses at sill and lintel levels and the front has also a circular window at the gable head and a plaque marking the laying of the foundation stone in 1897. A Baptist chapel noted in the 1851 ecclesiastical census may have been a predecessor to that of 1863 though there appears to be no other record of it.[120]

Wesleyan Methodist Chapel, Sheppards Cross, west end of Church Street, now a house. Built in 1879 in brick and flint, it has window dressings in stone and a roof of bands of plain and scalloped tiles. The long side facing the road is of three bays with arched windows and the entrance gable end has tall lancets either side of the porch, with a circular window above incorporating a four-leaf clover design. The lower extension to the west end, probably the vestry, has a modern plaque. The chapel closed in 1982 but may not have been converted until c1996.[121]

Primitive Methodists were renting a building for use as a chapel in 1859 and may have been using it for some time before then. It was closed by 1864.[122]

Box

The distribution of chapels here reflects the split of the village, with separate communities at Box Hill, Kingsdown and Ashley of which only Ashley seems to have had no chapel. Box was a stronghold for United Methodists but it is notable that there was no Baptist chapel, with local Baptists having to travel to Corsham.

*Ebenezer United Methodist Chapel, High Street,** in use. The original chapel of 1834 was replaced by the present one alongside in 1897, designed by A J Pictor of Bruton at a cost of £1200. The 1834 chapel, which was smaller and set at right angles to the present one, was then demolished along with the cottages in front of it to allow construction of schoolrooms in 1907, also by Pictor. The chapel is of gable-end type in ashlar under slate with large pointed-arch windows containing Gothic tracery either side of and above the porch; there are prominent pilasters at

the corners, buttressed to the sides. The inside has been modernised but retains a gallery now housing an 1850s organ in a mahogany case, acquired in the 1920s. The schoolrooms are of similar mass, again gable-ended but more Tudor with mullioned windows and drip mouldings. The two together have a strong presence in the village centre. The schoolrooms were sold off in 2001 and the money used to refurbish the chapel.[123]

Box High Street United Methodist of 1897, schoolrooms to the right.

United Methodist Chapel, Box Hill, just north of Quarryman's Arms, now a house. Built in 1868 under the influence of the Ebenezer chapel to 'combat riotous and drunken living' prevalent among quarrymen living on Box Hill, it is of ashlar under slate. The gable facing the road has a large pointed window which may be an extension of the original; otherwise it has been altered out of recognition. It closed in 1967.[124]

*United Methodist Chapel, Kingsdown,** Lower Kingsdown Road; now a house. The original chapel of 1869, also built under the influence of the Ebenezer chapel,

Box Kingsdown United Methodist of 1926

was attractively rebuilt in 1926 in ashlar under tile. The gable facing the road has a six-light mullioned and transomed window, the top sections round-headed beneath a drip moulding, above which is a date plaque. The porch is to the side and there is a lower floor to the rear where the ground dips away. It closed in 1967.[125]

Primitive Methodist Chapel, Beech Road, south end, now a house. This was probably built in the 1890s and is an extension to an existing terrace. The original, in ashlar under a slate roof, had two round-arched windows to the street, one of which remains, and a porch in the end gable wall. At a later date, probably after closure in 1957/8, it was extended by a further bay, the porch and door brought round to the front wall and one of the round-arched windows replaced by conventional windows above and below.[126]

Plymouth Brethren Gospel Hall, Quarry Hill; just north of Brunel Way junction; converted to a house but semi-derelict in 2021. Of ashlar under a hipped tiled roof, the north and east walls now each have two small square windows, probably converted from round-arched, and the west wall has similar windows either side of a replacement porch. It is believed to have been built in 1882 by Brethren originating from Bath and to have closed in 1964.[127]

A mission hall, denomination unknown, was built at **Prospect, Kingsdown** in 1936. A painted notice board 'Prospect Mission Hall 1936' remains, attached to a new fence, and the timber building set back from and below the road is probably a replacement for the original. It now operates as a holiday cottage as does the small roadside building in rubble-stone under a tiled roof which retains a Gothicised window in one gable. This is perhaps of the 1940s and may have served as a vestry.[128]

Boyton

Corton Particular Baptist Chapel, north end of Coomb View; now a house. This now looks like something from the Mediterranean but was built in 1828 as a chapel of conventional appearance. The south gable, where there is now a chimney stack, once housed the door, tall lancets either side, a plaque 'Ebenezer Chapel AD 1828' which has been retained on the chimney, and a truncated Gothic window above. The side facing the road, which now contains a complicated mix of openings, was built with three broad Gothic windows, and beyond that was the schoolroom, tapering in plan and with a plain door and windows. The schoolroom seems to have replaced two cottages predating the chapel and was enlarged in 1854. Inside the chapel there was a gallery at the south end and a smaller gallery, described as a balcony, over the pulpit. It closed in 1965, was sold in 1967, was used for a time as a store but was converted to a house in the 1980s at which time the chapel was substantially altered and the schoolroom rebuilt to a much larger size.[129]

Corton Baptist New Hall. 50 metres south of the chapel and built in 1914 to provide extra accommodation, particularly for young people. It is of brick under slate; the end gable has pebble-dashing above and a date plaque '1914' above a round-arched window. The rest was much altered and extended on conversion into a house, presumably after closing at much the same time as the chapel.[130]

Bradenstoke – see Lyneham

Bratton

Baptist Chapel,** off Redlands, Grade 2* listed, in use. This is externally one of the most appealing chapels in the county, in red brick under a semi-hipped roof of graduated stone tiles. Built in 1734 by a group from both Bratton and Erlestoke, it was originally a modest 30ft by 20ft but has had numerous extensions through the years, most noticeably the east wing for a vestry added in 1784, a 12ft extension to the rear in 1786, addition of the west wing for schoolrooms in 1818 and the raising

Bratton Baptist

of the roof by four feet in 1858. The front has a round-arched double door under a stone hood and tall round-arched windows either side with ashlar surrounds and prominent keystones. Above the door is a round window with similar ashlar surround, inserted when the roof was raised. The wings, with sash windows and conventional tiles, are more plain but the rear of the chapel is of similar pattern to the front and carries a date-stone for 1786. The schoolrooms were extended a further 10ft back in 1874. Inside, a first gallery was added in 1807 but the 1858 works increased this to three, approached by staircases in the wings. Late 20th century internal alterations included replacing the pews by chairs and introducing

Bratton Baptist interior – the woodwork now stripped of its previous dark stain

a screen across the rear to create a corridor inside the door.[131]

An **Independent Methodist** chapel was built here in an unknown location some time before 1800, seating 150. It was still in use in 1851 but seems unlikely to have survived long after that date.[132]

Wesleyan Methodists built a small chapel west of Stradbrook in 1870. It closed in 1952 and was demolished in 1957.[133]

Braydon

Primitive Methodist Chapel, in countryside at SU032873, in use. A green corrugated iron chapel built in 1889 for members of the Brinkworth circuit at a cost of £109, it has a small porch, rectangular windows and wavy bargeboards. The flat-roofed rear extension dates from 1970 as may the side arcade. Despite its remote position it had a regular congregation and still had a weekly Sunday service in 2020.[134] *Photograph on page 37.*

Bremhill

This widely spread parish had an early **Quaker** presence, the Friends meeting in a cottage in Charlcutt from at least 1696, but their meeting house had apparently gone out of use by 1783 and was given up to the lord of the manor in 1808.[135]

Moravian Church, East Tytherton, ** Grade 2* listed. An important example of a Moravian settlement, still in use. The main range is of brick with ashlar dressings under graduated stone slates, in three units. The chapel at the centre, dated 1792, is on the site of the original of 1745. It has tall round-arched windows either side of a classical columned porch with wide double doors, added in 1882; above this is a broad lunette and to the left a date stone for 1792 above a large plaque, now blank. There is a small hexagonal bell-turret over the right hand end. The inside is plain save for a gallery on iron columns, the centre broken forward and holding an organ.

The manse is to the left, of three bays with two tiers of sash windows, the outer ones paired; the door has a flat hood. To the right Church Cottage, the girls' school, was added by 1794. Originally of two bays, it was later extended to three and has similar windows to those of the manse. Behind these and separate from them, Kellaways House was the sisters' house, a little earlier, dated 1785. This is a larger, more severe affair, ashlar-fronted, of three storeys divided by bands and three wide bays. There are triple sash windows each side with the doorway and single windows in the middle.

Beyond Kellaways House is the distinctive graveyard with oblong gravestones

East Tytherton (Bremhill) Moravian

East Tytherton (Bremhill) Moravian – the interior

lying flat amongst trees. The chapel is still in use and the manse and Church Cottage are let out in four flats. Kellaways House has been sold.[136]
Photograph also on page 28.

Baptist Mission Hall, Ratford, ST982719; built 1900 as a mission church of Calne Castle Street Baptist, closed c1970 and now used as a store. This is a small brown corrugated iron chapel with wavy bargeboards, extended to the rear and in good condition.[137]

Wesleyan Methodist Chapel, Spirthill,* south end of village, now a house, Grade 2 listed. Simple and dignified in brick with ashlar dressings under tile, the rear wall rendered, it has two Y-traceried Gothic windows on the long side facing the road. There is a smaller version of the same over the double door in the gable end and above that a plaque dated 1828. It was closed in 1982, sold and used as a store and later converted to a house with an inserted floor replacing the original gallery, the floor marked across the windows by a line of darker glass. It provides a good example of how to insert a floor without ruining the external appearance of the windows.[138]

Spirthill (Bremhill) Wesleyan   Foxham (Bremhill) Wesleyan

Wesleyan Methodist Chapel, Foxham,* east end of village, now a house. This was built in 1855 close in front of existing cottages, in brick with ashlar dressings under slate. The well-detailed facade has two tiers of small round-arched windows and a pedimented plaque dated 1855. The porch, probably later, is harmonious but the chapel might have looked even better without it. There are two bays of larger round-arched windows to the sides. It closed in the 1980s.[139]

A **Primitive Methodist** chapel is listed in 1855, but not in the 1851 religious census. It is possible that this was a forerunner to that at Stanley, below.[140]

Primitive Methodist Chapel, Stanley, east of bridge, boarded up in 2019. Built 1865 and closed by 1986, this is a plain chapel in brick under slate with round-arched windows and ashlar dressings. The gable front has tall windows either side of the door, which has a lunette window above and a date plaque for 1865. The two-bay sides have similar windows.[141]

Brinkworth

The **Society of Friends** registered a meeting house in Brinkworth in 1690 but attendance had declined by the mid 18th century and the meeting house probably closed around then.[142]

Independents built a substantial chapel at **Causeway End** (SU007846) in 1741; this became a village mission of Malmesbury Silver Street Congregational. It was closed c1952 and subsequently demolished.[143]

Vine House, Grittenham, Grade 2 listed, was a farmhouse but was used by **Moravians** for a period in the late 18th and early 19th centuries. Long since converted back to a private house, it has a 16th century core but with substantial additions and alterations later.[144]

The **Brinkworth Circuit**, central to the spread of Primitive Methodism across much of southern England, had its origins here in 1824, at which time the village was said to have 'contained so many of the vilest characters that for years it had been perilous for a stranger to ride through the village alone.'.[145] On this unpromising ground the first *Primitive Methodist Chapel*, actually the fourth in the Brinkworth circuit, was built in 1828. This is the building, now a house inappropriately called Wesley Hall, just west of the later chapel and for long used as an assembly room. It is in rough stone blockwork under a modern tiled roof and very much altered, but it previously had round-arched windows, a circular window above the door and two tall windows to the sides; it retains only a trefoil-shaped ventilator at the gable head. Enlarged in 1839 with the installation of a gallery, it was replaced in 1860 by the new chapel.[146]

1860 Primitive Methodist, Brinkworth

Primitive Methodist Chapel, Brinkworth,[*] in village centre, now a house. Tall for a village chapel, as if to represent the status of the Brinkworth Circuit, it is built of rough stone with ashlar dressings under slate, to the design of T S Lansdown of Swindon. The gable facing the road has angled buttresses at the corners, a Gothic doorway, lancets either side and a triple lancet above, the windows all retaining their original coloured glass. An ornate scroll above the door reads: 'Primitive Methodist Chapel Jubilee, AD 1860'. There are two pairs of lancets to the east wall and probably the same originally to the west but one pair is now filled in. The former manse is alongside.[147]

Primitive Methodists of the Brinkworth circuit also built a chapel east of the road at **Callow Hill** in 1889 after meeting in a cottage from 1870. It was of conventional design with round-arched windows either side of a porch and was two bays deep. The **Salvation Army** shared it for weekday services around 1896 and the chapel closed between 1955 and 1971; it was subsequently demolished. A house called Whitegates now occupies the site.[148]

Primitive Methodists of this circuit built a further chapel at **Grittenham** (SU028827) in 1894 after more than 40 years of meeting in a cottage, searching for a site for a chapel but without success because of the opposition of a Roman Catholic landowner. The chapel was built at this relatively remote spot to be as close as possible to the cottage previously used and was an iron building, though relatively elaborate with shaped glazing bars to the windows and a round window above the porch. It appears otherwise to have been of conventional design, two bays deep. The chapel closed between 1955 and 1971 and was subsequently demolished.[149]

Britford

No chapels recorded.[150]

Brixton Deverill

An **Independent Methodist Chapel** was built c1843 but was no longer in use by 1867. It is believed to have been demolished.[151]

Broad Chalke

Congregational Chapel of 1801, Chapel Lane off North Street, Grade 2 listed, now a house. The chapel is of flint and stone and is attached at right angles at the west end of an earlier brick cottage, the whole unusually under thatch. A garage door replaces the previous chapel doorway, above which used to be a window to the gallery. To the rear, two tall round-arched windows give the main clue to the building's past, though now split by brickwork to reflect the insertion of a floor. The windows to the west wall have been altered. This chapel was replaced by the High Street Congregational in 1864 and subsequently became a temperance hall and a school before conversion to a house in 1986.[152]

1864 Congregational, Broad Chalke

Congregational Chapel of 1864, High Street. * This is Gothic, by W J Stent of Warminster, the front section now a village shop and the rear a cafe, though services are still held. Of flint and stone under slate, its most notable feature is the recessed central arch in the gable facing the road, the shape and large size of which make it look like a whale's jawbone. Within this and above the protruding porch are two cusped two-light lancets with a trefoil over and there are further lancets either side of the porch. The sides are of four bays with a lean-to extension beyond. It was said to have been built at the bicentenary of the original Independents meeting in the village.[153].

Primitive Methodist Chapel, South Street. Previously of cob under thatch and attached to the east end of Yew Tree Cottage, this was used from c1843 as a chapel until closure in 1965 and sale to the owners of the cottage. The back wall collapsed in 1970 and the remainder of the chapel was demolished and replaced by a single storey extension to the house of brick under tile.[154]

Broad Hinton

Primitive Methodist Chapel, now a house called Chapel Cottage, south of Horton Way at north end of village. By Read and Osborne of Swindon, this is of brick under slate. Originally with arched windows either side of a porch in the gable end facing the road, it has three bays between buttresses to the sides. It has been altered almost out of recognition, with the former door bricked in, windows re-shaped and a dormer inserted. Primitive Methodists from here had been meeting in neighbouring villages from the early days until a revival in 1906 led to a cottage being fitted up for worship and then this chapel being built in 1907 as part of the Brinkworth circuit. It closed in the mid 1930s and was sold in 1944.[155]

Exclusive Brethren from the early 20th century used a **Mission Hall** and after that a purpose-built wooden building. By 1937 they were using the building on the main street, a painted brick extension to a thatched house behind, which later became the Post Office and in 2019 was a tack shop. They stayed there until c1963.[156]

Broad Town

Wesleyan Methodists built a chapel at the end of Chapel Lane in 1868. It was closed in 1938 and demolished soon afterwards. The chapel stood in the angle between two roads and had a half-hexagonal front, the central portion with pilasters and a pediment.[157]

Primitive Methodist Chapel, on Wootton Bassett road north of village, now a commercial garage. A mission chapel for Brinkworth was built in Broad Town in 1827, the second chapel in the new Brinkworth circuit. It was elsewhere in the village, converted to cottages called the 'Chapel Houses' and still standing in 1907. The 1827 chapel was replaced by another in 1842, side on to the road with a burial ground to the south; this had a gallery added in 1858 for the use of children attending the Sunday services. The Primitive Methodists had a strong following here and in 1866 built a third chapel, the one still standing, almost opposite that of 1842 which then became the Sunday school. Both were renovated in 1900 but the 1842 chapel was closed by 1953 and demolished some years later. The 1866 chapel has its gable to the road with a broad pediment and round-arched windows, probably in two tiers. There were two bays of tall round-arched windows to each side and a slate roof. It has been a commercial garage since at least 1968, painted white and substantially altered. The burial ground opposite remains.[158]

Brokenborough

Primitive Methodist Chapel, by central triangle, derelict in 2019. This is a small chapel of one bay depth, rendered, with segmental-arched windows and a brick porch under a tiled roof. The gable plaque is now illegible. It opened in 1873 and closed c1963.[159]

Bromham

The **Society of Friends** first registered a meeting in 1690 and built a meeting house 'in a common near Bromham' in 1711. It closed in 1814 and was demolished in 1863.[160]

General Baptist Chapel, School Lane, now a house. Built in 1873 to replace a smaller one of 1828 elsewhere in the village, this closed during the Second World War. It is of brick with ashlar dressings under slate; the gable faces the road with a round-arched door and windows likewise. It was disfigured on conversion by the infilling of the top halves of the windows in white render.[161]

*Wesleyan Methodist Chapel, Church Hill,** in use. It was built on a steep slope,

Bromham Church Hill Wesleyan

hence the large plinth with cellar to the west side and the door not in the gable but to the east side. In brick with ashlar dressings under slate with a simple porch, it has a stepped triple lancet to the front, paired lancets to the west side and rear, and the east side is blank. The interior is plain with the former gallery now walled off. It was built in 1799 and enlarged in 1815 and c1880 but retains some of the 1799 fabric in the west wall.[162]

Netherstreet Primitive Methodist Chapel, now a house, No.66. This was built in 1848, closed for a period and reopened in 1934. It closed finally and was sold in 1950 and was converted to a house in 1951. It has been altered and extended almost out of recognition, the original being the left-hand one of what are now two gables. The whole is now rendered white under a tiled roof and a gable plaque carries initials and the 1951 conversion date.[163]

*Chittoe Heath Primitive Methodist Chapel,** ST966667, closed in 2016 and in 2019 being converted into a house. A neat, almost toy-like chapel in brick with pale brick dressings and some ashlar, it has round-arched windows and a slate roof. The chapel of three bays stands in front of the 1914 schoolroom which is a smaller version of it, also of three bays. The porch, which could be later, has windows either side and above it is a plaque stating in large script: '1882 Primitive Methodist'. The original chapel of 1840 was in the village centre but was rebuilt here in 1882 because the singing of the Methodists allegedly disturbed those worshipping in the Anglican church which had been built adjacent in 1845.[164]

Photograph also on page 35.

Chittoe Heath (Bromham) Primitive Methodist

A **Mission Room** present in Jockey Lane in the 1890s was used by both Anglicans and nonconformists but was later used solely by the Anglican church.[165]

A house called **West View, 5 Church Hill**, Grade 2 listed, may have been used as a chapel for a period from 1724, though its denomination is unknown. It is of brick under tile – originally thatch – and when built had a symmetrical facade of two tiers of two round-arched windows and a central door. It was later extended to the right and split into two cottages.[166]

Broughton Gifford

Particular Baptist Chapel,* east side of Broughton Common, Grade 2 listed, in use. The chapel was built in 1806, probably on the initiative of members of Old Broughton Road Baptist, Melksham. It is of squared stone with ashlar dressings and round-arched windows

Broughton Gifford Baptist

under a hipped slate roof. The well-composed front facade has three windows above and two below with a central but later and slightly unharmonious porch. The sides have two tall round-arched windows with unusual central mullions and to the rear are the single-storey, twin-gabled 1830 schoolrooms partially covering the rear window of the chapel which is now blocked.[167]
Photograph also on page 47.

Wesleyan Methodist Chapel of 1828, west of village street just north of Newleaze Park, now a house. This was the original Wesleyan chapel, small and neat in coursed rough stone with ashlar dressings under a hipped slate roof. There are two tall flat-headed windows to each side and the flat-headed front door has a window above placed asymmetrically, something very rarely found and probably a later insertion. This chapel was replaced by the new one in 1907 and in 1909 was presented to the village as a reading room by Sir Charles Hobhouse. It ceased to be used as a reading room in 1937 and was sold and subsequently converted to a house.[168]

Wesleyan Methodist Chapel of 1907, approximately 200 metres north of 1828 chapel, now a house. Designed by A E Bush, surveyor to Melksham Rural District Council, this is of coursed rock-faced stone blocks with ashlar dressings under tile. There are three pairs of lancets on the left side and two on the right; the gable facing the road has a large triple lancet above a lean-to porch with the door to the side and a double lancet to the front. The schoolroom extension of c1936 overlaps the rear. The chapel was converted to a house c2010.[169]

Bulford

Independent Congregational Chapel, Watergate Lane, listed Grade 2, in use. The chapel was originally of 1806, sponsored by Salisbury Scots Lane Congregational, but was rebuilt in its present form in 1828 with the lean-to Sunday school at the north end added late in the century. It is rendered under a hipped slate roof with overhanging eaves. The door was probably in the south wall originally, where there is now a low window, but was moved later to its present position on the east side where it now has a 20th century porch. The two-bay sides have tall windows with rectangular cast-iron frames but glazing bars in a semi-circular pattern at the top; the south wall has two similar but smaller windows high up. There is an original gallery at the south end.[170]

Bulkington

Wesleyan Methodist Chapel, Mill Lane at junction with High Street, now the village hall. This was built in 1816 of rough stone with brick dressings under a hipped slate roof. It is now largely hidden by a lean-to brick front extension probably dating from around the time of its conversion to the village hall in 1966.[171]

Burbage

Wesleyan Methodist Chapel, Eastcourt, off footpath west of Eastcourt, now a house. Erected in 1822, this chapel was closed in 1906 on the building of the new chapel in High Street. It is small, rendered under a hipped tile roof and extended to the left side. The timber porch is modern and it has been generally much altered.[172]

Wesleyan Methodist Chapel, High Street, north end, now offices. Of brick under slate, with ashlar dressings mainly applied to the west gable facing the street, which is handsome. This has three ashlar bands, a line of donors' plaques at the base and a substantial five-light Gothic window under which is the inscription 'Wesleyan Church 1907.' The rest of the building, designed by Thomas Price of Birmingham, is plain and not helped by the replacement glazing. The sides are of three bays with the door on the south side and there is a substantial schoolroom block to the rear at right angles. The chapel closed in 1996 and was sold in 1998 for use as offices.[173]

Burcombe Without

There is no further information on a **Wesleyan Methodist** chapel registered in 1846, which presumably had a short life.[174]

Bushton – see Clyffe Pypard

Buttermere

No chapels recorded.[175]

Callow Hill – see Brinkworth

Calne Without.

This large parish comprises the rural area to the west, south and east of Calne.

Derry Hill Little Zoar Baptist (Calne Without)

*Derry Hill Little Zoar Strict Baptist Chapel,** east end of Derry Hill close to junction with A4, in use, Grade 2 listed. A small chapel of 1814 in coursed rubble-stone with ashlar dressings under a semi-hipped stone tile roof. The long sides each have one central round-arched window with two lights and Y-tracery; the door is at the north end of the side facing the road, with an inscription above 'Little Zoar 1814'. The south end has two arched windows, the north two similar to light the gallery there; these are truncated by a later lean-to vestry extension.[176]

*Providence Particular Baptist Chapel, Sandy Lane,** west side, 150m north of junction with Back Lane, Grade 2 listed, now a house. Highly unusual design in ironstone blockwork and ashlar dressings under slate, with windows mullioned and transomed in six-light sets, round-arched below flat heads. The door surround is equally distinctive with its miniature blind arcade. There are hood moulds over the door and windows and a date plaque for 1817. A cross in ashlar is inset to the gable head, allegedly at the insistence of the landowner. Inside there was originally

Providence Baptist, Sandy Lane (Calne Without)

a gallery above the door and also a central baptistery. A schoolroom was added in 1825. The chapel was closed in 1978 and reverted to the Bowood estate; it was then sold and converted to a house in 1984. At that time the windows in the two-bay sides were placed lower down the walls so as not to overlap ground and first floors: it was neatly done.[177]

Studley Wesleyan Methodist Chapel, east side of Studley Lane north of A4, in use. This simple chapel in brick with ashlar dressings under slate is set at an angle to the road. It has round-arched windows to front and sides, a protruding porch with lunette over the door and above that a plaque dated 1855. The single-storey schoolroom to the side, parallel to the road and hence at an angle to the chapel, is of stone block with ashlar dressings under slate and dated 1896.[178]

Wesleyan Methodist Chapel, Theobald's Green, just east of central crossroads, now a house. The original chapel is in rough stone blockwork and of three bays, Gothic with a three-light stepped lancet in the end gable wall, a protruding porch on the long wall facing the road and angled buttresses to the corners; the gable is dated 1866. It closed c1960 and on conversion the windows facing the road were replaced by modern ones in two tiers and a one bay extension was added to the east. The tiled roof is probably a replacement.[179]

Primitive Methodist Chapel, Derry Hill, south of Old Derry Hill 300m east of A4 junction, now a house. A neat small gable-end chapel in brick with ashlar dressings under slate, it has round-arched windows either side of the porch. Its most distinctive feature is the pedimented plaque at the gable head, '1857 Primitive Methodist Chapel'. There are two arched windows each side and a lower schoolroom at the rear, the roof of which was raised to allow insertion of a second floor on conversion. Although the building is dated 1857 there is evidence for a chapel built here in 1849 and it is known that Primitive Methodists were meeting here by 1851: the apparent discrepancy is unexplained. The chapel remained open until probably the 1980s before eventual conversion to a house.[180]

Another **Primitive Methodist** chapel was built east of **Stockley Lane**, at SU002677, in 1841, with capacity for 70, which at the time appeared 'likely to be soon too small'. It proved not to be and it was closed and demolished in 1963.[181]

Castle Combe

Congregationalists worshipped from 1743 in a cottage in the village but moved from there to **The Hill** because neighbours objected to their singing; they met first in a cottage but in 1757 built a chapel. A schoolroom was added in 1846 but the lease expired in the early 20th century and the Congregationalists moved to the old malt-house in Upper Combe (see below). The chapel was demolished in 1935 but the schoolroom had various uses including as a telephone exchange and then from 1984 until 2012 as the village museum. It is now a holiday cottage.[182]

Congregational Chapel, Upper Combe, 100m east of centre, in intermittent use, Grade 2 listed. A former malthouse, bought by Congregationalists in 1903 for £327 to replace the chapel on The Hill, it was refurbished and opened in 1914. It is a long building in rubble-stone with ashlar dressings under stone slates; a porch was added to the front with a plaque at the gable head dated 1914. The adjoining house became the manse but was sold in 2016. Buildings to the rear were used as schoolroom and vestry.[183]

Baptists used a building as the **Lower Chapel**, probably from 1846. This was an extension to the rear of a cottage, now called Unicorn Lodge, west of the main street and almost opposite the old rectory. The chapel was accessed via a side passage to the cottage and, though small, had a gallery. It closed in the early 20th century and was demolished c1925, to be replaced later by new rear extensions to the cottage.[184]

Methodists are believed to have had a chapel in the village from the 1760s but it is not known where or for how long this lasted.[185]

Castle Eaton

No chapels recorded.[186]

Chapmanslade

Congregational Chapel,* north of main road, just west of turn to Cleyhill Gardens, now a house. The original chapel opened in 1771 and was enlarged in 1810 but was demolished in the mid 19th century after the entire congregation joined Chapmanslade Baptists following a dispute with the minister. The present chapel, by Joseph Chapman of Frome, opened in 1867 and is in an unusual Gothic style in coursed stone with ashlar dressings under tile. The most prominent feature in the heavy gable end is a trefoil window made up of three smaller trefoils. Below are lancets either side of a three-light stepped cusped lancet within a larger arch. The doors are in hipped-roof extensions to either side at the front, each with a small trefoil window above, and there are further extensions to the rear. It closed in 1985 and was converted to a house.[187]

Chapmanslade Congregational   *Chapmanslade Baptist.*

Baptist Chapel,* west side of Wood Lane, now a house. This was built in 1799 to accommodate 140 people; there was originally a rear gallery and side galleries were added later, probably in the early 19th century, increasing capacity to 280. The attractive facade in coursed rubble-stone has segmental-headed windows in substantial brick surrounds; there is a discordant modern porch and a hipped tiled roof. The chapel was converted to a house in 1975, though it was said to be in disrepair from the start of the 20th century and the congregation rejoined the Congregationalists around then.[188]

Charlton (North)

Primitive Methodists built a small chapel at **Stonehill**, east of the village, in 1836. It was closed by 1882 and is believed to have been demolished.[189]

Charlton (South)

Wesleyan Methodists built an iron mission hall on the north side of the village street near Friday's Lane in 1893. It was closed by 1925 and later demolished.[190]

Cherhill

Zoar Wesleyan Methodist Chapel, Marsh Lane, ST025705, west of road. This was built in 1832, closed by 1922 and later incorporated into Old Chapel Farm. The chapel is the lower hipped-roof section closest to the road with two blank rendered walls; behind was the minister's house now greatly extended. The chapel door originally faced the road and there was a gallery giving a total capacity of 80 despite the tiny size of the room. There is a plaque dated 1832 under new barge boards on the gable immediately behind the chapel.[191]

A **Wesleyan Methodist** chapel at **Yatesbury** opened in 1839 but from 1874 was used by **Baptists** as a mission room of Castle Street, Calne. It was located east of The Street, just north of the house which is now No.19. Open in 1939, it has since been demolished. The **Wesleyans** considered building another chapel c1881 but it was not built.[192]

Primitive Methodists were active in the parish from around the same time, registered various houses and in 1851 had a chapel, said to have been built in 1846 but perhaps part of a house. They probably continued to meet until c1900.[193]

Chicklade

No chapels recorded.[194]

Chilmark

Union General Baptist Chapel, Ridge, ST954320, now a house. This was built in 1861, before which meetings were held in houses and possibly in a previous chapel. It is of red brick with dressings in alternate light and dark brick giving it a vivacious if slightly garish look. The sides are of three bays with round-arched windows inset into large blind arcades. On the side facing the road is a porch and door in the right hand side arcade; a further smaller porch and door are in the lean-to extension to the left in the same style, presumably a vestry: the porches fit oddly with the arcading and they, or perhaps just their roofs, are probably later. The land falls steeply to the rear necessitating a substantial basement in stone. Redundant in 1996, it has since been converted to a house with an inserted floor.[195]

A **Mission Hall** was built in 1890, north off Ridgeway and west of Becketts Lane. Not strictly nonconformist, it was built by parishioners objecting to the High Church services of the parish priest. It was paid for by Mrs Whitehead of Chilmark House, was of iron, timber-lined, and held 200 people. The offending priest left in 1894 and the parishioners returned to the parish church, but the mission hall remained in use for some years for weekday meetings and Bible classes. It was eventually demolished and a house called Kent's Cottage built on the site.[196]

Chilton Foliat

Wesleyan Methodist Chapel, north of village street towards east end, now a house. To the rear is the original chapel of 1796 which might once have been interesting but is now largely hidden behind the 1932 enlargement. The front of this is in brick with stone quoins under tile with a date plaque and three stepped Gothic windows, the porch to the left side. The original is also in brick, with a higher roofline, three bays of much altered windows and a more recent lean-to porch to the right side. The chapel closed in 1988 and was then converted.[197]

Chippenham Without

This is the rural area immediately to the west of Chippenham

General Baptists built the **Ebenezer Chapel** in a field west of what is now The Grange, north west of Bolehyde Manor, at ST887757. It was probably built in 1832 but was disused by 1877 and subsequently demolished.[198]

Chirton

No chapels recorded.[199]

Chiseldon

Wesleyan Methodists opened a chapel in a farmyard at the north end of **Hodson** in 1798. This was the first Wesleyan chapel in the Swindon area and was very small, of wattle and daub with a thatched roof. In 1895 it was replaced by a red-brick chapel a little further south. This chapel seated 100 and had a conventional appearance with a circular window above the porch and the name in a band above that, all under a slate roof; it became derelict around the time of the First World War and the old chapel was brought back into use for a period. The brick chapel was renovated and reopened in 1924 but it closed by 1954 and was subsequently demolished. The old chapel had reverted to use as a farm building but was demolished in 1964.[200]

Wesleyan Methodist Chapel, Chiseldon, north of Turnball up an alley just short of the junction with High Street. There are three linked buildings, all now houses and all very much altered. That to the rear carries a plaque 'Methodist Chapel 1861' and is probably the original chapel of 1809. The building attached in front of it, perhaps a schoolroom, may have been added in 1861 at which date there were presumably other alterations made. The chapel brickwork is now painted and the building altered out of recognition. It had closed by 1967 and the congregation joined that at Turnball (see below).[201]

Wesleyan Methodists built a brick chapel in **Badbury**, behind cottages opposite Badbury House, now The Manor, probably in 1863. It closed in 1936 and was later demolished. **Primitive Methodists** were also active there but met in a house.[202]

Primitive Methodist Chapel, Chiseldon, north of Turnball, now a house. The chapel replaced a previous one of 1853 south of Turnball, a little to the west and now demolished, which in turn replaced the original of 1835. This one is of 1896, by R J Beswick of Swindon, and is of brick under slate with some stone dressings; the schoolroom, probably contemporary, is at right angles to the rear. The gable is a strange mixture: it starts conventionally enough with the Gothic-arched doors and windows either side but above that, in a space for paired Gothic windows, are two cusped round-headed windows with coloured glass and above them a pattern of multiple small shields in stone. The central section of the gable, which projects forward slightly, is then carried upwards above the roofline and incorporates a plaque in large text, '1896 Primitive Methodist Church;' stone-capped pilasters at the corners complete the ensemble. The three-bay sides are more restrained. It closed in 2007 and was converted to a house with an extension to the rear.[203]

Primitive Methodist Chapel, Coate, south of A4259 at SU184827. Small and derelict in rendered brick under slate, this chapel of 1888 has three bays to the side, the central one originally a door with a small porch. A small pitched-roof extension to the east was added, probably in 1919, with a new door, and the original door was converted into a third side window. It was out of use by 1964.[204]

A wooden **Primitive Methodist hut** was built at Chiseldon Camp during the First World War. It was demolished after the war.[205]

Chitterne

General Baptist Chapel, south of Bidden Lane, 80m west of junction with Townsend, now a house. The original section is to the west with its gable facing the road, built by **Wesleyan Methodists** by 1846 but not well supported and later given to the Baptists. It was constructed of rough stone blocks under thatch but fire in the thatch in 1903 largely destroyed the building and it was rebuilt with a four-bay extension at right angles to the side in brick with arched windows under tile: there is a memorial stone carrying that date. The arched windows to the original section, dressed in brick, presumably date from this time as does the untidy flint and stone used to complete the gable end: was it originally rendered? The chapel closed c1969 following a collapse of the hillside behind and was sold in 1978.[206]

Cholderton

No chapels recorded.[207]

Christian Malford

Shecaniah Congregational Chapel,* on B4069 at ST958792, Grade 2 listed, now a house. An impressive gable facade in squared rubble with ashlar dressings has two large pointed windows with Y-tracery above a similar door. The gable is pedimented and

Shecaniah Congregational, Christian Malford

carries a plaque 'Shecaniah Erected A.D. 1836.' The sides are of rubble-stone with a Y-traceried window at the east; there was probably a similar window to the west but that is now covered by the single-storey brick schoolroom added in 1909. An original chapel here, half-timbered under thatch, was probably built in the early 18th century and became a village mission of Malmesbury Silver Street Congregational. This chapel closed in 1998.[208]
Photograph also on page 27.

Chute

Wesleyan Methodists built a timber-framed chapel between **Cadley and Lower Chute**, at SU313533 in 1844. It was closed in 1990 and subsequently demolished.[209] **Primitive Methodists** built a small chapel of corrugated iron in 1879, south of Malthouse Lane and just east of its junction with Forest Lane. It closed in 1927 and was subsequently demolished.[210]

Chute Forest

No chapels recorded.[211]

Clarendon Park

No chapels recorded.[212]

Clench Common – see Wilcot

Clyffe Pypard

Bushton Primitive Methodist Chapel, north end of village, now a house. This is built of brick under slate. The north end gives an indication of the original appearance with a porch and round-arched door and two similar windows, the latter now part bricked in; all these are under arches of alternate red and pale yellow brick and the gable is extended to the side as a buttress with stone caps. The plaque, now moved to the south end, is dated 1874. All else follows the conversion: the roof was raised to allow a full first floor and the tall side windows were split; a large extension was built to the rear and the buttresses from the south side of the original chapel were moved there. The chapel opened in 1874, replacing a cottage elsewhere in Bushton converted in 1856/7, and was enlarged in 1894. It was still in use in 1968 but was sold in 1983 and converted.[213]

Coate – see Bishops Cannings and Chiseldon

Codford

The two rectors of Codford united in their efforts to stifle nonconformity here but a **Congregational Chapel** was eventually built in 1811, paid for by a London benefactor and placed in trust for Hackney College there. It was north of High Street about 200m west of Chitterne Road. Enlarged in the 1850s, a schoolroom was added to the south east with a manse beyond that. The chapel was of plain brick, side on to the road and with three tall pointed-arch windows. It closed in 1964 and was demolished in the 1970s as unsafe. The schoolroom is now a house called Hamewith, originally single-storey but now with inserted dormers; it has large pointed-arch windows and an extension and driveway where the chapel used to be. The former manse is a stuccoed building attached to the other side of the school.[214]

Colerne

Congregational Chapel, Chapel Path, in use, Grade 2 listed. The front is in ashlar with a date scroll for 1824 in a pedimented gable, two segmental-headed windows and a central door in a raised surround. A raised band at first floor level continues round rubble-stone sides which each have two round-arched windows breaking through it. The roof is of slate and there is a lean-to extension to the rear. Inside is a panelled rear gallery on iron columns. The chapel was built in 1824, renovated in 1924, renamed Evangelical in 1974 and a baptistery inside the chapel added in 1984 as the congregation, now independent, believes in full-immersion baptism.[215]

Providence Baptist Chapel; High Street,* just east of Chapel Path, Grade 2 listed, now a house. Most members of the Congregational Chapel had become Baptist by 1855 and after a legal case they left in 1866 and in 1867 built their own chapel here. It became Christian Fellowship in 1984 but the trustees were unhappy with their mode of worship so they left in 1986 and the chapel was subsequently sold and converted into a house in 2003. A rear extension in stained wood by Jonathan Tuckey Design was added in 2009. The ashlar front has a pedimented gable of unusually steep angle with a plaque dated 1867. Below it two round-arched windows flank a central projecting Roman Doric porch. The rubble-stone sides each have two similar windows and the roof is of slate. The schoolroom

Colerne Providence Baptist

is to the rear and beyond that the modern extension. The panelled gallery, and its hat pegs, have been retained in the conversion.[216]

Primitive Methodists built a chapel at **Thickwood** in 1860, on Thickwood Lane at ST827727. The Colerne High Street chapel built in 1895 probably removed much of this chapel's congregation and it was demolished in 1904.[217]

Primitive Methodist Chapel, west end of High Street, now a house. The gable facing the road is of stone block with ashlar dressings and has a projecting porch, a gable roundel dated 1895 and two round-arched windows with complex glazing bars nearly identical to those of the Providence Baptist. There are similar windows to the two-bay rubble-stone sides and there is a small contemporary schoolroom to the rear. The chapel opened in 1895 at a cost of £495. It closed in 1984 and was subsequently converted.[218]

Collingbourne Ducis

1849 Primitive Methodist Chapel, Cadley. A first chapel was opened in 1849 and described as thatched and whitewashed. It closed on construction of the 1880 chapel and a pair of brick and flint cottages, now one, at 67 Cadley Road now stands on the site. The right hand rear wing of the pair may contain some of the original chapel fabric.[219]

1880 Primitive Methodist Chapel, Cadley, now a house, 100m east of Saxon Rise. This replacement for the 1849 chapel is small and simple in render under slate with flat-headed windows which may have been reduced from their original height. The gable facing the road has a round-arched door, windows either side and a plaque dated 1880. It closed in 1983 and was converted to a house in 1988.[220]

Collingbourne Kingston

*Wesleyan Methodist Chapel.** On Chapel Lane at south end of village, now a house. The original, of 1819, was immediately north but demolished in the late 20th century. This new chapel, in brick and stone under slate by S Watson of Caversham, was built in 1914 and linked to the old chapel via the vestry. The gable is distinctive, dominated by pilasters either side of a central window, extending as octagonal shafts above the roofline and terminating in blunted ogee caps. The protruding porch has a nearly flat pediment with a modernist look; below that is an inscription 'Wesley Church 1914' and below that a door with a segmental arched top. Above is a three-light stepped

Collingbourne Kingston Wesleyan of 1914, distinctive but hard to see

mullioned and transomed window, again with shallow segmental tops, and there are similar single windows either side of the porch. The sides are, as so often with chapels of this period, much more calm, with three bays of paired windows, wooden-framed. The chapel closed in 1985 and was subsequently converted; a modern garage block occupies the approximate location of the 1819 chapel.[221]

Primitive Methodists were said to be meeting in the village in 1864 but there appears to be no other evidence for this.[222]

Compton Bassett

No chapels recorded.[223]

Compton Chamberlayne

No chapels recorded.[224]

Coombe Bissett

Baptist Chapel, on Homington Road at east end of village, in use by the Coombe Fellowship. Meetings in a cottage in the 1840s ended when the cottage leaseholder lost his tenancy through opposition to his faith. Eventually the village reading room was opened for meetings in 1892, with Brown Street, Salisbury supplying preachers, and this chapel followed in 1895; the gable plaque is dated 1894, when the memorial stones were laid. It was designed by A C Bothams of Salisbury. Of brick under tile, the sides are of three bays with flat-headed windows under dormer heads. The front originally had similar windows with a quatrefoil window above but these are now obscured by the 20th century porch extension. It closed by 2002 but was subsequently taken over by the Coombe Fellowship.[225]

Primitive Methodist Chapel, Homington, west end of village, now a house. A small chapel in brick under slate with round-arched windows and most dressings of pale brick; the gable plaque is dated 1877. The porch is later and there are side and rear extensions in timber. This is the 1877 rebuilding of the 1841 original; it closed in 1967 and was converted to a house after 1991.[226]

Corsley

Corsley Whitbourne Baptist in rural isolation just north of Longleat

Corsley Whitbourne Baptist – the side view gives hints to its complex building history

Whitbourne Particular Baptist Chapel, ** set well back east of road from Temple to Longhedge, ST825446, in use. This is a fine chapel with a complex building history. The gable front of 1811 has five simple segmental-headed windows, a later open porch and, above, a cusped stone niche for a ventilator. The north side shows its history: the first two bays are in rubble-stone with brick dressings and a blocked-in doorway. The roof was raised several feet some years after building and the upper windows, as well as the three galleries inside, may date from this time. At each level one window is segmental-headed and the other flat but possibly all were originally segmental-headed. The chapel was extended a further bay east, perhaps at the same time as the roof was raised, and two-storey schoolrooms were added to the

rear with a lower roofline; they have a separate door with porch and there are tall sash windows in the rear gable, which is hipped. The roof is of slate. The whole interior was renewed in 1882 and an organ acquired, said to have come from Longleat, and placed in the rear gallery. There is a circular open-air baptistery to the rear. The chapel, surprisingly, is not listed.[227]
Photograph also on page 25.

Wesleyan Methodist Chapel, Lane End,* east side of Greys Hill, now a house, listed Grade 2. The facade is neat, in coursed dressed stone with ashlar dressings under a hipped tiled roof. A central door and two tiers of symmetrically placed windows are all round-arched and there is a gable plaque 'Wesleyan Chapel Sacred to God 1849'. The sides are of rubble-stone, each with two tall round-arched windows. A schoolroom extension to the rear is of brick. The

Corsley Wesleyan

chapel was built in 1849, replacing the 1773 original, and the schoolroom was added in the late 19th century. It closed in 1966 and was converted to a house in the late 1980s.[228]

Corston – see Malmesbury Without

Corton – see Boyton

Coulston

General Baptist Chapel,* north west corner of village at ST951544, now a house. A small chapel unusual for its overhanging eaves roof and for having the door on the side. In brick with ashlar dressings under slate, it has pointed-arch windows, two to the south side and a three-light lancet to the front gable; also a prominent roof ventilator. The north side is blank, presumably because of the adjacent house. A long run of single-storey outbuildings stretches to the rear. It was built as an associated chapel of Bratton, the date stated to be 1872 but could be a few years earlier. It closed in 1937 and was sold and converted to a house in 1963.[229]
Photograph on page 34.

Covingham – see Swindon

Croucheston – see Bishopstone South

Crudwell

Particular Baptist Chapel, west of main road at south end of village just north of Rommel Lane junction, now a house. This has a semi-hipped gable in coursed rough stone under a tiled roof with two square windows probably replacing a window over a door. On the south side is a flat-headed door with windows either side, replacing two previous tall sash windows, and there is a substantial modern extension at right angles to the rear. The chapel opened c1840, closed between 1915 and 1920, became the village hall in 1934 and was converted to a house after 1966.[230]

Primitive Methodist Chapel, north of Tetbury Lane, now a house. Now linked to the adjacent former farm building of similar age and called Cleaver House, it is built of stone under tile but so altered that only the gable plaque dated 1866 shows it was once a chapel. It opened between c1867, closed during the Second World War and was later converted.[231]

Dauntscy

A small **Independent Chapel** was built at Dauntsey Common in 1824 or 1825 and was still in use in 1851. This was taken over in 1863 by **Strict Baptists** and thereafter rebuilt in 1875 as the *Providence Particular Baptist Chapel.* It is situated east of the stump of Sodom Lane, just south of the M4 at ST995815, and is now a house. Of brick under slate with ashlar dressings and round-arched door and windows, it originally had three bays, the west one with a small low window. It was extended to the west at a lower height in the 20th century with a door crowded in alongside a central window in the gable and the repositioned plaque 'Providence Chapel 1824 Rebuilt 1875'. There is a modern low extension to the rear. It closed in the 1960s, reopened in the mid 1980s but later closed finally and was converted.[232]

Derry Hill – see Calne Without

Dilton Marsh

Penknap Providence Baptist, Dilton Marsh

Penknap Providence Particular Baptist Chapel,** immediately east of railway line at ST858498, in use, Grade 2 listed. An impressive large chapel with an important place in the history of the Baptist Church locally, it was built in 1810 after the minister and some of the congregation of nearby Westbury Leigh Baptist withdrew from there over doctrinal differences. It was named after the field on which it was sited. The gable facing the road has a pointed-arch door and similar Y-tracery windows in two tiers; the gable head above is pedimented and has a pointed lunette window with 'Providence Chapel' and a date, probably 1810, in faded lettering. The sides were originally of three bays, with similar windows, and at that stage there were probably galleries inside on all four sides. A fourth bay was added when the chapel was extended backwards by 12ft in 1835, after which it retained three galleries; the new rear wall had two pointed-arch windows and also external stairs to two doors giving direct access to the side galleries. Schoolrooms were added at this date but in 1853 two new classrooms and a vestry were built against the back wall of the chapel, necessitating the closing off of the doors to the galleries; later on a lean-to roof was added to the schoolrooms and at this point, if not before, the rear chapel windows were blocked off.

The interior dates mostly from renovations of 1892 which included new pews. The galleries, with panelled fronts now painted, are on cast iron pillars and the former rear doors are still in place. The organ is at the entrance end above a glass-panelled lobby screen between the twin gallery staircases which each carry a wrought iron patterned grille on the enclosing panelling. Similar grille-work is to be found on the raised pulpit, and the blocked-off windows above now have painted texts added. As a last detail, and highly unusual, there are three wall ventilators each side to supplement the two roof ventilators: these are small boxes attached to the wall at head height, the top open to the inside and the bottom venting to the exterior, with a closable flap to shut them off.[233]

Photographs also on page 17, 48.

Penknap Providence Baptist, Dilton Marsh, interior; lower photograph shows rear screen from the 1892 alterations.

Particular Baptist Mission Chapel, Stormore, south of road west of junction with B3099, in use. This simple brick chapel is of three bays with pointed-arch windows and door. A lancet is set at the gable head and below that a plaque, 'Baptist Chapel Rebuilt 1884.' Built in 1829 as a mission chapel of Westbury Leigh Baptist, it was rebuilt in 1884 after the old chapel became unsafe; the architect was Henry Reeves of Bratton. After the closure of Westbury Leigh in 2016 this has now become the centre of local Baptist worship.[234]

Dinton

Primitive Methodist Chapel, Hindon Road, north of road at east end of village, now a house. In brick under slate with ashlar dressings, this typical turn of the century design has all the detail in the gable facing the road. This has a stepped three-light round-arched window above in a large semi-circular arch carrying the inscription 'Primitive Methodist 1895.' Below are round-arched windows either side of a five-sided porch, added in the early 20th century, which has two angled doors and a small central window. The sides have three bays and the lower rear is of rough stone block. The chapel opened in 1895, closed and was sold in 1988 and was much later converted into a house.[235]

Donhead St Andrew

No chapels are recorded here, though the **Wesleyan Methodist** chapel in **Berwick St John**, was actually in Donhead St Andrew parish when it was built in 1875. It is described under Berwick St John.[236]

Donhead St Mary

Birdbush Chapel was built in 1723 for **Presbyterians** who had previously been supported by the owner of Ferne House in Donhead St Andrew and had met there. The chapel derived its name from the local area and was set back east of Dennis Lane at the east end of the village. It was reorganised as **Congregational** in 1798-9, became dilapidated and was rebuilt in 1871. The rebuild was of substantial size, Gothic with three stepped lancets above twin doors in the entrance gable end, three windows with twin lights to the sides and, in front of those, three single lancets of increasing size seemingly there to provide side light to the rear gallery. It closed finally in the late 1980s though it had been struggling for some time before that date: the main part of the chapel was then demolished leaving only the former part-attached schoolroom standing. This, more like a barn than a chapel building, is a single room of much-altered rubble-stone and brick under a tiled roof, with twin lancet windows in the gable ends. The house in front is the former manse of 1803-4.[237]

*Wesleyan Methodist Chapel,** south of village street just north of lower junction with Watery Lane, now a house, Grade 2 listed. This is grand for a village chapel but hard to see. Of dressed limestone with ashlar dressings, the gable front has two windows and a large doorway at the lower level and three windows above, all round-arched. Above these is a pedimented gable with coped verges and a plaque 'Wesleyan

Donhead St Mary Wesleyan.
Photograph courtesy of Wiltshire Buildings Record

Chapel AD 1868'. There are three bays of tall round-arched windows to the sides, a slate roof, and a small low extension to the rear, possibly the former schoolroom. The original chapel was built on the opposite side of the street in 1837 but replaced by this one, which was built at a cost of £750. It was said to seat 400 and had a rear gallery. It closed in 2007 and was then converted with the insertion of a floor to the rear bay.[238]

Primitive Methodist Chapel, south side of A30 in centre of Ludwell, now a house called The Old Chapel. An inserted door and landscape windows make this small chapel unrecognisable. It was built in 1861 and closed in 1965.[239]

Downton

South Lane Particular Baptist Chapel,✶✶ in use, Grade 2 listed. This is a splendidly original design with an Alpine feel. In brick with patterned vitrified headers and stone dressings under a projecting slate roof on conspicuous wooden brackets,

Downton South Lane Baptist – subsidiary rooms to the rear maintain the distinctive styling

the whole is topped by an ornate ashlar bellcote. The gable facing the road has a projecting central section with a rose window above a tall two-light round-arched window; there are lancet round-arched windows either side and a lean-to porch with double doors attached to the north. The sides have brick pilasters slightly buttressed and two pairs of tall narrow windows with modern glazing reflecting the insertion of a floor. To the rear the church rooms are a smaller scale version of the main chapel. Inside, the inserted floor has created a top level for worship, accessed via the original gallery stairs and with the ornate hammer-beam roof visible; the ground floor is used for meeting rooms and offices. This chapel is of 1857, by Henry Crisp of Bristol, and replaces an earlier one of 1794 built by a group of Particular Baptists who had seceded from the Gravel Close chapel in 1734 and founded a first church here c1738. The 1794 chapel was built at right angles to the present one but only its baptistery remains.[240]
More photographs on pages 36 and 54.

Gravel Close General Baptist Chapel, now used by a band. A plain chapel of brick under tile, the gable faces the road with two altered round-arched windows; the modern porch is on the three-bay south side and there is a rear extension. The chapel's dull appearance belies the long history of Baptists in Gravel Close, the first church, by tradition, having been founded in 1666. A new chapel was built in 1715 and in 1835 was replaced by the present building, itself enlarged in 1845. The Gravel Close congregation united with that in South Lane in 1894 but this chapel remained in use until 1939 though the gallery was removed c1900. It has since been used by a local band as well as for some years by a pre-school.[241]

Rehoboth Strict Baptist Chapel, Lode Hill, north side just east of Barford Lane, now a garage for a house. The most noticeable feature of this small brick chapel is the garage door inserted into the centre of the gable facing the road. Previously there were Gothic-arched windows with Y-tracery either side of and above the porch. The eaves roof is of slate. The chapel was built in 1845, closed in 1955 and was converted by 1975.[242]

Wesleyan Methodists Chapel, Lode Hill, south east corner of junction with Slab Lane, now two houses, Grade 2 listed. This was built in 1814. There was a secession to the New Wesleyan Reformed (see below) in the 1860s and other members left to form the High Street United Free Methodist in 1884: it is not clear whether the chapel closed then or, as has been suggested, stayed open until c1919. Nor is it certain whether, as has also been suggested, it was used as a cottage hospital for a period after closure. What is certain is that it became a butcher's shop before ultimate conversion to residential. The result of all these changes is that it looks not at all like a chapel. It is of brick under tile with a substantial central chimney block; the gable to the main road has various alterations including a bricked-in former shop window and the remains of a large painted advertisement for the butcher. The side facing Slab Lane has at lower left another shop front with doors either side of a pair of sash windows. Above and to the right are segmental-arched sash windows and this facade probably originally had four of these in two tiers, perhaps with a central doorway forming the original chapel entrance. The south gable has two similar windows off-centre.[243]

The **New Wesleyan Reformed chapel**, south east of the road by Downton corn mill, was opened between 1851 and 1864 by a group who broke away from the Lode Hill Methodist chapel. Of gable-end form with pointed-arch windows, it closed in the early 20th century and was replaced in the 1960s by a house called Chapel Cottage.[244]

United Free Methodist Chapel,* south of High Street towards west end, closed and sold in 2019, planning approval given for conversion to residential in 2021. The strong facade is in brick and stucco under slate with channelled pilasters to the corners. There are round-arched windows either side of a prominent door-case which has a circular window over, and the pedimented gable has a date plaque for 1884. The sides have flat-headed sash windows, four to the west and two to the east where the chapel is joined to another building for part of its length; the roof is hipped to the rear and there is a lean-to single-room extension. The date refers to the date of formation in two cottages on this site and this chapel was built in 1896. It was said to have been formed by people leaving the Lode Hill chapel.[245]

Downton United Free Methodist

Wesleyan Methodist Chapel. Charlton All Saints, now a house, just north of All Saints church. A small chapel of 1864, built on a site given by Lord Folkestone, it closed in 1971 and became Wesleyan House, with the addition of substantial extensions. It is now rendered and the windows are much altered, but it was presumably originally brick. The porch is retained in the gable facing the road and there is a plaque above, 'Wesleyan Chapel 1864.' The roof is of slate.[246]

The British School for Girls, opened at the **Headlands** in 1846, was said to have been located in a former *nonconformist chapel*. No more is known about this chapel but the school closed in 1896 when the pupils moved to the new school in Gravel Close; the building later became the Headlands Garage and in 2016 was converted to residential. It is on the south side of The Borough, close to the junction with the Salisbury road, and is of brick under tile, much altered.[247]

Durnford

Wesleyan Methodist Chapel, Netton,* west of road at SU127369, now a house. A lively if cluttered turn of the century composition, this is built in red brick with plentiful pale brick dressings. The gable facing the road has pilasters at the corners, a projecting porch, a pointed-arch window to the right and a door to the left where a window used to be. The pedimented gable, with a stepped pattern in pale brick under the eaves, has a round window and the inscription '1895 Wesleyan Chapel' on inset tiles. The sides are of four bays with similar pointed-arch windows, all under a replacement tiled roof, and there used to be a lower vestry or schoolroom extension to the rear. The chapel was closed in the early 1970s and converted c1980, the rear section being increased to two storeys. In 1989 a separate building to

Durnford, Netton Wesleyan

the rear was demolished and a much larger extension built at right angles. Both conversion and subsequent extension were by Robert Townsend.

This chapel replaced the original, probably of 1812, which was on the opposite side of the road immediately north of and linked to a house now called Cobweb Cottage.[248]

Durrington

Congregational Chapel, Bulford Road, * just north of School Road, now the Congregational Free Church. More modern in appearance than many chapels of this period, it has a long low facade in brick under a hipped tiled roof. The doors are at either end of this facade and there is a central gable projecting upwards with a large nine-light window. The chapel was built in 1905 at a cost of £1150 to replace the original of 1824, altered in 1860, which stood on the opposite side of Bulford

Durrington Congregational of 1905 – distinctively modern for the date

Road and was demolished when this was built.[249]

East Chisenbury – see Enford

East Hatch – see West Tisbury

East Kennett

There is a report of two Baptist chapels here in 1864 but no further evidence has been found.[250]

East Knoyle

In 1827 **Independents** opened a cottage for worship and built a chapel alongside. The chapel, which may have been originally Baptist before becoming Independent, was apparently paid for by a lady who, in 1849, was persuaded by a new rector to sell it to him. He evicted the congregation and they then had to meet in a cottage again until 1854 when the new ***Congregational Chapel**** and schoolroom, paid for by Charles Jupe of Mere, was opened. This is now a house towards the north end

East Knoyle Congregational – schoolroom, manse and chapel in a line

of The Street, Grade 2 listed, and forms an appealing ensemble with the manse and Sunday school immediately south. In dressed limestone under slate, the gable facing the road has a large central window of four cusped lancets with trefoils over. There is a pointed-arch doorway below and a quatrefoil window above, together with buttresses and coped verges. The four-bay sides have pointed-arch windows, also buttressed. The last service was held in 1986 and it was then converted into a house, retaining its hammerbeam roof.[251]

Ebenezer Primitive Methodist Chapel, The Green, immediately north of the Fox and Hounds, now a house. Built in 1857 and closed in 1974, this is now a house with an inserted first floor. It is small, the brick gable at right angles to the road with a modern lean-to porch and a plaque above dated 1857. The two-bay side is rendered with round-arched windows. Primitive Methodists registered premises in The Holloway in 1843 and had some presence at the Green by 1851 in what may have been a temporary predecessor to the present building.[252]

East Tytherton – see Bremhill

Eastcott – see Easterton

Easterton

Wesleyan Methodist Chapel, west of High Street in village centre, now a house. A simple chapel in brick under tile, the gable facing the road has lancet windows, lengthened downwards on conversion, either side of a door with a modern hood replacing the previous porch. Two bands of vitrified headers relieve the otherwise plain front and there is a plaque above dated 1868. The sides are of three bays with lancet windows and the 1928 schoolroom to the rear has now been turned into a courtyard garden with the original door becoming an entrance arch. Fussy replacement windows are split to accommodate the inserted floor. It closed in 1984 and was converted in 1985.[253]
Photograph on page 56.

Eastcott was an early centre for **Wesleyan Methodism:** there was certainly a house used for worship there in the 18th century and a chapel may have been built though, if so, its location is unknown.[254]

Easton

Wesleyan Methodist Chapel, west of village street towards north end, now called Chapel Cottage. The original chapel of 1834 was in ruins by 1862, at which time meetings were held in a converted barn until this chapel was built in 1898, in brick under slate. It was side-on to the road with tall pointed-arch windows either side of a porch. The chapel closed in the mid 1950s and was converted to a house in 1965, with an extra bay to the right, an inserted floor, dormers and new windows. Only the porch was retained to give some small hint that this was once a chapel.[255]
Photographs on page 55.

Easton Grey

No chapels recorded.[256]

Ebbesbourne Wake

*Congregational Chapel,** east side of The Cross, in use. The exterior of this neat small chapel is characterised by its flint construction and paired round-arched windows, one set above the porch

Ebbesbourne Wake Congregational – a modest design by W J Stent. Note the overthrow, lacking its lantern, at the gate

and three to each side, their appeal somewhat reduced by the modern glazing. There is a battered plinth and corner buttresses, and stone is used elsewhere particularly for relieving arches above the windows and string courses to the sides. The interior is almost unaltered Victorian save for the plain walls. There is a panelled rear gallery on wooden pillars, the original pews, a low pulpit and communion table, and a double-angled panelled ceiling, the whole appropriately simple and dignified. The **first meeting house**, used from 1782-91 with the support of Mrs Turner of Tisbury, was a conversion of an existing building which still stands east of The Hollow at the south end of the village: it is square, with rubble walls, ashlar quoins and a hipped thatched roof. Its replacement in 1791 was a former coach house, which seems to have started out as Methodist before becoming Congregational. This may have been abandoned in 1812, with the congregation worshipping instead at Broad Chalke, but there was an active meeting locally again in 1857 when the present chapel was built to designs by W J Stent of Warminster.[257]

Edington

The **General Baptist Chapel, Court Lane, Tinhead**, was the upper floor of a former malthouse opened in 1794 but closed in 1897 when the lease expired; it was soon demolished. It was attached at right angles to the rear of the three-bay house at the junction of Charlton Hill and Court Lane which was perhaps the manse. The lease was held by the Bratton Baptist church from 1801.[258]

Wesleyan Methodist Chapel, Tinhead, south side of Salisbury Hollow south of main road, now two houses. Here are two buildings at right angles: that to the left is the chapel built in 1828, of brick under a hipped pantiled roof with three pairs of tall double round-arched windows with ashlar dressings. This was extended, re-windowed and a gallery added in 1848 to increase capacity to 360. To the right is the schoolroom of 1877, its gable with two tall round-arched windows facing the road. The chapel was 'practically rebuilt' in 1904. It closed in 2006 and was subsequently converted.[259]

Enford

A **Particular Baptist Chapel**, owned by Sir Edmund Antrobus of Amesbury Abbey, was built on Enford Hill, just west of what is now the A345, c1819. It was of brick under a semi-hipped thatched roof, side on to the road with the door unusually placed in the second of five bays; windows facing the road were round-arched, that in the end gable segmental. The chapel became War Department property in 1899 and was destroyed by fire in 1959. 1960 plans for a replacement seem not to have been acted upon.[260]

East Chisenbury Primitive Methodist Chapel, east of street in centre of village, now a house. A typical small brick chapel of the late 19th century, this has round-arched windows dressed in pale brick, the gable facing the road having windows either side of and above the door, the latter now replaced by French windows. There was previously an added porch but this has been removed. Above the door is a plaque dated 1896. The sides are of three bays, that to the left having the central window replaced by a door on conversion. The glazing is all modern and reflects the insertion of a floor; there is also a modern lean-to extension to the rear. The chapel was closed by 1981 and converted in 1988.[261]

A previous chapel was opened by **Independent Methodists** in 1821. It is possible that they became the Primitive Methodists who later built a further chapel, possibly converting a house, in c1845. This was a single-storey thatched building on the opposite side of the road from that of 1896 which replaced it. The 1845 chapel was probably demolished in the mid 20th century.[262]

Erlestoke

There was early activity by Independents or Presbyterians and Quakers but no meeting houses seem to have been built. Baptists were also active here in the early 18th century, associated with those of Bratton, but the decision was taken to build their chapel in the latter place. Methodists met in a cottage for a period in the early 19th century.[263]

Etchilhampton

Baptist Mission Room, north of road at east end of village, SU049603. A tiny corrugated iron building now in the owner's front garden, it is used as a garage. Brick lined, it has the original door at the west end though perhaps not in the original position. It was erected in 1890 after many years of meetings in a house, and was sold in 1962.[264]

Everleigh

No chapels recorded.[265]

Figheldean

Primitive Methodist Chapel, east side of High Street, now a house. The gable facing the road is austere despite its brick and flint construction. There is a protruding porch, round-arched windows either side and a plaque dated 1882; a further plaque above the door says 'Primitive Methodist'. The sides were originally of three bays with round-arched windows which, like those to the front, have brick dressings to the sides and ashlar to the heads. It was extended backwards, possibly as late as 1966. The roof is of slate. This building replaced a previous chapel in a house, certified in 1838 and also on the east side of High Street. The chapel closed sometime after 1975 and was sold for conversion in 1988.[266]

Firsdown

No chapels recorded.[267]

Fittleton

No chapels recorded.[268]

Fonthill Bishop

No chapels recorded.[269]

Fonthill Gifford

No chapels recorded. That at The Dene, Hindon, became part of Hindon parish in 1934 and is described there.[270]

Ford – see Laverstock and North Wraxall

Fovant

Congregational Chapel, * set well back west of lower end of High Street, Grade 2 listed, in use. Austere but dignified in ashlar under slate, the gable facing the street has a round-arched door surround and a lunette window above for the gallery but no other windows. There are two bays to the sides and the west end has one round-arched window high up. Inside, the central portion of the rear gallery, carrying a clock, is projected forwards. The chapel was built in 1820 as a mission chapel of Tisbury, perhaps designed by its builders the masons Francis and William Jay, and the gallery was probably added in the mid 19th century.[271]

Fovant Congregational – the simple and dignified interior

Foxham – see Bremhill

Froxfield

Primitive Methodist Chapel, south east of Brewhouse Hill, now a house. The unusual appearance of this small brick chapel is explained by the fact that it used to be longer, with a flat-headed door in the conventional place in the gable wall, pointed-arch windows either side and a small lean-to extension to the left. It was built in 1909, primarily for farm labourers, closed c1962 and at some point in the late 20th century the front wall fell down. This was then rebuilt further back and the strange front window inserted; the side door is also of this date. The original plaque dated 1909 has been replaced in the new gable.[272]
Photograph on page viii

Fyfield

Primitive Methodists had a chapel at the east end of the village, south of the main road, in the later 19th century. It was taken over by a **Congregational** mission, moved from Lockeridge, in 1884 and survived until demolished in 1938 to make way for widening of the A4.[273]

Garsdon – see Lea and Cleverton

Goatacre – see Hilmarton

Grafton

Wilton (Grafton) Wesleyan, showing its history on the front gable

Bethel Wesleyan Methodist Chapel, Wilton,✱ east of Grafton Road at west end of village, now a house. The history of this chapel is plain to the view. It was built in 1811, the schoolroom to the side added in 1843 and the walls raised between 1860 and 1870; this may have been the time when the rear gallery was added. The 1811 building had two flat-headed windows with keystones above what may have been a simple flat-headed door, all in brick with a pattern of vitrified headers. In the rebuilding these windows were infilled in brick and replaced by a single central one with a four-centred arch; this sits below a gable head with wavy bargeboards and a plaque, 'Bethel AD 1811'. Below are round-arched windows either side of a protruding porch with the initials AE above the door, probably all added in the rebuilding. The sides are plain with segmental-headed windows. The schoolroom is set back to the north side in plain brick with replacement windows and a plaque 'Wesleyan Schools.' The chapel closed in 1992, being deemed unsafe at that time, and was sold for conversion in 1996.[274]

Primitive Methodist Chapel, West Grafton, west of village road towards south end, now a house called Chapel House. The chapel, set back to the south, is now integrated into the neighbouring house which was possibly the manse and has since been extended. It is built of brick under slate, the windows much altered from what were probably tall round-arched originals, and with inserted dormers. The chapel was built in 1859 at a cost of £90 and closed by 1964.[275]

Primitive Methodist Chapel, Wexcombe, west of road at south end of village, now a house called Chapel Cottage. Another much altered chapel, now rendered under slate with a modern extension to the rear right. The gable facing the road has modern rectangular windows in what may be the original segmental-arched apertures; the porch is either an addition or a replacement. The chapel was built c1880 and closed by 1966.[276]

Great Bedwyn

Wesleyan Methodists built a chapel in **Church Street**, north west of the street near the church, c1810. Its exact location is not known but it was presumably replaced by the Brown's Lane chapel and later demolished.[277]

Brown's Lane Wesleyan Methodist Chapel, near junction with High Street, now a house. Built in 1875 of brick under slate, this chapel has the long side facing the street, with five bays of round-arched windows with cast iron glazing bars, the windows separated by buttresses. The south gable has a flat-roofed wide porch with bands of vitrified brick and small windows either side of an arched doorway with the inscription 'Wesleyan Methodist Church.' Above that is a double round-arched window contained in a single round arch surround and there is a similar window in the north gable. There are ancillary rooms to the north and a separate schoolroom to the west built c1904. The chapel closed in 1967.[278]

Great Cheverell

First Zoar Baptist Chapel,* adjacent to 1 The Green at junction with High Street, for some time used as an outhouse but now residential. This chapel was converted from an outbuilding sometime between 1760 and 1780 but abandoned after the High Street Baptist was built in 1833. Of brick under tile with a lean-to extension to the

The first Zoar Baptist, Great Cheverell – much altered but probably originally a chapel of 'long wall' type

north, it has a more recent chimney flue on the gable end, the top capped. The south side gives more clues to its past, with window and door openings, much altered, suggesting possibly that originally there were doors towards either end and a tall central window. The roof has been raised by around two feet, either during or after chapel use, and there is possibly still a baptistery under the floor.[279]

Little Zoar Baptist Chapel, not far west of the first chapel and south of High Street. This was built in 1833 as an Independent chapel, becoming Strict Baptist in 1842 and later General Baptist. When the lease was put on sale in 1907 the parish priest outbid the Baptists in an attempt to stamp out nonconformity in the village and converted it to a parish room; it later became the village hall. Rendered under slate with brick detail at the eaves perhaps indicating it was once all brick, it has two large

12-pane sashes to one side and two smaller blocked segmental-arched windows high up in the front gable. The original porch is of painted brick and offset in front of that on falling ground is a more modern second porch also in painted brick. This chapel and its successor were for long associated with the Bratton Baptist chapel.[280]

Baptist Chapel of 1907, built 1907 to replace the above, just to the east of it, now a house. This riposte to the parish priest is small and pleasing in brick with stone dressings, pointed-arch windows and bands of shaped tiles in the tiled roof. The side facing the road has two large windows with interlaced Y-tracery; there are later inserted dormers above and the porch to the left side has a plaque dated 1907 above a further window. The north east gable has a stepped three-light window. A schoolroom is offset to the rear. Henry Reeves of Bratton designed the chapel without charge: the original intention was to have only the chapel but success at fund-raising made it possible to add both the schoolroom and a baptistery. The chapel closed in 2000 and was sold for conversion in 2001.[281]

A **Wesleyan Methodist** mission room in the village was active for a few years from 1891, probably closing c1900. Its location has not been identified.[282]

Great Hinton

Wesleyan Methodists built a chapel c1864, south of Main Street and just west of the junction with Back Street. It was a small wooden structure of conventional gable-end shape with a plain door under a small pediment flanked by round-arched windows. Sold in 1935, it was demolished in the 1960s.[283]

Primitive Methodist Chapel, 25 Main Street, now a house. Built 1859 and originally intended as a pair of brick houses, one side was then left without a middle floor so that it could be used as a chapel. The other side became a house and externally it retained the appearance of a pair of houses. The two doors were at the centre under a flat hood: the left hand one had 'Primitive Methodist Chapel' written

Great Hinton Primitive Methodist – semi-detached houses, the chapel one side and a shop the other. It looks nothing like this now. Photograph courtesy of Diane Norris

above and that to the right for a while had advertisements for the shop which occupied the ground floor room. The chapel closed by the time of the Second World War and was used for storage until conversion in the 1970s. It is now rendered under tile with a modern brick porch and with nothing to indicate its previous purpose. The front openings are in their original positions but much altered with a window replacing the second door.[284]

Great Somerford

An **Independent** chapel of c1800 was recorded in Great Somerford in 1851 but nothing more is known of it.[285]

Primitive Methodist Chapel, Startley, west of road towards north end of village, now a house. The gable end at right angles to the road is in smart ashlar with round-arched windows either side of a replacement brick porch; above is a plaque dated 1854. The long side is of brick with a single tall round-arched window and the roof is of slate. Attached to the end is the jubilee schoolroom of 1860 with segmental-headed door, windows either side and a plaque above, 'Jubilee 1860'. There are modern extensions to the side opposite the road and, inside, the wainscot and ceiling panelling have been retained. The chapel was built in 1854 and closed in 1983. It may have been a successor to an earlier chapel of c1820.[286]

*Primitive Methodist Chapel, Great Somerford,** at junction of Top Lane and Park Street, in use. This is very Gothic in brick under slate with ashlar dressings, and makes an appealing group with the manse attached next door. The gable facing the road has a single large three-light window with a quatrefoil incorporated above. On the north east side are cusped lancets either side of the doorway

Great Somerford Primitive Methodist

with a probably later twin-gabled porch. The manse is also in brick and stone but with rectangular mullioned windows and wavy barge-boards. The chapel was built as a reading room in 1872 and bought and converted by the Methodists in 1882, this probably explaining its unusual side entrance.[287]

Great Wishford

Independents converted a house in West Street into a chapel in 1839 but it did not last long and may have closed well before the end of the century. It was attached to the west side of Chequers Cottage, diagonally opposite to the Royal Oak, and was probably of cob construction under a thatched roof; it was demolished in the 1920s or 1930s.[288]

Primitive Methodists registered **Cobb's Mill** as a meeting house in 1832 and used it, in increasingly decrepit condition, until 1912 when, having petitioned Lord Pembroke for a new site, they opened a new United Methodist chapel at Stoford.[289]

Grimstead

Wesleyan Methodist Chapel, West Grimstead, west of Chapel Hill, now a house. Plain brick under slate, it has an austere gable facing the road with strangely small round-arched windows either side of the porch, which carries the date 1869. At the gable head is a plaque, 'Wesleyan Chapel,' and above that is a pierced circular ventilator. The sides have two bays of round-arched windows of conventional size and there is a schoolroom extension to the rear. The first chapel here was built c1820 but replaced by this one on the same site, designed by G L Young of Salisbury, in 1869. The schoolroom was added in 1885 and the chapel was converted to a house in 2012.[290]

Free United, Methodist Chapel, East Grimstead, west of Grimstead Road just south of Long Drove junction, now a house. This 1907 chapel is built of brick under slate with an unusual projecting central section to the gable facing the road. The previous pointed-arch window at first floor level has been removed since conversion and the space left open to create an internal balcony. Two other windows on the gable are of similar shape but tall, and above is a plaque, now illegible. The door is in a projecting porch to the left hand side and the right has four bays of similar windows, all with keystones, separated by buttresses; there used to be a large roof ventilator shaped like a font on stand with cover. There is a small original lean-to room to the rear but the long building to the right with linking glass porch is modern. The chapel was converted to a house in 1966 but at that stage was said to have been disused for 20 years.
Photograph on page 49.

This chapel succeeded a **previous corrugated iron chapel**, probably of the 1880s, which was situated nearby, north of Bugmore Lane in what is now the garden of Holly House. This seems to have gone out of use on the opening of the 1907 chapel but may not have been demolished until the 1970s.[291]

Grittenham – see Brinkworth

Grittleton

Strict Baptist, *** set well back south of The Street, Grade 2* listed; now in the care of the Historic Chapels Trust and access can be arranged via their website. This is one of the oldest chapels in the county and has a remarkable early interior.
It is generally stated as built c1720 but a meeting house certificate, probably of

Grittleton Baptist, the east wall

1709, suggests it might actually have been built then, soon after the marriage of Priscilla White, heiress of Grittleton House, to Robert Houlton. It stood in the grounds of Grittleton House and was originally accessed through these grounds, with the support of Robert Houlton and also because most worshippers approached from that direction, development of The Street coming a hundred years later. A

Grittleton Baptist, the vestry beneath the north gallery, with pulpit in front

later owner of the house, probably Joseph Neeld in the second quarter of the 19th century, was less sympathetic to nonconformity and built the walls screening the chapel from his grounds, so access then had to be from The Street. The chapel was closed in 1982 and eventually repaired in 1985 after an attempt to sell it off for conversion to a house. It was transferred to the Historic Chapels Trust in 2011.

It is built of rubble-stone, probably originally limewashed, with ashlar dressings and segmental-arched windows, mullioned and transomed at the lower level, mullioned above. The hipped roof is tiled. There are two tall windows to the west side, four smaller ones to the east with four smaller still above. The doorway, again segmental-headed, is at the south end with a short moulded cornice above, and the north wall is blank.

The exterior suggests the pulpit was originally at the centre of the west wall between the two windows, with a gallery on the east wall. Now, though, there are north and south galleries. Beneath the north one, built or altered in the mid 19th century, is a vestry with partly glazed screen towards the chapel. The pulpit is placed centrally in front of what was once a door to the vestry, which has a fireplace and may also have been used as overnight accommodation by visiting preachers. The south gallery is 18th century with seating of the same date; in the main chapel at the south east corner there are three oak 18th century box pews; the remainder are 19th century pine including a charming child's seat.

Grittleton Baptist, a raised box pew especially made for children

The burial ground stretches north from the blank rear wall of the chapel, previously walled off.[292]

Congregational Chapel, Littleton Drew, west of village street towards south end, listed grade 2. At first sight a farm building, this is actually a chapel erected in 1815 but empty since perhaps as long ago as the 1960s. The gable facing the road belongs to a side extension, probably the schoolroom, and the chapel itself is behind with the long wall to the road. It is built of rubble-stone, previously rendered, under slate. There is a 16-pane window to the road side, the crude wooden lintels over both this and an adjacent blocked door, exposed by the decaying render, underlining the agricultural feel. A simple porch is alongside and there are further flat-headed windows in the right and rear walls, the latter of 24 panes. Inside is a simple gallery with steep stairs.[293]

Ham

No chapels recorded.[294]

Hanging Langford – see Steeple Langford

Hankerton

Rehoboth Strict Baptist Chapel, on Chapel Lane at east end of village, now a house. The chapel was built in 1837, of rubble-stone under a hipped slate roof. The door was in the south end with a simple wooden porch, the window above blocked off well before conversion, and on the long side facing the road were two tall sash windows of 30 panes each. Now the door in the end wall has been replaced by French windows and the tall windows by two tiers of smaller ones. A modern porch on the side at the north end replaces what may have been the vestry. The chapel closed in 1971 and was sold for conversion in 1975.[295]

Hannington

No chapels recorded.[296]

Hawkeridge – see Heywood

Haydon Wick

Emmanuel Congregational Chapel, by junction of High Street and Green Valley Avenue, in use. The original chapel of 1849 is tall and of rubble-stone with ashlar quoins under tile. A schoolroom was added at right angles to the rear in the late 19th century, in brick and buttressed between tall pointed-arch windows and with a first floor inserted later. The porch has gone through various stages from the first addition in 1897 to the present tall tile-hung effort from c1986. Further side and rear extensions complete the confusing picture and the interior has been modernised. The chapel, originally seating 200, was built at the sole expense of a village resident, a Mr Slye.[297]

Wesleyan Methodist Chapel, east side of The Brow, now the Sea Scouts' HQ. Very plain, of brick under tile with arched windows and two bays deep, the gable facing the road has had its porch replaced by wide double doors though it retains windows either side and a plaque dated 1869 above. There was previously a small single storey extension to the rear, perhaps a vestry and now gone. The chapel was sold to scouts in 1962 as part of the series of changes arising from the construction of by St Andrew's in Moredon Road, Swindon and a lean-to extension was subsequently added to the side.[298]

Heddington

Wesleyan Methodist Chapel, south of road a little way east of Heddington Wick, now a house. This small chapel, of brick under slate, was opened in 1854, closed c1950 and was turned into a scout hall in 1962. It was empty by 2011 but has now been converted to a house. The rectangular windows under stone lintels appear to be of original shape though one has been converted into a door, but the porch is a replacement. There is a gable plaque dated 1854.[299]

Heytesbury (see also Imber)

The **Congregational Chapel**, at the north end of Chapel Road, was built in 1868 to replace a chapel of 1812 on the same site. It was a large Gothic building in brick and stone with double-arched doors, a triple window above and pilasters either side of that. Closed in the mid 1950s, it was replaced by a new house, No. 18a. The 1812 chapel was itself of substantial size, with a hipped roof and, very unusually, three tiers of windows, the top two tiers round-arched.[300]

The surprisingly large 1812 Congregational, Heytesbury, in an early photograph. It was demolished c1868. Photograph courtesy of Salisbury Museum

Primitive Methodists built a chapel and schoolroom in **Tytherington**, south of the church and behind a row of cottages, now replaced by 'New Cottages.' It was built in1863 at a cost of £111, closed sometime shortly before the Second World War, and was demolished by 1957.[301]

Heywood

Congregational Chapel, Hawkeridge, * set back south of village street east of Royal Oak pub, in use. This is an excellent example of a small and largely unaltered village chapel. Conspicuously plain on the exterior in pebble-dash under a hipped tile roof, it has a simple door at one end, with a window above, and two rectangular windows to the north wall which have replacement glazing, as do all the others. To the south is the brick schoolroom, originally accessed via a door in the chapel but now with its own external door. The roof of this has necessitated the shortening of

Hawkeridge (Heywood) Congregational, complete with tiny gallery

one of the chapel windows on that side; the window at the further end of the south side has been made more shallow but wider, for unexplained reasons. Inside is equally plain, with a gallery up steep stairs at the doorway end and pews and pulpit by Reeves of Bratton, dating from 1901. Land for the chapel was bought as early as 1816 and it may have been built in 1844, although another source suggests 1859. As an Independent, and later

Congregational, chapel it was a mission station of the Old Congregational at Westbury. The schoolroom was added in the last years of the 19th century.[302]

Independent Methodists met in the village from c1819 and are known to have built a chapel with capacity for 140 before 1842. Although mentioned in the 1851 ecclesiastical census, their absence from directories from the 1850s suggests that the meeting did not last many years.[303]

Hilcott – see North Newnton

Hilmarton

Congregational Chapel, Goatacre, on a private drive running east from main road towards north end of village, now a house. The chapel is the section parallel to the road at left with the manse joined to it at right angles, the whole now rendered under slate with much-altered windows. The porch protruding forward from the junction of the two buildings is probably original. The rear section of the manse, in coursed stone blocks, may show what the whole chapel once looked like. Registered in 1824, it closed c1917, was used for a time as a club room, became the village shop c1967 and was later converted to a house. The considerable distance from the parish church may have helped make Goatacre stand out as a centre for nonconformity.[304]

Particular Baptists built a **Strict Bethel Chapel**, surprisingly next door to the vicarage, in 1849. It was replaced by the 1924 chapel but the building, of corrugated iron, survived until recent times in the grounds of the vicarage, now called Sunnyside.[305]

Zoar Baptist Chapel, built 1924 and now in use as an Independent church, at the east end of Church Road. A neat small building of stone blockwork under diamond-set tiles, it has pointed windows and a porch with a date plaque over. The sides are of four bays.[306]

General Baptists in **Clevancy** first met in a cottage but by 1881 had built a small corrugated iron chapel, known as the mission hall, on the road north from the hamlet and just north of Chapel Cottage. It was derelict by the 1980s and demolished soon afterwards.[307]

Primitive Methodist Chapel, Goatacre, * on corner of main road and the road to New Zealand, now a house called Primitive House. Primitive Methodists of the Brinkworth circuit had been meeting here from the 1820s but were only able to built a chapel in 1867 when the Quakers agreed to lease them their former burial ground at SU023766; the 1867 chapel was of conventional appearance with tall round-arched

Goatacre (Hilmarton) Primitive Methodist of 1909

windows either side of the doorway in the gable end facing the road. The site was considered too remote and it was replaced by this chapel in 1909; the original was demolished soon after. This is of brick with ashlar dressings under tile. It faces the main road and has a porch and triple lancet window above on this side. The schoolroom, of the same date, is at right angles by what is now the entrance drive and has paired and triple lancet windows. It closed in 1994 but the external appearance is remarkably unchanged following conversion: unassuming but well executed.[308]

Hilperton

Particular Baptist Chapel, east side of Hill Street, shortly before it joins Church Street, now four flats. This was built in 1806 by people who had previously worshipped at Back Street Baptist, Trowbridge. It then had an ashlar front with a shouldered gable, two tiers of plain windows, lately sashes, and a gable plaque for 1806; the sides were of rubble-stone and the roof slate. The vestry was enlarged and a schoolroom built above in 1821. The chapel closed in 1978; by 1982 it was derelict and there was an application to demolish and replace with a house but instead it was converted into flats in the 1990s. The proportions of the front were always uncomfortable but it has now been made worse by the application of ugly blockwork cladding and the fitting of ill-proportioned modern windows.[309]

*Wesleyan Methodist Chapel,** junction of Church Street and Hill Street, now two houses. The original chapel of 1819 may have had a schoolroom added in mid-century and both were rebuilt in 1891. The chapel is to the left and the schoolrooms to the right, both in smooth-faced stone of less than ashlar quality; the roofs are tiled. Their design is characterful, particularly the gable end of the chapel which has a central door under a Gothic arch and three rising diamond windows to the right for the staircase. Above is a ten-light mullioned and transomed window within another arch, with rough stonework infill above perhaps indicating second thoughts on the design. There are two bays with triple rectangular windows to the road side, then a third like a transept with a gable and six-light stepped window within another arch, topped by three small circular windows. Inside, the organ was previously placed

within an arch behind the pulpit. The schoolrooms to the right are of four bays with paired windows, round-arched above and flat-headed below; the door has a small protruding porch. The chapel and schoolroom closed in 1988, survived an application to demolish and replace with houses and flats, and were both converted by c2001.[310]

Hilperton Wesleyan

Hindon

Congregational Chapel, north side of The Dene at south end of High Street, now a house called The Old Chapel. The chapel origins of this building are far from obvious from its present appearance. It was built in 1810, paid for by the Revd Joseph Berry of Warminster who put it in trust for Congregational use. Of squared stone under a tiled roof, it has a rubble-stone east gable, originally the chapel entrance and now with infilled door and gallery window above; the door arch was pointed and that of the window round. The north side had two bays of large three-light pointed windows and the south side probably the same; all have been replaced by two tiers of modern windows, with a new door to the lane. A small house is attached to the west end and opposite the east end is a detached house which may have been the manse. Closed in 1972, it was then sold and converted.[311]

Primitive Methodist Chapel,* north east of High Street towards lower end, now a house. The original chapel was built in 1840 west of the upper High Street and set a long way back opposite the parish church; it was replaced by this chapel in 1896 and soon demolished. The 1896 chapel was built to designs by a Mr Hudson of Wincanton and Gillingham. It has a handsome Classical facade in ashlar with a round-arched door-case, circular window above, tall round-arched windows either

side and a shouldered pedimented gable with a plaque dated 1896. The sides are of squared stone blocks with brick dressings for three tall round-arched windows. A brick schoolroom to the rear was built at the same time and separated from the chapel by a sliding partition. The chapel closed in 1981, served for a time as an antiques shop and was converted to a house c2007, at which date the front windows were neatly deepened by just over one foot to their present extent.[312]

Hindon Primitive Methodist

Hinton Parva – see Bishopstone North

Holt

Holt's two *Congregational Chapels*** share the same site. The original, of c1810 and Grade 2 listed, has an interesting building history but the particular delight is the unaltered 1880 interior of its replacement.

The original chapel was Independent until 1859 when it became Congregational. Built at a cost of £220, it was extended in 1846, being thereafter divided with the chapel on the first floor and schoolrooms below. After the opening of the new chapel in 1880, this one continued in use as a school until 1962; it was renovated in 1977 and now has community use.

It is tall, under a hipped slate roof, and must have been almost cubic in shape before the one-bay extension east of 1846. From at least that date it seems that the entrance was in the south wall, as shown by the two blocked Tudor-arched doors which are accompanied by a smaller window between and three Gothic windows above, two with interlacing Y-tracery and one blocked. The join in the coarse ashlar masonry is apparent here as on the rubble-stone north wall, where there are now three similar windows at first floor

North wall of the original Congregational, Holt – the extension eastwards is obvious, other changes less so. Note the roof ventilator

level, one presumably moved sideways at the time of the extension to maintain symmetry; the three rectangular windows below presumably date from 1846 and may have replaced Gothic originals. The 'new' east wall, again in coarse ashlar, has two Gothic windows with recessed panels stretching down from them to flat-headed windows below, and dentil moulding across the wall at the level of the window arches, an unusually exuberant display of decorative detail. These windows are set unusually off-centre towards the north, perhaps reflecting the provision of original gallery stairs to the south, and so are the windows on the rubble-stone west wall. This has more Gothic windows with Y-tracery, probably originally taller, and altered openings below including the present main door.

Stent's 1880 Congregational, Holt

The 1880 chapel was built to provide more capacity, to the design of W J Stent of Warminster. It is in Early English style, of rock-faced squared stone with ashlar dressings, the roof banded with fish-scale tiles, and has a bell tower, a west aisle and an apse. From the outside it could be taken for an Anglican church of the period and Pevsner, who had no liking for Stent's work, called it obtrusive.

The inside is another story: here are the 1880 fittings more or less complete. The pine pews, each ornately numbered, are in two main blocks with the wider ones to the left divided into two by staggered panels. To the left behind arches on circular columns is the aisle containing the substantial organ, and the apse contains the pulpit. The gallery, well integrated to the structure above the porch, has a complex panelled front with inset stencilled floral decoration. The roof has corbels supporting the principal rafters and further timber supports, proud of the wall face.[313]

Photograph also on page 36.

Homington – see Coombe Bissett

Hook – see Lydiard Tregoze

Horningsham

Congregational Chapel,** on Chapel Street south of village centre; listed Grade 2*; in use. One of the most famous of all Wiltshire chapels and amongst the

Horningsham Congregational, the entrance front and north wall

oldest, though not as old as has been claimed. By tradition built in 1566 for Scots Presbyterian masons working for Sir John Thynne on the building of Longleat House, it carries the date 1566 on the west gable. Scots Presbyterians may well have been worshipping locally from this date but not in this chapel, which was built c1700. It was Presbyterian during the 18th century but later became Congregational. Of rubble-stone with some brick dressings under a half-hipped thatch roof, it was extended to the east in 1754 and to the west in 1816. In further renovations in 1863 the 18th century box pews were removed, and there were several further renovations in the 20th century.

Various blocked doors and windows show its history. There was initially a central entrance on the south side, closed apparently in 1863 and sited where there is now one of two buttresses built in 1925. The later east wall has a central doorway between two blocked windows and the west extension included a doorway in the north wall, blocked in the 1863 works. Most windows are modest in size, including eyebrow dormers to illuminate the galleries, but at the west end are two large ones, wooden-framed.

Horningsham Congregational. Note hat pegs for the men's gallery but not for the women's

The interior is even more compelling than the exterior, with a host of details to note including galleries around three sides supported on turned wooden columns, that to the east dating from the mid 18th century but those to north and south of c1816. They retain seating of that date though the box pews in the body of the church were replaced in 1863. The north gallery, where men sat, has wooden hat pegs; there is a central clock on the east gallery with a music stand for a choir behind, and some candle holders remain. There is a high early 19th century pulpit and the plaster ceiling is irregularly curved.

The adjacent schoolroom, of rubble-stone and render with some brick dressings under a half-hipped tile roof, was apparently originally the manse but converted to a schoolroom c1860.[314]

More photographs at frontispiece and on pages 22-4.

Horton – see Bishops Cannings

Huish

A **Primitive Methodist** chapel was built on **Huish Hill**, SU155641, c1863. It was abandoned when the hamlet here was deserted in the 1920s and demolished c1940. It is possible that the chapel started as **Wesleyan** but changed allegiance later.[315]

Hullavington

The **Society of Friends** built a meeting house in what is now **Watts Lane** c1697. It closed c1817 and was later used as a school for a period before at least partial demolition and the erection of a Methodist chapel on the site by 1843 (see below).[316]

General Baptist Chapel, Newtown, at junction of Newtown and Latimer Gardens, listed Grade 2, derelict in 2019. Barn-like in coursed limestone rubble under a part-hipped roof of graduated stone slates, it has pointed-arch windows with ashlar dressings and the remains of iron Y-tracery. There are two windows to the left side, one to the right and one above the flat headed door to the front; the rear wall is blank. It was built in 1821 and appears to have been substantially unaltered through its life, though changing during this period from Independent and Baptist to just Baptist. Closed in 1929, it was later used for agricultural storage but in 2019 was heavily overgrown and derelict. Attempts have been made to secure planning permission for conversion to a house: it is a building of character which deserves to be revived.[317]

Mount Zion Particular Baptist Chapel, Gibbs Lane, almost opposite the church, now a house called Watersmeet. In rubble-stone with ashlar quoins under a slate roof, this chapel has a gable plaque, 'Mount Zion Particular Baptist Chapel 1843,' on the north wall mounted above what was previously an upper square-headed window and below that a porch; this is now all blocked and there is an outbuilding there. The side facing the road used to have large conventional sash windows where now there are two tall round-arched windows, split to accommodate an inserted floor. The chapel closed in 1985 and was sold for conversion in 1991.[318]
Photograph on page 56.

Primitive Methodist Chapel, Watts Lane, No.7, now a house. Methodists rented the Friends' Meeting House from 1842, improving it in 1858 and buying it from the Friends in 1902. It was closed in 1985 and converted in 1991. Of rubble-stone with brick dressings under tile, the door at the gable end is blocked in but there is a window in perhaps the original opening above. The roof has been raised about three feet. Two flat-headed windows facing the road on the long side have been replaced by two dormers above and a window and French doors below; on the opposite side there are similar changes with a new door and porch inserted. The whole is almost unrecognisable as having once been a chapel.[319]

Idmiston

Baptist Chapel, Porton, south end of High Street, in use. The chapel has a plinth of brick and flint; the walls are rendered cob and the roof of slate. The gable facing the road has paired lancet windows above a large replacement porch. To the side are three pairs of lancet windows, those at the west end being part of a 1922/3 extension which also saw the creation of a Sunday school at the basement level.

The interior is now plain, though not many years ago it had a stove, pews and 'Sing unto the Lord' and 'Praise ye the Lord' in scroll painting on the pulpit wall. Porton was the centre of the Particular Baptists in South Wiltshire from 1655 until around 1710 but activity here declined with the building of Brown Street Baptist in Salisbury in 1719 and there seems to have been little Baptist presence until this chapel was built in 1865, itself part financed by Brown Street.[320]
Photograph on page 53.

Wesleyan Methodist Chapel, between Idmiston and Boscombe, west of main road, now a house. An earlier small chapel, west of the main road at SU195380, may have been that mentioned in the 1851 religious census as built in 1818. It was replaced by the present one in 1901 and demolished sometime after the First World War. This chapel, by Gordon and Gunton of London, is of strange white-faced brick under slate. The gable facing the road has pointed-arch windows either side of the porch and a wheel window above. There are three pairs of lancet windows with brick buttresses on the long side. It closed in 1970 when the Bourne Valley Methodist chapels combined into the Bourne Valley Methodist Church and was sold for conversion in 1973.[321]

Imber *(now in Heytesbury parish)*

A **Baptist Chapel** was built here in 1833; a school was attached in 1858 and the chapel was repaired and partly rebuilt in 1868. It was closed on the evacuation of the village in 1943 and demolished in the 1970s. The chapel had a semi-hipped roof and a side door with two bays of single windows to the left and one bay of windows in two tiers to the right, the latter probably the schoolrooms.[322]

Imber Baptist. Photograph courtesy of Salisbury Museum

Inglesham

No chapels recorded.[323]

Keevil

Wesleyan Methodist Chapel,⁎ Main Street east of village centre, Grade 2 listed, now a house. This is an imposing group, particularly the original chapel of 1833 to the right, in brick with ashlar dressings under a hipped slate roof. To the road side it has two large triple-lancet windows,

Keevil Wesleyan before front windows were lowered on conversion. Lighter brickwork may indicate some yet earlier change to the windows. Photograph courtesy of Wiltshire Buildings Record.

Keevil Wesleyan

extended three feet down on conversion to a house and so altering greatly the front appearance. As a chapel it was orientated parallel to the road with a gallery at the entrance end. To the left are the 1901 Sunday school rooms in similar materials but more Gothic in feel with a pitched roof, a gable facing the road with a triple stepped lancet window and a small cross-wing behind with a similar window to the south gable. A string course in stone runs at the original level of the window sills, the front windows also having been deepened on conversion, this time by four brick courses. The door to the chapel was originally in the south wall but a corridor here now links the two buildings and the door faces the road. The chapel closed in 1987 and was converted in 1989, the external signs the window deepening already noted and new glazing. The floor then inserted is neatly hidden behind the central row of lights in the lengthened chapel windows.[324]

Kilmington

Wesleyan Methodist Chapel, south of The Street at ST780359, Grade 2 listed, now a house. The gable facing the road is of dressed limestone with pointed central double doors and two lancets above; a platband above them has a worn inscription. The sides were previously of render over rubble-stone with ashlar dressings but the render has now mostly gone; each side has two tall pointed windows with stone Y-tracery. The roof is of slate, hipped to the rear. Built in 1847, it closed in 1969, was derelict by c2000 but has since been converted into a house.[325]

Kingsdown – see Box and Stratton St Margaret

Kingston Deverill

Wesleyan, later Primitive, Methodist Chapel, south of road at ST851371, now part of a much larger house. Built in 1825, it was disused by the early 20th century but then rented by Primitive Methodists in 1908 following closure of their own chapel (see below). They gave it up in 1912 after which its condition worsened until it was sold to the rector in 1926, with the intention that it should become a parish club room. It had various uses before being converted finally into a house. The chapel forms the front portion of the present house; all is much altered but the gable is of painted rubble-stone with a perhaps original pointed-arch window above. A bay window below may be in place of the original door.[326]

Primitive Methodists built a chapel at Whitepits, ST845375, which was there by 1887 but demolished by 1901. They subsequently rented the Wesleyan chapel for a short period.[327]

Kington Langley

Moravians had a presence here from 1748 but it is not known when they left.[328]

Union Chapel; **built for Countess of Huntingdon's Connexion**, south side of Middle Common at ST922768, Grade 2 listed, in use. This handsome chapel has its gable facing the road and is built of squared rubble-stone with ashlar quoins. The later ashlar porch has a two-light double-arched window above, and above that is a charmingly mis-spaced inscription on a band under the pedimental gable, 'O come let us enter into the house of our God.' Finally, above that, is a plaque, 'Union Chapel 1835'. There are two arched Y-tracery

Union Chapel, Kington Langley – the gable inscription

windows to the left side and one to the right, behind which is a projecting vestry wing with a round-arched window above, a flat-headed window below and a further door. The roof is of slate and there is a rear gallery on iron columns inside. The chapel appears to have been changed little during its life, though the lower seating was renewed in the late 19th century. Independents were meeting in the house of James Pinnegar, a builder and mason, in 1834 and it was he who built this in 1835. Although built for the Countess of Huntingdon's Connexion, it is said to have been placed in trust for the joint use of Moravians, Independents and Baptists, hence the name.[329]

Photograph also on page 33.

Primitive Methodist Chapel, Silver Street, north of Lower Common, ST926771, now a house. The small original chapel of 1844 was attractive with two pointed-arch doors in the ashlar front facing the street and a similarly sized window with stone Y-tracery between them. Above each door is a small blind window with traces of inscriptions; the rubble-stone sides each have two substantial pointed windows and the whole sits under a hipped slate roof. The purity of this design was compromised early with a small side extension of c1900, now made larger. On conversion to a house two small windows have been inserted high up on each side and, more intrusively, one of the doors has been blocked and a metal flue pushed through it. The chapel closed in 1987.[330]

Plymouth Brethren moved from premises in Goldney Avenue, Chippenham to a new site on Plough Lane, immediately west of the A350 by the traffic lights, in 2015; they are registered here as the **Down Gospel Trust**. Their premises look like

a large warehouse with a curved metal roof, set in a vast car park.[331]
Photograph on page 52.

Kington St Michael

Bethesda Congregational Chapel, east of village street north of The Close, now a house. This may have been built in 1830 for the Baptists and taken over by Independents in 1835 but more likely was newly built for the Independents at the latter date; it later became Congregational. A schoolroom was added at right angles to the rear c1875 but was demolished after the chapel closed. The gable facing the road is of coursed worked stone with ashlar dressings, two round-arched windows above a modern porch and a now-illegible plaque within the pedimented gable head. The sides are of rubble-stone and the roof tiled. It was closed and converted probably not long before 1985.[332]

Knook

No chapels recorded.[333]

Lacock

Lacock Congregational

Congregational Chapel,* Chapel Hill, off Cantax Hill, Grade 2 listed, now a house. An eye-catching chapel, tall for its plan dimensions, it is built of squared rubble-stone with ashlar dressings under a hipped roof of graduated stone slates. The entrance front facing the road has double doors under a hood on brackets and a Y-tracery two-light pointed window above; there are two similar windows on each side. The interior, panelled to waist height and with a later rear gallery, was plain. The chapel is usually dated to 1812 but a meeting house certificate for 1808 suggests it might be earlier. The later and lower schoolroom extension to the rear, probably added mid-century, has a tiled roof and was enlarged c1913. Redundant in the 1990s, the chapel was converted in 2003.[334]

Lacock Congregational. The later gallery overlaps the windows and there are three blocks of pews despite the modest overall width.
Photograph courtesy of Wiltshire and Swindon Archives.

Wesleyan Methodist Chapel, east of river at foot of Bowden Hill, now a house. The gable of this chapel faces the road and has a porch with a pointed-arch door under three stepped pointed-arch windows; above these is an inscription scroll now blank. Each side has three tall pointed-arch windows with buttresses between and there is a lean-to schoolroom extension to the rear. The whole is of ashlar under tile. It was built in 1863 by Joseph Gale of Lacock, replacing a 'preaching room' of 1828, and abandoned in the 1970s when the Methodists joined the Congregational chapel. Advertised for sale in 1981, it was not converted until after 2003.[335]

There were plans in 1932 to build a **Gospel Hall** on Lovers' Walk, east of Cantax Hill. It seems the hall was never built.[336]

Landford

Primitive Methodist Chapel, west of Lyndhurst Road towards north end of village, in use but undergoing renovation in 2019. A cob-walled chapel was built here in 1825 but, with a limited life, it was replaced by this building in 1866 at a cost of £167. The layout is conventional, the gable facing the road with what looks like a later porch and, either side, tall round-arched windows with ashlar heads; there is a plaque above dated 1866. The chapel is built of pale brick but the bottom twenty courses of the south wall are in red brick, for no clear reason, and this wall has two tall flat-headed windows. A small lean-to extension to the rear is in red brick with a new door and the Sunday school, added in 1956, is at the rear to the south. The chapel roof is of slate, that of the Sunday school of tile.[337]

*Landfordwood Mission Hall,** north of Stock Lane in Landfordwood, Grade 2 listed, in use. This was built in 1899 for £300, to designs by Rawlence and Squarey of Salisbury. It is made of stained timber on a brick plinth with long ranges of windows to the sides and dormers with trefoil windows above. The porch is to the front and the roof is of tile, converted from wooden shingles in the 1950s. On top at the front is a surprising Classical bell turret on six wooden pillars with ogee roof. Inside is a single space, timber-lined and with a hammer-beam roof. Built on the estate of Lady Ashburton, paid for by her and using estate timber, the hall was closely associated with

Landfordwood Mission Hall

Landford Methodist chapel until it became a Free Evangelical mission between the wars. It was listed as recently as 2020.[338]

Langley Burrell Without

No chapels recorded.[339]

Latton

No chapels recorded.[340]

Laverstock

Wesleyan Methodists were active in **Ford** from at least the 1840s, meeting initially in a house. In c1878 they built a small chapel almost opposite Ford Mill, in what is now the garden of Riverbourne Cottage, formerly Down Cottage. It was probably of conventional stone construction. Closed perhaps during the First World War, it stood empty for a time but was then adopted as a chapel of ease of Laverstock parish church, called St Francis first but later St Christopher. It closed in 1980 and was demolished.[341]

Lea and Cleverton

Zion Baptist Chapel, Lea,* east of The Street, in use. An attractive simple chapel of coursed squared stone with ashlar dressings and pointed-arch windows under a slate roof. Its gable faces the road and has a porch with two windows above and a worn gable plaque. Stone on the front is rock-faced but is smooth on the two-bay sides with their Y-tracery windows. The original chapel, of 1808, was built for Calvinistic Methodists but had been taken over by Independents by 1855. It was replaced by the present building in 1861: this was used by Independents, later Congregationalists until at least 1916 but it had been taken over by the Baptists by 1928.[342]
Photograph on front cover.

Jubilee Primitive Methodist Chapel, Garsdon Heath, north east of Garsdon at ST975884, now a house, set back north west of the road. The plain rendered gable has a porch with tall segmental-arched windows either side and a plaque dated 1860. The chapel was built in 1860, closed in 1995 and was converted to a house after 2009.[343]

Cleverton (Lea & Cleverton) Primitive Methodist

Primitive Methodist Chapel, Cleverton,* just south of village T-junction, in use. A good example of a small and modest village chapel, it is built of coursed squared rubble-stone under slate and has round-arched windows with brick dressings. The gable, at right angles to the road, has a replacement porch with windows either side and a plaque above dated 1874. There is one window to the road side and a small lean-to rear extension. Inside are original wainscotting, panelled ceiling and hat pegs. The original chapel, of 1832, was probably on this site and was replaced by this one in 1874.[344]

Quakers had a burial ground at Lea, south of the road a little way west of the parish church. It was last used in 1771 and by 1879 the **Primitive Methodists** were attempting to buy it to erect a chapel on. The parish clergyman also wished to buy it, to erect a schoolhouse, but in the event neither succeeded and it remained open ground until a modern house, Willow Tree House, was built there.[345]

Leigh

Primitive Methodist Chapel, south of B4040 at SU067919, now a house. The chapel is small, rendered though perhaps originally brick, with a slate roof and extended on conversion from two bays to three. The gables are at right angles to the road and that at the north east end has a new porch with tall round-arched windows either side, now reduced slightly in size. The side facing the road is now blank though originally it had one window; it carries a modern replacement plaque dated 1860. The south east end appears to have had the original doorway, between two similarly tall round-arched windows and with a circular plaque above. Farmers assisted in building the first chapel here in 1840, apparently in the hopes of reducing thieving in the parish, and it was rented to Primitive Methodists of the Brinkworth circuit until they bought and converted a cottage in 1859/60. This served until the present chapel was built in 1867. The chapel closed in 2003 and was converted in 2008.[346]

Liddington

Wesleyan Methodist Chapel, south of The Street, now a house. The chapel is of brick under tile with ashlar dressings, much altered on conversion with inserted dormers, new windows and a front extension. The gable is at right angles to the road with flat-headed windows either side and a round window over. The later schoolroom is to the west, making this a long building overall. The chapel was built in 1870 and closed in 1982.[347]

A **Methodist** chapel of 1842 was further east but demolished by 1900. It may have been Wesleyan and hence a predecessor of that of 1870 but there are suggestions that it was Primitive.[348]

Limpley Stoke

Baptist Chapel, Middle Stoke, east of road, Grade 2 listed, now a house. The simple and handsome gable facing the road seems earlier than the stated date of 1888: did they retain the facade of the original 1815 chapel which became dilapidated and was replaced by this? In ashlar, it has a round-arched door and tall round-arched windows either side, with buttresses at the corners and a date 1815 at the gable head. Falling ground behind means the rubble-stone sides are on two levels. There is a cottage attached to the rear, probably the manse. It was built for £300, closed in 1987, was proposed for demolition in 1988 but was then turned into a house, the front set back about 12 feet but then re-erected in identical form.[349]

Little Bedwyn

Primitive Methodists built a chapel in 1846 at the south east end of the village by the Harrow Inn. It was demolished, probably in the mid 20th century, and was replaced in 1992 by a house.[350]

Little Cheverell

No chapels recorded.[351]

Little Hinton – see Bishopstone North

Little Somerford

No chapels recorded.[352]

Littleton Drew – see Grittleton

Littleton Panell – see West Lavington

Lockeridge – see West Overton

Longbridge Deverill

Congregational Chapel, Crockerton, south of Clay Street, now in commercial use. Very Gothic, in rock-faced stone with buttresses under a tiled roof with bands of diamond tiles, it has three bays to the right of the porch, forming the chapel, and a two-light window to the left, part of a schoolroom extension. Built in 1860 and paid for by Charles Jupe of Mere, it was closed in the late 1940s, sold in 1952 and has since been used by a joinery company. Its history lies with the **Wesleyan Methodists** and is explained below.[353]

*Baptist Chapel, Crockerton Green,** east of A350 at ST868432, Grade 2 listed, empty in 2019. An early chapel, built probably soon after 1704 while Crockerton was the centre of a network of local Baptists because of its convenient position

 mid-way between Warminster and Horningsham. This is interesting but hard to view because of an overgrown hedge and a busy main road alongside. It is built of squared rubble-stone with ashlar dressings under tile. There are three tall round-arched leaded windows to the road side and to their right is the door with a smaller window above lighting

Crockerton Baptist (Longbridge Deverill), nearly hidden by trees

the gallery. The rear has three tall square-headed windows and two windows above each other to the left, equivalent to the door and gallery window on the front. Attached to the south is the early 19th century one-bay schoolroom of similar shape and beyond that a house, perhaps of the same date. The chapel interior retains a Georgian pulpit and some 18th century panelling. It closed in 1979; the schoolroom had commercial use for a few years but now both are empty.[354]

Crockerton Baptist less overgrown in the 1980s, the schoolroom at that date in use as a shop. Photograph courtesy of Wiltshire Buildings Record.

Wesleyan Methodists were active in Crockerton from 1755 and built a chapel here, but it was not put in trust and they were expelled when the owner died. They then met in a house until in 1808 they took possession of a building which they used as a chapel, extending it twice and adding a total of three galleries. In 1835 they fell out with the Methodist Conference and became a separate society and by 1859 they were Independents, transferring their property to Charles Jupe. The old chapel was pulled down in 1860 and the new Congregational chapel, described above and paid for by Jupe, was erected on what was probably the same site.[355]

An **Independent Methodist** of about 1811 was open in Longbridge in 1851 but does not seem to have survived long afterwards. It is possible that this is the same group as that from Crockerton, above.[356]

Primitive Methodist Chapel, off east end of Sand Street behind Wellington Cottage, used as a store. Single-storey in rubble-stone with brick dressings under tile though perhaps once thatched, and looking nothing like a chapel, it opened in 1846 and was for a time linked to other buildings to both north and south. Those to the north are now gone and a later gable wall has been built with bands of brick; a blocked doorway is visible inside. The west side is blank but for a doorway at the north end and the east side has three small flat-headed windows. The chapel was closed in 1971 and was bought by the owners of Wellington Cottage.[357]

Luckington

Providence Strict Baptist Chapel, Chapel Row, now used as offices. This is rendered under slate with ashlar dressings including raised voussoirs as well as keystones to the round-arched windows. The gable faces the road and has a porch, tall sash windows either side, a circular plaque above dated 1866 and a shouldered gable head. There are three similar windows to each side and all have complex glazing bars in an attractive pattern copying the originals, although those had some panes blanked off to create an even more interesting effect. To the rear, with a lower roofline, is a small vestry probably added before c1880. The chapel closed c1990 and has since been used both as a house and as offices.[358]

Primitive Methodist Chapel, east of The Green, in use. A standard corrugated iron chapel of 1903, it has three windows to each side, all with modern glazing. It is well maintained, as are most of the county's remaining 'tin tabernacles'.[359]

Ludgershall

Strict Baptists built a chapel on the east side of St James's Street just north of Chapel Lane, probably in 1810 or 1818. It was ruinous by the end of the century but replaced by an iron chapel in 1902, supplied by Browne and Lilly of Reading. This also became ruinous and was sold in 1915, to be replaced by the row of terraced houses which is still there.[360]

Wesleyan Methodist Mission Hall, south side of Andover Road, in use. A mission hall was built on the north side of Winchester Street (now Andover Road) in 1904; it was in use in 1909 but later became a Territorial drill hall before being demolished, perhaps after the Second World War. A new hall was registered on the present site, south of the road and a little further east, in 1921 though it may have been built earlier. It was added to in 1948 when the former mission hall from Tangley was acquired. Both are of corrugated iron; that closer to the road is the original, larger and with five windows one side, four the other.[361]

Primitive Methodists built a chapel immediately south of the Crown Inn, probably in 1844. It closed between 1885 and 1889 and was demolished early in the 20th century.[362]

Lydiard Millicent

Primitive Methodist Chapel, Nine Elms, south of Old Shaw Lane just west of Roughmoor Way, now a house. A small chapel, now with rendered walls between brick pilasters under a slate roof, it may have been originally all of brick with stone dressings. It has three bays with round-arched windows and has been extended at each end, the west end extension probably before conversion: there used to be a conventional porch with windows either side here. A gable plaque at the west end is dated 1852, referring to the original chapel built in that year, probably on this site. This one is from 1882 and closed in the late 20th century.[363]

*Primitive Methodist Chapel, Lydiard Green,** south of road, now a house. Primitive Methodists of the Brinkworth circuit were active here from 1828 but were only able to construct this chapel, against strong local opposition, in 1863. The original building is to the east, tall in Classical style with prominent pilasters made more so by the application of render over the original brick. It has round-arched windows with ashlar heads and keystones, now painted, and the roof is of slate. The gable facing the road has a porch dating from 1909, a flat-headed double door with lunette over and very tall windows either side now with modern glazing. A plaque above is dated 1863 and the pedimental gable head has a circular ventilator. There is a single tall window to the east side and to the west is the 1909 schoolroom extension, originally separated from the chapel

Lydiard Green (Lydiard Millicent) Primitive Methodist, painted render and ashlar an uncomfortable mix with the brickwork

by a sliding partition. It is at right angles to the original and of similar design with a single tall window to the gable, pedimented above with the date 1909. In the angle between the two main buildings is a two-bay classroom with lean-to roof, of the same date and making the whole a substantial size. There is a more modern single-storey extension to the rear. The chapel was still in use in 2004 but has since been closed and converted.[364]

Holy Trinity Church, Shaw village centre, in use. This large modern church is adjacent to the shopping centre and is made of brick under a tall tile roof. The cross-wing at the east end has a tall gable to the south with a full height window and a spire above. It was built in 1989 to serve all Anglican and nonconformist denominations.[365]

Lydiard Tregoze

Primitive Methodists from the Brinkworth circuit built a chapel in **Hook** in 1840 but the lord of the manor claimed the land it stood on was his and it had to be surrendered to him at valuation. The later police station was said to contain some of its fabric.[366]

After a long period meeting in a partially converted cottage, **Primitive Methodists** built another chapel in **Hook** in 1886, west of the road just north of what is now Windsor Close. The chapel was of iron and enlarged in 1889 but remained squat with a low roof angle. It closed in 1965 and has since been demolished and a new house built on the site.[367]

Primitive Methodists also built a chapel on **Hay Lane**, just south of the bend in the B4005 at SU110820. It too was of corrugated iron, with three windows each side and a small front porch. Erected in 1887, it had a capacity of 80 and was said to have had a typical congregation of 60 after the First World War. It closed in 1967, was used as a store for some time, then converted with double garage doors at the front and later apparently moved to a farm at South Marston.[368]

Lyneham

Providence Particular Baptist Chapel, Bradenstoke,* north of road at west end of village, Grade 2 listed, in use. The chapel is early, and notable particularly for its tall facade, in brick with ashlar dressings under a part-hipped roof of stone slates. This is dated 1777 and has tall segmental-headed windows, perhaps enlarged from the

Bradenstoke (Lyneham) Providence Baptist

originals, either side of and slightly above a 19th century porch in ashlar carrying the legend 'Providence Chapel' in faded lettering. Above is a similar but smaller window and the whole is topped by a wooden bell cupola: this is said to have been the only Strict Baptist chapel in England to have had a bell. The left and right sides each have a single tall window, blocked, and to the right there is also a bricked up further doorway. At the rear is a rubble-stone gable with two similar windows, a central brick chimney and two square attic windows above. Attached, and forming an L, is the minister's house of similar early date in the same materials with sash windows to the left. In the re-entrant angle is an unfortunate later porch, formerly lean-to but now with a room over, rendered and with a flat roof. There is a 20th century timber schoolroom to the rear. The interior, with simple pews and a gallery over the entrance, was remodelled at an early date: it has been suggested that the side door was the original entrance and that the remodelling was carried out when this was closed. An attic room is now accessed via the house.

The chapel was erected in 1777 as a result of the preaching of John Cennick, though the direct inspiration was Isaac Turner of Calne. In the 1830s the congregation was a mixture of Baptists and Independents and when the minister died the Independents of Christian Malford tried to take control, going so far as to nail up the doors. The Baptists prevailed, however, and the chapel was established as Strict Baptist in 1843. It closed in 1996 but reopened in 1998.[369]

Primitive Methodist Chapel of 1828, Bradenstoke, north of road in village centre, now a house. A low building in brick under a modern tile roof with rendered, previously brick, sides. It has a modern door and windows with awkward infilling of the original round-arched tops at the front; even the original dentilled bargeboard has been lost. The gable plaque is the only interesting feature: 'He gave Himself, a Ransom for All. Primitive Methodist Chapel 1828'. The chapel was founded as the third in the Brinkworth circuit and was improved in 1853, at which time the original earth floor was replaced by a boarded one: it is possible that the building was also re-faced at this time. Closed on the opening of the new chapel in 1887, it presumably continued to serve as a Sunday school for many years before eventual conversion.[370]

*Primitive Methodist Chapel of 1887, Bradenstoke.** This is the more attractive replacement for the above, built next door and now a house. Made of brick with ashlar dressings under tile, the much-decorated gable facing the road has tall round-arched windows either side of a gabled porch which has a double round-arched window in front and doors to the sides. A large roundel above has the inscription 'Primitive Methodist 1886' surrounding a six-pointed star window. The sides each have three round-arched windows. It was converted in 2016.[371] *Photograph on page 35.*

Primitive Methodists of the Brinkworth circuit in Preston, south east of Lyneham, met in cottages for 66 years until 1906 when they built a corrugated iron chapel at the east end of the hamlet. Services continued until at least 1968 but the chapel, which was of conventional appearance for an iron chapel, has now been demolished.[372]

Lyneham Methodist Church, north end of village, in use. The brick gable is behind a more recent flat-roofed brick porch, placed asymmetrically. The gable has a triple lancet window with lively stained glass and the inscription '1934 Gaisford Memorial Methodist Church.' This was a new foundation in 1933, not a replacement for a previous building.[373]

Maiden Bradley

*Congregational Chapel,** south end of village, set back to east, Grade 2 listed, in process of conversion into exhibition space in 2021. A tall chapel, rendered under a slate roof, it has segmental arched sash windows, two bays to the side with two tiers of windows. The front gable facing the road has a small Tuscan portico for the door, a window over and the date 1820 above that. The inside is much more interesting, with galleries on three sides on iron pillars, complete with twin access stairs, the whole producing a remarkable effect in such a small space. A single bay two-storey extension to the rear, with flat-headed sash windows and probably of the late 19th century, provides a schoolroom below but above that an

Maiden Bradley Congregational

arch has been broken through into the main body of the chapel so as to create an organ loft above the pulpit, its gallery front at a slightly lower level than that of the other three galleries. The organ, organ gallery front and pulpit with wrought iron panels are all of this date and have been retained on conversion. The chapel was built in 1820 and closed before 2013.[374]

Malmesbury Without.

This is a large rural parish wrapping round the town mainly to the south and east but also to the north.

A **Congregational Chapel** was built in **Corston**, north east of the church, in 1821 as a village mission of the Malmesbury Westport Congregational. It was repaired and enlarged in the 1830s, but replaced at the turn of the century by the second chapel (see below). Access was via a long drive immediately east of the church: the older house which stood alongside at right angles is still there but the chapel itself has been replaced by a modern bungalow.[375]

Congregational Chapel, Corston, * west of main road opposite Rodbourne Road, now a house. The appealing if fussy facade is typical of the turn of the century, in brick with ashlar dressings, bands of darker brick and pointed-arch windows. A pattern of five windows defines the front, with one on the porch, larger ones either side and two smaller above. There is a plaque below the porch window, now illegible, and a quatrefoil ventilator at the gable head. The sides are of three bays with similar

Corston Congregational of 1897 (Malmesbury Without)

windows. Built in 1897, it replaced the 1821 chapel but itself had a short life, closing probably in the 1930s. It had other uses before becoming derelict and finally being converted to a house c2006.[376]

Independents built a chapel in **Rodbourne** by 1823. It is presumed to have closed sometime after 1860 and subsequently to have been demolished.[377]

Zion Particular Baptist Chapel, Corston, north side of Mill Lane, now a house called Chapel House. Built in 1857-8, it closed by 1899 and was later very much altered into the present house of rubble-stone under tile with a rendered rear extension. The south gable facing the road has a heart-shaped plaque at its head dated 1857 and below that is a segmental-headed window, originally taller. A new ground floor window probably occupies the space where the door was originally. The sides, also much altered, appear to contain some original fabric.[378]

Manningford

Ebenezer Particular Baptist Chapel, Bottlesford, north east of Seven Stars pub, now a house called The Old Chapel. It looks like a small double-fronted cottage with dormers above, pebble-dashed under a slate roof, though with substantial modern extensions to the rear. Before conversion it was very different: single-storey chequerboard-effect brick using what seem to have been vitrified stretchers, with a central porch, double segmental-arched windows either side within rectangular openings and a plaque above the door, 'Ebenezer Chapel 1842.' Conversion involved raising the roof and inserting a floor and dormers, lowering the ground floor windows and altering the porch as well as extending to the rear in two phases. The plaque is still in place though hidden by vegetation and the lower tiles of the previous hipped roof are visible at the ends, otherwise all trace of the chapel is lost. It was built in 1842, closed in 1937, left empty for many years and converted before 1971.[379]

Strict and Particular Baptist, Manningford Bohune,* south of main road at SU138578, in use. A simple and attractive chapel in brick with some ashlar dressings under a slate roof, it looks modern for its date, the appeal enhanced by the

brick dressings to the round-arched windows. The gable facing the road has a porch, three stepped windows above and a diamond-shaped plaque at the gable head, 'AD 1869'. There are three windows to the sides and a lower rear schoolroom extension of two bays. The interior has a rear gallery and some original panelling. It was opened in 1870 to designs by J A Randell of Devizes, replacing an adapted cottage, and may have been General Baptist in its early life.[380]

Manningford Bohune Baptist

Manton – see Preshute

Marden

General Baptist Chapel, west of The Street towards lower end, now a house. This is built of brick, unusually in English bond, under a slate roof with overhanging eaves; it has a new porch and new fenestration. Only the plaque, 'Baptist Chapel 1899' on the otherwise nearly blank end gable clearly betrays its history, though the fence and gate may also be original. It is side on to the road and tall, with no evidence that the roof has been raised on conversion. Attached to the south, with a slightly lower roofline and now also a house, is the former Sunday school. The chapel was built in 1899 at a cost of £441, to designs by Henry Reeves of Bratton. It was closed and sold in 1951.[381]

This chapel was a replacement for the original **General Baptist chapel**, south of Church Mill at SU081578, which was built c1870 but demolished soon after the new chapel was constructed.[382]

Market Lavington

Society of Friends Meeting House, later Congregational,* west of road towards north end of High Street, listed Grade 2, lately an artist's studio. The monthly meeting of Quakers in Market Lavington was the focus for central and south Wiltshire in the late 17th and early 18th centuries and this building was constructed as their meeting house in 1716. Quakerism declined through the 18th century and they gave up this building in 1795, selling it to the Congregationalists in 1809. The Congregationalists enlarged it, doubling its size and adding a gallery to give a capacity of over 300, and used it until it was replaced by the new chapel opposite in 1892. Thereafter it served as a Sunday school until sold off in 1968 and converted into a house.

The outline of the 1716 building can be seen in the east side facing the road, in rubble-stone with brick quoins and a single segmental-arched window. The tiled roof above, previously hipped, shows where it was extended north in 1809. The symmetrical north front, of brick, is that of 1809 and has five bays, three windows alternating with two doors on the ground floor and five windows above, the windows all segmental-arched. The complicated tiled roof is part hipped and part pyramidal. The inside retains a gallery to the north wall.[383]
Photograph on page 29.

Congregational Chapel of 1892, at north end of village almost opposite the former chapel, now a house. This handsome building by William Smith of Trowbridge is in brick with some ashlar dressings and a tiled roof with bands of fish-scale tiles. The gable facing the road has a lean-to porch with three small flat-headed windows to the front, doors at the ends and a memorial plaque dated 1891 below. Above that is a large 'sun and planets' circular window. The sides are of five bays with pointed-arch windows between buttresses. The chapel closed in 2008 and was sold for conversion in 2010. The congregation now meets as the Trinity Church in the village's community hall.[384]

Strict Baptist Chapel, Chapel Lane, just south of Market Place, now the servery for a fish and chip shop. The last in the row of buildings, it still retains two segmental-headed windows to the side with remains of a string course above and a slate roof hipped to the rear; it was originally brick but now rendered. Built c1832, it closed in 1929 and was sold in 1931, the proceeds being divided between the chapels at Allington, Bottlesford, Enford, Manningford and Upavon. It was thereafter converted to a fish and chip shop.[385]

Particular Baptist Chapel, 7 Church Street, now a house. Built by 1855 as an offshoot of that in Chapel Lane, it was closed by the turn of the century and thereafter was for many years a shop before being converted to a house, perhaps in the 1980s. It was originally all brick though the first floor front is now rendered and all the brick painted; the bricked-in former shop-front is clear. The chapel front originally had elaborate detailing with two tiers of arched windows but the only evidence remaining are the pilasters at either side. Its orientation and the hipped tiled roof provide further slight clues to its origins.[386]

Marston

Primitive Methodist Chapel, ST966568, set back to west of road at south end of village, in use. A modest chapel with capacity for 90, in brick under slate, the simple gable facing the road has the doorway in a porch and round-arched windows each side. A plaque at the gable head is dated 1835. The sides each have two round-arched windows.[387]

Marston Maisey

No chapels recorded.[388]

Melksham Without.

This large rural parish covers an area to the north, east and south of Melksham.

General Baptist Chapel, Beanacre, west of A350 at junction with Westlands Lane, now a house. This was originally of two bays in coursed shaped stone with ashlar quoins under a slate roof. The gable facing the lane is dated 1846 and below is a modern single-storey extension southwards where the porch and door used to be. The windows to the sides are all much altered and dormers inserted. The schoolroom extension to the north, of 1925, was originally single-storey but the roof was raised after 1994. The chapel closed in 1967.[389]

Wesleyan Methodists built a chapel at Berhills, north east of Sells Green, c1850 but there is no further evidence of it.[390]

Wesleyan Methodist Chapel, Whitley, south of Top Lane near junction with Middle Lane, in use. The chapel is built of coursed stone blocks with ashlar dressings and a tiled roof. The gable facing the road has a tri-partite stepped pointed-arch window in a larger arch and a gable head plaque, 'Wesleyan 1867'. There are two tall pointed-arch windows to the left side and, to the right, the 2013 extension in stone with glass double doors providing a new porch and other facilities. The Sunday school was added to the rear c1923. The interior was remodelled in 1985 and is now plain, the pews having been replaced by chairs in 2008. An **earlier chapel** of 1824, elsewhere in the village, was replaced by this one in 1867 and later demolished.[391]

Primitive Methodist, later Wesleyan Methodist Chapel, Redstocks, south side of lane left off the Redstocks road at ST932627, now a house. The full history is not known but the chapel could have been as early as the 1830s and was acquired by Wesleyans from the Primitive Methodists in 1886. To the lane is a long side of coursed stone blocks with two round-arched windows with brick dressings, close together high up: it is possible that this whole wall has been rebuilt. The east gable is confusingly of lower quality rubble-stone with a window where once the doorway may have been. The chapel was extended to the west, presumably for a schoolroom, and to the south is a modern wing. It was sold in 1950 and has been much altered since.[392]

Non-sectarian Chapel, Sandridge Lane, north end of lane at ST944654, now a house. This is a tiny two-bay chapel in brick under a slate roof. The side windows are square-headed and there is a replacement round window above the porch in the gable end. Meetings had previously been held in a cottage for 'upwards of 40 years' until this chapel, seating 80 to 100, was built in 1882 at a cost of £110. It was non-sectarian from the start with trustees representing the Church of England, the Baptists, Wesleyans and Congregationalists. It closed some time after 1955 and was unobtrusively converted.[393]

Mildenhall

No chapels recorded.[394]

Milston

No chapels recorded.[395]

Milton Lilbourne

Wesleyan Methodists built a chapel in **Littleworth** c1854, immediately north of the central road junction. It was closed in 1932 when the successor chapel was built and was subsequently demolished. The second *Wesleyan Methodist Chapel*, now a house called The Chapel, was built a short way north of the crossroads at SU188612 in 1932, to designs by Cripps and Stewart of Oxford. The gable facing the road contained two narrow windows either side of the pulpit and a large lunette over; the door was in a side extension towards the rear and the schoolroom was separated from the chapel by a removable partition. It closed in 1967 after which the schoolroom section was replaced by a new and much larger two-storey house: the remaining two bays of the chapel remain as a single room, overlooked by a lunette window in the gable of the new house but almost unaltered.[396]

Primitive Methodists opened a chapel in the parish in 1843 but this was closed by 1864 and is believed to have been demolished. Its location has not been established.[397]

Minety

A **Strict Baptist** chapel was built south of what is now Chapel Lane, **Sawyers Hill**, at the west end. The original of c1840 was wattle and daub with a thatched roof. It was rebuilt in 1862 in rubble-stone with brick quoins under tile, small with square-headed windows and door and no ornamentation. It carried the inscription 'Peculiar Baptist Chapel', supposedly an engraver's mistake. Closed in 1970, it was demolished c1988 though the graveyard remained.[398]

Primitive Methodist Chapel, Sawyers Hill, east of road towards north end, now a house. A meeting of the Brinkworth circuit was held here from 1844, variously in a barn, a cottage and the open air, and this chapel was built in 1865. Tall but shallow, it is made of brick with the front gable rendered. The windows are round-arched, very tall either side of the porch with a smaller one recently inserted above it where there used to be a plaque. There are pilasters at the corners and a circular ventilator at the gable head. All glazing is new. The left side is blank and the right was the same but acquired a small lean-to extension later which in turn has been replaced by a modern extension. The chapel was renovated in 1916, closed by the early 21st century and then converted.[399]

Monkton Farleigh

No chapels recorded.[400]

Netheravon

Particular Baptists built a chapel down a passage accessed off the north east end of High Street in 1820. The chapel was burnt down in 1946; the vestry was rebuilt and services were held there but that closed in 1967 and had been demolished by 1974. The graveyard remained.[401]

Primitive Methodist Chapel, High Street, on the opposite side of the same passageway, now a house. It is small, one of a short terrace, of brick with crudely done bands of flint, a segmental-arched door at the centre and similarly arched windows either side. This represents the original disposition of openings but at the time of conversion the central doorway was bricked in and an entrance had been made at the left hand end of the front; this has now, in its turn, been bricked in. All this indicates that the chapel was probably originally of 'long wall' type, with the pulpit in the centre of the long wall opposite, but was reorientated when the new door was inserted. Built in 1847, despite its modest size it was stated in 1851 to be capable of holding 150 people. It was sold in 2003.[402]

Netherhampton

No chapels recorded.[403]

Nettleton

Particular Baptist Chapel, Nettleton, east of road to Nettleton Shrub at ST823779, in use. The gable facing the road is rendered with a plain ashlar porch and a Y-tracery pointed-arch window above. The sides are of coursed rubble-stone with two Y-tracery windows and the schoolroom wraps around the back, lower with square-headed windows and a door to the rear. The chapel roof is tiled, the schoolroom roof of slate hipped to the south end. The chapel opened in 1823 and the schoolroom was added c1843. In 1899 the chapel was considered 'dingy and dilapidated' and it was refitted with larger windows, the old straight-backed pews replaced by ones of varnished pine and the pulpit replaced by a reading desk on a low platform. The supervising architect was a Mr Roach of Charfield.[404]

General Baptist, later general nonconformist, Nettleton Green, east of road on easterly fork at ST817785, now a house, 'Beckett House'. The chapel is the more northerly of two houses here, both with blank gables facing the road and linked by a cross-wing to the rear. It is of coursed rubble-stone under tile with rectangular mullioned windows in the south wall. The north wall is much altered but might have contained the original central doorway; the road gable contains a blocked ground floor window. Used by General Baptists from at least 1847, it was marked as 'nonconformist meeting place' on maps by the turn of the century and probably went out of use between the wars. It is not clear what denomination was using it in the later period.[405]

Mount Zion Particular Baptist Chapel, West Kington, set back east of road at ST807772, opposite Latimer Farm, in use. This is built of coursed rubble-stone with ashlar dressings under a slate roof. The plain gable facing the road has no windows, just an ashlar porch and a plaque, 'Mount Zion Baptist Chapel 1882'. There are two six paned mullioned windows each side and a long schoolroom to the rear, lower and with smaller windows. Calvinistic Baptists split from the Nettleton chapel and built this in 1882 after meeting in the open air and in a cottage for a number of years.[406]

The Brethren had a meeting room in **West Kington** for a period in the 1880s and 1890s; its location is unknown.[407]

Netton – see Durnford

Newton Tony

Wesleyan Methodist Chapel, set back east of street in village centre, now a house. Big for a village chapel and handsome before conversion, this is built of brick with pale brick dressings under slate with the gable facing the road. Originally there were round-arched windows of medium height either side of the porch with a round-arched door to the front. On conversion the gable windows have been truncated and new round-headed windows inserted at first floor level with brick infill between; at the sides one round-arched window remains but the others have had similar treatment to the front. The gable plaque says 'Wesleyan 1877.' To the rear is a long but low Sunday school which was added after 1918. The chapel closed in 1981.[408]

North Bradley

General Baptists built a chapel north west of Little Common, adjacent to what is now King's Lodge. The chapel was opened in 1780 but progressively altered and enlarged until it ended up a substantial building in brick with ashlar dressings, two tiers of pointed-arch windows and three galleries. A schoolroom was created in 1831 and replaced by a new one to the rear in 1852. King's Lodge may be the 1896 rebuilding of a manse originally bought in 1869. For many years there was a wish for a new chapel in a less inconvenient position and this was eventually built in 1961. The 1780 chapel was then demolished, though several monuments remain in the graveyard.[409]

North Bradley Baptist, 1961.

Baptist Chapel of 1961, * north of Westbury Road close to junction with Little Common, in use. Built in 1961 to replace the above, to designs by T W Snailum of Bath, this is an impressive piece of post-war design. The building is wide and low with a concrete frame clad in brick under a low-pitched roof of metal sheet. An angled clerestory behind and above the porch ties the whole together effectively. The manse of 1980 is next door.[410]

General Baptist Chapel, Yarnbrook, east of A350, a little way south of roundabout, in use. In ashlar with pointed-arch windows under a tiled roof, the gable facing the road has a three-light stepped window above the porch; the north side has four pairs of lancets and there are two to the south with a lean-to extension beyond. Built in 1874 to designs by Noah Hobbs, it closed in 1956 but was sold in 1957 and has since been used as a non-denominational chapel.[411]

North Newnton

Independents opened a chapel at the west end of **Hilcott** village in 1798. It is believed to have closed between 1848 and 1851.[412]

Primitive Methodists took over the Independents' chapel in 1852. It was closed between 1880 and 1885 and is believed to have been demolished.[413]

North Wraxall

Congregational Chapel, Ford, high up north of the A420 at ST838750, now a house obscurely called 'Bishop's Gambit' and hard to see. The chapel is a neat box in coursed rubble-stone with ashlar dressings under a hipped tiled roof, containing originally a single gallery. It has been well converted, retaining the segmental-headed windows, three to the south side, and two to the east end above the porch. It was built in 1820, closed in the late 1960s and was sold in 1970.[414]

Congregational Chapel,* midway between North and Upper Wraxall at ST812747, Grade 2 listed, now a house. The manse next door is as prominent as the chapel and the two are now combined into a single house via a glass corridor between altered extensions at the rear. The chapel is of coursed squared rubble-stone with ashlar dressings under slate; the gable facing the road has tall round-arched windows either side of a projecting porch, ashlar quoins and a plaque dated 1862. There are similar tall windows to the sides. The manse is a double-fronted cottage in the same materials, said to have been the building in which meetings were held from 1812 until the chapel was built in 1862. The chapel closed finally in 2013. The site is unusually isolated even for 1812, possibly located to be within equal reach of the two settlements.[415]

North Wraxall Congregational.

Norton

No chapels recorded.[416]

Norton Bavant

No chapels recorded.[417]

Oaksey

Primitive Methodist Chapel, north of road at west end of village, now a house. This chapel of coursed rubble-stone under a tiled roof originally had a single round-arched window to the street side gable end and a similarly arched doorway with a small window above in the gable, topped by a plaque: 'Primitive Methodist Chapel AD 1842. We Preach Christ.' Added later is: 'Rebuilt AD 1874'. The chapel was built as part of the Brinkworth circuit in 1842. It closed c1956 and was used as a hay store before conversion to a house, perhaps in the 1970s, with unfortunate new window openings and only the plaque remaining as a reminder of its former role.[418]

Oare – see Wilcot

Odstock

Particular Baptist Chapel, Bodenham, south of road in Bodenham, now a house. It is unusual for its triple-gabled porch, the smaller central gable containing the door joined each side by larger ones forming rooms in front of the main building, a neat way of providing more space on a limited plot and found nearby also at the Barnard Street mission in Salisbury. The front rooms have segmental-headed windows which were rectangular and taller before conversion, and above the porch is a round window in the chapel front. The sides are of two bays with tall square-headed windows and a further bay extension, added post conversion. The whole is painted brick under slate. The original chapel was built in 1839, served by Baptists from the Brown Street chapel in Salisbury; it was either much altered or rebuilt in 1860. Major alterations were made in 1900: the roof was raised three feet, the rooms at the front were added as schoolrooms either side of a vestibule, the tall windows inserted and the interior completely refurbished. The architect was A C Bothams and the work was again largely funded by Brown Street. There was a further restoration in 1964 but the chapel later closed; it was converted in the late 1990s.[419]

Photograph on page 34.

Perhaps surprisingly, there appears to have been no chapel built in either **Odstock** or **Nunton.** It is, however, suggested that a barn at Manor Farm, Odstock, may have been used as a chapel for a time and that there was a group of Baptists in Nunton in 1864, though whether worshipping in a house or a chapel is not clear.[420]

Ogbourne St Andrew

Independents built a chapel by 1820, probably that known as Zion Chapel in 1858, on the village street just west of the junction with Sheepridge and behind the house now called Crowlynch. It was conveyed to the **Particular Baptists** in 1860, closed in 1903 and was demolished not long afterwards.[421]

Ogbourne St George

Independents, sponsored by the congregation at Marlborough, built a chapel in 1842. The chapel, probably on the site of the later Wesleyan, did not last long, being mentioned in the 1851 religious census but not in any directories from the 1860s onwards.[422]

A **non-denominational chapel** was built on land belonging to Joseph Phelps in 1847. It was recorded in the 1851 religious census but may not have survived long afterwards. The location is not known but it is possible that it was on the site of the later village hall, having been bought in 1882 by the vicar and churchwardens for use as a reading room.[423]

Baptists opened their chapel in 1857 – an event accompanied by the considerable coup of having the famous Rev. C H Spurgeon to preach at the opening service – and may have used the Phelps chapel. They did not survive long, not being mentioned in directories after 1867.[424]

Wesleyan Methodists built a chapel in 1864, north of the junction of the village street with the Swindon-Marlborough road. A pre-existing building there was probably the Independent chapel which the Wesleyans adapted. It seems that the Wesleyans leased the building, finally buying it in 1906. It closed in 1956 and was later replaced by the houses of Chapel Close.[425]

Primitive Methodists built their chapel in 1852 at the junction of the Swindon-Marlborough and Aldbourne roads. In 1904 they expressed an interest in buying the Wesleyan chapel from the owners, the Congregational Union, but this came to nothing. This implies that their own chapel was not in good condition and indeed it was disused early in the 20th century and the chapel was soon demolished.[426]

Orcheston

No chapels recorded.[427]

Patney

No chapels recorded.[428]

Penknap – see Dilton Marsh

Pewsey

Independents bought a house in **Easterton Lane**, south of the High Street, in 1817. They used it as a chapel for some years and it or a replacement on the same site was also used for a period up to 1873 by **Wesleyan Methodists** (see below). It was sold by the Wesleyans to **Strict Baptists** in 1875 and in 1880 they in turn sold it on to **General Baptists** who used it as the Zion chapel and may have at least partially rebuilt it in 1893. The General Baptists remained there until it was finally closed; it was sold in 1955. By 1968 it was decrepit and was soon afterwards demolished and later replaced by a garage block for an adjacent house. It was located south west of the lane, opposite the south end of the allotments, of brick under a hipped roof with at least one wall rendered and a gallery at one end.[429]

The **Strict Baptists** built a chapel on **High Street near Brunkard's Lane**, probably in 1832; the exact location is not known. It may have been this group who had the brief ownership of the Easterton Lane chapel before moving to the *Strict Baptist Chapel near the Town Mill* c1880. The Town Mill chapel is on the approach to the Heritage Centre. Largely disguised by added-on single-storey buildings, the segmental-headed windows at first floor level on both ends and the pattern of vitrified headers to the west end give some clue to its previous appearance: it was probably newly built by the Baptists but could have been an adaptation of an existing building. This chapel closed in its turn and was sold in 1920. After serving for an electric power company and as a club it is now a furniture workshop.[430]

Wesleyan Methodist Chapel, North Street, west of road, in use. The original Wesleyan chapel was a metal building of 1834 off High Street, possibly immediately on the left up Brunkards Lane. The Wesleyans seem not to have stayed there long for it seems they then bought the Easterton Lane chapel from the Independents and used this until their new chapel in North Street was built. The North Street chapel is of 1873, to designs by Lansdown and Shopland of Swindon, in brick under a tiled roof with ashlar dressings and round-arched windows; a gallery was added in 1898. The gable facing the road has an inscription over the door, 'Wesleyan Chapel 1873'; there are windows either side and a triple stepped window above. To the side are four bays then the long 1928 schoolroom, known as the Wesley Hall, linked to the chapel by a modern tall glass porch facing Goddard Road.[431]

Primitive Methodist Chapel, King's Corner, south end of Easterton lane, now a house. This is a very small building in brick under slate. The gable facing the road has the door, flat-headed windows either side, a plaque above - 'Church Mission Room' - and above that a later square window with a separate lunette over. The overhanging eaves and shaped barge-boards are modern. The sides are of two bays with one window on the left replaced by a new door, and there is a rear extension. It was built in 1879 to designs by W E Baverstock but superseded by 1895 by the Brunkard's Lane chapel. It is thought to have been taken over by the Anglicans as a church mission room – hence the plaque – until at least 1936 and later served as a school lunch room before its eventual conversion.[432]

Primitive Methodists built a *Mission hall* near *Brunkard's Lane* c1895 to replace that at King's Corner, having obtained the premises as early as 1886. It was advertised by a large sign attached to the front of the house at the High Street corner, now No.61, and it seems that the front section of this house was converted for the purpose. It is likely that there was also a metal chapel on the left just up Brunkards Lane, possibly that used previously by the Wesleyans. It is not certain whether the Primitive Methodists used this as well as the converted house. The house was originally near-identical to the one to which it is joined, in brick under tile with a three-sided bay window, but has had a number of alterations since. It did not last long as a chapel, closing between 1915 and 1920, and was then reconverted. The metal building was moved for re-use in Hampshire.[433]

Pitton and Farley

Wesleyan Methodist Chapel, Farley,* South of village street, now a house. In brick, with exuberant pale brick dressings and round-arched windows under a slate roof with overhanging eaves and shaped barge-boards, this has its gable facing the

road with the door in a truncated porch, tall windows either side with replacement glass, a circular window above that and a lozenge pattern at the gable head. There are three bays to the sides and a modern extension to the left rear. An attractive example of a common late 19th century type, it was built in 1883 as a successor to an earlier small chapel in Ben Lane, described as a wooden temporary building in 1864. It was still in use in 1982 but was sold in 1987.[434]

Farley Wesleyan (Pitton & Farley)

Wesleyan Methodist Chapel, Pitton, South of White Hill, now two houses. Of a similar pattern to that at Farley, this is more austere in brick with pale brick dressings to the gable only, under a slate roof with overhanging eaves and decorated barge-boards. The gable facing the road has a protruding porch, a circular window above and a plaque, 'Wesleyan 1888,' at the gable head. The chapel is of four bays with round-arched windows and the schoolroom at right angles to the rear, dated 1934, adds two bays to the right hand side and extends to the left. The chapel was closed by 2007; from 2008 to 2011 it was used by an independent school and in 2013 it was converted into the two houses, the chapel being one and the schoolroom the other. The first Wesleyan chapel was built in 1835 immediately north west of the church but became too small, was replaced by this building in 1888 and soon after demolished.[435]

Porton – see Idmiston

Potterne

In 1813 **Strict Baptists** built a chapel, probably at an unknown location in Lower Street, now Whistley Road. With a capacity of 180, it was used through much of the 19th century but is believed to have been demolished since.[436]

Wesleyan Methodist Chapel, now a house, Applecross, Coxhill Lane. This is a substantial building of brick under slate, extended to the rear, but the west side so altered with inserted bay windows as to make it unrecognisable as a chapel. Only the gable facing the road betrays its origins, with steps up and infill brickwork where once were a door and two adjacent tall windows. Built c1841, it declined in the late 19th century, closed during the First World War but was not sold until 1938 then converted soon afterwards.[437]

Reformed Methodist, later Open Brethren, Chapel, south of Mill Road, now a house. A group seceded from the Wesleyan chapel c1852 and by 1859 were able to build this chapel. It is plain, of brick under slate, the gable facing the road having a hooded door and a plaque over, 'Wesleyan Reform Chapel erected AD 1859'. There are two round-arched windows to the west side with a further door, perhaps later, to the south. A flat-roofed extension, perhaps of the 1950s, is to the east. The chapel closed by 1907 but the residue of the congregation became the nucleus of an Open Brethren meeting and the building was reopened by them as a mission room, lasting probably until c1960.[438]

Poulshot

Wesleyan Methodist Chapel, * west of village street towards north end, now a house. This was built in 1886 to designs by C E Ponting of Marlborough, in brick with an eaves tiled roof and a prominent ventilator. The brick dressing is neat and the proportions of the pointed-arch door and two windows in the end gable create a tension which is resolved by the harmonious march of the four-bay sides, the whole very much of its time but without resorting to the multi-coloured brickwork which is elsewhere so common. A plaque confirms the date 1886. The linked schoolroom

Poulshot Wesleyan – sophisticated design by Ponting in 1886.

at right angles to the rear, probably contemporary, has been altered. The chapel was sold in 1977 and converted to a house.[439]

Preshute

Quakers built a burial ground at **Manton Corner** in 1658 and this was followed some time later by the erection of a meeting house there. This may not have lasted long as by 1727 they were in High Street, Marlborough.[440]

Primitive Methodists registered premises in **Manton** in 1817 and in 1860 replaced these with a chapel at Manton Corner, south of the A4 and immediately east of what is now Manton Corner House. This seated 100 and was built in the Friends' burial ground. The chapel was probably still open in 1931 but was closed and demolished soon afterwards.[441]

Gospel Hall, Manton, 16 High Street, now a house. This is a small building of painted brick under slate, the gable facing the road much altered with a modern doorway replacing what were originally double doors under a segmental arch. It opened in the late 19th century and was probably used by the Open Brethren from c1904 to the mid 1930s.[442]

Purton

Independents built a chapel south of the **High Street** and immediately east of the Workhouse in 1829. In 1922 it was offered for sale to the Primitive Methodists but only rented by them from 1929 until 1947 for social events and a Sunday school. It was demolished in 1969 and replaced by a scout hut.[443]

Wesleyan Methodist Chapel, Play Close, south of east end of High Street, in use. The original chapel of 1869, designed by Thomas Smith Lansdown of Swindon, was replaced by this larger one on the same site in 1882, built at a cost of £460. Cottages behind served as schoolrooms until, on merger with the Upper Square Methodists in 1969, the cottages were demolished and rebuilt. The chapel is a neat building of coursed rubble-stone with ashlar details under slate and pointed-arch windows. The gable facing the road has a protruding porch, tall windows either side, a circular window above now filled in but dated 1882 on the surround, and a diamond-shaped ventilator at the gable head. The front windows are linked by an ashlar string course to the heads of the four windows at the sides. The two-bay two-storey rooms to the rear as rebuilt have an incongruous partly flat roof.[444]

Primitive Methodist Chapel, Upper Square, now Hoggs Lane, * now a house called Hafawey House. The original chapel was converted from a cottage in The Row in 1843. It seated 120 but was not successful in that out of the way location and was replaced by one here in 1856, then sold. The first chapel here was extended forwards to make a double pile building in 1893, giving more seating space as well as schoolrooms. In 1969-70 Methodists in Purton joined together at the Play Close chapel and this one was sold; the 1856 section to the rear was demolished on conversion in 1972-73 (hence the house name), leaving the 1893 block. This is highly unusual and shows how much more experimental chapel architects were prepared to be towards the end of the century. It has a long brick facade to the road with three small gables, each above a two-light round-arched window with smaller circular window above in an ashlar round-arched surround. The inscription 'Primitive Methodist' is still just visible on a string course linking the windows at mid height. Even more unusual are the single-storey porch and rooms to the front and below, apparently of the same date: the porch is gabled with double doors; the rooms either side each have three small round-arched windows. The sides are of coursed rubble-stone with a large Y-traceried window, perhaps shortened, to the south and two smaller windows in original positions to the north; the roof is of slate. Remarkably, much of the glass is original. Some of the wall of the 1856 building at the rear remains.[445]
Photograph on page 36.

Primitive Methodist Chapel, Purton Stoke, on Pond Lane, south of village road, now a house. **Quakers** had built a meeting house on Purton Stoke street by 1705; it was probably located almost opposite the old post office, now 16 Stoke Common Lane. They had disbanded by 1759 and in 1832 sold their meeting house to the Primitive Methodists. By 1868 the Methodists had outgrown this building and material from it was used to make the present chapel on Pond Lane. A schoolroom was added to the side c1908. The chapel is in brick of uneven colour and has a slate roof. The gable facing the road has a later protruding porch, perhaps of the same date as the Sunday school. Tall round-arched windows either side of the porch have fussy modern glazing designed to disguise the inserted floor; between them is a plaque dated 1868 and above that the gable head is rendered with a ventilator. The north side is blank and to the south is the lean-to schoolroom with door and two windows, all round-arched, to the front with a plaque, 'Centenary Sunday School,' above and three flat-headed windows to the side. The chapel closed c2012 and was subsequently converted.[446]

Primitive Methodist Chapel, Braydon. This corrugated iron chapel, close to the border of the two parishes, is described under Braydon.

Quidhampton

Baptists built a chapel in 1835 in an unknown location but it had gone out of use by the turn of the century and is believed to have been demolished.[447]

Ramsbury

Presbyterians built a chapel on the north side of **Oxford Street** in 1716 but by 1766 it had been demolished.[448]

Ebenezer Congregational Chapel, set back south of High Street opposite church, now a house. The gable facing the road, now rendered, has a Tudor-arched door, round-arched windows with Y-tracery either side and a Venetian window above, all under a prominent date plaque for 1839; the Venetian window was originally a round-arched window with smaller flat-headed windows either side. Congregationalism revived here in the 1820s and in 1830 a building was licensed for meetings. This chapel followed in 1839. It was enlarged c1850: alterations probably included the addition of a gallery, a schoolroom attached to the east side, and the manse fronting the street, now 27 High Street. The chapel was repaired in 1894 and the schoolroom lengthened in 1897. In decline after the First World War, it suffered a fire in 1961 and closed in 1982.[449]

Congregationalists built a chapel on a track north of **Axford** village street at SU238703, probably in the 1850s although there had been a mission in the village since the 1830s. The chapel had been closed and demolished by 1899.[450]

Wesleyan Methodist Chapel, High Street, south of High Street and accessed via an alley between the former bank and the hairdresser's, now a house called Gilwell House. This was built c1805, enlarged and rebuilt in 1833, closed in 1944 when the Wesleyans joined with the Primitives and later became a scout hall before final conversion to a house c1990. It is tucked away out of view but attractive, with bands of brick and flint and a hipped slate roof. The north wall, with a date plaque for 1835 and now painted, has an altered doorway but original flat-headed windows above, probably indicating the presence of a rear gallery. On the east wall are two tall round-arched windows and on the south wall two round-arched windows above and more recent insertions below. The west wall is joint with the adjacent building.[451]

Wesleyan Methodist Chapel, Axford, north of road just west of church, now a house. A small brick chapel with a slate roof, this has a protruding porch, segmental-headed windows either side and a plaque dated 1888. There is a substantial modern extension to the rear. It opened in 1888 and closed between 1972 and 1975.[452]

Primitive Methodist Chapel, Chapel Lane, east side of Chapel Lane, now a house. Primitives Methodists came to Ramsbury c1830, probably in a carpenter's shop in

Crowood lane. They built this c1842 and it was replaced by the Oxford Street chapel in 1876; thereafter it was used as a Sunday school until 1886 and later had some commercial use before ultimate conversion to a house. It is built of bands of brick and flint under a slate roof and the chief interest lies in the south entrance front which has tall round-arched windows either side of a central round-arched door. The plain gable facing the road now has three segmental-headed windows but it is not possible to tell the original pattern and the ground floor had for some time large garage doors inserted into it. The rear appears to have had a tall round-arched window centrally placed but now blocked: if that was the case it might imply that the chapel, despite the entrance front, was not of the 'long wall' type.[453]

*Primitive Methodist Chapel, Oxford Street,** closed in 2020 and for sale for conversion in early 2021. A grand town chapel in brick with ashlar dressings, the gable facing the road has two tiers of windows inside a triple arch with four rusticated piers, the outer arches more narrow. At the centre a triple round-arched window is set above the modern porch and, either side, a round-arched window is separated by a stone rosette from the flat-headed window below. A gable plaque, 'Primitive Methodist Church,' sits below the shouldered gable with modillion detail. The sides are plain.

Ramsbury 1876 Primitive Methodist.

Built in 1876 to replace the smaller Chapel Lane chapel, it had a schoolroom added to the rear in 1885 and there were further alterations in 1952.[454]

*Primitive Methodist Chapel, Witcha Farm,** north east of Whittonditch at SU301737, Grade 2 listed, now used as a garden room. This is an exquisite tiny chapel but very hard to see in the grounds of Witcha House. The gable is in English-bond brick with vitrified headers and tall round-arched windows either side of a round-arched door. There is a plaque and a diamond-shaped window above, the latter perhaps originally a ventilator. The sides are of brick and flint with two sash windows in brick segmental-headed openings and the roof is of slate. It was built in 1859 and 180 people attended the opening despite the remote site. It closed in the mid 20th century.[455]

Almost hidden, the Primitive Methodist at Witcha Farm, Ramsbury

The **Salvation Army** arrived here in 1881 and opened a barracks on the west side of **Union Street**, then called Blind Lane, in 1881. They were unusually successful for a village setting and in 1908 they replaced this with the brick building on *High Street* just west of the church, now the public library; the Union Street barracks was demolished soon afterwards. The High Street barracks, now with shortened windows and an inserted floor creating a flat above the library, has four characteristically fortress-like brick pilasters on the gable end facing the street. The Salvation Army were present here up to the First World War, revived in 1939 but had left by 1942.[456]

Salvation Army Citadels had foundation stones too – examples on the front of the Ramsbury citadel of 1908.

Ratford – see Bremhill

Redlynch

Particular Baptists built a chapel in **Harthill Drove** in 1824, possibly south of the road and just east of Harthill House. It remained open in 1864 but was probably closed by 1882 and has since been demolished.[457]

Baptist Chapel, south side of Grove Lane, now a house called The Old Reading Room. This was built in 1878 as a combination chapel and workman's hall, paid for by trustees of South Lane Baptist, Downton. In 1899 a cottage behind was replaced by a new reading room whereupon the original building became solely a chapel. It was refurbished in 1907 with the old partition, presumably between the chapel and reading room sections, removed. The congregation joined with South Lane, Downton in 1961 and the chapel was sold and converted to a house in 1980. It is small, of brick with some patterning in vitrified headers under a tiled eaves roof. The gable has a flat-headed door and two windows below and an altered window above. There are two bays to the side and the windows to the rear gable are much altered. The reading room, at right angles, has two floors with segmental-headed windows, semi-dormers and again some use of vitrified headers. A plaque dated 1899 commemorates the benefactor of the new reading room, William Taunton.[458]

Wesleyan Methodists built a chapel in 1812 in **Warminster Green**. It was still operating in the 1860s but may have closed soon thereafter and the congregation transferred to the new chapel in Chapel Lane.[459]

Wesleyan Methodist Chapel, Chapel Lane, off Quavey Road, now a house called Chapel Cottage. Wesleyans had been meeting in Harthill Drove, possibly in the former Baptist chapel, and it is believed that they founded this chapel c1873. A schoolroom to the rear, now demolished, was added probably in 1877; a fire c1930 led to the necessity for repairs and there was a further schoolroom extension to the rear in 1951. The chapel closed c1975 and was converted in the early 1980s. It was of conventional appearance with round-arched windows either side of the door and a date plaque above, but the front gable is now rendered and completely altered. Some hint of the original appearance comes from the sides, which are of English bond brick with vitrified headers and show evidence of infilled windows.[460] *Photographs on page 56.*

Wesleyan Methodist Chapel, Hamptworth, by road junction at SU243194, now a house. The austere gable front facing the road is of brick with a protruding porch which may be later. The door is round-arched as are the windows either side. A plaque is dated 1876 and the quoins and eaves detailing are in pale brick. There are two bays to the side with tall round-arched windows, now made even taller by being brought down to ground level. A linking section with two segmental arched windows joins to the later schoolroom, probably early 20th century, at right angles to the rear and in similar style. The roofs are slate. The chapel closed between 1973 and 1975.[461]

Previous Wesleyan Methodist Chapel, Hamptworth, about 150 metres further south down Lyburn Road from the 1876 chapel, now a house. The house called Chapel Cottage is believed to have been the original Wesleyan chapel here, dating probably from 1825 and closed when the 1876 chapel opened. The building, rendered under a slate roof and with a gable wall to the road, bears no signs of its previous life other than perhaps the flat-headed window in the first floor of the gable. It was used as a smithy for many years after closure before being turned into a house.[462]

Woodfalls Primitive Methodist Chapel, junction of The Ridge and Vale Road, in use. The chapel is of red brick with plentiful pale brick dressings and round-arched windows under a slate roof. The gable facing the road has a central arch and four pilasters; the porch is modern and there are plaques within the arch bearing the dates 1932 and 1874. The sides are plain and of three bays and there is a large schoolroom to the rear. The original chapel of 1833, towards the east end of Slab Lane, was of cob and thatch, enlarged with a gallery in 1843 but replaced by this in 1874. The original schoolroom was replaced with a hall and classroom in 1926 and the chapel was refurbished in 1933 and 2003.[463]

Ebenezer Primitive Methodist Chapel, Morgan's Vale Road, east of road about half way along, now a house. This is built of red brick with intricate pale brick detailing, particularly at the string course and the eaves. The gable facing the road has two windows above each other and above these is an unusually decorated plaque dated 1877 but with the words beneath erased. The barge boards also are highly decorative. The side windows, originally tall, are partially infilled and reconfigured and there is a new porch to the left hand side. The chapel closed perhaps as early as 1934 and was later converted. It originally had a pointed-arch door and similar windows slightly above and to each side: had they left these alone it would have been a gem.[464]

Nomansland Primitive Methodist Chapel, on Forest Road adjacent to Lamb Inn, in use. The gable facing the road is of brick with prominent pale brick pilasters topped by stumpy columns. Above is a central two-light window with small circular window over in a single arch with the date 1901 and there are windows either side, all round-arched. The original porch reflected the pattern of these windows, as does its larger modern replacement of c2009 which is however so big that it obscures much of the front. The sides are of three bays with round-arched windows and there is a later lean-to extension behind. The roof is of slate. This chapel replaced an earlier one of c1881, 200 yards south on the same side of the road, later a schoolroom but now gone. That in turn replaced the original cob-walled chapel of 1846, possibly on the same site.[465]

Redstocks – see Melksham Without

Rodbourne – see Malmesbury Without and Swindon

Roundway

No chapels recorded. Much of the parish now lies within the **Devizes** urban area – see the entries for there.[466]

Rowde

Wesleyan Methodist Chapel, west of Marsh Lane, now a house. The serious-looking gable facing the road is of plain brick with two large round-arched windows, a round-arched door and a plaque dated 1838. There is a single similar window to the right side and to the left is a lean-to extension of c1980. The roof is of slate and there is a late 19th century schoolroom offset to the rear. The chapel opened in 1838, closed c1979 and was converted in 1980/1.[467]

Rushall

Baptists built a chapel north of Pewsey Road at the north end of the village in 1760. A low three-bay brick building, later rendered at front and sides, with segmental-arched windows either side of the door on the long side and a hipped tiled roof, it was refitted and had a vestry added to the east in 1839. A porch was added in 1919 but the last service was held in 1970 and the chapel was demolished in 1982. A thatched building called Chapel House, the former manse, stands directly opposite where the chapel once was.[468]

Sandridge – see Melksham Without

Sandy Lane – see Calne Without

Savernake

No chapels recorded.[469]

Seagry

Primitive Methodist Chapel, Upper Seagry, south of Henn Lane, now a house.

A small brick chapel of conventional shape, its significance lies in its being the first chapel built for the Brinkworth circuit, in 1825: the site was given by two brothers who built the wing at right angles to the rear as their own home. The brickwork is now painted and the far side rendered, with conventional tall round-arched windows, the central doorway replaced by a window and a plaque above dated 1825. This is all modest enough but before 1875, when it was altered, the roof was six feet lower and the windows square-headed. There were further alterations at the centenary in 1925 and the chapel closed c2008, the two buildings then being combined into a single house.[470]

Sedgehill and Semley

General Baptist Chapel, Semley, set back west of road towards south of village, Grade 2 listed, now a house. This is an interesting chapel but hard to see. It is distinguished by the paired round-arched windows, rather monastic in appearance, which are probably later than 1823 when the chapel was built and may date to c1841 when it was extended to the rear to create a vestry and schoolroom. It is constructed of dressed limestone under a slate roof and the gable facing the road has paired windows in two tiers, a porch with round-arched doorway, and a date-stone for 1823. The left side shows the original two bays with round-arched pairs above and flat-headed below. The third bay, of 1841 and built of more random stone, now has a modern porch and window above, and there is a modern rendered extension beyond that. The interior originally had three galleries. The chapel probably closed c2000.[471]

*Wesleyan Methodist Chapel, Barkers Hill,** South of road at ST907256, now a house. Although now converted and with an inserted floor, this remains a good example of a small village chapel. In brick with pale brick dressings, the gable facing the road has round-arched windows either side of a later porch which, surprisingly, has a Gothic doorway. There is a small circular window above the porch, a plaque dated 1877 and ornate barge-boards. The sides have three bays with round-arched windows, many retaining their original crimson glass in the edging panes, and there is a later one-bay schoolroom extension to the rear, probably from the early 20th century. The chapel was built in 1877 and closed by 1964.[472] *Photograph on page 22.*

Seend

*Wesleyan Methodist Chapel, Seend,** end of Factory Row at west end of village, Grade 2 listed, closed in 2020 and for sale in 2021. An important early Methodist chapel. Wesley preached in Seend in 1749 and in 1775 Methodists built the present chapel, which he opened. It is of brick with ashlar quoins under a hipped slate roof. The facade is of its time but lifted by a surprisingly imposing pedimented hood above the double doors; above that is a two-light Gothic window with 'Wesleyan 1774' inscribed in the spandrel. A further inscription above the door, added in 1929, states 'This chapel was opened by the Rev. John Wesley A.M. on March 4th 1775.' There is a small blocked window in the left side, perhaps closed off when the adjacent building was erected, and the right side has two, each of three lights

Seend Wesleyan, the simple interior with ubiquitous clock facing the preacher.

and again Gothic; the rear has two two-light windows. It is believed that the roof was raised and the windows given their Gothic heads c1830, the former possibly to accommodate the panelled gallery on cast-iron columns over the doorway, which is of similar date. The interior was, as one would expect, simple but dignified, and it is to be hoped that this is not entirely lost in future.[473]

Photograph also on page 28.

Primitive Methodist Chapel, Seend Cleeve,* in the angle of Pelch Lane and the village street, Grade 2 listed. This is built of brick with ashlar quoins under a hipped slate roof, the general appearance not dissimilar from that of the Seend chapel. The main access was from the village street through the burial ground to a facade with double doors in a plain surround; above that are two

Seend Cleeve Primitive Methodist, conversion stalled in 2020.

flat-headed sash windows and a plaque at the head, now removed, which stated 'Primitive Methodist Chapel Erected AD 1741 Rebuilt AD 1849.' The sides have two large sash windows and the rear facing the street behind has a subsidiary door between two tall round-arched windows. The plaque was mistaken: the first chapel was built in 1841, with round-arched windows, and rebuilt in 1849. A Sunday school, probably the building to the north east, ruinous in 2019, was added at some

Seend Cleeve Primitive Methodist, the plaque with its incorrect date now detached from its place. Photograph courtesy of Wiltshire Buildings Record.

point in the 19th century. The chapel was closed in 1979, has suffered unsuccessful attempts at conversion into a house and remained empty and near ruinous in 2020.[474]

Semington

Wesleyan Methodist Chapel, at junction of Church Street and High Street, now a house. This is an attractive mixture of brick with profuse ashlar dressings and lancet windows under a slate roof. The gable facing the road has lancet windows either side of what was the door. This was probably turned into a garage door on conversion, creating a problem which has now been neatly solved with a wide glass door and screen. There is a stepped triple lancet above and an inscription, 'Wesleyan 1884,' at the head. The four-bay sides have pairs of double lancets and the schoolroom is built in similar materials at right angles to the rear. A previous chapel of 1819, almost certainly on this site, was replaced by this one in 1884 and the schoolroom of 1912 was probably a rebuilding of a previous version built with the chapel. The chapel was closed and converted in 1981-2 and the Methodists then joined the Anglicans in the parish church.[475]

Shalbourne

Wesleyan Methodist Chapel, Ivy House, north of village street at SU317632, Grade 2 listed. Wesleyans had been worshipping for some years at an unrecorded location in the village before, in 1873, they moved into the former school by the drive to Shalbourne Manor, an attractive Tudor Gothic building in ashlar, dated 1843 and Grade 2 listed, which had become too small for its previous use. By 1884 the school had become too small for the Wesleyans also and in the late 1890s they moved into a chapel created from the north end of Ivy House. The house is of brick, banded with flint, and the only external evidence remaining for the chapel may be the 12-pane sash window at an intermediate level in the east wall towards the north end. The entrance was in the north wall, with steps curving down to the road.[476]

Wesleyan Methodist Chapel of 1911, west of road in village centre, now a house called The Old Chapel. In 1911 the new owners of Ivy House, wanting more privacy, built this chapel as a replacement. It is of brick, now painted, under slate with ashlar dressings. The gable facing the road has pointed-arch windows either side of the protruding porch which has a three-light window to the front. There is a circular sun-and-planets window above and a date plaque for 1911. The three-bay sides have paired pointed-arch windows in flat-headed surrounds. The chapel closed in 1968 and was converted after 1979.[477]

Primitive Methodists had been meeting in various cottages since the 1830s but in 1894 built a chapel outside the village at the junction of the **Hungerford Road**

with **Daniel's Lane**, SU323645, at a point accessible to Ham and Bagshot as well as Shalbourne. It closed c1950 and is believed to have been demolished.[478]

Sherrington

Wesleyan Methodists met in a cottage in the late 19th century but in 1890 opened a **Mission Room** at an unrecorded location in the village. This was of corrugated iron, lined in match-board and seating 60. It was short-lived, lasting barely beyond the turn of the century.[479]

Sherston

Congregational Chapel, Cliff Road, empty in 2019. This is substantial but plain apart from the windows. The rendered wall facing the road has three large round-arched windows with intersecting wooden Y-tracery and a tablet over the central one dated 1825. The south wall, of rubble-stone, has a single similar window over a plain pair of doors. The roof is half-hipped, now tiled but previously having stone slates. There was a gallery at the south end. To the rear at right angles is a smaller and lower extension in similar style and probably of similar date; this was said to have been the vestry though it is large for that purpose. The chapel was opened in 1825 and was converted from a barn, which may help to explain its appearance. The congregation built the British School just along the street in 1844; the British School closed in 1895 but continued as a Sunday school and is now used for worship after the chapel closed c2013.[480]

General Baptists built a chapel on the north side of Back Lane, now **Grove Road**, in 1837. It was rendered to the front and rubble stone to the sides under a semi-hipped roof; the porch was on metal pillars below a large round-arched window with Y-tracery and there were two smaller round-arched windows to the side. It closed probably around the time of the First World War, was sold and used for storage and survived a long time, not being demolished until after 1971. It was replaced by a bungalow, No.6a.[481]

Particular Baptists built the small Zion Baptist on **Gaston Lane**, c1860. It may have been in an outbuilding behind 6 Gaston Lane, since demolished, or it might have been the house itself. Nothing more is known of its history but it seems unlikely that it continued in use beyond the First World War. No.6 is one of a curving terrace of two-storey rubble-stone cottages with roofs of graduated stone slates.[482]

Primitive Methodist Chapel, Grove Road, at north east end, in use. This small chapel in coursed rubble-stone under a slate roof is side-on to the road with two round-arched windows and high up between them a plaque dated 1851; alterations in the stonework show that the door was originally centrally placed between these windows. There is a single round-arched window in the rubble-stone south wall and the north wall is also of rubble-stone and was previously attached to a neighbouring cottage. There is now a porch there in industrial brick, dating from 1964 when the adjoining cottages were sold and demolished and a small extension housing kitchen and lavatories was added to the rear.[483]

Shrewton

Independents opened a chapel in **Maddington** some time before 1858. It did not last very long.[484]

*Zion General Baptist Chapel,** junction of Salisbury and Amesbury roads, now a house. In brick with some ashlar under a slate roof, this chapel has an impressive gable at right angles to the road with a pedimented doorway, flat-headed windows either side and three round-arched windows above, the central one taller; the gable head plaque is no longer legible. There are four round-arched windows to the side and beyond that the schoolroom with four flat-headed windows, increased in height since conversion. A cob building of 1796-7 was replaced by another in 1816 and this in turn was rebuilt here in 1846 when it was noted as having a capacity of 800 persons, though the 1851 religious census gives it as 550. Closed in 1997, it was converted to a house by Arts, Lettres, Techniques of London.[485]
Photograph on page 55

A second **Baptist** chapel, the **Bethesda Baptist**, was built by 1831 in what is now called Chapel Lane. However, it was probably closed by 1851. It may then have served as a British School until some time after 1878 before being demolished.[486]

Wesleyan Methodist Chapel, High Street Maddington, in use. This broad and sombre brick chapel with raised brick dressings under a slate roof has a pointed-arch doorway, lancets either side and plaques above reading '1861' and 'Methodist Church'. There are two bays of sash windows to the sides and a late 19th century schoolroom to the rear, with further small extensions. The chapel was built in 1861 by people who had seceded from the Zion Baptist.[487]

Slaughterford – see Biddestone

Sopworth

No chapels recorded.[488]

South Marston

Wesleyan Methodist Chapel, Chapel Lane, empty but maintained in 2019. A tiny chapel – 'no bigger than a poor man's dwelling' - in brick under a slate roof, its gable of conventional design has a protruding porch, the door and windows either side all segmental-headed. The south side has three bays with flat-headed sash windows and the north only one as there was previously a building attached at the west end. There was an earlier Wesleyan chapel here from at least 1855, possibly on this site, and this was built in 1878. It may always have struggled to attract a congregation - in 1912 an evening service was reported as attended only by the preacher, his wife and one old woman who died soon afterwards – but it struggled on until closed in 1974. It was then sold in 1977 to the owners of the house opposite.[489]

South Newton

Wesleyan Methodists built a chapel east of the road, just north of what is now Forge Close, in 1812. By 1879 it was being used by **Primitive Methodists** but it was demolished before 1900. A house called Tehran now stands on the site.[490]

United Methodist Chapel, Stoford, east of road at south end of village, now a house. L-shaped in brick under tile with arched sash windows and wooden frames, possibly original. The gable facing the road has three stepped lights in a single arch and a plaque above dated 1912. There are three bays to the side and the schoolroom to right rear has two bays. The porch, which appears original, is in the re-entrant angle and has a gable with a two-light window to the front and the door to the side. It has wall plaques from various donor United Methodist congregations but also one from 'Primitive Methodist Friends'. The congregation had been meeting in Great Wishford but their premises there grew decrepit; they petitioned Lord Pembroke for a site for a new chapel but in the end the present site was given by a Mr White of Porton. The chapel, which opened in October 1912, seated 100 and was linked by sliding doors to the schoolroom. It closed in 1986.[491]

South Wraxall

Congregational Chapel, Lower Wraxall, north of path alongside stream at ST834643, now a house called Rose Villa. This is built of coursed rubble-stone with ashlar dressings under slates set in diamond pattern. The gable facing the path had the original door, now a window; there is a 6-pane flat-headed window above, and above that a date-stone for 1832. The side windows are altered, with one to the east originally substantially taller and the door to the west probably inserted later. A slightly lower bay to the north in rubble-stone was the schoolroom, added sometime before c1880. The date on the plaque perhaps relates to the formation of the meeting, for the chapel was built in 1844. It became a mission station of Holt and was sold in 1925 and converted to a house.[492]

Wesleyan Methodist Chapel, Bradford Leigh, south of road at ST838625, now a house. This is large for a corrugated iron chapel. The gable has a lean-to porch with the door to the side and above that is a three-light stepped window with modern glazing. The sides have modern glazing and an inserted dormer. The chapel was built in 1892 as a mission chapel attached to that at Coppice Hill, Bradford on Avon. It closed c1950 and had various uses before being adapted as a house.[493]

Southwick

*Old Baptist Chapel,*** Wynsome Street, in use, Grade 2 listed as are its gates and railings and the nearby baptistery. This chapel is distinguished not only by its appearance but also as the central point from which so many Particular Baptist churches in the west of the county sprung. There was very early Baptist activity here from soon after 1662, first in Witch Pit Wood and later in a converted barn at Pig Hill, on the road from Bradley to Southwick, where it was said that up to 1000 people came from all around to worship. After the Act of Toleration congregations formed elsewhere, often under the auspices of Southwick, and the first chapel here, for a now smaller congregation, was built in 1709. This had a thatched roof and a gallery over the door but the roof was so low that people in the gallery could not stand upright. It stood in front of where the present chapel is and, being in a 'decayed state', was replaced by it in 1815. It was left standing until the new chapel was complete and the best materials were then used to build the original vestry and schoolroom to the rear. Improvements were made in 1845, including moving the pulpit from a side wall. There were further renovations in 1872 and in 1878 the

Southwick Old Baptist – twin gallery staircases for symmetry even in a building of such modest size

Southwick Old Baptist

chapel reopened after erection of a new schoolroom and a new vestry, allowing the old vestry to become another schoolroom. There was a new extension to the side furthest from the road in 1980.

The chapel is of brick with stone dressings under a hipped slate roof, and nearly square. The north west entrance front has three bays of segmental-headed windows with raised keystones and imposts; these are placed either side of the door below with three above, and between the levels is a pattern of three lozenges in vitrified headers. There are two pairs of similar windows at each level in the side walls, placed close together, those at first floor on the road side joined to those on the entrance front by a continuous stone band at sill level; the wall facing away from the road is rendered. To the south east is the 1878 schoolroom and vestry, with gable in brick and stone but the south east wall in rubble-stone; it has a tiled roof. There is a stepped three-light round-arched window in the gable and a separate doorway in the lean-to porch alongside, with the modern extensions to the rear. The chapel interior has been substantially stripped out but retains a panelled and painted gallery round three sides with a clock centred on the gallery front opposite the pulpit.

The open air baptistery is 100m north west alongside the river, square and with surrounding rubble walls, rebuilt in 1937 but no longer used.[494]
Photograph also on page 32.

*Providence Strict Baptist Chapel,** Frome Road, just north of Wynsome Street junction, Grade 2 listed, now a house. A group of people who objected to the dismissal of a minister from the Old Baptist left with him and built this attractive chapel in 1861. Of ashlar under a slate roof hipped to the rear, and with round-arched windows, it has a gable end facing the road with a door and five windows in two

tiers, raised quoins and a pedimented gable above with a plaque dated 1861. The sides each have two tall windows and their lower walls are in coursed rubble-stone. The later and lower schoolroom to the rear has sash windows. The chapel closed in the 1990s and was later well converted into a house.[495]

A **General Baptist** con-gregation deriving from that at the Conigre chapel in Trowbridge had built a chapel in Goose Street, south of the Old Baptist, by 1714. It was closed and demolished c1800.[496]

Southwick Providence Baptist – an attractive if perhaps amateur take on a Classical facade

In 1818 **Methodists** built a chapel at the north end of the lane to Poles Hole Farm, now Wesley Lane. It closed in 1876, was then converted into a blacksmith's forge and much later into a house called The Old Forge which may contain some of the old fabric.[497]

Spirthill – see Bremhill

Stanley – see Bremhill

Stanton Fitzwarren

No chapels recorded.[498]

Stanton St Bernard

In 1841 **Wesleyan Methodists** built a chapel in a cul de sac east of the village street at SU094623. It was closed by 1920 and has since been demolished.[499]

Stanton St Quintin

Primitive Methodists built a chapel at Lower Stanton in 1873, towards the end of a cul de sac in the east of the village at ST918808. It may have been unsatisfactory from the start because it seems the Primitive Methodists were negotiating in 1879 to buy the disused Quaker burial ground, set back a few yards behind the garden of what is now 14 Seagry Road, to build a chapel on. They were unsuccessful but the first chapel was replaced in 1905 by another north of the village road at the junction with **Avil's Lane**. Services were still held there in 1989 but it has since been demolished and a new house, Chapel House, built on the site. The original chapel was demolished probably sometime in mid century at the time a new house, 'The Old Orchard', was built adjacent.[500]

Stapleford

In around 1820 **Wesleyan Methodists** built a small chapel on what became Chapel Lane, on the central section which is now a footpath. It was closed in around 1946 and demolished c1970.[501]

Startley – see Great Somerford

Staverton

Wesleyan Methodist Chapel,* just south of bridge, Grade 2 listed, now a house. A satisfying example of an unspoilt simple chapel of early design. Tall pointed windows of uniform size have Y-tracery, the front is coarse ashlar, the sides are of coursed rubble-stone and the hipped roof of slate. The front has an arched doorway with double doors, windows above at either side and a plaque dated 1824. Each side has a centrally placed window. Built in 1824, it closed in 1985, was sold to Nestlé for storage associated with their factory next door and was later sold again and neatly converted to a house with an unobtrusive inserted floor.[502]
Photograph on page 32.

Steeple Ashton

General Baptist Chapel, Sundial House, 19 High Street, Grade 2 listed, now a house. This building, then a house and probably quite newly built, was converted into a chapel in 1864 as an outstation of that at Bratton, under the direction of Robert Reeves. A Sunday school was added in 1874. The chapel closed c1940 and was sold in 1947 to be converted back into a house. It is double-fronted in ashlar with sash windows and a door within an Ionic portico, all under a tiled roof. The entrance when a chapel was by the present front door – the porch previously carried the words 'The Baptist Chapel' - and it seems likely that the whole ground floor was converted into a single large room for worship. The schoolroom was the long single-storey extension stretching

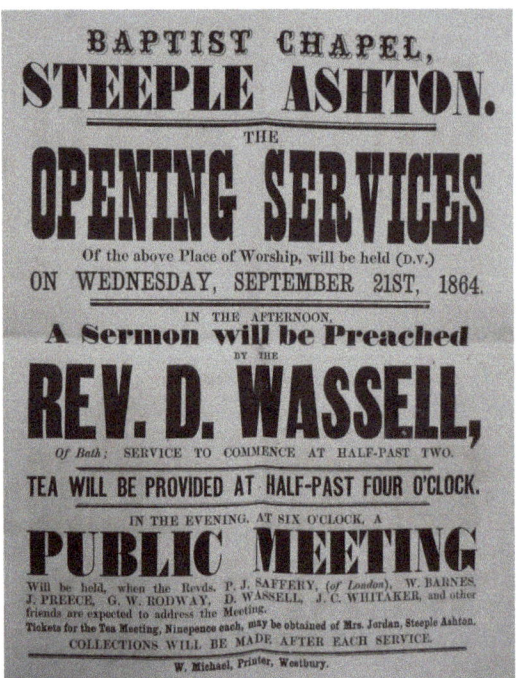

Opening services, as here at Steeple Ashton Baptist, were both celebratory and fund-raising to help pay off the construction debt. Photograph courtesy of Wiltshire & Swindon Archives.

across the rear of the house, brick to the front and gabled ashlar to the side, where there was presumably a separate entrance.[503]

Primitive Methodist Chapel, on village street just north of parish church, in use. The original building of 1854 is of brick under a slate roof with ashlar dressings and two tall windows to the road side. The entrance was in the north gable with a porch and two sash windows above. That is now hidden by the 1991 extension in similar materials, the new gable to similar design but with asymmetrically placed porch. On the side of the extension is the repositioned plaque dated 1851, 1851 being the year of the church's foundation here. Inside, there is a rear gallery. To the south an attached two-storey one-bay building in similar materials was built as a house at the same date or very shortly afterwards. This was presumably the manse and was placed in front of a pair of earlier cottages, one of which it has now become a part of. By 1864, when some presumably transient crisis caused the chapel and manse to be offered up for auction, the manse was tenanted by a cordwainer.[504]

Steeple Langford

Primitive Methodist Chapel, Hanging Langford, west end of village in Chapel Lane, now a house. This is of brick, with dressings of pale brick, under slate. The gable end has a round-arched door between two similar windows and a lunette over. The west side originally had three similar windows but dressed in red brick, the rear two now bricked in. The east side has one window then a substantial modern extension at right angles, in render with a metal roof. The chapel was built in 1849 but rebuilt in 1868. It closed in 1960 and was subsequently converted though the rear wing and interior of the main building are much more recent.[505]

Stert

General Baptist Chapel, south of village street, now a house called Maitland. The three bays to the west are the chapel, but much disguised by later alteration. The porch is probably original and was symmetrically placed with windows either side on the long side. The dormers and the one-bay extension to the east are additions since conversion. It is rendered and has a tiled roof with bands of fish-scale tiles; there are modern extensions to the rear. It was built c1869 for Methodists but sold in 1887 to the New Baptist Chapel, Devizes. It closed in 1957 and was bought by a builder who extended and renovated it.[506]

Stockton

No chapels recorded.[507]

Stourton with Gasper

No chapels recorded.[508]

Stratford Tony

No chapels recorded.[509]

Studley – see Calne Without

Sutton Benger

Quakers were active here from the late 17th to late 18th centuries, supported by the family which later founded Fry's chocolate in Bristol. They may have met only in houses.[510]

Wesleyan Methodists built a chapel here in 1850 but it is not known where. It may not have lasted for long.[511]

Sutton Mandeville

No chapels recorded.[512]

Sutton Veny

Independents built a chapel on the north side of High Street in 1793, opposite what is now Walnut Close. A schoolroom and burial ground were added in 1818 and the chapel was rebuilt in 1869-70 in Romanesque style by W J Stent of Warminster. It was demolished in 1970. A British School to the rear, also built in 1869, remains and has been converted to a house.[513]

A **Wesleyan Methodist Mission Hall**, set back north east of High Street about 100 metres from the central cross-roads, was built c1890 but had closed by 1907 and was soon demolished.[514]

By 1864 **Primitive Methodists** had built a chapel at **Little Sutton**, ST914410, almost in Tytherington. It went out of use between the wars and in 1959 was demolished and new houses built just to the north.[515]

Swallowcliffe

A **Catholic Apostolic** Irvingite chapel was built south east of Pole's Farm at ST965269 in 1837. It was closed in the early 20th century and later demolished.[516]

A **non-denominational** corrugated iron mission hall, perhaps sponsored by the **Band of Hope**, was opened opposite and just north east of the Royal Oak between 1886 and 1890. It closed c1920 and was subsequently demolished.[517]

Teffont Magna

Primitive Methodist Chapel, Teffont Magna, west of road towards north end of village, now a house. This small chapel was built in 1820 but closed in 1905. It may have been used by **Open Brethren** for a period after that but by around 1920, in very dilapidated condition, it had been let out and converted to a house. A proposal to reopen it as a chapel in 1925 came to nothing. The door with two-centre arched windows either side is in the long side facing the road, in brick; the porch hood is modern. The gable ends are in rubble-stone, possibly rendered previously, and there are two low windows to the south end which may not be in original positions. The roof is tiled and modern extensions to the rear are in keeping with the chapel's modest scale.[518]

Tidcombe and Fosbury

No chapels recorded.[519]

Tidworth

The **Presbyterian Church of St Andrew and St Mark** was built in 1909, mainly for Scots soldiers based at the newly-built garrison. Anglican and Roman Catholic churches were built nearby in 1912 and survive but the Presbyterian church, known as the Scottish church, closed in 1964. It was at the junction of St Patrick's Avenue and Kirkee Road and was a substantial building with side aisles, a clerestory and a bellcote. After it closed another building was used for some years until St Michael's church became inter-denominational.[520]

Tilshead Baptist

Tilshead

General Baptist Chapel,* next to Rose and Crown, empty in 2019. A good example of a late small village chapel, this is of brick with pointed-arch windows and doorway under a steeply pitched tiled roof. The side facing the road has two windows with interlacing tracery and a protruding porch with double doors. The west gable is blank but for a small lancet at the gable head; the east has a similar lancet but also a tall stepped triple lancet and a plaque dated 1882. The small schoolroom was added at right angles to the rear c1927. Built in 1882 to designs by Henry Reeves of Bratton, the chapel was closed in 2015, advertised for sale for conversion but still empty in 2019.[521]

Tisbury

Congregational Chapel, High Street,* set well back opposite the Boot Inn, Grade 2 listed, now a house. An interesting early chapel but hard to see. It was built against local opposition in 1726 as Independent but became Congregational in 1797 and remained in use until replaced by the larger Zion Hill chapel (see below) in 1842. Thereafter it was used as a British School and later a board school. It was restored in 1906 and eventually converted c1989 to a house now called Morgan's Chapel. The front is of ashlar under a pyramidal tiled roof with a weather vane dated 1726 and two octagonal ventilators; a coved plaster cornice goes round the whole building beneath the eaves. There are mullioned and transomed two-light windows with round-arched heads either side of the similarly round-arched doorway on the front wall and two flat-headed windows to the rear mark the site of the pulpit. The sides each have two upper windows of two lights. Inside, there are 18th century galleries on the south and east sides.[522]

A glimpse of Tisbury High Street Congregational, now almost impossible to see. The photograph does show the near-square pyramidal roof, the twin ventilators and the plaster cornice

Mrs Turner's Congregational Chapel, south of Weaveland Road, just west of High Street junction, now a house. Mrs Turner, a founder of the Tabernacle Congregational Chapel in Trowbridge, moved to Tisbury in 1781 and did not like the Presbyterian teaching in the Independent Chapel. Against local opposition she

opened her own house - perhaps The Old House in High Street - for worship
and then built this chapel in 1782. By 1797 the original chapel had adopted a
Congregational form of government and the two factions merged. This chapel was
sold, being used for business purposes before eventual conversion into a house.
The street side is of ashlar under slate with a blocked arched door to the east and
a later extension to the west; the windows are much altered but there could have
been three bays originally, pointed-arched if the windows matched the door. The
south side, also in ashlar, has four pointed-arch windows.[523]

Tisbury Zion Hill Congregational

Zion Hill Congregational Chapel, Cuffs Lane,* Grade 2 listed, now nine flats.
The 1842 replacement for the first Congregational chapel in the village, large and
prominently positioned above Cuffs Lane. In Early English Gothic, ashlar under
slate, the front has a stepped gable with pilasters at the corners, the design reflected
in the porch below whose door has now been turned into a window. There are two
tiers of two-light lancets either side of the porch and, centrally above, a stepped
triple lancet. The sides have two pairs of tall lancets with buttresses between and,
on the east side, the new entrance. There was originally a south gallery on cast
iron columns. The chapel closed in 1978 after the need for substantial repairs
was revealed; the congregation merged with the Methodists and the chapel was
eventually converted to flats c1996.[524]

Wesleyan Methodist Chapel, The Quarry, empty in 2021. Small and unusual with
its semi-hexagonal front, this was the first Wesleyan chapel in the village, replaced
in 1902 by the new Wesleyan in High Street (see below). It is of ashlar under slate
with round-arched windows and despite its small size had capacity for over 100
worshippers. The front has a later porch obscuring what was probably a lunette
window above the door. It is dated 1846 below the eaves and opened in May of that

year.[525]

Wesleyan Methodist Chapel, High Street, in use. This was the 1902 replacement for that at the Quarry and was designed by Thomas Wonnacott of Southsea in rock-faced Gothic, the stone quarried on site. The gable facing the road has a five-light window above a long but shallow blind arcade and the entrance is through the base of a tower on the south side, with a Continental feel and a pyramidal roof. Set back behind that is the slightly later schoolroom block, with grouped pointed-arch lancets to the front but the south side in ashlar with segmental-headed windows in brick surrounds. The north wall of the chapel is in ashlar with paired lancets but again in brick surrounds. The inside was stripped out in c2006 with a false wall inserted at the pulpit end to create more rooms behind; the organ and pews were removed.[526]

Mission Hall, Weaveland Road, almost opposite Mrs Turner's chapel, now a pair of houses. A Mission Hall of unknown denomination opened here c1900 with seating for 200 and services on Sunday afternoons. Construction is of smooth-faced rubble-stone with brick dressings and a slate roof, the windows segmental arched. The building was apparently intended as a pair of houses but was turned into the mission hall on completion. It was in use in 1915 but closed by 1920, then auctioned and later turned back into the two houses originally intended.[527]

Tockenham

Primitive Methodists built a chapel to the west of the village street at SU038794 in 1863, part of the Brinkworth circuit and seating 120. It was no longer used by 1961, derelict in 1968 and subsequently demolished. The chapel had tall round-arched windows either side of the door, corner pilasters and a coped gable.[528]

Tollard Royal

*Primitive Methodist Chapel,** north of road towards west end of village, now a house. The characterful gable facing the road makes quite an impact. It is in brick and flint above a brick plinth with a round-arched doorway inset into a further tall arch which also carries a plaque, '1879 Primitive Methodist'. Tall round-arched windows are placed either side of the door and the eaves have a stepped pattern in raised brickwork. There are three similar windows to the sides and a tiled roof. Built in 1879, it closed in 1957, was used for a time as a workshop but had been well converted to a house by 1988.[529]

Tollard Royal Primitive Methodist, appealing in brick and flint, if hard to see

Tucking Mill – see West Tisbury

Turleigh – see Winsley

Tytherington – see Heytesbury

Upavon

Cave of Adullam Baptist, Upavon – the south wall which previously had the door at its centre

*Strict Baptist Chapel, Cave of Adullam,** west side of Chapel Lane, Grade 2 listed, in use. A chapel bearing the scars of its long life, it is made of rendered brick under a half-hipped slate roof, with some walls battered and a buttress. The south wall has two round-arched windows and between, above where the door used to be, a cast-iron plaque 'Cave of Adullam Baptist Chapel AD 1838'. The gable facing the road has a small late 19th century porch containing the new door, moved there at that time, and a sash window above. There is one round-arched window in the north wall and the west wall has a further sash. Inside there is a panelled gallery and a raised pulpit. It was built in 1838 on the site of, and possibly as a conversion of, a previous building and was a successor to another chapel elsewhere in the village. After consideration of closure a programme of restoration was started and the main windows were replaced by 2021, at which date services were held fortnightly.[530]
Photograph also on page 33.

Primitive Methodists built an iron mission hall in 1886 at the north end of Chapel Lane, north of the junction with Jarvis Street. It was out of use c1950, demolished not long afterwards and replaced by a modern bungalow.[531]
A new **Methodist** chapel was erected in 1966 in **Avon Square**, south east of the main village. By 2006 it had been closed and replaced by further housing.[532]

Upton Lovell

No chapels recorded.[533]

Upton Scudamore

General Baptist Chapel, later Wesleyan Methodist, east side of road running south from the Angel Inn, now a house. The unusual ashlar gable facing the road has the central lower section brought forward as if for a porch; the section above that, projecting to a lesser degree, contains a circular window and culminates in a raised and shouldered central gable. There is a dentil-like pattern in stone stepped up the eaves. The north wall is in coursed rubble-stone with two of three original round-arched windows blocked; the south wall is now thickly rendered with a door, altered windows and inserted dormers. The front contains three flat-headed windows and it seems may always have contained only windows, albeit round-arched, with the door being in its present position to the side. Built in 1850 by Warminster Baptists, it was disused from 1907 and sold in 1920 to the Wesleyans who used it for a short period, probably until the late 1920s, before it was closed finally and converted to a house. The modern extension to the rear is much more recent.[534]

Urchfont

Independents built a chapel at The Green in 1817 and added a schoolroom in 1825. By 1851 it was being shared with **Baptists** and by 1886 had been taken over by **Open Brethren**. It was in what is now Chapel Lane and was a square red-brick building which was eventually sold in 1969 and demolished in 1971. 'Chapel House' was built on the plot.[535]

Wesleyan Methodist Chapel, Wedhampton, on The Cartway, now a house. The building is of brick under a tiled roof with some ashlar dressings. The gable facing the road contained the original porch and door with a three-light Gothic cusp-headed window above and a plaque dated 1867 which is still there. The north east wall has four bays, the rear two having similar cusp-headed windows with the arch attractively outlined above in dark brick. There is a modern porch and to the front a similar window but with two lights. The chapel was built in 1867, closed c1964 and by 1969 was being converted, with modern windows and a garage alongside the new porch: several of the cusped windows are therefore well-made replacements.[536]

Wanborough

Independents built a chapel in 1806 and it was used until at least 1829. It may not have lasted long after that date.[537]

Baptists opened the **Adullam Chapel** in Rotten Row, Kite Hill in 1856. It was bought by the **Primitive Methodists** in 1882, though they had been renting it for a number of years before that. A schoolroom was added in 1905 but the chapel closed in 1956 and was demolished in 1965. It was at the south west corner of the junction with what is now Orchard Close. Constructed of brick with stone dressings, the original had three bays with a porch and two Gothic windows. The schoolroom extension to the west had a large Gothic window with interlacing Y-tracery facing the road.[538]

Wesleyan Methodist Chapel, Lower Wanborough, east side of Chapel Lane, now a house. It has a broad gable facing the road, now pebble-dashed but probably originally brick, with a brick porch of 1901 and unsympathetically altered windows. Above the porch is a quatrefoil window with the inscription 'Wesleyan Church 1818' and above that a prominent ventilator; the gable is shouldered with small pinnacles. The sides are of four bays, brick with much-altered window openings, and there is a slate roof. The chapel was built in 1818 and a schoolroom added to the front in 1892: this would have obscured the whole right side of the facade but it has since been demolished, perhaps on conversion. The chapel closed in 1978 and was sold for conversion soon afterwards.[539]

Wedhampton – see Urchfont

West Ashton

No chapels recorded.[540]

West Dean

Wesleyan Methodists built a chapel on Moody's Hill c1860, by the road in what is now the front garden of a house called Whitegates. It was closed and sold in 1971 and subsequently demolished though a small part of one wall appears to be still standing.[541]

West Kington – see Nettleton

West Knoyle

Primitive Methodists were meeting in 1851, perhaps at Oxleaze Farm, ST851317, and a chapel may have been built there. A section of wall finally demolished c1978 was thought to have been part of this.[542]

West Lavington

An **Independent** chapel, later **Congregational**, was registered in **Littleton Panell** in 1834 at an unknown location. It went out of use c1880 and was presumably demolished soon thereafter.[543]

Ebenezer General Baptist Chapel, Littleton Panell, High Street, south of central crossroads, in use. Of brick with ashlar dressings and pointed-arch windows under a slate roof. The gable facing the road has a protruding porch and arched double doors with a triple stepped lancet above and a gable plaque dated 1895. There are three windows with interlaced tracery on the north side and two on the south. To the rear is a lower three bay schoolroom with separate door and two sash windows, perhaps contemporary. A Baptist chapel was registered here in 1839 and was probably that sited immediately south east of the central crossroads. It had a short life for it was replaced in 1848 by a chapel built on the present site; the 1839 building was marked as disused on an 1884 map and had been demolished by 1899. The 1848 chapel on the present site, said to have been made by voluntary labour using chalk dug from the adjacent hillside, was in turn replaced by the present chapel, by Henry Reeves of Bratton.[544]

Wesleyan Methodist Chapel, Littleton Panell,* west of central crossroads, now St Joseph's Catholic church. A chapel of rich Arts and Crafts detail, if now unhappily screened by trees. Of brick under a tiled roof, its gable facing the road has a very broad four-centre-arched lunette window with elaborately cusped tracery above the original door which has small windows either side and is now bricked in; the door head is of an almost flattened ogee shape. There are four bays to the sides with three-light windows, slightly stepped and with flattened arches in shallow segmental-headed surrounds, all with leaded coloured glass. A block to the rear at right angles, originally the schoolroom, now serves as the entrance. The chapel was paid for by two brothers as a memorial to their father and built in 1900 to designs by Read and Macdonald of London; the schoolroom was probably concurrent. The chapel had been preceded on the same site for a few years beforehand by a much smaller Wesleyan chapel, presumably of iron. The 1900 chapel closed in the 1960s and was bought by the Catholic church in 1967. They reversed the orientation, placing the altar where the door had been originally. The interior retains its hammer-beam roof.[545]

Photograph on page 50.

West Overton

Overton Heath Wesleyan Methodist *chapel is in* ***Wilcot*** *parish and is described there.*

Wesleyan Methodists built a chapel at the west end of Overton village in 1901, at SU128678. It was of corrugated iron with pointed-arch windows, three bays to the sides, a small porch and a circular window above. Closed in 1966, it was demolished and Chapel Cottages built on the site.[546]

Open Brethren opened a mission hall in Lockeridge some time after 1906 and before 1915, a little way north of the Who'd 'A' Thought It pub and on the same side of the road. It was plain and timber-boarded and was in use until the 1950s when it was demolished to make way for housing. It was replaced by a smaller chapel a little further south on the same side. In use until c1983, this was later demolished and replaced by a house called Chapel Lodge.[547]

West Tisbury

Primitive Methodist Chapel, East Hatch, set well back immediately south west of Hatch Farm at ST926285, empty in 2019. The gable facing the road is of rock-faced block with ashlar dressings. There is a Gothic doorway in the protruding porch with small matching windows either side and a gable plaque, also Gothic-arched, dated 1872. The sides are of three bays; the interior is now stripped of fittings and panelling. A first meeting house was certified in 1846, by reputation in the field opposite, and this one was built in 1872. It was unused after c1941 and sold to Hatch Farm in 1945.[548]

Primitive Methodist Chapel, Tuckingmill, at start of Hatch Lane west of Tisbury centre, now a house. This simple chapel is of brick with pale brick dressings including horizontal bands and has uniformly-sized round-arched windows beneath a tiled roof with overhanging eaves. The gable has a round-arched door with windows either side and a lunette plaque above dated 1877; there are three bays to the sides. Built in 1877, it closed c1939 when the congregation joined the Tisbury Methodists and may have been used as a store or workshop before eventual conversion into a house c2010.[549]

Westbury Leigh – see Westbury in Smaller Towns gazetteer

Westwood

Particular Baptist Chapel, Lower Westwood, set back immediately east of Orchard Close, now a house. Small, in neat ashlar under tile, the gable has a round-arched doorway with similar windows either side and the date 1865 above; the doorway has a flat hood above but previously had a pediment. The sides are of three bays with sash windows. This was built in 1865 as a village station of Back Street, Trowbridge, to seat about 100. A Sunday school in the chapel started in 1871 but proved too small and in 1885 a new schoolroom, a little further into what is now Orchard Close, was built to designs by W Smith of Trowbridge. This is a much larger Gothic building of rock-faced stone under tile. The chapel was closed some time after 1950 and used as a store before conversion to a house. The schoolroom was used as a primary school for a period before being used as a store and then converted into a house.[550]

Wesleyan Methodist Chapel, Upper Westwood, north of road near west end of village, now a house called Broadview. Recognisable by its shouldered and coped gable but much altered, it is made of ashlar under a slate roof. The gable facing the road used to have a projecting flat-roofed porch with double doors and typical tall round-arched windows either side, with date plaque above. All this is now gone and replaced by two pairs of nearly square windows. The east side wall seems always to have been blank, with stone of near-ashlar quality. The west side had a small vestry or schoolroom and this was extended in 1926 to make a larger schoolroom: two tall round-arched windows on the west gable remain but are now largely blocked in. Built in 1862, the chapel closed before 1971 and was made into a house in 1972 before people started to convert chapels sympathetically.[551]

Whiteparish

Wesleyan Methodist Chapel, south end of Dean Lane, now converted as a holiday cottage. This is of red brick with pale brick dressings under a slate roof. The gable end facing the road has a round-arched doorway, tall round-arched windows either side and a plaque above dated 1859; the coped gable is decorated with bricks set at an angle. The north wall has two bays of round-arched sash windows and the south wall is the same but rendered. To the rear is the Hayter Memorial school of 1903, in brick with four bays of similar windows. The chapel was built in 1859 though an original chapel of 1826 may have been on the same site. It was sold c2008 and converted.[552]

Primitive Methodist Chapel, north end of Clay Street, now a house called Hopway. Of painted brick under a slate roof, the gable facing the road has an altered porch and windows, though the location of a previous tall window can be made out. The chapel was built in 1860-61 with the adjoining cottage, probably the manse, at a cost of £204, and originally had 'four good windows', presumably two in conventional positions to the front and two to the north side. It closed in 1940 following the 1932 Methodist Union, after which all Methodists used the Wesleyan chapel. It was converted to a house c1944.[553]

Whitley – see Melksham Without

Wilcot

Wesleyan Methodist Chapel, Oare, Pound Lane, now a house. A plain brick chapel under a hipped slate roof, the side facing the road has a later porch carrying a plaque 'Methodist Church'. The sides are of two bays with replacement segmental-headed sash windows to the south and possibly original ones to the north. It was built in 1841, altered c1905, closed in 1976, used as a store until at least 1992 and subsequently converted.[554]

Wesleyan Methodist Chapel, Overton Heath, south of A345 on bend at Clench Common, SU173656, now a house called Foxhill Chapel. This faces the main road but is screened by a tall hedge so is hard to see. It is built of brick under a slate roof with altered windows, all originally round-arched. The gable facing the road has windows either side of a two-centre-arched door and is otherwise plain except for a circular ventilator at the head. The sides are of two bays. The south wall face has a window with a circular window above. Certified in 1846, it was rebuilt in 1882, closed and was sold in 1931 and was then used as a store until conversion to a house after 1977.[555]

Wilsford

A chapel of unknown denomination was built at the south west corner of **Wilsford Street**. It was there in 1844 but nothing more is known of it.[556]

Wilsford cum Lake

No chapels recorded.[557]

Wilton – see Grafton and Smaller Towns Gazetteer

Wingfield

A **Baptist** chapel of corrugated iron was built on Chapel Lane in 1896, founded by a mission band from Emmanuel Church, Trowbridge. It was demolished c1981 and Chapel House was built on the site.[558]

Winsley

Particular Baptist Chapel, Turleigh,* immediately east of Turleigh Manor, now part of a house. It looks as though someone has altered a chapel

Turleigh (Winsley) Baptist – could the highly elaborate glazing bars in the front window be original?

by inserting coach doors at the street level but in fact the chapel was built above an existing coach house and accessed via steps through the door in the wall to the right. Of rubble-stone with ashlar quoins, it has a slate roof and round-arched windows to the gable and the east side; that to the east is a sash and that to the gable has complex curved iron glazing bars which could be original. There is a gable plaque, now blank, and it is joined at right angles to another building at the rear. Promoted by the owner of the manor, the chapel was registered in 1819. From c1869, struggling, it came under the care of the Zion chapel in Bradford and it closed in 1885.[559]

Wesleyan Methodist Chapel,** south end of village, Grade 2 listed, in use. Unassuming on the outside, this is as good an example of an unaltered small turn of the century interior as one could hope to see. The first Methodist chapel was built 20 yards further back down the footpath which runs alongside the present building. It was opened in 1811, a small building with a gable facing south of conventional appearance with central door and round-arched windows either side and above. After a decline in attendance a revival in the 1890s led to plans from 1901 to provide a larger chapel and the present site was bought. Drawings were provided by George Brooks, a local builder and member of the church, and the building opened in 1903.

　　The chapel has its gable facing the road with the schoolroom to the right, the whole in free Gothic style with coursed rock-faced stone, ashlar dressings and a slate roof. Most windows are of two lights with Y-tracery but the north and south windows of the chapel are much more elaborate, particularly the south with its

Winsley Wesleyan – there is no clear reason for the door on the slant but it adds to the building's character.

Winsley Wesleyan — note the raised choir seating behind the pulpit with its exuberant wrought ironwork

integrated rose window. Below that are two small two-light windows with ogee heads in square frames and to the east is a porch with ogee heads to the openings. A door to the west is cut on the angle, also with ogee head. The interior is a treat, with original pews and panelling, much of the boarding placed on the angle. There is a central aisle, less unusual by this date. The fronts to the gallery and pulpit surrounds are particularly attractive with angled boards below and elaborate wrought iron tracery above.[560]

Winterbourne

*Independent, later Methodist, Chapel, Winterbourne Dauntsey,** east of main road in village centre, in use as **Bourne Valley Methodist Church**. The interest lies in the original chapel of c1799, unusually made of cob on brick footings under a half-hipped thatched roof. The end facing the street had the doorway with a window above; a porch was added later. In around 1980, with the arrival of the new building, the porch, door and window were removed and replaced by a single tall narrow window. There are three windows to each side, the central ones of two lights, though one of the windows on the left side is a more recent addition. There was originally a gallery which was removed c1910. The chapel was built as Independent, sponsored by Salisbury Scots Lane, but in c1844 passed into the hands of the Methodist New Connexion and was bought by the Wesleyans in 1899. It was extended to the rear in the early 20th century.

The Bourne Valley Methodist churches had already part amalgamated by 1970 and around that date they combined here. In 1980 they opened the much larger new chapel of brick with tile-hung gables, five bays deep, which has a porch with Gothic windows. It cost £40,000 and is linked to the old chapel which is now

Winterbourne Dauntsey before the original chapel was altered. Photograph courtesy of Salisbury Museum

Wesleyan Methodist Chapel, Winterbourne Gunner, north of main road opposite entrance to East Farm, now two houses. This is probably made of cob on a brick and flint plinth and has a hipped slate roof. There are few clues that it was ever a chapel but the narrow end facing the road used to have a porch where there is now a lean-to extension and there is an altered window, formerly round-arched, above: there used to be

used as a meeting room and Sunday school.[561]
Photograph also on page 27.

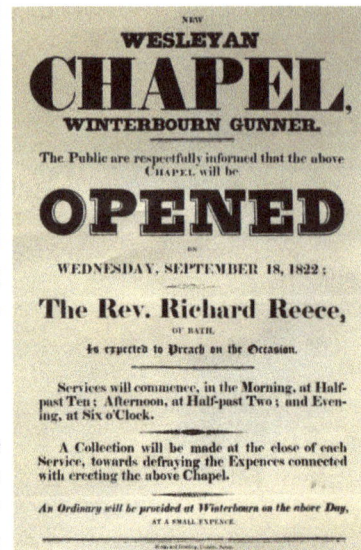

Winterbourne Gunner Wesleyan – the opening day, 1822. Photograph courtesy of Bourne Valley Historical Society

unusually large plaques saying 'Wesleyan' and 'Chapel' either side of this window. The sides have two tiers of two windows with altered brickwork showing where there were single taller round-arched windows before. Opened in 1822, it closed c1927 when the congregation joined with that of Winterbourne Dauntsey and was later converted.[562]

Winterbourne Gunner Wesleyan in use – it is now scarcely recognisable as the same building. Photograph courtesy of Bourne Valley Historical Society

Wesleyan Methodists built a chapel on Black Horse Lane in **Hurdcott, Winterbourne Earls** in 1843. It was a small building, 22ft by 18ft, with a hipped roof, protruding porch with flat-headed windows either side and a date plaque squeezed in above. It closed in 1967 when the congregation joined with Winterbourne Dauntsey and was subsequently demolished.[563]

Winterbourne Bassett

Primitive Methodist Chapel, west end of village, now a house. Built of brick with some ashlar dressings under a slate roof, it has its long side, with three round-arched windows, parallel to the road. The entrance end has similar windows either side of a porch with the door facing the road. The window above, formerly circular with an inscription, has been altered as has that at the opposite end which has a small lean-to extension below. The round-arched windows are now part blocked in for modern window frames with unfortunate effect. Primitive Methodists of the Brinkworth circuit were active locally from early in the 19th century but only managed to build this chapel in 1904. It closed in 1958 after an unusually short life and was sold for conversion in 1960.[564]

Winterbourne Monkton

No chapels recorded.[565]

Winterbourne Stoke

No chapels recorded.[566]

Winterslow

Former Baptist Chapel, West Winterslow, on Weston Lane nearly opposite present chapel, now a house called Bemerton. Of around 1828 in date, the original chapel included the porch and windows either side, to the west end of the building; the porch is modern but the low windows may be in original positions. The tiled roof is hipped. Inside was a larger room to the east, presumably the chapel, and a smaller to the west. Closed in the early 20th century, probably when the iron chapel opened, it was used as a tannery for some years before conversion to a house and extension to the east.[567]

Baptist Chapel, West Winterslow, on Weston Lane, in use. This is a well-maintained corrugated iron chapel of two bays and a porch. The interior is timber-lined with a modern baptistery in the floor and there is a flat-roofed modern extension to the rear. It was built in 1908.[568]

Wesleyan Methodists built a chapel on **The Common** in 1810. It was closed and demolished after the new chapel opened in 1865. It is believed to have been immediately adjacent to the new site, probably to the west.[569]

Wesleyan Methodist Chapel, Winterslow Common, north of The Common, in use. This is built of brick under a slate roof, the gable rendered and with incised lines in imitation of ashlar; the open porch is modern. There is a plaque dated 1865 above that between round-arched windows containing dark stained glass. The plain brick sides have three round-arched windows and there is a lower schoolroom extension to the rear. It was built in 1865, the schoolroom added in c1907 and extensive alterations made from 1983.[570]

Gospel Lifeboat Mission, Middle Winterslow, on Middleton just north of Yarmley Lane, in use. The present building was opened in 1979 and replaced the original mission hall of 1891 on the same site. It is of brick under a tiled roof, the gable with inset doors and walls curved in to create an internal porch. 'Gospel Lifeboat Mission' is written over that and there is a tall window above, pointed to follow the roofline.[571]

A second **Gospel Lifeboat Mission** hall was built in 1893, at **Winterslow Common,** immediately east of St John's church on Gunville Road. This closed in the early 1920s and was later demolished; it stood in what is now the garden of a house called Sunways.[572]

Woodborough

Wesleyan Methodist Chapel, Chapel Lane, off Church Road, now a house. This is of brick under a hipped slate roof. The entrance front has a replacement porch and a small circular window above replacing a plaque; there seem never to have been other windows in this wall. The north side has two tall round-arched windows, now split either side of an inserted floor, and there is a modern extension to the south. The chapel opened in 1820, with capacity for 134 people including 32 in the gallery. It closed in 1970 and was converted c1983.[573]

Woodford

No chapels recorded.[574]

Wootton Rivers

Wesleyan Methodist Chapel, on Forest Road towards north end of village, now a house. This simple brick chapel has a replacement porch with round-arched door in the gable facing the road, small round-arched windows either side and a plaque dated 1881. Its most unusual feature is the clock over the porch which has the hours marked by the words 'To God Be Glory' and which was apparently made by one Jack Spratt, a village craftsman. The sides have two bays of round-arched windows and the roof is of slate. Built in 1881, there were proposals in 1903 to build a substantial extension to the south as the new chapel, the original becoming a schoolroom. These were not acted upon and the chapel closed in 1967; it was converted to a house with an inserted floor c1980.[575]

Worton

Wesleyan Methodist Chapel, north of High Street towards west end of village, now a house. In brick with ashlar dressings under a slate roof, the gable facing the road has tall round-arched windows either side of a similar door which has a later ashlar porch in front like a sentry box. The ashlar quoins act as pilasters to the shouldered gable and a plaque is dated 1849. To the rear is a lower schoolroom extension added some years before 1900. The original Wesleyan chapel of 1824, probably elsewhere in the village, was replaced by this building in 1848. It closed and in 1993 was sold to the Anglican Catholic church which reopened it in 1994 as St. Brithwold's. This in turn closed in 2002 and the chapel was then converted to a house.[576]

Wroughton

Wesleyan Methodists from Hodson are said to have built the first chapel in Wroughton on the corner of **Wharf Road** and High Street around 1805. This burned down and was replaced by a chapel in **The Pitchens**, built c1823 and extended in 1855. This in turn was replaced by a chapel on **Devizes Road** of 1878 to designs by Orlando Baker of Swindon. The new chapel was in brick with contrasting bands, generally Gothic in style and with what was probably a schoolroom at right angles to the rear. It was empty for many years prior to its demolition in 1972 to make way for the Ellendune Community Centre. The Pitchens chapel was absorbed by the adjacent stables but demolished some time around the end of the Second World War.[577]

Primitive Methodist Chapel of 1879 south of High Street towards west end, in use. The front of painted render stands proud of the painted stone dressings and hence probably covers the original brick. The chapel is aligned at right angles to the street but short sections of wall and roof either side of the front gable and at right angles to it give the impression otherwise: they were presumably built this way to align better with the adjacent terraces. These side arms each have a Gothic window and five more complete the facade: small lancets either side of the porch with its arched doorway and three more above, wider and stepped. A ventilator at the gable head is dated 1879. The brick side elevations have three bays of Gothic windows and the substantial schoolroom behind, added in 1904, has four more, with round-arched windows. The roof is tiled.[578]

Primitive Methodist Chapel of 1853, now two houses at 36A and 36B High Street. Built in 1853, this closed when the new one was opened in 1879 and was then offered for auction. It may have been split into two at that time but was used as a church institute for a period in the 20th century. Below a shouldered gable are what were presumably two tall round-arched windows with raised surrounds and imposts. Between the windows, where there are now two doors, a broad flat hood may have covered the original single one.[579]

Primitive Methodists had a second chapel, on **Wroughton Road**, west of the road just south of the motorway where the old road diverges from the A4361. Built in 1891, it was of traditional design with a stepped three-light window above the porch. It was later enlarged but was 'hit hard by the (First World) War'; it was still active in 1943 but may have closed soon after the war ended. A bungalow, No.123, now stands on the site and may incorporate some of the old fabric.[580]

The **Hay Lane Primitive Methodist** chapel is described under **Lydiard Tregoze**.

Brethren Gospel Hall, in use, west side of Markham Road. Brethren started outreach work here in the early 1920s and first built a timber meeting room in Markham Road in 1926. A larger wooden building was built on the present site in 1934; the meeting is believed to have closed between 1949 and 1959 but opened again and in 1968 built the present hall. It is single storey, of pale brick with a low roof angle and a flat-roofed porch across the front and part way down one side.[581]

Wylye

*Congregational Chapel,** east end of Teapot Street, now a house. Of Gothic design, this has an interesting pattern of flint and stone with a continuous stone band at window sill level, complemented by a roof of tiles laid in diamond pattern. The east gable has a porch with three stepped lancets above and a plaque which is no longer legible. The sides are of three bays and to the west end the gable of the schoolroom, contemporary with the chapel, faces the street with a three-light window with square cusped heads. There is a modern flat-roofed extension to the north side. Meetings started under the control of Codford in 1817 and a former malt house was adapted as a chapel in about 1827. This chapel was built in 1860, paid for by Charles Jupe of Mere. It closed in 2001 and was converted.[582] *Photograph on page 36.*

Yarnbrook – see North Bradley

Yatton Keynell

Ebenezer Baptist, later Congregational, Chapel, east of The Street by Grove Lane, in use. The entrance gable in coarse ashlar has a later porch with a lunette window placed awkwardly above double doors. There are two small round-arched windows above and a plaque dated 1835. The sides are of coursed rubble-stone, blank to the north but with three bays of round-arched windows to the south. The roof is of slate. To the rear is a schoolroom of two bays with a separate door. The chapel was built in 1835 for Baptists but taken over by Congregationalists in the 1870s. A schoolroom was added in the early 20th century and may have been substantially altered in time for the centenary in 1935. The interior, plain with no gallery, has been modernised.[583]

Zeals

Congregational Chapel, east side of Fantley Lane, now a house. This is an interesting building but hard to see. To the north is the original chapel of 1832, with gable facing the road in coursed stone block; it has a Tudor-arched doorway below, a two-light window above with segmental-heads under a drip mould and above that a trefoil former ventilator. The north side has one window like that to the gable but what was probably a second has been replaced by a garage door and there is an inserted dormer above. The roof has bands of fish-scale and diamond tiles. In 1856 this became the schoolroom on completion of the new chapel, paid for by Charles Jupe of Mere. This is attached to the south, plausibly Gothic, of coursed rubble-stone with a similar banded tile roof. It has three bays at right angles to the old chapel, a porch at the north end alongside the gable of the old and an apse at the south with a vestry to the east of that. Closed c1970, it was converted in 1980.[584]

Primitive Methodist Chapel, east of Chapel Lane towards south end, now a house. A building which it is hard to imagine as a chapel. The end gable is of coursed rock-faced stone and now has a large central chimney stack where once the door was. The west side is of rubble-stone with one modern window but the stonework indicates the two tall windows probably here previously; the east side has inserted modern windows. The roof is of slate. The lower schoolroom to the rear is in brick under a tiled roof with two round-arched windows. Built in 1852, it was enlarged in 1866, the schoolroom was added in 1915 and it was closed c1973 and converted.[585]

5. The Smaller Towns

Amesbury

Baptist Centre, Butterfield Drive. Baptists were active in the town from the 17th century but it seems there was never a chapel. However, a group formed in 1991 and built the Baptist Centre in 1997. It is a large two-storey block in brick under a heavy tiled roof with some tile cladding. A main space under a hipped roof has a subsidiary set of rooms attached at right angles.[586]

Wesleyan Methodist Chapel, High Street, in use. The original chapel of 1818 was set back behind another building on the north west side of High Street and was enlarged in 1835. It burned down in 1899 and the present chapel was built on the same site, to designs by Josiah Gunton of Gordon, Lowther and Gunton. This is a substantial Gothic building in brick with some stone dressings under a tiled roof. A five-sided porch in the gable end has double entrance doors with 'Methodist Church' in large lettering typical of the date. Above is a large pair of 6-light mullioned and transomed windows with decorated cusped heads and above that a triangular section of stepped blind arcading at the gable head containing two ventilators. The gable is shouldered with buttresses below. The sides, of cheaper brick, have four bays with buttresses between, and behind are first the schoolroom of 1931-2 by Bothams and Brown and then the 1961 hall. The chapel presents a severe face to the street and lacks the exuberance of many others of this period.[587]

Primitive Methodist Chapel, Flower Lane, now a house called Port Royal, south of road by bend. Built as a four-bay corrugated iron chapel between 1899 and 1910, and closed by 1922, it was converted to a house soon afterwards and now has external panelling, painted white and held in place by a timber frame.[588]

Bradford on Avon

It is no surprise that Bradford, with its woollen industry, has a strong nonconformist history. Indeed, at the 1783 Bishop's Visitation, the parish priest described it as having nonconformists 'of almost every denomination under Heaven innumerable'. It is impressive that this history is reflected in such an interesting and varied collection of chapels, all bar one listed and many of early date.

Quakers

The **Quakers** were probably the first dissenting sect to have a meeting house here, this being at **Cumberwell** on the Bath road. It is believed to have been built in 1676 and rebuilt in 1689 after the Toleration Act. It was replaced elsewhere in the town in 1718 but not sold until 1813. There is a claim that the meeting house can be identified with the end-terrace house at 119 Bath Road but although this is called 'Old Chapel House' it is surely 19th century and hence a replacement.[589]

The **1718 Quaker meeting house** was in the town centre in what is now **St Margaret's car park**. It was used until c1798 and taken over in around 1850, or perhaps earlier, as a British School. It was sold in 1902 and demolished in 1965.

Quakers have been meeting again in the town from 1971, in a building of 1890 in **Whitehead's Lane,** formerly part of Spencer's brewery.[590]

Independents, Congregationalists and Baptists

Grove Meeting House, Middle Rank, ** Grade 2 listed, in use. The oldest chapel still standing in the town and one of the oldest in the county. Built in 1698, it started as **Presbyterian** but doctrinal disputes led to a group seceding in 1739 to form the Morgan's Hill chapel (see below) while the Grove became **Unitarian**. It declined at the beginning of the 19th century and in 1815 was let to a group of **Independents** who had seceded from Morgan's Hill. Although they did not at first flourish they became strong enough to build in 1823 the adjacent **Zion Chapel** and became **Baptists** in about 1848 after being joined in 1842 by a group seceding

Bradford on Avon, the Old Baptist (R) and Morgan's Hill Congregational (L – both with hipped roofs) in close proximity south of the river

Grove Meeting House, Bradford on Avon, the rubble-stone east wall now containing the entrance

from the Old Baptist (see below). The Zion chapel was of Classical design, with a rusticated ground floor, two tiers of round-arched windows and a central pediment. The Grove was little used for the next 50 years and in 1859 was described as ivy-covered and 'fast hastening to decay', but in 1873 it was taken over by the Zion chapel for use as a Sunday school. It remained thus until 1939 when the Zion chapel was requisitioned for the Red Cross and the congregation moved back into the Grove, where they remain, the chapel now being called the Zion Baptist chapel. The 1823 chapel became dilapidated after the Second World War and was eventually demolished in the 1960s; the site is now a small car park.

The exterior of the Grove chapel is of exceptional interest, with a long side in ashlar of six bays facing south over the town. At the lower level are four rectangular four-light windows between doors either end, the doors now blocked. Above are two similar windows at each end with between them a round-arched pair. The whole thus represents the original layout with doors either end and a gallery round the west, south and east sides. The east end is of coursed rubble-stone but at some point, probably when the chapel was converted into a Sunday school in the 1870s, it became the entrance front, with a plain door below a large eight-light mullioned and transomed window, the latter perhaps original. At that time also the galleries were removed. The west end joins to the adjacent terrace, the end house of which could previously be accessed direct from the chapel and may have been the manse. The north wall abuts the hillside, though there was originally a passage-way behind it. The roof was of stone but replaced by tile in the 1870s renovations; it is hipped at the east end and double pile. The interior was stripped out on conversion to a schoolroom and is now very plain, only the ornate Gothic-fronted organ of 1858 moved here from the 1823 chapel adding some interest.[591]

Photograph also on page 26.

Old Baptist Chapel, (Particular Baptist) St Margaret's Street,** Grade 2 listed, in use. The original chapel was built on the same site in 1689, possibly as a daughter church of Southwick Baptist, though nearby 6-7 St Margaret's Street was also licensed for meetings in 1672. The congregation flourished but the chapel became both too small and dilapidated and was replaced by this one in 1797. Access had

Bradford on Avon Old Baptist, the street entrance

been via a narrow side passage but, on rebuilding, a house on St Margaret's Street was part demolished to create the archway which is still used and which bears the legend 'Old Baptist Chapel founded 1689 rebuilt 1797'. The building to the left of this opening became the Sunday school and that to the right the manse. The chapel facade is of ashlar with two tiers of pointed-arch windows with Y-tracery and a central doorway with pedimented surround and Tuscan columns; doors either side were inserted in the 19th century to give direct access to the galleries but

Bradford on Avon Old Baptist, the steeply tiered galleries and raised pulpit adding to the 18th century feel

are now blocked. The sides and rear are of rubble-stone with similar windows, three to the sides and two tall single windows to the rear now blocked following the addition of a lean-to vestry. The roof is of slate, hipped. Inside there are panelled galleries on three sides, of possibly slightly later date, and a tall raised pulpit at the east end. The gallery contains original seating, with some box pews remaining, but box pews below were replaced with bench pews in substantial renovations carried out in 1887. The combination of a light space with handsome windows, galleries on three sides and the high pulpit makes this one of the most attractive of town chapel interiors.[592]
Photographs also on page 8 and 49.

Morgan's Hill Congregational Chapel, St Margaret's Hill,* Grade 2 listed, in use as the **United Church.** This was founded in 1740 by members of the Grove Chapel who disliked the way that it was moving towards Unitarianism. It was lengthened by 12ft in 1798, possibly to designs by Robert Cadby of Bradford, and lengthened again in 1835, this time with the roof raised by 4ft and previous tiles

Morgan's Hill, Bradford on Avon, the Sunday school of 1835 to the left

replaced with slates. By then it had a capacity of 650. The Sunday school, at right angles to the chapel, was built at the same time on the far side of the three-storey annex, this latter perhaps the original minister's house. The chapel became Congregational in the late 1850s and in 1976 merged with the Methodists, who had abandoned the Coppice Hill chapel (see below), to form the United Church.

The facade is ashlar, Classical of five bays with a string course above raised over a plaque to suggest a pediment, this change made when the hipped roof was raised in 1835. Below are two tiers each of four windows, split either side of a central doorway with a blocked window above; this doorway replaces an original pair to either side. The sides and rear are of rubble-stone, the sides showing by retained quoins where the second rear extension was carried out. Windows to the sides are again rectangular, the two to the rear segmental-arched. Inside are panelled galleries on three sides on wooden columns, the rear gallery containing the organ, and early 20th century stained glass panels in some of the windows. The Sunday school to the north west is a substantial block, the long sides of ashlar, that to the front with four bays of rectangular windows with a blank wall beyond where a further building was joined at right angles until into the 20th century.[593] *Photograph also on page 46.*

Bearfield Congregational Chapel, Huntingdon Street,* Grade 2 listed, in use. This opened in 1787 as the Anglican but independent **Bethel** chapel; it closed after a few years and in 1802 was bought by a Bath clergyman and re-opened. He added the minister's house and a gallery but in c1816 the chapel was made over to **Lady Huntingdon's Connexion**. The chapel was renovated in 1849 and the association with Huntingdon's Connexion lasted until 1879 when it became **Congregational** under the auspices of the Wiltshire and East Somerset Congregational Union. It remained Congregational but did not join with the Presbyterians in the United Reformed church in 1972 and has stayed independent.

The building is of rubble-stone with ashlar dressings under a hipped roof of stone tiles. The entrance front faces a side path and has a porch with a later and perhaps incongruous pedimented doorway under a round-arched window with tall rectangular windows either side. The street side has three similar windows with the painted inscription 'Bearfield Church' above. To the rear is a low schoolroom extension in squared stone blocks under tile and to the north side is attached the former minister's house in

Bearfield Church, Bradford on Avon

ashlar, entered from the side and with a bay window to the front, which was used as schoolrooms from 1897 and in 1925 was reduced in height to a single storey with lean-to roof after it became unsafe. Inside the chapel, the former gallery was removed in 1892 renovations by T B Silcock of Bath: there is no evidence that the windows at that end were altered at that time so they must previously have overlapped the gallery. The renovations included re-seating, the long central pews divided and numbered, and the provision of a new pulpit with an ornate wrought iron surround.[594]

*Providence Particular Baptist Chapel, Bearfield Buildings,** Grade 2 listed, now two houses, Nos. 2A and 2B. This is a chapel which was converted from houses in 1858,

was closed c1980 and then converted back to houses c1990. Part of a terrace, it now has four bays in crude ashlar with round-arched windows above; there is a door below at either end with rectangular windows between; the door at the east end has a round arch above still carrying the inscription 'Providence Baptist Chapel'. Apart from the shape of the windows the present appearance is probably not too dissimilar to the original facade of the cottages, which were late 17th or early 18th century. When a chapel, it had three tall round-arched windows to the west, their heads in the same positions as now, and the same window and door configuration at the east end. The roof was of tile and inside there was a gallery at the door end. The Sunday school was in a lean-to extension in rubble-stone to the rear. The pulpit and other artefacts are preserved in Bradford on Avon Museum.[595]

Photographs also on page 45.

Providence Baptist, Bradford on Avon, cottages converted into a chapel. Photograph courtesy of Wiltshire Buildings Record

Methodists

*Pippett Street, now Market Street, Wesleyan Methodist Chapel,** behind the Bradford Town Club, Grade 2* listed, now a billiards room. A notable chapel even though it is invisible from the road, this was built c1756, was preached in by John Wesley and was the county's first purpose-built Wesleyan chapel as well as the centre of Methodism in North Wiltshire until 1790. The building in front was the Maidenhead Inn and it was the landlord of this inn who built the chapel behind on the site of a former malt-house. To the front is the former inn, re-fronted in Classical style in 1755, with double doors at the south leading to a side passage. It later became a Post Office before becoming the Conservative Club and finally the Town Club. The chapel is behind, up steps from the street entrance, and is in rubble-stone with ashlar dressings under a line of three transverse hipped tiled roofs. The exterior is not generally visible and is hemmed in by other buildings

Bradford on Avon Pippett Street Wesleyan. John Wesley is said to have preached facing this clock, which remains on the premises

including the former manse, but the original Venetian window at the east end can still be seen. The interior retains the rear gallery – there were once side galleries also - but a false floor has been inserted at this level and only the original ground floor is used, for billiards. Windows have been blocked in and the former pulpit, previously high up below the Venetian window and accessed by stairs both sides, is long gone. The clock from the chapel, allegedly one Wesley would have taken the time from when preaching there, is retained in the Town Club. The chapel became redundant in 1818 when the new Coppice Hill chapel (see below) opened, although some accounts indicate it closed as early as 1790 when the congregation transferred to a predecessor of Coppice Hill.[596]

*Coppice Hill Wesleyan Methodist Chapel,** Grade 2 listed, now a shell containing a private swimming pool. This grand replacement for the Pippett Street chapel is still prominent in the view north from the south of the town, like a ruin on a Tuscan hillside. It is possible that there was an earlier replacement, of 1790, on this site but in any event this was built in 1818, perhaps to designs of T L Evans of London. It has a tall broad front of 5 bays of round-arched windows in two tiers, the door centrally below and the middle three bays stepped forward below a blind attic of three bays with a Greek pediment and giant scrolls either side, the whole of course in fine ashlar.

The sides have tiers of similar windows and at the north end two such windows flank a broad central arch which used to lead through to a communion recess. Inside was a U-shaped gallery on three sides. By the 1950s this vast space had become too large for the diminishing congregation and they moved in to the Sunday school, the round-arch-windowed single-storey building on the right on the approach path. In 1976 they abandoned the whole site and joined the Morgan's Hill congregation to form the United Church. By this stage the chapel was ruinous but it was saved from complete demolition and

Coppice Hill Wesleyan, Bradford on Avon, derelict and awaiting its fate. Photograph courtesy of Wiltshire Buildings Record

Still prominent in the townscape looking north, the shell of the Coppice Hill Wesleyan, Bradford on Avon

sold to the owners of an adjacent house who created a swimming pool inside the shell.[597]

Primitive Methodist Chapel, Sladesbrook, close to Mount Pleasant junction, Grade 2 listed, now a house. Built in 1845 by a group which had seceded from the main Methodist church in 1810, it had a short life, closing between 1885 and 1890. It was then used successively as a temperance hall and as part of the nearby school before final conversion into a house soon after 1979. In ashlar under slate, it has a fine pedimented gable facing the road, dated 1845, with round-arched door and windows above and to either side. The sides each have one flat-headed window; it is still joined to an adjacent building to the south and rubble-stone walling shows where there used to be an attached building to the north, demolished in the late 19th century. Replacement windows show where a floor has been inserted.[598]

Others

A **Catholic Apostolic** Church is believed to have been founded in the town in 1836 but probably did not last long.[599]

Calne

There was early dissenting activity in Calne – for example the over 200 people who attended a Presbyterian meeting in 1669.[600] – and the town had one of the longest-lasting Quaker meetings. Methodists were late on the scene, probably not meeting here until c1808, and the relatively limited presence of both Wesleyan and

Primitive Methodists is perhaps surprising. Seven chapels remain, two of them well worth seeking out.

Presbyterians and Quakers

Presbyterians built a chapel in **Back Road**, parallel to London Road, c1695. Joseph Priestley preached there in the 1770s while he was librarian at Bowood. By the early 19th century it was considered **Unitarian** and it closed in the late 1830s. **Primitive Methodists** used the chapel for a period from that date but could not afford the rent and switched back to a cottage in or near Back Road which they had registered in 1832. They returned to the chapel from 1846, at a lower rent, but in 1886 bought the former **Wesleyan** chapel, also in **Back Road**. After that the **Salvation Army** took it over, from 1899 or earlier, and continued to use it until the Second World War. The chapel, of four bays with a hipped roof, was demolished c1960 and replaced by a block of flats in Linden Close.[601]

Friends' Meeting House, Wood Street, east side of road, Grade 2 listed, now a shop with a blue plaque. Quakers bought land on Wood Street in 1672 and built a meeting house with a burial ground behind. They rebuilt it in 1838, with capacity for 100 plus 50 in a 'stepped loft', and remained here until 1908 when the meeting was discontinued. The building was leased to the YMCA c1921 and sold in 1962, with the street front altered to accommodate a shop window. The ashlar front now has doors either side of the shop window, that to the right leading to the flat above which has two sash windows to the street between pilasters and under a moulded cornice. Before conversion it had a central door between windows in a rusticated front. The walls to the rear are of rubble-stone and the former meeting house is set under a slate roof hipped to the rear.[602]

Baptists

General Baptist Chapel, Castle Street, set back south of street, in use. A Baptist chapel was first built on this site some time before 1703, in which year it was destroyed by a high wind. It was replaced a year later but that building in turn was replaced by the present chapel in 1817. This had a vestry added in 1832, a schoolroom to the east in 1857 and the main north front rebuilt in 1864 to designs by W J Stent of Warminster. There were originally cottages at the entrance to the site from Castle Street but these were demolished c1835. Only the main front is easily visible: before the 1864 works this had pointed-arch windows with Y-tracery and a hipped roof but now it has three cusped Gothic windows for the north gallery inset to the original ashlar above what was previously a wide lean-to Gothic porch; this was replaced in 1978 by the present unhappy effort in mainly glass. At the gable head is a trefoil window of similar design to those below. The sides have original Y-tracery windows under a tiled roof hipped to the rear and the various later buildings are attached to the east side and the rear. The inside is stripped out but the rear gallery and its pews remain, accessed by twin staircases from the lobby. A substantial organ from 1902, placed behind the pulpit in a space expanded in 1926, suffered woodworm and was replaced by an electronic organ in 1983.[603]

Zion Particular Baptist Chapel, Pippin Road (now The Pippin),* Grade 2 listed, in use. Small for a town chapel, this one was built by a group which seceded from the Castle Street Baptist in 1813 because they thought it was moving too far away from strict Calvinism. They met first in a converted cottage and then from 1824 in a converted warehouse at an unknown location in High Street before building this in 1836. It is of coursed rubble-stone under slate, the gable pedimented above with an inscription dated 1836. Below are two rectangular sash windows for the gallery and a late 20th century porch. The sides are of two bays with larger sashes and attached to the rear are the later schoolrooms and vestry with two gables and six windows in two tiers facing the street. The burial ground used to be west of the entrance front and was walled in.[604]

Zion Baptist, Calne

Methodists

Wesleyan Methodists started in a weaving shop in Kew Lane, using the ground floor and a room above with the floor cut away to form a gallery. By 1811 this was too small and they built a chapel in **Back Road**, parallel to London Road. They enlarged it in 1815 and again in 1828 and stayed there until 1876-7 when the Silver Street chapel was opened. The Back Road chapel, having been used for some years as an iron foundry, was taken over by **Primitive Methodists** in 1886 and used by them until 1965 when they joined the congregation at Silver Street. The Back Road chapel was subsequently demolished and Nos. 1a and 2a Back Road now stand on the site.[605]

Wesleyan Methodist Chapel, Silver Street, in use. This is a substantial town chapel, Gothic and rock-faced but maintaining nonconformist symmetry. It was opened in 1876 on land obtained from the Marquis of Lansdowne and was designed by

Mungo Hart with ashlar dressings, substantial buttresses, shouldered gables and a tiled roof with ventilators. The gable facing the road has a large window of four lights with three quatrefoil lights above; there is a modern porch below, and to either side is a small transept with smaller windows to the same pattern. The sides have four bays with similar windows of two lights with alternating trefoils and quatrefoils above. A schoolroom block at right angles to the rear may post-date the chapel but not by much. Inside, a panelled rear gallery remains but the former pews, together with the raised pulpit and the organ behind it, were stripped out in modernisation work completed in 2001.[606]

Others

Free Church, Church Street,* Grade 2 listed, in use. In 1866, led by members of the Harris bacon family, 89 parishioners left the parish church in protest at the high church ministry of the new vicar. They met for a time in the town hall but this church, designed by W J Stent of Warminster, was opened in 1868. A separate block of schoolrooms behind was built concurrently, served as a British School for a period and was still in use until 1930 whereupon it became the church hall. The church at first used the Anglican liturgy but became gradually more nonconformist until eventually no liturgy was used.

The chapel is of substantial size in squared rock-faced stone with ashlar dressings and angled buttresses under a tiled roof. Early Gothic in style, with a flat-topped tower to one side, it has a clerestory of paired mullioned windows and a semi-circular apse to the rear. The front gable is dominated by a large window with four lights below and intricate circular tracery above. The interior is modest and equally Anglican in appearance, even down to the central aisle and the pulpit placed to one side at the crossing. The apse, however, is remarkable, with its five tall stained glass windows carrying geometrical designs and between them panels of glazed tiles painted with mottos on scrolls around olive branches in William Morris style. Nikolaus Pevsner may have thought this building 'terrible' but we would perhaps be more generous in our assessment today.[607]
Photograph on page 40.

Plymouth Brethren met in Calne from c1848 and may have been meeting in Wood Street from 1849; Brethren were certainly meeting there from the late 19th century. From c1899 **Exclusive Brethren** met in a new building called *Stanley Home* down an alleyway west of **North Street** just north of the Oxford Road junction, and from at least the 1950s, and probably from the 1930s, this building was used only by them. They continued to meet there until the 1970s and perhaps as late as 1989, after which it was converted into a private house. The meeting house, No.15, is of brick under tile, the gable facing the road originally having two tall windows and the east side two door openings and two tall windows beyond, but all now very much altered.[608]

The *Oxford Hall on Oxford Road*, now called the Calne Evangelical Church and in use, was built in the early 1930s and later rebuilt; **Open Brethren** had been active in the town from 1919 and met in this hall from c1933. It is a low building in stone blockwork under tile. Brick pillars separate the four bays of its sides.[609]

Plymouth Brethren Meeting Room, No.199 Quemerford, now a house. This was built in 1860 and in use until c1963 when it may have been closed as part of a general centralisation of Brethren premises at that time; it was converted to a private house in the 1970s. The front is rendered with modern windows and gives no clue to its past but the tiled roof is hipped and a visible section of the side towards the rear is of brick with neat ashlar quoins.[610]

Corsham

Though not now thought of as a substantial town, Corsham and the hinterland within its parish had a population large enough in the eighteenth and nineteenth centuries to sustain a considerable number of chapels. Amongst their number is the incomparable Monks chapel.

Quakers, Independents and Congregationalists

Monks Lane Chapel,** Monks Lane, ST876686, Grade 1 listed, in use. A near-perfect example of a late 17th century interior in a small country chapel, without pretension and with a complete focus on the preacher. It was built by the Quakers in 1662 and sold by them to Independents in 1690 shortly after the Act of Toleration. The chapel became Congregational and now continues as United Reformed.

The interior fittings date mainly from 1690 or shortly afterwards and consist of densely packed box pews below and a three-sided gallery above with access stairs either side, centred on a tall pulpit in the centre of the wall opposite the door; all have fielded panels. The pulpit is illuminated by a small window above and other rectangular mullioned windows of modest size illuminate the lower level; the upper window was allegedly placed there so that the minister could see any 'trouble' approaching and make good his escape if necessary.

The box pews are solid and well built; the gallery provides much more crudely finished seating and some of the hat pegs up here, which are of turned wood elsewhere, are simply nails hammered into the wall. There are texts above the pulpit and above the eyebrow window, and two long cast-iron bars with hooked ends are joined to thinner bars fixed to the rafters to support the roof structure, later additions but of considerable age. There was once a fireplace at the north end of the west wall, the stump of its chimney still visible outside: this was replaced by a stove in the centre of the floor in front of the pulpit, its flue running horizontally to the west wall, but this in turn is now gone.

The exterior is of rubble-stone with ashlar dressings under a roof of graduated stone slates. To the front, a long drip-mould covers the door and windows either side. Above the door a sundial in a Classical frame with a broken pediment provides an unusual degree of ornamentation and above that is the chapel exterior's most conspicuous feature, an eyebrow window of five leaded lights with the roof curved up above it and at its head the inscription ' Keep thy foot when thou goest to the house of thy God Ec 5. 1'. This harmonious addition, which helps to illuminate the preacher, is believed to be late Georgian in date although there could have been a smaller window here before this. Other sides of the chapel are plain, though

Monks Chapel, Corsham. Amongst many details note the tall back to the pulpit, the biblical text above, and substantial bars holding the roof together

Monks Chapel, Corsham, the intimate ground floor interior with panelled box pews, raised pulpit and timber supports for the galleries

the rear also has a long moulding above three windows, the central one of which, behind the pulpit, is half blocked in.[611]

Photograph also on page 21.

Quakers had a strong presence in Corsham and Pickwick in the late 17th and early 18th centuries. They built a meeting house in the town early on, perhaps immediately after selling the Monks Lane chapel to the Congregationalists in 1690, and this was located near the Horsefair and what is now the cricket club. Their burial ground at Pickwick may pre-date this and may have been bought as early as 1659. Pickwick became the centre of their activities locally but it is not certain when they built their meeting house here: it may have been in 1709 or might not have been until 1774 when a new meeting house was erected in exchange for that in the town. The Pickwick burial ground and meeting house were located immediately west of the entrance to what is now Woodlands, on the site of the later house, 21 Pickwick. The meeting house closed in 1815, became a working men's club and reading room, was in a poor state of repair by 1885 and was probably demolished soon after that and replaced by the present house.[612]

*Congregational Chapel, Pickwick Road,** Grade 2 listed, now a cafe. Under the stimulus of the Wesleyan revival, Congregationalists met for some years in a malthouse in the town centre before building this chapel. The main building is of 1793, ashlar on the east entrance front, elsewhere of rubble-stone with ashlar dressings under a hipped roof of stone tiles. The entrance front has two round-arched doorways with curved hoods on brackets and above them circular windows for the gallery; there is a tall round-arched window

Corsham Pickwick Road Congregational

between them. To the sides are three bays of similar windows and to the rear the single-storey schoolrooms of 1902, at which time the west end of the chapel was also altered, the architect being William Harris Bromley. The schoolrooms are at right angles to the chapel, of stone block with mullioned windows under slate. The chapel closed in 1971 and by 1984 the congregation had merged with the Methodists to form the new church of St Aldhelm's (see below). The building was converted into offices in 1971 but was later turned into a restaurant by CMS Ltd of Corsham. The restaurant, accessed via the schoolrooms, retains the gallery of 1824 with its extended forwards central section.[613]

An **Independent**, later **Congregational, chapel** was built c1848 east of Velley and west of the road at ST888683. This was small, of stone block with a rectangular window above the door in the gable end but otherwise almost windowless. It may have been a conversion of an earlier building, was probably redundant before the Second World War and was ruinous when it was demolished c1960. A modern house, Chapel House, now stands on the site.[614]

Baptists

Ebenezer Baptist Chapel, Priory Street, * Grade 2 listed, in use. A handsome chapel, distinguished by pointed-arch windows with intersecting Y-tracery glazing bars. The front is of ashlar with three windows above and the porch of 1922 below

Ebenezer Baptist, Priory Street, Corsham

with a window either side; there is a date-stone for 1828 above the porch. The sides are in rubble-stone with ashlar dressings and two tiers of three similar windows. There are two taller windows to the rear and the hipped roof is of slate. Attached to the south is the Jubilee Memorial Hall, dated 1873, in similar style but of one storey, and left of that is a further small modern extension. The interior has been modernised and the previous panelled and bow-fronted gallery on columns, dating from 1838, has been replaced by an unsupported one with glass-panelled front. The congregation was formed in 1823 by members having doctrinal differences with the Congregational chapel and this chapel was built in 1828 after a converted cottage in Bence's Lane proved too small. The vestry was added in 1867.[615] *Photograph also on page 38.*

Ebenezer General Baptist Chapel, Velley, east of B3353 at ST884684, now a house. Gothic, of coursed rubble-stone with ashlar dressings under a graduated stone tile roof, the gable facing the road has a porch dated 1907 and a scroll above dated 1857. Either side of this are tall lancets neatly split into two tiers at the time of conversion to a house, to disguise the addition of a first floor: a good example of taking the trouble to get it right. There is a circular window to the gable head, perhaps previously a ventilator, and the sides have similarly split windows in two bays; there is a lean-to extension to the rear. A group of Baptists was meeting here from before 1850 and built this chapel in 1857. The porch was added in 1907 and it was converted on closure c1990.[616]

Zion Particular Baptist Chapel, Pound Pill, west of B3353 just north of railway line, now a house. Built in 1859 by a group which seceded from the Priory Street Ebenezer Chapel over doctrinal matters, this is small and unornamented with rectangular sash windows. The gable facing the road is of crude ashlar with windows either side of a door in a later open porch, and there is a plaque dated 1860 above. The sides are of rubble-stone with ashlar dressings and two windows, the rear one on each side blocked since conversion, and the roof is of slate. It closed in 1977.[617]

Ebenezer Particular Baptist Chapel, Moor Green, south of road at ST856687, now a house. A chapel of strange appearance, with single-storey outbuildings tacked onto the front of what was presumably a conventional ashlar gable end. The porch of classical appearance protrudes a long way but could well be original, and contains in the fanlight circular patterning in sympathy with that in the sun and planets window above. There is a plaque dated 1860 at the gable head and there were presumably originally more windows either side of the door, now hidden; a modern window has been inserted above left. The west side, of rubble-stone, has two tall two-light round-arched windows; the east side is now linked by a glass corridor to the adjacent building. The Sunday school to the rear, with a separate door, was added before 1884 and was renovated in 1905. The outbuildings at the front, likewise, might not postdate the chapel by long. The original chapel, probably on this site, was built in 1833 and replaced by this in 1860. It closed and was converted sometime after the 1950s.[618]

Methodists

Wesleyan Methodist Chapel, now St Aldhelm's, Pickwick Road, in use. Behind is the first chapel, of 1878, built to the rear of the plot with the intention that a larger chapel would be built in front to replace it, at which time the original would become the Sunday school. It was designed by William Harris Bromley of Corsham and is conspicuously plain, as if they were saving their money for the larger chapel. The construction is of stone block; the west end has a stepped tripartite lancet but all the other windows are rectangular. The second chapel, also designed by Bromley, duly followed and opened in 1904. It is in Decorated Gothic style but symmetrically planned so that the side facing the road has five bays, the central one of double height with a six light window under a small gable, and above at the roofline a small fleche spire. The entrance gable, at right angles to the road, has a substantial four-light window, and below that is a flat-roofed porch. The roof is of tile and the interior is now plain and modernised, with no galleries though it does have an arched opening for the pulpit. Extensions for further service rooms were added in 1963 and 1972.[619]

Primitive Methodist Chapel, Station Road, at the junction of Hastings Road, in use as the Gospel Hall. A neat small chapel in ashlar under slate with round-arched windows. The gable facing the road has a door, now blocked, and tall windows either side; a plaque at the gable head is now blank. The sides have two similar windows each and the lean-to rear extension in stone block now contains the entrance. Primitive Methodists had been meeting in a house in High Street but opened this chapel in 1855. It was described then as being 33ft long by 22ft wide and 15ft high, with a floor of red deal, six windows and lighted by gas. The 'iron palisading' mentioned at that time remains. It was sold to the **Brethren** in 1926 to become a Gospel Hall.[620]

Brethren

Plymouth Brethren Gospel Hall, Corshamside, south of Chapel Lane, Neston, now a house. Corshamside was the centre of local activity by the Brethren from c1832 and this hall was given in 1856 by Mr Edridge of Pockeridge House for use as a Gospel Hall and associated graveyard. It was enlarged in 1903 to accommodate a growing Sunday school and by that time many people from Corsham were attending, a development which led to them taking over the former Primitive Methodist chapel in Corsham in 1926 (see above). The hall, of coursed rubble-stone under tile, is very plain with the gable facing the road having only a Gothic-arched doorway with 'Gospel Hall' incised above and a circular ventilator at the gable head. The sides have tall mullioned and transomed windows, four to the east and three to the west where a small wing, probably the former Sunday school, is attached at right angles. The hall became redundant in 2011 and was converted to a house, with an inserted floor, after 2015.[621]

Cricklade

The town's small size – it did not exceed 2,000 population until the second half of the 20th century - left it with one chapel each for the four main denominations, of which one is still in use.

Congregational Chapel, Calcutt Street, in use. Independents met in Cricklade from 1772 and constructed a chapel in 1799. This stands at right angles behind its 1878 replacement, built to provide more capacity; the original then became the church hall. The 1878 chapel, designed by Orlando Baker of Swindon, is in Early English style in rock-faced stone under slate. The gable facing the road has two stepped three-light lancets vertically above each other and entrance towers either side, that to the west larger and with a pitched roof, that to the east containing the doorway and apparently intended to carry a spire. The sides are of four bays, behind which is the original chapel, much altered in 1894 by William Henry Drew, of rubble-stone under slate but now with segmental-headed paired windows either end with brick surrounds. Beyond that is a further more modern extension. The chapel interior is modernised but retains a narrow gallery at the street end.[622]

Particular Baptist Rehoboth Chapel, Calcutt Street, now Cricklade Museum. Small and plain in coursed rubble-stone under slate, there is a round-arched window on the gable front above an ashlar porch with a similarly shaped double door; also a small brick side extension for the vestry towards the rear. The chapel was built in 1852, replacing an 18th century predecessor also in Calcutt Street; the vestry was added two years later. It closed in 1937 and was then used as a Women's Voluntary Service canteen until 1955 when it was taken over as a church by Roman Catholics until 1984. It was converted to the town's museum in 1986.[623]

Wesleyan Methodist Chapel, north of town bridge, now a public hall. The Wesleyans were late arriving in Cricklade, for once following the Primitive Methodists. They were meeting here in the mid 19th century but did not build this chapel until 1870. It is Gothic, of coursed rock-faced stone with ashlar dressings under a slate roof. The gable faces the road with a porch of c1902, windows either side and a date plaque above. There are two bays to the sides, a small lean-to extension to the rear and another extension, of 1955 by Cripps and Stewart of Oxford, to the rear south side. It closed and became a Sunday school after union with Primitive Methodists in 1938 and was a schoolroom from 1945. It is now known as Thames Hall.[624]

Primitive Methodist Chapel, Calcutt Street, Grade 2 listed, disused in 2020. Primitive Methodists were active in the town from 1824 as part of the Brinkworth circuit. They are believed to have met in Calcutt Street in 1832 and may have rented the building, still standing off Gas Lane, which later became the British School. The meeting almost collapsed at various times in these early days but other premises at that time are said to have included both the Independent chapel and a chapel built for the Wesleyans 'but not used for them': the identity of the latter is a mystery and, if the assertion is correct, it seems that the Wesleyans were here earlier than previously thought. Two cottages were torn down in 1855 to make way for this, the Pethahiah chapel, and their materials were apparently used in the new building. A schoolroom and vestry were added in 1893. The two sets of Methodists combined in this chapel in 1938 but it closed in 1969 after which Methodists shared the Congregational chapel. It was sold c1977 and became a doctors' surgery from 1980 to 2000 and later offices. Set back from the road, it is of brick with ashlar dressings, a shouldered gable and a slate roof. The protruding porch is later and has tall round-arched windows flanking it; above is the inscription, 'PRIMITIVE METHODIST. PETHAHIAH. AD 1855'. There are two similar windows to the rear with a small lean-to extension to the east side and the single-storey schoolroom attached at right angles behind.[625]

Devizes

Nonconformists were active in Devizes from an early date. In 1661 the bishop of Salisbury found the people 'not good'; from 1662 ejected ministers began to settle here and in 1670 the borough had the reputation as being one of the two most notable places in the diocese for 'great and outrageous' meetings. By the end of that century several leading Devizes families were dissenters, a prelude to the rapid growth of nonconformist worship in the town.[626]

Quakers, Presbyterians and Congregationalists

Quakers had a significant presence from the 1660s, acquiring a burial ground in Hillworth Park in 1665 and registering a meeting house there in 1690. The location out of town was inconvenient and they built the replacement **Quaker Meeting House**, now **23 High Street**, in 1702. This continued in use until 1826 and was sold in 1840. The Quakers revived in the 1850s, the meeting house was repurchased and remained in use until 1879 after which the building was again sold in 1884. They reoccupied it finally between 1903 and 1907 but from 1929 it was taken over by the **Exclusive Brethren** who used it until c1970. In 1981 it was converted into a house. An ashlar screen wall now faces the street, with doors either end and pilasters separating these from two rectangular four-light windows. There is a parapet above and the building proper is set back behind what was a forecourt but is now further rooms. The meeting house has a central door with a small window above set between two tall windows with flat-arched brick heads; the west wall is gabled and has an extension built against it which means it is no longer possible to access the building from St John's Alley as was the case in earlier days. The roof is tiled, hipped at the front with an inserted dormer.[627]

There was a revival of Quaker belief in the town from c1975 and the new **Quaker Meeting House**, on **Sussex Wharf** by the canal, was built in 1994 to designs by William Barnes of Letchworth. It is a single-storey building of brick under slate; the meeting room is semi-octagonal with substantial glue-laminated rafters reaching down to ground level like crucks. A pre-existing house of the 1960s is linked to it.[628]

Presbyterians built a chapel in 1734 behind houses at the south end of **Long Street**. This fell into decay and they moved to a site on the east side of **High Street**. In 1791 they opened a new chapel in **Sheep Street**, located next to where the New Baptist chapel now stands and accessed via the passage of a house in the street. In 1820 they joined with seceders from the Old Baptist and in 1852 the New Baptist (see below) was opened. The Presbyterian chapel was demolished in 1858.[629]

*Congregational, 'St Mary's', Chapel, Northgate Street,** almost opposite Wadworth's brewery, Grade 2 listed, now split into flats. All that is easily visible is the street gable of the lecture hall and schoolroom added in 1868-9 in Early English style to designs by Benoni Mullings. This is a striking facade in ashlar with a pair of doors, a large four-light window above and lancets either side at two levels, with buttressed pillars at the corners. The sides are in brick with two-light windows under slate, and behind, unfortunately very hard to see, is the real treat, the original chapel of

Devizes Northgate Street Congregational, the 1868-9 lecture hall and schoolroom facing the street

1776. This is of brick with ashlar dressings and Y-tracery windows under a multi-part hipped slate roof. On the east side, the most easily visible, are four windows above, separated by a string course from three windows and two doors below, the bottom level now altered with the windows reduced in height. Inside there were galleries on two sides, the third gapped for an organ, and a raised pulpit opposite. The chapel has a complicated history: built for Calvinistic Methodists, it became Congregational by the late 18th century. It was originally oblong and entered from the east; in 1790 it was extended eastwards and made square; schoolrooms and an assembly room were added to the south, probably in 1810-11, and the extension northwards was added in 1868-9, the entrance then moving to that side. Even before that extension it was attracting congregations of 500. Other alterations were made at different dates, including in 1876 by J A Randell. The chapel closed in 1984 and was converted to a house and six flats, the congregation joining that of the Long Street Methodists.[630]
Photograph also on page 29.

Baptists

*Old Baptist Chapel, Particular Baptist,** south end of Maryport Street, in use. Baptists had been active in the town from as early as the 1640s and by the 1670s were meeting in a building behind **22 The Brittox**, accessed via an alleyway which has now been built over. This apparently attracted congregations of 300 in the 1720s and was not replaced until the present Old Baptist was built in 1780. The Brittox chapel, which had mullioned windows and a mansard roof, was sold in 1834 and demolished c1970; the site is now part of a car park.

The successor chapel had an east gallery added in 1785 and in 1818 a vestry, schoolroom and side galleries were built. In 1860-1 the windows were altered and

Devizes Old Baptist, Maryport Street

two porches added at the east end. In 1895 the congregation of the Salem chapel (see below), who had split off in 1837, rejoined and the schoolrooms were enlarged for the extra children. In 1922 an apse was added – at only two bays deep the chapel was short for its width - and the side galleries were removed.

The interior is plain, with round-arched windows, those on the left obscured by the two-storey schoolrooms which were built alongside and stretch the length of the chapel; a vestry to the right rear extends alongside the apse. In recent times the rear gallery has been walled in to create a further meeting room. All is of brick, under a hipped slate roof, but the Classical stuccoed front with its segmental-arched windows and later ashlar porch is handsome: it takes a second look to notice that it is not symmetrical, being extended one bay at the left hand side to cover the front of the schoolrooms.[631]

Photograph also on page 53.

Another **Baptist** chapel is said to have been opened in **High Street** before 1815 and lasted until at least 1851. There appears to be no further evidence of it.[632]

Salem Particular Baptist Chapel, New Park Street, * Grade 2 listed, in use by Rock Community Church. George Wessley was appointed pastor of the Old Baptist in 1836 but left in 1837 because of divisions in the congregation and founded this chapel in 1838. In 1895 the congregation rejoined the Old Baptist and this building was then used by **Open Brethren**, and bought by them in 1929; it was last listed as in use by them in 1995. It has a domestic feel, in brick with rectangular windows, all originally sashed, under a hipped slate roof; the front has three windows above and two below flanking a broad doorway with elliptical arch. There are small single-storey extensions to the side and rear.[633]

Photograph on page 22.

Devizes New Baptist, Sheep Street

New Baptist Chapel, General Baptist, Sheep Street, * Grade 2 listed, in use. Built in 1852 by a group of Presbyterians (see above) who many years before had joined Baptists who had seceded from the Old Baptist. This building replaced the Presbyterian chapel next door which was demolished in 1858. It is a large town chapel, designed by Thomas Hardick of Warminster with accommodation for 700, in tall spiky Gothic with an Italianate feel. The ashlar street gable has tall lancets either side of a projecting central bay delineated by buttresses and pinnacles; a stepped triple lancet stands above a similarly stepped doorway with windows either side. The rubble-stone sides are of five bays with tall lancets and more buttresses and to the rear there was originally a single schoolroom, with rectangular windows with hood-moulds to the side and a triple pointed-arch window to the rear; a second storey was added to this in 1894, containing 10 small schoolrooms.

The interior has galleries to all four sides; the fourth originally contained the organ above the pulpit but this, along with the pulpit itself and the pews, was stripped out in modernisation in 1989. The galleries are accessed by twin staircases and are held on slender cast iron columns; their fronts have a pattern of blind arcading, probably originally in stained wood but now painted. There is original patterned stencilling at the wall heads, and the roof structure, with queen trusses and harmoniously curved braces, is appealing.[634]

Methodists

Wesleyan Methodists built a chapel in **New Park Street** in 1818-9, set back north of the street alongside where the police station now is. It lasted until 1898 when it was replaced by the Long Street chapel (see below) and was then taken over by the **Salvation Army**. It was derelict by 1971 and soon afterwards demolished.[635]

Wesleyan Methodist Chapel, now St Andrew's, Long Street, in use. Opened in 1898 to replace that on New Park Street, it is Gothic, in brick with some ashlar dressings under tile, to designs by Isitt, Adkin and Hill of Bradford, Yorkshire and with stained glass by John Hall and Sons. The broad gable facing the street has a very large five-light window above what was originally a further five-light window but which was converted in 2003 to glass entrance doors. The original entrance doors to the right are contained within a small buttressed semi-hexagonal tower and a similar opening to the left may also have contained doors. The schoolrooms are to the rear, at right angles to the chapel and probably contemporary. The interior, with a chancel-like recess perhaps originally for an organ, has an attractive double-curved ceiling; it has been modernised but retains a panelled rear gallery. The church joined with the North Street Congregational in 1984 to become St Andrew's United Reformed.[636]

Primitive Methodists had no significant presence in the town. A building on **The Green** was certified for Primitive Methodist worship in 1853 but had probably closed by 1882 at the latest and may not have been a purpose built chapel.[637]

Brethren

Exclusive Brethren certified a room in **Couch Lane** in 1873 and were there until they took over the former Quaker meeting house in High Street in 1929 (see above). The two-storey brick building is still there, on the west side with a bricked-in arch for wagon access towards the north end.[638]

Open Brethren used the **Salem Baptist** chapel as noted above.

Salvation Army

The **Salvation Army** met from 1881 in various premises before taking over the former Methodist chapel in New Park Street in 1900. They left here in 1967 and moved in 1971 to the former Civil Defence headquarters in Station Road: this was later closed and demolished.[639]

Highworth

Highworth was a market town comparable in size to many others in the county at the start of the 19th century but it failed to grow from there, perhaps because of its proximity to rapidly developing Swindon. Indeed its population at the end of the century was smaller than that at its start and it was not until the second half of the 20th century that it started to grow significantly. This small size restricted the number of chapels built, though the main denominations were all represented.

Zion Congregational Chapel, High Street, * Grade 2 listed, in use. A house on this site was fitted out as a chapel and registered for Independent worship in 1788 but seems not to have thrived and it was only after a missionary campaign that the present chapel was built in 1825, designed by Thomas Angell of Highworth. It was enlarged in 1848 to give a capacity of over 400 and the following year a British School, still there, was built on Brewery Street with a cemetery behind. The chapel is set back from the street with an entrance which retains its original iron overthrow. The front is of ashlar in two storeys with five round-

Highworth Zion Congregational, the front Classical but uncomfortably proportioned

arched sash windows and a central pilastered doorway; the gable is pedimented with a plaque dated 1825 and two blank plaques below. Above was a small bellcote which remained in place until at least 1924. The gallery is reached by twin stairs and was originally U-shaped but replaced by a single rear gallery in 1888; the gallery front with scrolled metalwork has been retained but the gallery itself is now partitioned off to form a room. The interior is otherwise modernised but retains the 1888 pulpit, behind which to each side are windows from 1925 with stained glass figures.[640]

Photograph also on page 53.

Particular Baptist Chapel, The Elms, next to recreation centre, now split into three houses, that to the east modern. Very much altered, the side facing the road now has two tall arched windows with obtrusive glazing, set in a rubble-stone wall under a slate roof. Previously there were two smaller arched windows high up, one with a later door inserted beneath. At the lower level are four unexplained bricked-up arches, springing from ground level either side of each window. The original door was in the east gable wall where the new extension is now attached and the Sunday school was probably in the lean-to section to the rear which has since been demolished. The chapel was opened in 1862 and went out of use in 1933. It then became a club and, perhaps in the 1990s, was converted finally to housing, with the extension to the east.[641]

Wesleyan Methodist Chapel, east of A361 by junction with Westrop Road, now premises of the Highworth Silver Band. Mr Bush of Lambourn, famous for spending most of his income over many years to build Wesleyan chapels through the Vale of the White Horse in both Berkshire and Wiltshire, funded this chapel in 1842. It was in use until sold in 1963, the Wesleyans combining with the Primitive Methodists in the new church in 1964. The gable facing the road is in coursed squared rubble-stone with brick dressings to two pointed-arch windows and has a modern replacement porch; a plaque is dated 1842. There are brick quoins, blank rubble-stone sides and a slate roof. The inside, seating 140 with no gallery, is now stripped out.[642]

Primitive Methodist Chapel, The Elms, now a house. It has a gable facing the road; the front and the west side are now rendered, the remainder in rubble with brick dressings, and the roof is of slate. To the front are Y-tracery pointed-arch windows above and either side of a door with a modern open porch. A plaque above states 'Primitive Methodist Chapel' with an illegible date. There are small flat-roofed extensions each side and it is connected to another building at the rear which could have been the manse or Sunday school. The windows have stained glass with an early 20th century feel so presumably inserted well before conversion. The original chapel of 1838, on this site, became too small and was replaced by this one in 1851, a larger building with a gallery. It closed and the congregation joined with the Wesleyans in the new chapel in 1964.[643]

New Methodist Church, east of main road just north of parish church, in use. This was built in 1964, at which time the former Primitive and Wesleyan Methodists moved here from their existing chapels; it was much extended in 1992. It is a sprawling building, in brick under tile with windows angled up to two low gables and a partial cladding of random cut stone.[644]

Malmesbury

Malmesbury is notable as a centre for the Moravians from the 1740s and for the late and short-lived presence of Wesleyan Methodists. The town was and remained small but it was also the centre for a surrounding rural area, hence increasing the strength of nonconformity there.

Ebenezer Chapel, Independent, Silver Street, now a masonic lodge. Independents first converted two cottages for use as the Ebenezer chapel before 1800, perhaps in 1797. In 1812 they united with the Westport Congregational and sold the chapel, which was then used intermittently by Primitive Methodists. A new meeting house was opened in Silver Street in 1836, initially as a branch of the Westport church but from 1841 separate. It was enlarged in 1848 and new seating for 300 was provided in 1885; at the same time an adjacent cottage was acquired to provide two classrooms. After an initial proposal to reunite with the Westport church in 1914 they eventually joined them in 1952. The chapel became a hall for a while but was then taken over by the Masons from 1973: they extended it to the rear at a slight angle. The rendered gable facing the road, perhaps over stone, has two large round-arched windows with prominent keystones either side of and above a similarly shaped door. The lower level is semi-rusticated, there are raised quoins, and at the gable head is a lunette-shaped ventilator. Below that is first a plaque 'Ebenezer Chapel Enlarged 1848' and then a masonic symbol carrying the date 1902, the date of foundation of the lodge.[645]

Westport Congregational Chapel, between West Street and St Mary's Street, in use. A big town church with an Italianate feel, by W J Stent of Warminster and largely funded by Charles Jupe of Mere. The east gable facing St Mary's Street has a large rose window in a recessed arch, with below that five narrow windows in a three and two singles; the rubble-stone is strangely inset with random ashlar blocks. The doors are at the bottom corners, that to the left below a low side extension and that to the right below a tower with an octagonal spire containing a bell cote. The sides are of four bays with paired round-arched windows and to the west, at right angles, is the substantial Sunday school block. A first Presbyterian chapel was built near this site but rebuilt in the Horsefair in 1788. That church probably became Congregational from 1811 and this chapel was built as replacement in 1867.[646]

Malmesbury Westport Congregational

Abbey Row Particular Baptist Chapel, set back north of Abbey Row, Grade 2 listed, in use as The King's Church. The first Particular Baptist chapel was built near here shortly before 1695 and replaced by this building in 1802, after which it was used as a stable for a time before being demolished. The chapel has an austere exterior of coursed rubble-stone with ashlar dressings, the gable facing the road having pointed-arch windows either side of a porch with Tuscan columns, with a plaque overhead no longer legible but which used to say 'Abbey Road Baptist Chapel 1802, Restored 1910'. The sides are blank save for two small windows at gallery level but the north end, which was extended in 1816, has two windows similar to those at the south. Inside there are three galleries on wooden columns, added in 1814 and giving a total capacity of 400. The chapel was refurbished in 1910 at which time the Sunday school to the rear was built, and continued in use until the mid 1980s. It was bought by The King's Church in 1997.[647]

Moravian Chapel, Oxford Street,* Grade 2 listed, now the Julia and Hans Rausing Building of Athelstan Museum. Moravians were active in the town from the 1740s, initially under the influence of East Tytherton (Bremhill), and a malting house on this site was fitted up as a meeting house and remained in use until it was replaced by this chapel in 1770; the manse attached to the south was obtained at the same date. The panelled gallery, now with a curved dip at the centre, was added in 1787 and the building partly rebuilt and enlarged to the west in 1859. Under a slate roof, the long rendered east front to the street has three round-arched windows with late 19th century stained glass, the north one shorter and with a door underneath with an 18th century moulded canopy. The north wall, of rubble-stone, used to have a building against it. The west wall has two windows similar to those on the east and a long staircase wing in brick at the north end. On this side is a courtyard containing the burial ground, entrance gates and, at the west end, the schoolroom of 1860, sold in 2019 for conversion to a house. The interior has been stripped for its new use but retains the gallery. The Moravians left the chapel in 1997 and met in the old school room until the meeting closed in 2008. The Athelstan museum bought the chapel in 2017 after it had stood empty for nearly two decades.[648]

Moravian Chapel, Malmesbury

Wesleyan Methodist Chapel, Oxford Street, now part of the town hall. Wesleyans had a short-lived presence in the town and this chapel, which might easily be confused with the town hall of which it is now a part, was not built until 1886, to designs by Robert Curwen of London. It was closed by 1919, converted to a YMCA in 1920 and in 1970 incorporated into the town hall. The whole is in shaped rubble-stone with ashlar dressings under slate. The west entrance front facing Market Lane has a pointed-arch doorway and, above, a large four-light Gothic window with tracery; either side are flat-headed four-light windows in two tiers. The east end is blank but the long side onto Oxford Street has two tiers of six-light flat-headed windows, probably originally four at each level but the west one at the ground level now replaced by doors. The chapel was built at first floor level over the schoolroom and two classrooms; it was of substantial size and is now stripped out as a meeting room with hammer beams and panelled ceiling retained.[649]

Primitive Methodist Chapel, Bristol Street, now a house. Primitive Methodists were very early to break away from the main group of Methodists locally, in 1812, well before the formation of the Brinkworth circuit. They met in various places including the Ebenezer Chapel in Silver Street before building their own chapel here in 1856. By 1899 it was too small and was replaced by the new chapel in the Triangle. The Bristol Street chapel was used as a warehouse between 1932 and 1968, then as living accommodation before full conversion to a house in 1998. Originally of brick with stone dressings, the front and back are now rendered and various windows altered or blocked. The front gable was originally of conventional form with tall round-arched windows either side of a central door and a gable plaque, 'Primitive Methodist Chapel Erected 1856' above. On conversion to a warehouse a large central opening was made with a canopy of corrugated iron. Final conversion to a house might have involved just reinstating the smaller doorway but instead a garage door in a crude surround replaces the warehouse entrance and new doorways, narrower than the windows above, have been inserted at either side, the existing windows being truncated to this end; the gable plaque has been retained and a small circular window inserted above the garage door. The symmetry has been respected but what was once an attractive facade has been despoiled.[650]

Primitive Methodist Chapel, The Triangle, now a house. This was built in 1899 to replace the Bristol Street chapel, in shaped rough stone with ashlar dressings. The gable facing the road has a broad window of five lights with tracery above, all under a segmental arch and typical of this period. There are pointed-arch windows either side and below is a porch, perhaps later, in ashlar with an oval-headed doorway and small pointed-arch windows either side, now blocked in. The porch is aligned to follow the kerb line so is at an angle to the building. '1899' is inscribed on the main window keystone and 'Primitive Methodist Church' above. There are three bays to the sides and a schoolroom behind. The Primitive Methodists were joined by the Wesleyans in 1932 as a unified Methodist church but the chapel closed some time after 1989 and was subsequently converted.[651]

Marlborough

In 1676 there were 250 dissenters in Marlborough, more than in any other Wiltshire town, and in 1681 its inhabitants were considered a 'seditious, schismatical people'. Despite this early strength, the nonconformist presence here in later times was relatively modest.[652]

Quakers initially met in premises at **Manton Corner** in Preshute parish, established some time after the burial ground there was created in 1658, but in 1721 they bought land north of the **High Street**, behind No. 113, and built a meeting house there which was registered in 1727. This was repaired in 1759 and 1772 but the meeting declined by the 1790s and had dissolved by 1800. In 1816 it was in use as a British School and was sold in 1831 but not demolished until 1935. Friends started meeting again in the town from 1962 and in 1985 bought the former hall of the **Congregational** chapel on *The Marsh* (see below). It was altered to designs by John Bangma and opened in 1986 with the meeting room upstairs and a classroom below.[653]

*Congregational Chapel, The Marsh,** west of The Parade, Grade 2 listed, opened as a cinema in 2021. Presbyterians and Independents had their own chapel in **Back Lane** from 1706 but also met in **Herd Street**. Later in the century they were reorganised on Congregational principles, apparently with support from Lady Huntingdon, but in 1802 were left without a home when the Back Lane chapel was forcibly closed by its owner. This state of affairs continued until the present handsome building, with capacity for nearly 400, opened in 1817 at a cost of £1800 including the land. The adjacent manse, which had been rented, was given

to the chapel in 1863. In 1867 a schoolroom and lecture room were added as a separate building, the latter now used by the Quakers, and an additional lecture room was added in 1895. In 1873 major internal alterations included new pews, a new platform and reading desk in place of the 'old-fashioned' high pulpit, and the installation of gas lighting. The chapel closed in 1984 and the congregation moved to the Methodist church. After a long period standing empty it was converted to a cinema in 2021, with the manse opened out into the chapel.

Marlborough Congregational, renovated and about to reopen as a cinema in 2021

The building is of brick with a hipped tiled roof, the front elevation with three round-arched sash windows to the first floor and two below flanking a substantial stone Doric porch with pilasters and columns. A small brick pediment above carries the dates 1817 and 1873, the latter being that at which the porch was added. The interior, which has a rear gallery, was refitted also at that date.

The schoolroom to the side, dated 1867, is in brick and much altered, with the 1895 lecture room a two-storey brick building attached at right angles to the rear and also dated. The manse, joined with its back to the side of the chapel, has the appearance of a double-fronted suburban villa.[654]

Particular Baptists built the **Zoar Chapel** on the north side of St. Martin's, behind No. 9, in 1876, though there may have been Baptist activity here from as early as 1814. It closed in 1921 and has since been demolished.[655]

Marlborough New Road Wesleyan, the 1811 chapel to the left

Wesleyan Methodist Chapel, (Christchurch) Oxford Street/New Road, Grade 2 listed (the 1811 chapel), in use. The 1811 chapel, in brick, had its entrance to Oxford Street with a central door and tall round-arched windows either side below a pedimented gable. The doorway looks to have been altered and there is a circular panel above it which may be a later insertion: the windows are now blocked, masonic symbols added to the centre of the panel and 'Masonic Hall' added in a plaque at the gable head. This was extended in 1872, a polygonal rear bay being added to the south end.

In 1910 a new chapel was built alongside, with the entrance at the New Road end. This was designed by Gordon and Gunton of London and is a much larger affair, also in brick under slate, with a combination porch and window at the south gable end with ashlar tracery in a free Gothic style within an ogee arch. At the east end of this gable is a stair tower with belvedere top; the chapel sides are of four bays with two-light windows and tracery playing another variation on the Gothic. The inside is now modernised but retains a rear gallery and a hammer-beam roof. Behind the chapel and of the same date is the schoolroom, now the Wesley Hall and linked to it with a new porch. The congregation united here with that from the United Reformed Church in 1984 and it was re-designated Christchurch. The Masons took over the old chapel in 1910.[656]

Ebenezer Primitive Methodist Chapel, Herd Street, now a house, No. 34a. Unlikely as it may seem, this ordinary-looking house was once a Primitive Methodist chapel. There are some clues: the hipped slate roof indicating an older building, the fact that though the building is of brick the front behind the additions is rendered and lined to look like ashlar, and the out-of-sequence numbering which is so often a sign that a chapel in a street has been converted to a house. However, the comprehensive alterations have hidden all sign of previous windows and doors. The chapel was built in 1823 and closed between 1923 and 1925, then being used as a hall for some time before conversion to a house.[657]

A group of '**Peculiar Calvinists**' met at the **Providence** chapel in **Kingsbury Street** in the mid 19th century. The chapel is believed to have been demolished long since.[658]

Exclusive Brethren met in **Kingsbury Street** in 1851 and may be the people who registered a meeting at **High Wall, New Road** in 1866 and met there until 1906. Probably the same group registered premises in **St Margaret's** in 1931 and continued meeting there until the late 20th century.[659]

The **Salvation Army** occupied premises in **London Road** from 1887 to 1903 and then in **New Road** until 1910.[660]

Christadelphians had a hall in **New Road** in 1923 or earlier and met there until c1930.[661]

Melksham

As with many other Wiltshire towns, there was a strong nonconformist presence in Melksham from an early date, and by the early 19th century it was recorded that, of the population, 'much the largest portion are dissenters'.[662] The total number of chapels built was modest but there are several of considerable interest.

Quakers and Congregationalists

Quaker Meeting House, King Street,* west of road just south of Market Place, Grade 2 listed, now offices. Melksham was an important centre for Quaker activity. They started in Shaw c1669 but by 1690 were active in the town and in 1698 bought this site. The original meeting house was enlarged in 1704 but rebuilt in 1776/7 in 'a style befitting a substantial town meeting'. The meeting lasted much longer than most others in the county, not closing until 1950; thereafter the meeting house was used successively by the **Plymouth Brethren** and the National Spiritualist Church before conversion to offices in 2013.

The meeting house is of ashlar, nearly square, with a hipped stone slate roof. The side facing the road has two, originally three, segmental-arched sash windows below a moulded cornice and parapet which run also round the two sides,

Melksham Quaker Meeting House

each of which has two similar windows. The entrance was originally to the rear but moved to the south side when in the later 18th century a women's meeting house was built against the rear wall, in rubble-stone with ashlar dressings and two segmental-arched windows; this was later extended to the south in the same style. A small pavilion built onto existing rubble-stone walls has been added to the front.[663]

Congregational Chapel, Market Place, * Grade 2 listed, now the Rachel Fowler Centre. This was built by Independents on a site obtained in 1780. It was enlarged c1835 and a Sunday school was added in 1883 to the north side at the rear, on land given by Miss Rachel Fowler. The chapel was apparently originally hipped-roofed with stone tiles but changed to gabled ends in 1900, the stones replaced by slates; there was also a plan for a Sunday school alongside and of almost the same size as the chapel but this was not built. At this time also the three round-arched windows with Y-tracery

Melksham Market Place Congregational

Melksham Market Place Congregational, the interior substantially unaltered as the Rachel Fowler Centre

Melksham Old Broughton Road Baptist, the interior largely of 1879

were added in the ashlar front, the central one taller. Below is the Classical flat-roofed porch of 1928 by Sir George Oatley of Bristol, with pedimented door-case said to have been the original. The chapel sides are in rubble-stone, each with two tiers of windows, those at gallery level having Y-tracery and round heads. Inside there are galleries to four sides on cast iron columns, the ornate cast iron fronts with an Art Nouveau feel replacing wood-panelled fronts in 1889. The chapel, which had become Congregational by the early 20th century, closed in 1975 after the congregation united with the Methodists and from 1979 became the Rachel Fowler Centre. It has lost the pews and high pulpit but is otherwise intact inside, with the 1894 organ still installed above where the pulpit used to be.[664]

Baptists

General Baptist Chapel, Old Broughton Road, ** Grade 2 listed, in use. The schoolrooms facing the road are unassuming but behind them sits a chapel of real interest. Baptists may have met in Melksham as early as 1669 and a first chapel was built, probably immediately behind this site, in 1714-16. By later that century it was too small and this successor chapel was built in 1776-7. The gallery was added in 1795; in 1806 a vestry was built and the chapel was extended to the south, increasing its capacity to over 500. It was restored in 1879 by William Hardick of Warminster, the restoration including new galleries and pulpit. A Sunday school room had been built before 1840 but the present schoolrooms, facing the road, were added in 1909 to the designs of Walter Wadman Snailum of Trowbridge; cottages facing the road were bought and pulled down to create room for them. For a period the roles of the two buildings were reversed but now the original chapel is again used as the main worship space.

The chapel is of rubble-stone with ashlar dressings under a steeply-pitched hipped tiled roof. The original entrance is at right angles to the road and has three round-arched windows above and flat-headed windows below, either side of a pedimented door with pilasters. The sides each have two similar round-arched windows above and flat-headed ones below; a tall window to the north west was presumably blocked when the galleries were added. The round-arched windows in the south end are also blocked, apparently because low sunlight made it difficult to see the minister. Inside is a gallery on three sides with cast iron supports and an elaborate cast iron front. The pulpit, gallery pews and probably the organ are from the 1879 works but other fittings are modern.

Melksham Old Broughton Road Baptist – the schools of 1909 face the road with the 1776-7 chapel behind. Photograph courtesy of Melksham Historical Association

The schoolrooms have a central hall facing the street with lower sets of rooms either side, all gable-ended in stone blockwork and the central door with a curved hood. To the rear is a further block at right angles and of the same date, linked to the old chapel at the rear by a short narrower section.[665]

Photograph also on page 30.

Ebenezer Particular Baptist Chapel, Union Street, set back down alley north of street, Grade 2 listed, in use. There was a Particular Baptist congregation in the town by 1794, possibly comprised of people who had seceded from the Old Broughton Road chapel, and it is thought that there was a 'Zion' meeting house by 1829, perhaps in Watson's Court off High Street. This chapel was built in 1835 and the schoolroom to the rear added in 1853. It is small, simple and modest with no town-church pretensions, of coursed squared rubble-stone with ashlar dressings under a slate roof of low pitch. The gable facing the street has flat-headed windows, one above and others either side of a door set in a stone porch with pilasters and a cornice; there is a worn date plaque for 1835 at the gable head and a modern plaque below marks its restoration in 1990. The sides each have one window and the Sunday school is at a lower level behind. An external baptistery in the grounds behind was in use until well into the 20th century and an internal one was finally added in 1994. There is believed to have been a rear gallery at one time.[666]

A **General Baptist Chapel** was built in 1840 at what is now the junction of **Snarlton Lane and the A3102, Forest**. It was closed in 1905, sold in 1906, was still in place until well into the 20th century but has now been demolished. There is a petrol station on the site.[667]

Methodists

Wesleyan Methodist Chapel, High Street,* Grade 2 listed, in use. It is likely that there was a Methodist presence in the town, and perhaps a chapel, by 1783. The first chapel on this site, however, was opened in 1808 and enlarged in 1821. It was replaced in 1872 by the present one, designed by Wilson, Willcox and Wilson of Bath. Nikolaus Pevsner described its facade as 'showy and somewhat painful' but we might now be more charitable about its four giant Corinthian columns supporting a big pediment, and the pilasters with Corinthian capitals at either end, all beneath a balustraded parapet with stone urns. The two doors have highly decorated segmental-arched pediments, perhaps a main cause of Pevsner's distress, and above are three very conventional round-arched windows. The sides each have four tall round-arched windows. Inside, there is an early 19th century organ, moved here from elsewhere, in a bay at the east end. There is a wooden-fronted gallery at the west, the rear now screened off to create a separate room, and the interior is otherwise modernised. A Sunday school was established in a three-storey ashlar building a short way north on High Street in 1860 - a bridal shop in 2021 - but the chapel was extended back to create school-rooms c1906 and the other building was then leased out.[668]

Photograph also on page 39.   *Melksham High Street Wesleyan*

Wesleyan Methodists formed a separate meeting in **Semington Lane**, now Semington Road, in 1889 and built a chapel there west of the road by 1896. Small and red brick, it was side on to the road with three bays, a porch to the left end and a schoolroom to the right. It was in use until well into the 20th century, was still standing in 2016 but has since been replaced by modern houses.[669]

Primitive Methodists built a chapel in **Forest** in 1856. They had been active in both the town and the Forest area since 1829 but the town meeting struggled and eventually collapsed and it was not until 1852 that they bought a pair of cottages in Forest and converted them into the chapel, which opened in 1856. It was replaced in 1904 by the new chapel a few yards south and was soon demolished: the pair of brick houses which are here now were then built, No 4 Woodrow Road being on the site. The chapel formed one of a row with No 2, next door to the south, and another to the north. It had a narrow frontage of perhaps barely 15ft, with tall segmental-arched windows either side of a similar door; the worship space extended to the rear under what appears to have been a hipped roof.[670]

*Primitive Methodist Chapel of 1904, Forest,** at junction of Forest Road and Church Lane, now a veterinary surgery. Designed by W W Snailum of Trowbridge, this opened at the end of 1904 as successor to the previous chapel a little way north of here. It is of appealing straightforward Gothic in coursed rock-faced stone with ashlar dressings under slate with a prominent central lantern ventilator. The gable

facing the road has lancets either side of a buttressed porch and a three-light window above in a larger arch which incorporates a lozenge with the date 1904. The sides have four paired lancets with buttresses between and to the rear are the contemporary church rooms, including a schoolroom originally separated from the chapel by a removable partition and a small wing at right angles. Immediately south east is the new Sunday school room of 1938 with plain mullioned

Melksham Forest Primitive Methodist, still with prominent roof ventilator

windows, by Sir George Oatley. The chapel closed before 2010, at which date it was sold and converted into a veterinary practice.[671]
Photograph also on page 48.

Others

Salvation Army, off Church Street, now flats, set back just to the right of what is now the information centre. The Army leased this building, formerly a malt house, before buying it in 1929. They occupied it until c1970 and it was converted to flats in the 1990s. It is a long plain block, originally of red brick but now rendered.[672]

Queensway Chapel, Pembroke Road, in use. Built in 1967 for this evangelical church associated with the Open Brethren, originally called the Christian Assembly and active in the town from at least 1924. The chapel is a low sprawling building of stone blockwork under tile with large windows up to the roof angles in the gable ends.[673]

A **Catholic Apostolic** Church was registered in a 'house or building' in 1836 and may have survived until after 1868.[674]

Mere

The two most notable characteristics of nonconformist development here were firstly what appears to have been an almost complete absence of Wesleyan Methodists and secondly the remarkable success of the Congregationalists, whose first chapel was enlarged twice in the early 19th century before being replaced by two increasingly large chapels in quick succession.

Quaker Meeting House, Salisbury Street, south side, marked 'Lecture Hall', now function rooms run by a charity. A Quaker meeting house was registered in the town as early as 1701 but there seems then to have been little further activity until a small group settled in 1853 and in 1863 built a meeting house on Salisbury Street as the north part of an existing lecture hall. In c1927 a small room was added to the east end and in 1928, the street becoming too noisy with motorised traffic, the Quakers moved to the small lecture room for meetings. The meeting closed in 1987 and a charitable trust now runs the three rooms: the main lecture hall seating 100, a smaller room to the side and the original meeting house fronting the street. The wall facing the street is of squared coursed rubble stone under slate with a door either end and a group of three sash windows at the centre with stone mullions between and 'Lecture Hall' incised on the lintel. The interiors are modernised.[675]

The first **Congregational Chapel** was founded in 1795 as an expression of thanksgiving for his cure by Ronald Butt, a successful grocer. It was on the north side of the corner of Boar Street and **Dark Lane**, later the site of the 1853 chapel. Of small size, it had three Y-traceried Gothic windows to the sides and attached was a small house with a mansard roof, apparently for Butt's own occupation. The chapel was enlarged in both the 1830s and the 1840s but even so, and despite a capacity said to be over 300 in 1851, proved not to be big enough and was demolished and replaced in 1853.[676]

Congregational Chapel of 1853, Chapel Street, now in use as commercial premises. This replaced the 1795 chapel and is attributed to W J Stent of Warminster with funding, at least in part, by Charles Jupe, a silk merchant and prominent supporter of nonconformity. It was on two floors with a large schoolroom below the church. It had a short life as a chapel (see below) but a much longer life as a school. Built of blocks of local stone, now eroding, under a slate roof, it has five bays of tall lancets to the sides with intervening buttresses. The front gable facing the road has lancets either side of a triple stepped lancet but these are now partially obscured by a single-storey room and new entrance, with a short tower to the south, added in 1868 for the use of the British School then occupying it. It became the Mere junior school in 1922 and remained in that use until 1972.[677]

*Congregational Chapel of 1868,*** adjacent to the 1852 chapel, in use. This much more ambitious chapel, wholly funded by Charles Jupe and designed by W J Stent, replaced the second chapel in 1868. It is of squared rough stone, much buttressed, with mostly ashlar dressings under tile. The side facing the street makes a considerable impression, the entrance in a pyramidal-roofed tower at the west end, transepts at the east and a polygonal apse beyond, with a nave of four bays of multiple lancet windows in two tiers with cusped heads of unusual design. The transept has a large four-light window above and three lancets below.

Mere Congregational, the galleries awkwardly supported by the aisle columns

Inside is an impressive space, the main body of the church separated from aisles by slender cast iron columns and with galleries on three sides, that on one side apparently originally for boys and the opposite one for girls. The south transept gallery contains the organ and that to the north has rows of tiered pews; there is an apse at the east end and an entrance lobby at the west leading to two sets of gallery stairs. The ceiling has arched braces, tie-beams and king struts. Intrusive partitioning off of the west end of the church and the north aisle may be improved by works planned for 2021.[678]
Photograph also on page 41.

Primitive Methodist Chapel, North Street, * Grade 2 listed, now a house. A handsome chapel in strikingly rock-faced but eroding stone, with round-arched windows under slate. The gable facing the road has windows either side of the door, which has a fanlight; there are three taller windows above, buttresses to the corners, a date '1846' and a coped gable. Two bays to the sides have very tall windows and there is a schoolroom to the rear with, on the east side, narrow windows either side of a door in an arched porch, again with fanlight. The schoolroom has a large Venetian window at the north end and a tiled roof. The chapel was built in 1846, the gallery on cast iron

Mere North Street Primitive Methodist, the schoolroom of 1874 behind the chapel

pillars added in 1859, the schoolroom added in 1874 and new pews and windows in 1877. It became Mere Methodist Church after the Methodist union in 1932 but closed in 2017 and is now a house. The house conversion, which has retained the gallery, the pulpit and much of the original glazing, won a Salisbury Civic Society award in 2020.[679]

Photograph also on page 39.

Exclusive Brethren Meeting House, corner of Manor Road and Castle Hill Lane, now flats. This is of red brick under tile with three bays to the sides between brick pilasters and three bays to the gabled front. The windows are tall, now modern and split between two floors but perhaps originally of double height and round-arched, though the changes are such that it is not possible to visualise its original appearance with any confidence. The Brethren were active in the town from the early 1870s, meeting initially in the Ship Inn but building this c1880. They were here until at least the early 1940s but may have left soon thereafter.[680]

The **Salvation Army** were said to have opened a barracks in **Barton Lane** on the site of what is now the Grove building. The date given – 1865 – is suspiciously early for the Army's appearance in Wiltshire: whatever the date, they must have left there by 1899 when the Grove Buildings were opened.[681]

Stratton St Margaret

U ntil it was absorbed into the expansion of Swindon in the 20th century, Stratton was a collection of four small separate communities. Kingsdown, the smallest, and Lower Stratton the largest were about a mile apart from each other on Ermin Street; Upper Stratton and Stratton Green were a shorter distance respectively south west of those places. Their chapels are described together but they developed separately.

The Baptists were strong here from the mid 18th century onwards and Stratton was until the end of that century the centre of worship for Swindon Baptists.[682]. Primitive Methodists were later also strong whereas the Wesleyans arrived late and appear to have had limited impact.

Baptists

Stratton Green Baptist Chapel, now Storehouse Christian Fellowship, west of Swindon Road opposite Marshfield Way. The first chapel on this site was built in 1751 and for the rest of that century was the only permanent meeting place for Swindon nonconformists. The roof was raised and a gallery inserted in 1801. The chapel had its long wall parallel to the road, was of rubble-stone and had a semi-hipped slate roof, the extra height after raising, without added windows, giving the front an unbalanced look. By the early 20th century it was in poor condition and was replaced in 1934 by the present building, designed by Walter Rudman of Chippenham. A Sunday school – the Burson Memorial School - was added in 1937, possibly also by him; this was to the rear of a row of three houses which had been built directly behind the old chapel in the 1920s and which the Baptists later purchased. The chapel closed in 2014 but was taken over by the Storehouse Christian Fellowship in 2015.

The 1934 chapel stands with gable to road, the whole in render under slate with a look slightly reminiscent of cinema architecture. Corner pilasters and the projecting central section of the entrance front each have small hipped slate roofs and there is a large round-arched window above the doors; other windows are flat-headed. The chapel retains interesting stained glass, characteristic of the period, and has a similarly characteristic plaque above the door 'Stratton Green Baptist Church Founded 1751 rebuilt 1934', now obscured by a sign for Storehouse Christian Fellowship. A diamond shaped tablet re-attached to a small outbuilding right of the entrance states 'TS 1801', Thomas Smith being the minister at the time of the 1801 works. Inside, there is a rear gallery and wall panelling to shoulder height, all in dark stained wood.[683]

Lower Stratton's Baptist chapel was the **Zion Baptist**, set back west of **Ermin Street,** just south of the junction with Swindon Road. This was formed from a coach house, converted in 1830 to create a chapel and enlarged in 1835 to hold a congregation of 150. It was on a narrow plot with its gable facing the road containing a round-arched door with tall windows either side; a plaque was dated 1835. Worship ceased in the 1930s and the chapel had various other uses before final demolition in 1990. A new house was then built on the same footprint.[684]

The **Providence Chapel** on **Green Road, Upper Stratton,** just north of the Upper Stratton Baptist, was built in 1838 as **Independent** but was described as Baptist in 1851 when it shared a minister with Stratton Green. It closed when the adjacent Upper Stratton Baptist opened and was then used by Primitive Methodists until their own iron chapel in Dores Road opened in 1890. It is believed to have survived until the 1960s when it was demolished and replaced by a bungalow.[685]

Upper Stratton Baptist Chapel,* Green Road, in use. An appealingly simple Gothic chapel, with a long wall facing the road of two bays either side of a projecting central porch; this has a bellcote above which carried a bell until 1886 and the whole has the look of a school. It is in coursed shaped rubble-stone under slate and the interior, modernised, is open to the ceiling with shaped exposed rafters. It was built in 1862 to designs of a Mr George, probably of Stratton. A British School

Upper Stratton Baptist, simple Gothic with a hint of the Scottish Highlands

was built a short distance south on Green Road, later demolished, and the adjacent Sunday school hall was added in 1929. A further building was added to the rear in 1954 and in 1995 the hall and church were linked by a glass corridor and porch.[686]

Methodists

Wesleyan Methodist Chapel, Upper Stratton, St Philip's Road opposite Farrfield junction, in use as Swindon Chinese Christian Church. The Wesleyans' only church in Stratton, dated 1870, it is now rendered but was probably originally exposed brick. It has pointed-arch windows either side of a broad porch, ashlar dressings and a shouldered gable. There is a quotation from Psalm 100 above the windows, three bays to the sides and a single-storey Sunday school extension to the rear in brick, built c1900. The chapel closed in 2001 and had other uses before becoming the Chinese Christian Church in 2008.[687]

Primitive Methodist Chapel, Swindon Road, Lower Stratton, * east of road by Hobley Drive junction, now two houses. This was Stratton's first Primitive Methodist chapel, built in 1830 apparently in the space of just one month. It was enlarged c1842 and in use until 1883 when it was replaced by that further north by Ermin Street. It was then intended to become the Sunday school but that did not happen and instead it was converted to two houses c1891. The origin of these houses is still obvious, with a central lunette-shaped plaque proclaiming 'Primitive Methodist Chapel 1830 Prepare To Meet Thy God'. The round-arched first floor windows are the tops of the originals which stretched down to the ground floor and were placed either side of a round-arched door-case. The chapel was of brick with stone quoins, still visible though the brick is now rendered. Although it now has a conventional pitched roof, when it was in use it had a parapet in front of a much more shallow roof angle.[688]

left: Lower Stratton Primitive Methodist, Swindon Road. Photograph courtesy of Clive Carter. right: The same, now converted to two houses

Primitive Methodist Chapel, Lower Stratton, * by Ermin Street/Swindon Road junction, in use. The 1883 replacement for that further south on Swindon Road, to designs by William Drew of Swindon, it is of brick with copious ashlar dressings and round-arched windows under a slate roof. The gable facing the road has five tall windows, the central three stepped, and four assertive pilasters topped by metal finials; the central window has a 1930s clock inserted at its head. Above is a plaque dated 1883 and above that a circular ventilator. The porch is of c1900 and has two sets of three small windows with cusped heads. The sides have five bays with similar windows separated by buttresses, and to the rear is the much more plain meeting room of 1998 by Wyvern Architects, beyond the original Sunday school of 1891 by R J Beswick.[689]

Primitive Methodists built a corrugated iron chapel in **Dores Road, Upper Stratton,** in 1895. It had a short life, being replaced by the nearby chapel in Beechcroft Road (see below) in 1907. It was used as a coach garage in the 1950s and 60s before eventual demolition in the 1970s. A modern house, 11a Dores Road, now stands on the site.[690]

Primitive Methodist Chapel, Beechcroft Road (formerly Kingsdown Road), Upper Stratton, opposite turn to Dores Road, in use by Church of God of Prophecy. Built in 1907 as a replacement for the small iron chapel on Dores Road, it was constructed at the rear of the plot because there were aspirations to build a new chapel in front of it, at which point it would have become the

Lower Stratton, the 1883 Primitive Methodist

Sunday school. This never happened. It is of brick under replacement tiles with two segmental-arched windows and a door on the long side facing the street. The gable end, barely visible, has a protruding porch with the main door, segmental-arched windows either side and a circular window above with inscription 'Primitive

Methodist Church and School 1907'. It closed in 1973 when the congregation joined the St Philip's Road chapel and was sold in 1975. It was taken over by the Church of God of Prophecy, which had previously been using the former workhouse chapel, c2010.[691]

Others

Kingsdown Gospel Hall, west side of Hyde Road just north of Arkell's brewery, derelict. This corrugated iron chapel was built by the Christian Brethren in 1924 on land leased by the Arkells. The Brethren previously met outdoors from 1881, then in a cottage and then in the flour loft at **Hayes' bakery at 46 Hyde Road**, a building which still has a plaque with 'Ebenezer' inscribed on it at the gable head and which seems also to have been used for a period by Primitive Methodists. The gospel hall remained in use until closure in 1999 after which it was abandoned. It is of wood clad with corrugated iron under a corrugated asbestos roof.[692]

Warminster

There was a strong presence by nonconformists here in the years immediately after the Restoration, mainly Independents and Presbyterians, and amongst these were some of the most prominent townsfolk. This group later built the Old Meeting but many worshipped at the Horningsham chapel during the period of persecution. By contrast, it was over a hundred years before Baptists built their first chapel and most worshipped at Crockerton in the intervening years. Quakers met in a house in Common Close for a period from 1690 but never built a meeting house.[693]

Warminster Old Meeting, North Row.

The Old Meeting, Presbyterian/Unitarian, North Row,* Grade 2 listed, now Dewey House offices. In 1691 the Independents and Presbyterians built a 'plain barn-like' meeting house on this site. It was replaced by the present larger building, seating 500, in 1704; the opening preacher was the Rev. Cotton Mather from Boston, now infamous for his association with the Salem witch trials. The meeting became Unitarian in the late 18th century but thereafter declined; the last minister left in 1866, the chapel closed in 1868 and was sold in 1870. In 1872 it became the Girls' British School and remained in educational use until eventually being taken over by the town council as offices. The building is in brick with stone dressings under a hipped tiled double pile roof, the valley beam held up by two substantial oak posts. The west face is of five bays with mullioned windows in two tiers; a new porch was added when the building was converted to a school, with a plaque 'Girls' British School' above a Tudor-arched doorway. The rear has two large multi-paned cross-windows and a blocked door; the ends retain windows, some blocked or altered, similar to those on the front.[694]

Some members of the Old Meeting, dissatisfied with the preaching there, left in 1709, and more followed in 1719. They formed the **New Meeting** in **Common Close**, now The Close, and they were joined there by others who had been worshipping at the Horningsham chapel. The first chapel they built, in 1720, became too small and was pulled down bar the front wall and rebuilt in 1798 with new galleries and pews. Schoolrooms were added in 1836, apparently shared with the Baptists and Wesleyans, and British Schools were based there soon afterwards. The chapel was rebuilt again in 1839 in Gothic style, the centre of the gable end stepped forward between twin porches. Side galleries were added in 1846, increasing its capacity to over 700. Classrooms and a vestry designed by W J Stent were added to the north side in 1863, by which time it was Congregationalist. It declined in the 20th century and merged with the Methodists in George Street in 1983. The chapel and school were demolished in 1987 and Kyngeston Court was built on the site.[695]

The **Bread Street Independent Chapel**, an offshoot of the New Meeting in Common Close, was opened in 1802. The chapel seems to have been used intermittently by Independent Methodists before they established their own chapel in what is now Chapel Street. It is believed to have been destroyed by fire in 1857.[696]

Ebenezer General Baptist Chapel, North Row,* Grade 2 listed, in use. There was no early Baptist congregation in the town, people worshipping at Crockerton or at Common Close, but in 1810 this chapel was built in what was then called Meeting House Lane. It is of brick under a hipped tiled roof with a prominent circular ventilator. The gable facing the road has tall round-arched windows either side of a plain doorway with a plaque dated 1810 and above that a lunette. The windows have tracery of 1882 which might be thought not to add anything to their appearance. The three-bay sides, with round-arched windows above and flat below, also have tracery of this date. The adjacent schoolroom in ashlar was built in 1858 to designs by Thomas Hardick and has simple paired and triple round-headed windows. A central extension to the rear of the chapel through a large arch provides a bay for the organ behind the pulpit, moved there from the east gallery in 1882, and behind that are single-storey church rooms. Inside, the single gallery left from the three in place before the 1882 alterations has an ornate cast-iron balustrade. The 1882 alterations were by W Hardick and Son.[697]

A small group of **Strict Baptists** met in **Pound Street** between c1876 and 1907. It is possible that this group took over the Methodist mission hall (see below) for that period but they might instead have met in a house.[698]

Warminster Ebenezer Baptist, North Row

Wesleyan Methodist Chapel, George Street, in use. Methodists met in the town in the 1770s but were persecuted and it was not until 1804 that they were able to build a chapel in Chain (now George) Street. Numbers fluctuated thereafter but by 1861 the congregation was strong enough to have the chapel rebuilt to designs by W J Stent. It is Gothic, in exceptionally rough rubble-stone with ashlar dressings under slate. The gable facing the street has a large four-light window above what was originally a triple-arched entrance but this is now hidden by an unfortunate blockwork porch of 1976. The sides are of four bays and behind are lower subsidiary rooms probably built concurrently with the chapel. The interior in the early 20th century had the pulpit in front of a tall blind pointed arch, with arched doors either side, a large organ bought second-hand from elsewhere to the left, the whole under a hammerbeam roof. The 1976 alterations substituted chairs for the pews and a modern small organ for the old one; a suspended ceiling was also added to conserve heat. The Methodists merged with the United Reformed Church, formerly the New Meeting, in 1983 and meetings are held here.[699]

There was a **Methodist** presence in **Warminster Common**, at that date still a separate village, from 1803, and they borrowed the Independents' Bread Street chapel for some time. In 1818 a group expelled from the George Street chapel came to the Common, leading to the eventual construction of an **Independent** but essentially **Wesleyan Methodist** chapel in 1828 in what was later called **Chapel Street**. A gallery was added in 1838, increasing its capacity to over 300, and a vestry and schoolroom in 1844 and 1846 respectively. The school and chapel were on the north side of Chapel Street, just east of the junction with Bread Street. They were of brick, the chapel with a triple-gabled single-storey porch in front and the school east of it with three tall flat-headed windows facing the street. The meeting declined and the building was leased to the **Salvation Army** in 1882. Both chapel and school were demolished in 1983 and there are now two pairs of houses on the site.[700]

Independent Methodist Mission Hall, Pound Street, immediately north of the Maltings, now a house, No.35. Opened in 1842 in close collaboration with the George Street chapel, this was a conversion of a building from the 1760s. It closed in 1970 and became a private house. It is behind No.37, accessed via an alleyway, and though much altered appears to have had bands of pale brick and rubble-stone to the north and just rubble-stone to the south. The north side has three bays of two tiers of segmental-headed windows, the top tier now breaking through the roofline. The east gable is semi-hipped with altered openings and it has a tiled roof.[701]

Brethren were meeting in The Close in 1938 and at various houses in the town at different times but no more is known of their activities.[702]

Westbury

Westbury is in that area along the Wiltshire-Somerset border where dissent was strong in the later 17th and early 18th centuries. Independents and Baptists founded chapels here at that time and were soon joined by the Quakers. Methodists were relatively late in establishing themselves: John Wesley preached here in 1748 and 1749 but it seems the first chapel was not built until the early 19th century.[703]

Quakers were active in the town in the 18th century and had a burial ground outside the south west corner of the churchyard; this belonged to the Matravers family, leading members of the meeting. The graveyard, which contained the graves of up to 14 members of that family, was restored in 2019. The Quakers were said to have had a meeting house in a brick building adjoining the **churchyard,** but this was in use as a stable by 1894 and appears to have been demolished since.[704]

Old Congregational, Warminster Road, * set back east of road just north of Hospital Road junction, in use. Independents converted a barn on Leigh Road into a chapel in the late 17th century but this was burned down, perhaps deliberately, in 1711. They then built another chapel, probably on the present site, and this was subsequently rebuilt in 1821 at a cost of £2000. The brick gable facing the road was substantially altered in the 1860s, probably by Stent, and now has a double portico with columns and round-arched doors, tall round-arched windows either side with added tracery, a triple stepped round-arched window above

Westbury Old Congregational, showing the contrast between the 1860s front and the more sober original sides

the door, and pilasters in ashlar at the corners topped by urns; the gable itself is raised and shouldered at the centre. The sides, unaltered, are altogether more calm, with three bays of segmental-headed sash windows in two tiers, the upper tier of 36 panes, the lower of 24. The roof is of slate. Inside there are panelled galleries on three sides on iron pillars and an apse behind the pulpit contains the organ. There is a modern church hall to the rear beyond the apse.[705]

Upper Congregational Chapel, west of Warminster Road immediately south of nursing home, Grade 2 listed, now three houses. This was opened in 1763 by members of the Old Congregational who had left there in 1751 because they objected to the minister, who was suspected of holding unitarian views and who preached against slavery. It is believed to have been rebuilt c1790 with a capacity of 500. Various attempts were made later to reunite the two congregations but this did not happen until 1940. After that time the chapel was used as a store before being converted into three houses in 1988. The building is large and plain, of red brick with round-arched windows under a tiled roof, previously stone-slated, hipped to the rear. The front wall has two windows and a broad double door below, three windows above, and above those a lunette. The sides are of four bays, with round-arched windows above; the east wall has no windows below but the west side has flat-headed windows there, believed to have been added on conversion. The interior had galleries on three sides on cast iron columns.[706]
Photographs on pages 30 and 43.

Westbury Leigh Particular Baptist Chapel,* south of Westbury Leigh just east of junction with The Spur, Grade 2 listed, in process of conversion to housing in 2021. This church was 'planted' by Southwick, perhaps as early as 1662, and met from 1693 in a barn on the present site. The barn was converted into a chapel in 1714 and this in turn was replaced by the present substantial building in 1796-7. A schoolroom was added in 1819, the chapel was renovated in 1896 and closed some time shortly before 2012. It has an imposing facade in brick with ashlar dressings and round-arched windows. The broad pedimented door-case has windows either side and three above, and there is a lunette in the pedimented gable. The sides have three bays, each with windows in two tiers, and behind is the schoolroom of two bays with tall flat-headed windows and a steeper roof angle; there are lean-to outbuildings at the rear. The interior was remarkable, with galleries on three sides, their fronts panelled, lined and polished. A tall pulpit was reached by steep steps either side and there was a substantial organ in the rear gallery. The schoolroom opened into

Westbury Leigh Baptist – conversion work suspended in 2021

the chapel in what would have been the fourth gallery, above the pulpit, through an arched shuttered opening. It appears that the galleries and stairs are to be retained on conversion to a house.[707]

left: Westbury West End Baptist. right: Westbury West End Baptist – road widening and the loss of front railings have left the chapel looking much more exposed now than at the time of this photograph. Photograph courtesy of Wiltshire Buildings Record.

West End General Baptist Chapel, formerly Cook's Stile,* north of A350 in town centre, in use. Although there were Baptist chapels at Westbury Leigh and Penknap to the south west of the town by the early 19th century, there was nothing in the town centre. The opportunity was therefore taken in 1825 to acquire the chapel built in 1823 by a short-lived congregation calling themselves the 'New Lights,' at Cook's Stile, now West End. A schoolroom was added in 1853 and a baptistery in 1859 but in 1868 the chapel and schoolroom were replaced by a new chapel on the same site. This was designed by William Hardick of Warminster and could hold 400, in contrast to the 170 of the original; the schoolroom built at the same time was designed to hold 200. The chapel, in brick with ashlar dressings under slate, has a Greek temple feel with four pilasters to the front and a pedimented gable; there are tall round-arched windows either side of a round-arched doorway above which is a circular window. Railings which used to separate the forecourt from the street have gone, diminishing its impact. The sides are of four bays with tall round-arched windows between brick pilasters and the lower schoolroom behind has a hipped roof. The inside, now modernised, retains a rear gallery.[708]

Wesleyan Methodist Chapel, Warminster Road, set back down alley south of town centre junction of B3098 and A350, now a masonic lodge. This was the first Methodist chapel in the town, built in 1809 and replaced by the larger Station Road Methodist in 1926; it became a masonic lodge in 1927. Now rendered under a hipped tiled roof, it was probably originally exposed brick. One round-arched infilled window is visible on the south west face. A flat-roofed front extension dates from the 1927 conversion and obscures the original door, and there is a further hipped lean-to extension to the rear with two windows originally much larger. A separate hipped roof brick building behind, for long linked to the chapel but no longer, may have been a schoolroom.[709]

Methodist Chapel, Station Road,* south end of Station Road, in use. The larger replacement for the Warminster Road Methodist, which was too small and inconveniently situated 'adjoining a slaughterhouse yard', this was planned from 1904, the land purchased in 1915 but construction delayed by the First World War. The chapel, to designs by William Henry Ansell of London, eventually opened in 1926. It is of brick under slate in basilica form, five Diocletian windows at each side acting as clerestory above a nave and side aisles. The entrance front has a pedimented gable cut through by a tall round-arched window, with below that a broad flat-roofed porch in generally similar style dating from 1995 and designed by Eric Mammen; this replaced the original which was on a similar footprint but with flat-roofed porches either side of a lean-to central section. The interior was initially fitted with cinema-style tip-up seats and the organ from St Stephen's church in Trowbridge which closed in 1924. With its barrel vaulted ceiling it provides a successful light-filled space for worship. The schoolroom and further buildings are to the rear.[710]
Photograph on page 51.

Wilton

There was limited early dissenting activity in Wilton. Presbyterians were meeting by the 1720s and seemed to have prospered in the period of strong evangelism thereafter but Baptists had virtually no presence in the town. Quakers were here in the 18th century but not strong enough to establish a regular meeting. Growth after that was limited by the slow expansion of the town but despite this the chapels which are left are a varied lot and two are of particular interest.[711]

Quaker Meeting House, South Street, now the library. It was not until 1883 that a Quaker meeting was opened, at the instigation of Pardoe Yates, manager of the carpet factory. This was initially in Russell Street but later moved to South Street. The meeting there was discontinued by 1911 and the building is now the town's library. It has a gable facing the street in pale brick with red brick bands and dressings. The round-arched doorway has similar windows either side and one above. The sides are of red brick and the roof tiled.[712]

Presbyterians built a meeting house in **Crow Lane** in the mid 18th century. The Congregational chapel was built on the same site in 1791 and it is believed that the Presbyterians may have become Independent and then Congregational, and hence that the church had a continuous life.[713]

Congregational Chapel, Crow Lane,* now flats. This may have been a direct successor to the Presbyterian meeting house on the same site and was rebuilt in 1791, becoming the largest nonconformist church in the town. It prospered through the 19th century and was extended to the rear c1810. A Sunday school wing to the side was rebuilt in 1853 and further substantial alterations were carried out in 1872. Attendances later declined and the chapel was abandoned in the 1980s when the congregation moved to St Edith's Church in Kingsbury Square. It was converted to flats in 1987, the Sunday school being demolished in the process.

The building is of brick under a hipped tiled roof. The side facing the street, of three bays in two tiers, used to contain the entrance door, now converted to a window but with boot scrapers still in place either side. The windows are paired in single surrounds, round-arched above and cusped below in an intrusive style introduced with the 1872 alterations. The north east side is now of five bays but the rearmost was added c1810 and the front two were for many years covered by the attached Sunday school; this was removed on conversion and windows inserted in the same style as the remainder. These are again in pairs within single surrounds, round-headed above and flat-headed and cusped below. A central door was inserted, also at the time of conversion. A small extension to the north west contains what used to be the organ chamber, perhaps added in 1872. The interior before conversion had galleries on iron columns, numerous memorial tablets and a rose window above the pulpit.[714]
Photograph on page 31.

There is no evidence for early **Baptist** meetings in the town but a group of Baptists has met in the former **town hall** in the corner of the **Market Place** since 1981.[715]

Wesleyan Methodist Chapel, North Street, just south of Riverside; now a house called The Old Chapel. Built in 1831 and sold in 1933 after which the congregation joined the Primitive Methodists in Kingsbury Square; the building was then used for some years as a warehouse before conversion into a house. It is small and low, of pale brick under slate, the brickwork showing only headers. The chapel has been greatly altered, with the roof raised and a floor inserted, but the openings for the door and windows either side in the long wall may be in their original positions.[716]

Primitive Methodists opened a chapel in **West Street** in 1837 at an unidentified location. It had a gallery and an attached schoolroom and its construction was supervised by the Earl of Pembroke's carpenter. The chapel was closed soon after 1875 when the new chapel in Kingsbury Square opened (see below). It was later demolished.[717]

Methodist Reform Chapel, Kingsbury Square, now Town Council offices. This has a narrow late 18th century facade of painted brick in three storeys under a hipped mansard slate roof. Windows and doors, from the time it was converted into a chapel, are round-arched with prominent imposts: to the front a double door with window of equal size above and smaller windows at either side and at attic level; to the rear two windows split between floors, now blanked off. The chapel

Wilton Methodist Reform, Kingsbury Square, the meeting room now a council chamber. Photograph courtesy of Wilton Town Council.

interior, now the council chamber, was on the first floor, long and narrow with exposed tie beams and rafters. The chapel was opened in 1872 but closed by 1896. Thereafter it is thought to have been used by the masons before being taken over by the town council after they moved out of the town hall now used by the Baptists.[718]

Primitive Methodist Chapel, Kingsbury Square, * Grade 2 listed, now offices. The 1875 replacement for the earlier chapel in West Street, with a front in rendered brick reminiscent of an Italian palazzo. The ground floor is rusticated with two sash windows either side of a central door-piece having Doric half columns. Above are five sash windows, all pedimented; the central window also has a narrow balcony supported by the door-piece. There is a heavy entablature and a hipped slate roof which extends to the rear in two side arms. The left side wall has two bays in similar style to the front with two of the windows blind, and the right side and rear walls are almost blank. Highly unusual for a chapel, its appearance may be explained by the fact that it was built as a Temperance Hall and many of these did choose a strongly Classical facade. It was, however, sold to the Primitive Methodists before completion. In 1967 they joined the Congregationalists in Crow Lane and in 1969 the building became St Edith's Roman Catholic church. In 1984 the Catholics were joined by

Wilton Primitive Methodist, Kingsbury Square, amongst the most unlikely-looking of all nonconformist chapels

the Methodists and the United Reformed Church in a sharing agreement. In 2007 the building was converted by The Classic Architecture Co. into their own offices.[719]

Wootton Bassett

Hephzibah Congregational Chapel, Wood Street, Grade 2 listed, in use. This was built in 1825 to replace a 1797 meeting house, also in Wood Street. The gallery was added in 1828, schoolrooms and a vestry in 1862 and two more classrooms in 1870. The bleak gable facing the road is of ashlar with rectangular windows in two tiers of three bays. The porch of 1882 adds some life and has a round-arched door with a no-longer-legible date plaque above. The chapel has a gallery at the west end, a round apse, also of 1882, to the rear, and subsidiary buildings at right angles in brick under slate.[720]

The **Hope Baptist Chapel** was built at the west end of **High Street** in 1896 and was of brick with stone dressings, round-arched windows and a pedimented front gable. It was closed in 1939 and later used as a store and a primary school room before demolition in 1967. The original front wall and entrance steps were still visible in 2019 next door to No.178.[721]

Wesleyan Methodists built a chapel in 1855 at the entrance to **Coxstalls**. It stayed in use until the early 1960s at which time the Wesleyans joined the Primitive Methodists at the Hillside chapel. The chapel was demolished when Coxstalls was widened in 1964. It was Gothic, of substantial size, with five bays to the sides and a schoolroom behind. The chief element of the front facade was a large Gothic window above the porch containing circular tracery.[722]

Primitive Methodist Chapel, Hillside, set back towards lower end of High Street, in use. Two houses were bought here in 1831 and converted into a chapel. In 1838 a new and enlarged chapel was built on the same site; in 1841 a gallery was added and in 1842 a day school. The chapel was enlarged further in 1858/9. Later alterations included the new porch in 1975 and comprehensive internal refurbishment in the period up to 1993. It is built of rubble-stone with brick dressings, some of those rendered. The gable facing the road has two tall round-arched windows behind a large modern porch; at the gable head is a plaque dated 1838 and there are ornamental finials at either end of an otherwise plain roofline. The previous porch had an ornately curved ogee top. The 1859 extension to the rear is of similar design and behind that are other more modern buildings.[723]

6. Chippenham

There was some early religious dissent in Chippenham, with small numbers in the 1660s and 1670s refusing to attend church service or to have their children baptised. Presbyterians met in the town in 1669 and Quakers and Baptists were also active at that time, but the development of nonconformity thereafter through the 18th century appears to have been slow. More chapels were built in the 19th century, several of them interesting, but the total number remained modest, reflecting the relatively small size of the town until well after the main period for chapel building was over.[724]

Presbyterians, Quakers and Congregationalists

Presbyterians, who had for some time been meeting in a private house, registered a new meeting house at the back of the **Bell Inn, 39-40 Market Place**, in 1701. They were active in 1715 but their history thereafter is obscure. The meeting house is believed to have become **Methodist** by 1784 and to have been demolished in 1811.[725]

Quakers became strongly established in Chippenham in the later 17th century, despite persecution, and in 1670 opened a meeting house in the **High Street (later The Causeway)**, registering it in 1690 after the passing of the Act of Toleration. It was rebuilt in 1733-4 and remained in use until 1812 when, with declining attendance, they discontinued the meeting. The building was used from 1822 as a school room and in 1834 it was sold to the **Primitive Methodists** (see below).
A further Quaker meeting was established in Chippenham in 1935 and lasted until 1962. In 2002 the Causeway Primitive Methodist chapel, containing the remains of the original meeting house, was converted into The Cause and Quakers began meeting there. They continue to do so.[726]

Tabernacle Congregational Chapel, Emery Lane, * Grade 2 listed, now a nursery. Though Congregational for most of its life, the preaching of the Calvinist Methodist George Whitefield provided the inspiration for this chapel and he was one of the founding trustees: many of the chapels founded by his followers were called 'Tabernacle'. It was opened in 1770, apparently on a site corresponding to the rear half of the present building, and rebuilt to seat over 500 in 1826. A minister's house and schoolroom were added at the street side in the mid 19th century and the chapel was then entered through the arch in the front of that building, there being other buildings attached to the south.

Chippenham Tabernacle Congregational – the buildings were continuous alongside the road until recent times, requiring the chapel to be accessed through the archway on the left

The chapel interior was refitted in 1889 and further works in 1904 included alterations to the galleries, new window tracery and the opening up of the rear wall to create a separate space for the organ. It closed in 2016 and was re-opened in 2017 as a nursery.

The 1826 building, now partly hidden by the minister's house and school-room, has a hipped slate roof and a three-bay two-storey front in squared stone blocks with ashlar dressings, the central bay pedimented with a round-arched window. A plaque in the pediment reads 'Tabernacle, first erected in 1770, rebuilt in the year 1826'. The sides are also of three bays in two tiers, in rubble-stone. To the rear is a one-bay extension, stone below and brick above, the brick section added in 1904 and providing the space for the organ. At the front the schoolroom abuts the left hand side of the chapel facade and is of painted rubble-stone with ashlar dressings and two round-arched windows under a slate roof hipped at one end. At the outer end it joins the minister's house, which is of brick with an ashlar facade containing the arched doorway used to access the chapel before the adjacent buildings were demolished. A new lean-to porch was added to the chapel front, probably at the same time as the manse and hall were built. Inside, the gallery on three sides remains, supported on cast iron columns, probably altered in 1904 and now with trefoil designs in the panelling. The organ is set

Chippenham Tabernacle Congregational – the organ gallery with its inverted arch below was created as recently as 1904

in an arched opening at gallery level, the lower edge of the opening formed by an unusual inverted segmental arch.[727]

Baptists

Old Baptist Chapel,* Chapel Lane, off High Street just north of Market Place, Grade 2* listed, in use. There were Baptists active in the town in the late 18th century but they may not have been connected with those who founded this

Strict Baptist church in 1804, and there is a suggestion that this group seceded from the Tabernacle chapel. They first met in a building in St Mary's Street but opened this chapel in 1810, petitioning to have the former name of the street, Gutter Lane, changed to Chapel Lane. Baptisms were first carried out in the Avon but an internal baptistery was added in 1818. The building was originally almost square but a small extension to the north east was added in the late 19th century.

The domestic frontage of Chippenham Old Baptist

The chapel is of rubble-stone, coursed at the front, with ashlar dressings and a hipped slate roof. The front facing the lane looks like a house, with three bays and two tiers of flat-headed windows. The door, with a hood, is up steps at the centre. To the rear are two tall round-arched windows either side of the pulpit. The left side is joined to another building and at the right is the one-bay extension of similar height, ashlar to the front but brick to the side and rear. The interior is substantially original, with three panelled galleries on cast-iron columns, perhaps early nineteenth century and with a stand for choir music books in the rear gallery. There is a high pulpit of similar date between the windows with steps up from one side and a panelled back-board, and there are late 19th century pews.[728]

The **Bath Road Baptist Chapel** was founded some time after 1851. It was known to have been there by 1871 but closed in 1877 in what appear to have been controversial circumstances. It was small, with a gable facing the road and sash windows in a pedimented rear gable. Located north of Bath Road, it was replaced there by a storehouse which in turn was much more recently replaced by the Bath Road car park building.[729]

Interior of Station Hill Baptist, Chippenham before alteration. Note the organ, as so often a later addition and therefore awkwardly placed, and the labelling of pews to indicate those renting them. Photograph courtesy of Micah Leitch

Station Hill General Baptist Chapel, * corner of New Road and Station Hill, Grade 2 listed, in use. An appeal for funds to build this chapel was launched in 1854, apparently unrelated to any other Baptist congregation in the town and perhaps at the initiative of Bratton Baptists. The chapel opened in 1856, built to designs by Thomas Hardick of Warminster, and the schoolrooms to the rear facing St Mary's Place were added in the later 19th century. A refurbishment in 2018 replaced a lean-to extension in the rear north east corner with one of two storeys.

The large Classical facade in ashlar facing Station Hill is handsome though the pediment may be thought heavy. There are four substantial pilasters below an entablature and between them three flat-arched windows at the upper level and blind windows either side of a door under a shallow hood at the lower. The sides are of three bays in two tiers, in low-quality ashlar, with segmental-arched windows above and flat-arched below. The schoolrooms are slightly lower, again in low-quality ashlar, with two bays to the sides and three across the rear, the windows all flat-arched. There is a second small lean-to extension to the south west rear corner. The interior, perhaps surprisingly, seems never to have had a gallery. Old pews were removed as late as 1930 and it has now been further modernised, the replacement pews and the organ, formerly to the left of the pulpit, all having been stripped out.[730]

Photograph also on page 39.

In 1890 the minister of Station Hill Baptist, the Rev. H B Bardwell, fell out with the members on doctrinal grounds, resigned and started his own **Baptist** church in the private school he ran behind his house at **54-55 New Road**. This might have been in a partially bricked-in arch of the adjacent railway viaduct which had previously been used by the Salvation Army and perhaps other nonconformists. The Bardwell chapel may have continued until c1915.[731]

Wesleyan Methodists

Wesleyan Methodist Chapel, The Causeway, * set back east of south end of The Causeway, Grade 2 listed, now flats. Wesleyan Methodists are believed to have had a meeting house in the town by 1784, possibly that formerly used by Presbyterians. This was demolished in 1811 but another chapel was opened, probably at the north end of London Road and perhaps in a converted block of four cottages, in 1812. That was replaced in turn in mid century, perhaps in 1853, by this building. It was in use until 1909 when it was closed on completion of the Monkton Hill chapel. That same year it was sold to become Spinke's printing works, which remained in business until 1978; it was then converted into flats.

    The ashlar Gothic facade peers out between the ends of adjacent terraces and would make a considerable impression were it not so screened from view. At the

Chippenham Causeway Wesleyan

ground floor level are three openings, now two windows with Y-tracery flanking a door but believed originally to have been all doors; the present door still has 'Spinkes Works' painted over the arch. Above that is a larger four-light window with intersecting tracery and the gable head has low battlements; at the corners are octagonal pilasters terminating in pinnacles. The roof is of slate and the sides and rear of rubble-stone with three bays of pointed-arch windows to the side above round-arched windows at the basement level where the schoolrooms – later referred to as 'badly ventilated' - were placed. There was formerly a run of buildings immediately behind the chapel of which one, older than the chapel itself, remains.[732]

Wesleyan Methodists erected a corrugated iron hall and schoolroom, supplied by James Lee of Manchester, in **Park Street, later Woodlands Road**, in 1902. It was intended as a temporary chapel and was sold to raise funds for the new Monkton Hill chapel which opened in 1909. The hall was by the junction with Canterbury Street, at what was then the limit of housing development. It remained for some time but has now been replaced by a modern hall.[733]

Wesleyan Methodist Chapel, Monkton Hill, ** Grade 2 listed, in use. At the opposite extreme to those early chapels hidden away out of harm's way, the Central Methodist is graceful but highly assertive in its elevated position above the street, the chapel proper raised above a large suite of schoolrooms at road level. It was designed by Gordon and Gunton of London and was intended to mark the centenary of Methodism in the town, opening in 1909 after a long search for a more central site eventually produced results in 1900. The chapel provided a larger replacement for both the Causeway Wesleyan and the temporary building on Park Street.

The ashlar front facing down Monkton Hill is of two storeys, the corners stepped out to form one-bay staircase towers and between them three bays separated by engaged Ionic columns, in two tiers under a dentilled pediment. The windows and doors here are round-arched whereas those in the towers are round-arched above and flat below. The four-bay sides, also ashlar, have round-arched windows above and flat-arched below, separated by plain pilasters, and on the road side the fall in the ground level creates the space for the basement schoolrooms, in coursed rubble-stone with flat-arched windows. The hipped roof is of slate and there have been various minor alterations, including the addition of the Allden room to the left side in 2003 to designs by Julian Taylor Architects of Cherhill. This followed the closure of the Primitive Methodist chapel in The Causeway in 1996, the combining of the churches and the re-designation of this as the Central Methodist.

The interior is a delight, competing with Back Street, Trowbridge, as the culminating Wiltshire example of large chapel design and largely unaltered since first built. The galleries on three sides, with panelled fronts and metal grille inserts, are cantilevered, leaving the main space free of supporting columns, but the chief pleasure is the east end. Here a set of choir stalls, highly unusual, curves round the raised pulpit which itself stands behind a curved communion rail in harmonious combination. Behind them an arch contains the organ, probably originally contained within the space behind but now – this a war memorial replacement of the 1920s – brought forward. This arch, with its dentilled detailing, matches the lunette windows high up to either side. Other details all fit with the design and the

Chippenham Causeway Primitive Methodist

period, down to the tiered seating in the rear gallery between the two staircase towers and the circular windows in the various doors.[734] *Photographs on rear cover and pages vii and 39.*

Primitive Methodists

Primitive Methodist Chapel, The Causeway, ** south of Market Place, Grade 2 listed, now The Cause music and arts centre. The tall, twin-towered Gothic facade facing the street may be more reminiscent of rural France than Wiltshire but there is much more going on behind. At the rear is the original chapel, in rubble-stone with ashlar dressings under a hipped slate roof and two altered round-arched windows behind. This is certainly of 1834, when it was taken over by the Primitive Methodists from the Quakers, and very probably contains much of the original fabric of that building which opened c1734, closed in 1812 and was used as a schoolroom from 1822. The Methodists are believed to have used it much as it stood until they built the new chapel in front in 1896, at which time they inserted a floor and the sash windows with brick surrounds in the north wall. The interior is now plain.

The original chapel may have been accessed via the archway in the adjoining house on The Causeway which is still used. The buildings previously joined to this house were later demolished to make way for the much larger chapel which was added to the front in 1896, at which time the old chapel became a schoolroom again. The new chapel, designed by Thomas Holloway, has a three-bay front in rock-faced block with plentiful ashlar dressings, the two side bays brought forward to form towers. In the centre bay the minimal porch obtrudes slightly into the four-light window above with three quatrefoils at its head, and to the sides are two tiers of cusped pointed-arch windows. Each bay has a separate gable, those to the towers pierced by further Gothic arches, and there are pilasters to the tower corners with alternate ashlar stones creating the impression of ladders.

The interior retains galleries with blind wooden balustrading and original seating, supported on wall brackets on two sides but with a single supporting column to the rear where the seating is stepped up. The organ remains behind where once stood the pulpit, all under a hammerbeam roof. The whole interior is appealingly composed.

The chapel closed in 1996, the congregation merging with that at Monkton Hill, and reopened as The Cause in 2002.[735]

Chippenham Causeway Primitive Methodist, the 1896 interior – side galleries are on brackets but the rear gallery over the entrance vestibule is still supported by a pillar.

The **Primitive Methodists** built their **Lowden** chapel in 1855 near the junction with The Quadrangle. It closed in 1901 when the congregation moved to the Sheldon Road chapel and was then used as the Chequers Yard commercial premises for many years before demolition in 2020 pending redevelopment. In use, it had a broad gable end facing the road with twin porches for the two doors and a two-light round-arched window between them.[736]

Sheldon Road Primitive Methodist Chapel, junction of Sheldon Road and Audley Road, in use. This was built in 1901 to designs by J A Piccaver of Northampton as a larger replacement for the Lowden chapel. It is Gothic, in coursed squared stone with ashlar dressings under a tiled roof, and its most notable features are the broad four-light window to the gable end and the tall slated flèche at the centre of the roof. The door and adjacent windows have pierced spandrels over and the side is of four bays with tall pointed-arch windows. A schoolroom to the rear was replaced by a modern brick building in 1968 and to the west is the church hall, also with pointed-arch windows, added c1924. The hall is now opened out to create a single space with the main building, divisible by a folding screen, and the worship space turned at right angles.[737]

Others

Salvation Army Citadel, Bath Road, * town bridge end, now a shop below and hall for hire above. Very much a citadel, down to the castellations and the two ends of the elevation brought forward as miniature towers. The Salvation Army met in the town from 1881, perhaps initially in one of the railway viaduct arches west of

New Road which was bricked up with a window inserted. They built this citadel in 1903, as its plaque proclaims. Of brick and render with stone dressings, its walls are angled to follow the constrained site: the hall is on the first floor. It eventually became too cramped and the premises were liable to flooding so the Army purchased the Co-op hall in Foghamshire in 1970 and have met there since.[738] *Photograph on page 46.*

The Brethren established a number of premises around the town before moving in 2015 to a new meeting house at **Kington Langley**. From 1885 Exclusive Brethren were in a building in **Cook Street**, now the Market Place end of St Mary Street, or **Emery Lane**, perhaps the building now called Emery House. They were still there in 1913 but by 1933 they had a meeting room in *Cocklebury Road*, opposite what is now the station car park: no doubt altered from its first appearance, this is now a typically blank-walled building in render under a tiled roof. In 1969 they added a further meeting room on the bend in *Goldney Avenue*, an octagonal building in pale brick, used since 2005 by the **Emmanuel Church** congregation which used to meet in Hardenhuish school; the Brethren have retained a small adjacent building. Finally, by 2008 the Exclusive Brethren were also meeting in *Hill Corner Road*, some way east of the junction with Greenway Lane, this one again anonymous in brick under a tiled roof.[739]

Ladyfield Evangelical Church, junction of Hungerdown Lane and Ladyfield Road, in use. The church was founded during the Second World War and was originally part of the Brethren but later became an independent fellowship. It acquired this site in 1954 and built a succession of larger and more permanent buildings culminating in this chapel of 1996 with its extensive range of further buildings, replacing earlier ones, opened in 2009. All is of pale brick under low tiled roofs and the chapel is octagonal with a central clerestory. In recent years, after a period of use by Reformed Baptists, it has again become associated with the Brethren.[740]

Christian Fellowship Church, 205 Wood Lane, in use. This Elim Pentecostal church was built c1990. It is in plain brick with four tall narrow windows to the gable end, a porch and other rooms in a single-storey side block at an angle, and a tiled roof.[741]

New Testament Church of God, Lowden, immediately south of railway bridge, in use. Built in 1886 as St Peter's, a chapel of ease to St Andrew's, it was by Graham Awdry who also designed the adjoining almshouses. Closed c1968 on construction of the new church on Frogwell, it was later taken over by the New Testament Church of God. It is built of coursed squared rubble-stone with red brick dressings which are wearing badly. The windows are round-arched and the roof steeply pitched and tiled. The facade has a stepped three-light window above a large entrance arch, with smaller windows either side. There is a bell turret at the gable head and the sides are much buttressed. The interior has aisles and an apsed chancel.[742]

7. Salisbury

There was a Baptist congregation in Salisbury from as early as 1626 and activity continued through the interregnum and the years of persecution which followed, with General and Particular Baptists, Presbyterians, Congregationalists/Independents and Quakers all present although the last-named were relatively late on the scene. A census of 1675 revealed 63 protestant dissenters out of an adult population of 3609 but this small number may understate their activity. Nonconformity became strongly established in the city during the 18th century, particularly Wesleyan Methodism for which Salisbury was said to be the focus for the whole of southern England. The strength of nonconformity in the city in the 19th century produced many interesting chapels, though several have been lost.[743]

Quakers

Quakers were present here from the 1650s but not noticeably active until the 1680s. Various houses were used but the first purpose-built meeting house was that on the west side of **Gigant Street**, opened in 1712. It declined later in the century and may have been out of use by 1796. The Salisbury meeting was discontinued in 1826 and the Gigant Street premises were then registered as Independent. It is not known which group of Independents made the registration but in any case it seems to have been short-lived because the meeting house is reported as having been an infants' school from 1830. It was sold to the Temperance Society and, perhaps ironically, then survived in reconstructed form well into the 20th century at the south end of the Gigant Street brewery. It is now demolished and Charter Court built on the site.[744]

The meeting reopened in 1934 and met successively at the **Rechabites' Hall on Crane Street** until around 1962, then from 1964 until at least 1974 at **44 Harcourt Terrace (now Rectory Road)**. In 2003 they bought *Pembroke Lodge, 51 Wilton Road**, and this was converted for them in 2009/10 by Philip Proctor Associates after a prolonged period of fund-raising. The east end of this building is of early nineteenth century date and its original use uncertain, but later in the century it was extended to the west and became a private house. It was used from 1923 by the Fisherton Asylum and its successors until closed in 1997. The east end has a semi-circular front to the road and an overhanging first floor on Tuscan columns. To the west the later extension, also stuccoed, has three irregular bays facing the road, the west end carrying a parapet. The windows have four-centred arches and the whole Grade 2 listed building, though not built as a meeting house, is handsome.[745]

Salisbury Pembroke Lodge Quaker Meeting House

Presbyterians

Presbyterian Meeting House, now the Salvation Army, Salt Lane. Presbyterians were flourishing in the late 17th and early 18th centuries and built a meeting house here c1702, the first purpose-built nonconformist chapel in the city, set back south of Salt Lane. A minister's house was added in 1720 on the forecourt where the forward extension of the Salvation Army Citadel now stands. In the later 18th century, however, the church went into a decline, with many of the congregation seceding to the Congregationalists following the appointment of a new minister in 1756, and by 1773 it had probably more or less ceased to function. By 1815 the premises were ruinous and were then sold to the **Wesleyan Methodists** from St Edmund's Church Street as schoolrooms and a minister's house, the Wesleyans having to spend £500 to put them back into usable order. In 1882 they were sold on again, to the **Salvation Army**. They extended the main block forwards, rebuilt the minister's house in 1889 to form the present left side block at the front, and much later added the present porch. The original meeting house is now gabled and rendered under a slate roof but was originally of brick under a double roof, with a gallery. Its side and rear walls remain but the front one was lost in the extension and there are various blocked and altered windows in the side walls. The front block is of four bays, single-storey in brick with a parapet in front of a pitched slate roof.[746]

Congregationalists and Independents

The **Congregationalists** seceding from Salt Lane met first at the Crow Lane chapel in Wilton but in 1766 they were provided with two houses in **Scots Lane**, behind one of which a chapel was built and registered in 1767. It was enlarged in 1791 and 1808, and schoolrooms and a vestry were added in 1829. A group had seceded in 1806 to form the Endless Street chapel (see below) and the two groups reunited in 1860: Scots Lane was very much the dominant partner but the 800 seat capacity Endless Street was chosen because it was larger than the 530 seat Scots Lane. The Scots Lane buildings were then used as Sunday schoolrooms and for a British School until closed in 1888, and then as a Sunday school until 1890. They were then sold to the **Open Brethren** to help pay for the Fisherton Street chapel which had been built in 1879. The Open Brethren reopened the chapel as City Hall in 1895 but it was closed again in 1917 or possibly 1931. In 1932 it was taken over by the **Elim Four Square Gospel Alliance** and used by them until the late 1950s. It was demolished in 1960 and the west end of the telephone exchange now covers its former site.[747]

A group of **Congregationalists** seceded from the Scots Lane chapel in 1806 over the choice of a new minister and in 1810 registered a chapel in **Endless Street**. There were repeated disagreements during this chapel's short life and in 1860, with the acrimonious departure of another minister, the meeting more or less collapsed. The two groups then recombined here but the dominant Scots Lane group, anxious to erase memories of the secession, had the Endless Street chapel refurbished inside and re-fronted by W J Stent of Warminster, in stone in a 'bold Italian' style. The new Fisherton Street chapel was built in 1879 and the Endless Street chapel was then sold to help pay for it. It was converted into the city's first public lending library in 1890 and sold on again in 1905, for a while as a shop but eventually becoming the Royal British Legion Club. The front facade of the chapel was removed and its replacement brought forward: how much original fabric remains behind, if any, is not clear.[748]

Congregational Chapel, Fisherton Street, * west of river, Grade 2 listed, in use. The city's third Congregational chapel was opened in 1879 at a cost of £11,000 to replace the Endless Street chapel; it seated 650 people. By Tarring and Wilkinson of London in an early Gothic style, it was the first nonconformist building in Salisbury in Gothic. The exterior is in Purbeck stone block with ashlar dressings under a slate roof and the most prominent feature is the separate tower which has a spire, corner buttresses and the former main entrance below. The tower is linked to the chapel which has a further entrance door, now in glass, and a substantial five-light window above with tracery. The interior has aisles, clerestory windows and a chancel arch all in Anglican fashion, and equally Anglican was the lack of galleries. A separate lecture hall and classrooms were built behind in 1892 and seven more added in 1898. 1973 plans to sell the church and schoolrooms and re-build elsewhere fell through but instead the chapel was much altered in 1978 to the designs of Anthony Stocken; this included inserting a first floor with two new staircases. The ground floor is now plain meeting rooms but the first floor still contains the tops of the arches and much of the substantial and much-traceried north window. The schoolroom block was sold to fund this work and commercial buildings were erected on the site, themselves demolished and awaiting redevelopment in 2021. There were proposals in the early 1990s to demolish all but the chapel facade and the tower but these also were not carried through and the church continues to thrive. It is a good example of how far back towards Anglicanism some chapel design had travelled by the late 19th century, a long way from the symmetry and simplicity of early design.[749]

Photograph also on page 22.

Salisbury Fisherton Street Congregational

Congregational Mission Room, Dew's Road, now a house, 15 Dew's Road. This narrow three-storey brick building next to the former tanning factory had had previous commercial use and was opened as a mission room and Sunday school in 1867. The mission use lasted a relatively short time but it was still in use as a school until 1898 when the extra capacity then provided at Fisherton Street allowed it to be closed.[750]

Baptists

Brown Street Particular, Later General, Baptist Chapel, * in use. Brown Street became the mother church for Baptist worship in a wide surrounding area, the first chapel having been built here shortly before 1719 after the Salisbury Baptists parted from the original mother church at Porton in 1690. It was apparently rebuilt in 1750 and then, under pressure of numbers, replaced in 1829 with a chapel designed by William Henry Roe of Southampton with seating for 800. This was in what has been called 'debased classical style' with four pilasters under a pediment, three round-arched windows above and a door and two windows below, the latter heavily pedimented and with trapezoid framing in the 'Egyptian' style.

left: Salisbury Brown Street Baptist – Stent's assertive front with eccentric but effective truncated columns; schoolrooms to right. right: Salisbury Brown Street Baptist before alterations. Image courtesy of Wiltshire and Swindon Archives

W J Stent was employed in 1881-2 to make alterations: he refaced the building and re-modelled the interior but did not increase its capacity. A Sunday school was recorded as opened in 1873 and this could be the building immediately adjacent to the chapel, with its twin pointed-arch doorways. Stent added more schoolrooms at the time of his other works and the second adjacent building could be his, though surprisingly plain if so. In 1908 an Institute was built forwards from the Sunday schools towards the street but this was demolished in 1990. There are further rooms behind the chapel; these brought the total number of schoolrooms to 24 at the peak, with capacity for over 400 pupils.

Stent's Lombard-style front is in assertive red brick with the central section thrust forwards under a heavily coped gable; there is a round window above within an arch and below it the porch with truncated columns. Further round-arched windows complete the front and to the side, in less demonstrative brick, are two tiers of windows, round-arched above and mostly segmental-arched below. Inside, the building was split into two floors in 1989, with meeting and service rooms below and the chapel above, illuminated by the upper tier of windows and with Stent's ceiling and his organ arch at the east end still visible.[751]

General Baptists, said to have seceded from Brown Street in 1869, built a chapel on **Harcourt Bridge Road, now Mill Road**, in 1875 but left in 1893. It was later used as a furniture depository and eventually demolished in 1971, to be replaced in 1972 by the house which is now 12 Mill Road.[752]

Bishopdown Baptist Chapel, now Evangelical Church, at junction with Barrington Road, in use. This long timber shed with a brick porch was opened in 1959 to serve the growing Bishopdown community.[753]

Wesleyan Methodists

Wesleyan Methodist Chapel, St Edmund's Church Street, * Grade 2 listed, in use. The original chapel here, built in 1759, set back from the road and probably reached through an arch between cottages, was praised by Wesley as 'the most complete in England.' It was rebuilt in 1811 with seating for over 1000 and extended to the west in 1835, at which point it was claimed to have accommodation for 1500; the architect for the extension was a Mr Harding of Fisherton. A secession of 'reform' Methodists, who built the new Milford Street chapel in 1852, led apparently to a halving in attendance but recovery followed and the chapel was given its present appearance on the street side through alterations by Fred Bath in 1889. The striking five-bay stuccoed facade has round-arched windows with complex circular patterns in the glazing bars. This front was originally of 1835 but the outer bays were brought forward as stair towers in 1889 and the window tracery may also be of that date. Between the towers, the entrance-way is formed by a curving stone porch with Tuscan columns, also of 1889. The roof is hipped and of slate and the side windows are in two tiers, round-arched above and segmental below. Inside there were galleries on all four sides with curved open cast-iron fronts which were added as part of the 1889 works, their appearance remarkably similar to those still in place at Back Street Baptist, Trowbridge. Major alterations in 1992, however, left only a rear gallery, housing the 1930 organ moved from the opposite end: the

Salisbury St Edmund's Church Street Wesleyan

lines of the former galleries are still marked on the walls but the impact on the appearance of the interior has been severe.

In 1815 the Salt Lane Presbyterian chapel was bought and renovated for schoolrooms but it was not long before this chapel had a large set, including some facing Greencroft Street built in 1879 and demolished probably in the mid 20th century; a further set attached to the church was built in 1882. A young people's institute was added to the rear in 1912 and the remaining schoolrooms have been subject to various later alterations. The chapel facade, now such a notable feature, was until 1889 obscured by other buildings in front of it on St Edmund's Church Street. Methodists in Salisbury united in this church in 1987 and the Harnham and Dew's Road chapels then became redundant.[754]
Photograph also on page 53.

Wesleyan Methodists opened a chapel in **Church Street**, now **Mill Road**, in 1832, west of the road. It was located where the down platform of the present station now stands and was demolished to make way for the extension of the London and South Western Railway across the city in 1859. It was replaced by the chapel opened in Wilton Road in 1860.[755]

Wesleyan Methodist Chapel, Wilton Road, * north of road at east end, Grade 2 listed, in use as **Emmanuel Free Church**. This chapel, replacing that in Mill Road, opened in 1860 with seats for 250. Its capacity had increased to 400 by 1927, perhaps through the addition of the galleries on three sides, with inset iron panels, which remain in place. It also acquired schoolrooms at right angles to the rear, built in 1881 but increased in size in 1897. The chapel closed in 1962 and in 1967 it was taken over by the Emmanuel Free Church (see also below) who still worship here. The brick and ashlar front has a pediment broken into by a rounded architrave,

Salisbury Wilton Road Wesleyan

and round-arched windows in two tiers either side, their glazing almost identical with those of St Edmund's Church Street. These flank the chapel's most notable feature, the striking central domed porch in stone on fluted pilasters, probably added with the other alterations in 1897. Above this is a large pedimented and pilastered plaque, perhaps also of this date. The rendered sides have round-arched windows.[756]

Primitive and Other Methodists

Primitive Methodist Chapel of 1826, Fisherton Street, later a Conservative Club and now flats. 'Tent Methodists' were active in the city in 1823 but there is no evidence that the group which created this chapel in 1826 was the same. It may have been a conversion of an existing building rather than newly built and was set well back south of the street; it is accessed now by an alleyway adjacent to Myler and Mawes' furniture shop, being the building visible from the street end of the alleyway. Now divided into flats, it is rendered over brick with a slate roof hipped at the north west end where it joins onto another building. A parallel smaller block was joined to it to the south west after 1843 and the whole is now much altered with modern windows: round-headed windows on the south east gable end may be the only visible sign of its past. It was replaced in 1869 by the new chapel on the north side of Fisherton Street and later became a Conservative Club, perhaps before the turn of the century.[757]

The **Primitive Methodists** opened a second chapel in **Fisherton Street** in 1869, replacing that of 1826 and this time prominently on the street rather than hidden behind other buildings. It was north of the street, immediately east of Chapel Place. The facade was handsome with uniform round-arched openings across a slightly protruding central section, above which was a pedimented gable with a date plaque for 1869. There was a paired opening to an open lobby in the centre with a single window to each side, the same pattern repeated in windows at the first floor. It had capacity for 400 including a gallery, and to the rear were schoolrooms and a vestry. Prone to flooding and difficult to maintain, it closed in 1915 and the congregation then moved to their new chapel in Dew's Road. The Fisherton Street chapel was sold and, much to the distress of the chapel trustees, converted into a cinema, the front rebuilt in cinema style. From 1939 the Salisbury Playhouse was based there until it moved to a new building in 1976. The former chapel was later demolished to make way for what is now a bed shop.[758]

Salisbury Fisherton Street Primitive Methodist of 1869 flooded in 1915. Photograph courtesy of Salisbury Museum

Primitive Methodist Chapel, Dew's Road, at corner of Dew's Road and West Street, in use by the **Elim Church**. This was built in 1917 to replace the second Fisherton Street chapel, with capacity for 450 people. It closed in 1987 when Methodists combined in St Edmund's Church Street, but was taken over by the Elim Church in 1990. They remain there, having more recently bought the adjacent building, formerly a school and then a tanning factory, and turned it into a conference centre. At this late date the simplicity of early Primitive Methodist design is left well behind and this chapel in free Gothic style by George Baines and Son of London, in brick and stone, has a slim tower with spire to one side and a three-light north window with art-nouveau-influenced tracery very much of the period. The sides are of three bays with a transept behind and an apse at the south end, beyond which are other rooms, probably those of 1935. The interior is modernised with an altered rear gallery.[759]

Primitive Methodist Chapel, St Mark's Road, later used by Christian Scientists and now in use by Jehovah's Witnesses. This was built in 1890 to serve an expanding area of the town. It closed in 1971, was taken over by the Christian Scientists and in 1989 by the Jehovah's Witnesses who still meet there. It is of red brick with pale brick dressings but the gable facing the road has been rendered and the windows blocked in though still marked in curved string courses of brick. The door is modern, the gable head is dated 1890, the sides are in brick with four bays of round-arched windows, again blocked in, and there is a long single-storey pre-war extension to the rear.[760]

Methodist Reformed Chapel, Milford Street, then United Methodist Free Church and later Elim Pentecostal, * Grade 2 listed, now a nightclub. This opened in 1897 and has a lively exterior - Italianate in form but Gothic in detail - and a surprisingly well preserved interior. It was designed by W H Dinsley of Chorley and has an elaborate front of brick and stone, four bays wide with a pediment over the central two bays. These have large round-arched windows above and oddly more narrow round-arched doors below with pillared surrounds. Either side of these are round-arched windows below and flat-arched windows above with pilasters alongside and balustrades over. A triangular plaque in the tympanum has the entwined date 1896.

The front might be old-fashioned and an uncomfortable mix of design but it makes an impact, as does the interior which has a bow-fronted gallery on iron pillars, probably unique in the county. This faces the pulpit and the arch behind it which leads to the extra bay containing the organ. These, and many of the tiered pews, are still in place despite its current use as a nightclub: worth seeking out, though attending the club in order to do so may be a challenge too far for some.

The first chapel on this site was opened in 1852 by a 'reform' group which had broken away from the Wesleyan Methodists and a Sunday school was added behind c1880 to designs by John Wills of Derby. Acoustics, lighting and ventilation in the first chapel were poor and it was replaced by the present one which opened in 1897 with a number of schoolrooms behind and to the rear west side; these survive though much altered. The chapel closed in 1958 due to declining numbers and the remaining members transferred to St Edmund's Church Street. It was then taken over by the Elim church and used by them until 1990, at which point they moved to the former Primitive Methodist chapel in Dew's Road. An attempt at about this time to have the whole building sold and moved to serve as a school chapel for Pangbourne College in Berkshire was unsuccessful and it later became a nightclub.

The 1852 chapel was smaller, with three bays in two tiers facing the road, a door and two windows below, all flat-headed, and round-arched windows above; there was a pronounced string course between the floors and a parapet above in front of a pitched roof.[761]

Photographs on pages 40 and 44.

Under the auspices of the Milford Street chapel a further **United Methodist Free Church** was built on **Church Lane, Bemerton** in 1864, close to St Andrew's church. It was 38ft long by 23ft wide with 12ft high walls but its location and construction were such that by 1870 the trustees had to buy a new stove so as to attract more worshippers in winter and in early 1871 they noted that the harmonium in the chapel had been ruined by damp. In April 1871 the chapel was sold to Admiral Fulford, who lived at Riversfield House nearby, making it surely one of the shortest-lived of all purpose-built chapels. It is believed to have been demolished.[762]

Methodist Chapel, Roman Road, Bemerton, * just up from the skew bridge, in use. This was built in 1932 to serve the new housing in that area of the city and is an interesting example of the tensions sometimes found in architecture of the period. It is in brick and stone with Gothic windows including one in the gable end with trefoil tracery, yet the gable itself is stepped in 1930s fashion and below that, equally of its time, is a large ashlar porch with a central semi-domed doorway and

three-sided wings. The sides are of four bays with more Gothic windows and brick buttressing and there are transepts to the rear. A church hall at the back was added almost immediately and further single-storey schoolrooms were added later. The interior is plain and has an organ behind the pulpit. The architects were Bothams, Brown and Dixon of Salisbury.[763]
Photograph on page 51.

A **Methodist Chapel** was provided in **Saxon Road** for the growing area of West Harnham. It opened in the early 1950s and a hall alongside soon afterwards. In 1987 the Methodists united at St Edmund's Church Street and this chapel was demolished. The site is now occupied by a group of flats called Wesley Close.[764]

Others

The earliest of the new denominations coming into Salisbury was the **New Jerusalem or Swedenborgian** Church which first registered the freemasons' hall in George Yard in 1825 and then registered a chapel in **Crane Street** in 1828, premises of which there appear now to be no trace. Various houses were soon after registered by possibly more than one group of Swedenborgians, including in **Castle Street** from c1840: this building had capacity for over a hundred but is also believed to have been demolished. A further congregation met in **Fisherton Street** in 1872 but by 1878 had moved to **Antelope Yard**. This last congregation had disappeared by 1894. It has not been possible to establish with confidence exactly where any of these meeting places were located.[765]

Exclusive Brethren built a chapel in **Church Street, Fisherton Anger (later Mill Road)** in 1860, said to be a little way south of the Victoria Hotel, perhaps immediately north of No.66 Mill Road and now replaced by Mill Road Mews. It was still in use in 1969 but was probably closed soon afterwards.[766]

Open Brethren Chapel, Barnard Street, just east of Gigant Street, in use by the **Christ Church**. The **Open Brethren** were meeting in an iron mission room in **Guilder Lane** by 1885. In 1895 they took over the former Congregational chapel in **Scots Lane** as City Hall. They left there in 1917 and in 1929 bought this chapel, built in 1875-6 as the **Barnard's Cross Mission** Hall and originally serving as an evangelical mission to children, with trustees from five free churches in the city and from St Paul's church. The Open Brethren left here in 2015 and the building is now in the ownership of the **Christ Church**.
      The chapel is of basically conventional shape, in render with large round-arched windows with Y-tracery high in each gable, four bays to the sides and a small lean-to rear extension. It is however notable for the triple-gabled single-storey front extension, the central one a porch and the others rooms, the right hand one extending part way along the side of the chapel.[767]
      Open Brethren were also meeting in **Brown Street** in 1930.[768]

Exclusive Brethren met in recent times on **Middle Street, Harnham** and then **Netherhampton Road, Harnham**, both characteristically anonymous red brick buildings of modest size. Their largest premises in the area are now on **Pembroke**

Road immediately west of the skew bridge, a large warehouse-type building with a similarly large car park. They are also using the former **Christadelphian** hall on **Ashley Road** (see below).[769]

The **Catholic Apostolic** Church, which may have been active in the city by 1848, met in the Temperance Hall in Catherine Street from 1862 to 1876.[770]

Maundrel Hall, Fisherton Street, immediately west of the river bridge, now a public house. Named after an early Protestant martyr, the Maundrel Hall was provided by public subscription as a place for non-denominational worship and discussion, especially for poor people who were not regular churchgoers. Designed by Fred Bath and opened in 1880, it was soon followed by other buildings nearby also built for Christian purposes, including a hall, a temperance hotel and a hostel for women. The hall lost much of its usefulness after the building of a new Parochial Hall in 1937 and a shift of population westwards, and was sold with adjoining buildings in 1954. It was for some time used as a furniture shop but is now a public house.

The building is altered, rendered and plain but retains detail in the cusp-headed wooden framing of the rectangular windows. It is five bays deep, beyond which are two bays of successively lower roof height and an apse-like semi-circular end. Before conversion the front had densely applied half-timbering above the ground floor, with a third window at the centre which is now blocked in. Below were windows either side of a central door, each of the same width as those above.[771]

The **Railway (Emmanuel) Mission** built a chapel at what is now 63 Devizes Road in 1906. It was re-registered in 1954 as the **Emmanuel (Free Evangelical) Church** and they continued to meet here until 1966, moving in 1967 to the former Wesleyan Methodist on Wilton Road (see above), where they remain. The 1906 chapel was subsequently demolished and replaced by a small block of flats.[772]

Christadelphian Hall, Ashley Road, east of Coldharbour Lane; now used by the **Exclusive Brethren**. This is a small hall, rendered above a brick plinth, three bays deep and with an extended porch across the full width of the front with a lunette over. The Christadelphians were established in Brown Street in the early 20th century but built this in 1929.[773]

The **Elim Pentecostal Church**, formerly Elim Four Square Gospel Alliance, has had a relatively brief but mobile existence in the city, described above under the various chapels they have used but summarised here. From 1930 to 1958 they were at the **Scots Lane** chapel, initially Congregational and then Open Brethren. They then moved to the **Milford Street Methodist Reform** chapel until 1990 and finally on to the former **Dew's Road Primitive Methodist** chapel where they remain.[774]

Harnham Free Church, Hawksridge, south of Coombe Road, in use. This was originally the workhouse chapel, dating from around the turn of the 20th century. The original building is of brick in two shades under tile with fish-scale bands and half-timbered gable heads; the interior was also finished in two shades of brick. The Harnham Free Church was established in the 1970s and bought the chapel in 1980, extending it in 1988 to provide a hall and other facilities. The extension, also in brick, picks up some of the detailing of the original.[775]

8. Swindon

At the start of the 19th century Swindon had a population of barely over a thousand, making it smaller than almost every other town in Wiltshire. Nonconformists were not particularly active in this part of the county so it is no surprise that the only permanent meeting place for Swindon nonconformists throughout the 18th century was the Baptist chapel in nearby Stratton Green. This situation changed at first slowly - an Independent chapel was built in 1804, a Wesleyan Methodist was under construction from 1813 and Primitive Methodists were active from the late 1820s - but it was the arrival of the Great Western Railway works in 1843 which produced the major change.

The establishment of the works and the New Town, a mile away from the Old, led to rapid and sustained growth. The population increased from 4,900 in 1851 to 33,000 in 1891, during which time the two settlements, initially separate, increased in size and joined, and the New Town expanded northwards into Gorse Hill and Even Swindon. Many of the new residents were workers from elsewhere in the country, a good proportion of them nonconformists, so there was soon a vigorous programme of chapel building and enlargement. This covered the New Town and the Old as well as the expanding suburbs, and continued into the 20th century by which time Swindon was by a large margin the biggest town in the county.

More chapels were built in the early 20th century, some in the expanding suburbs and some for denominations new to here, and after the Second World War further rapid population expansion saw the building of chapels in new estates on a scale not witnessed in other Wiltshire towns. Although the general pattern of church amalgamations and closures is as noticeable here as elsewhere, there are nevertheless numerous new congregations, many evangelical, meeting throughout the urban area alongside the longer established denominations.[776]

The gazetteer for Swindon is set out in three sections to reflect this pattern of development. The first covers the limited initial development before the arrival of the railway. The second, and much the longest, covers the main period of chapel expansion up until around the beginning of the 20th century. The third covers more recent building, much of it post-war.

Haydon Wick, now part of Swindon, was previously a separate parish and is recorded in the villages gazetteer.

Swindon Before the Railway

Quakers, Congregationalists, Independents and Baptists

Quakers had almost no presence in the town in earlier days.[777]

The first **Independent/Congregational Chapel** was built in **Newport Street** in 1804. This was small and octagonal, standing on the north side of the street, with arched windows at ground and first floors and above the door a round window with a date medallion above that. Side wings to the gallery were soon added and in the 1830s the schoolroom of a British School was built on to the east side. Despite a secession

THE OLD INDEPENDENT CHAPEL.

Swindon Newport Street Congregational. Image courtesy of Local Studies, Swindon Libraries

to the Baptists in the 1840s, the congregation continued to grow but the building itself was described by the 1860s as a 'dismal cell' in which the ceiling was so low that the minister in the pulpit and people in the gallery could touch it. It was eventually replaced by the Victoria Street chapel in 1866 and is believed to have been demolished by the 1880s.[778]

An **Independent** house or chapel was registered in **Moredon** in 1839. Although it was still there in 1851 it seems that it may have already been out of use by that date.[779]

Although there are likely to have been a small number of **Baptists** in Swindon from the 17th century onwards, their activity only became significant in the 1840s.[780]

Wesleyan and Primitive Methodists

The **Wesleyan Methodist Planks Chapel** was the second nonconformist chapel in the town and was started in 1813 by a group of Wesleyans who had been meeting in houses for a number of years previously. Shortage of money meant it was not completed until 1824 and at that stage they even considered selling it. They were rescued by money from Mr Bush of Lambourn, famous for giving away most of his income over many years to establish Wesleyan chapels through the Vale of the White Horse in both Berkshire and Wiltshire.

The Planks chapel prospered thereafter, with a gallery added in 1842 and a schoolroom to the side. The front had tall round-arched windows either side of a similarly arched door above which was a plaque, 'Wesleyan Chapel 1816', a parapet and what seems to have been a hipped roof. The school was a lean-to at the side, tapering from front to back. It seems that an attempt was made in early 1861 to sell the chapel in order to build a replacement elsewhere but this was thwarted by the terms of the trust deed and in the end it was replaced on the same site in 1862 by a new octagonal building which had four gables and an octagonal pyramidal roof culminating in a stubby spire. This was designed by Thomas Smith Lansdown of Swindon. The site was south of the corn exchange, the 1862 chapel facing east in what is now the rear of the Planks car park. An adjoining house was either replaced by or converted into a schoolroom. The problems with the trust deed having finally been overcome, the chapel was replaced in 1880 by the Bath Road chapel. It was subsequently used for a while as a stable, then by the Salvation Army and later as a garage and a store before demolition in 1937/8.[781]

Primitive Methodism was introduced to the town in the late 1820s by preachers from the newly established Brinkworth circuit. There was continuing activity centred on the Eastcott Hill area but the opening of a first chapel only followed the arrival of the GWR works in 1843.[782]

The Railway Age

Quakers

It was not until 1899 that a meeting became established strongly enough for a meeting house to be built. This was the **Quaker Meeting House, 79 Eastcott Hill,** still in use. It was built in 1901, small and plain in brick with an entrance lobby under a hipped lean-to roof attached to the front. In 1976 the rear half of the building was demolished and replaced by a two-storey extension containing classrooms and a flat, the latter later converted to offices. Either then or in 1989, when further structural work became necessary, the lobby was removed, the front rendered and a half hip introduced to the roof. The doorway was moved to the side and the front now has three modern windows though it retains a long stone panel above inscribed 'Friends Meeting House'.[783]

Congregationalists, Independents and Unitarians

The successor **Congregational Chapel** to that on Newport Street was built at the corner of **Bath Road and Victoria Street** (now Victoria Road) in 1866, part-funded by the ubiquitous Charles Jupe of Mere. There was controversy over the move, which had been planned since the 1840s, and when the new chapel opened only five members, not including the minister, transferred to it though numbers soon rose. Although plans had been drawn up by George Bidlake of Wolverhampton the final design was by W J Stent of Warminster, chosen perhaps because of his association with Jupe elsewhere. Seating 550, it was built of rough stone with 'heavy stone' dressings, had a rose window at the south end and a square tower at the south east corner giving the whole an Italianate feel. The choice of location, in the old town, was not well suited to where most of the congregation now lived and in 1877 a group left to form a new chapel in Sanford Street. By 1916 the chapel was in poor condition and it was later threatened by a street widening scheme but it was not until 1938 that a site for a replacement was chosen in Upham Road, Walcot. The Victoria Street chapel was demolished shortly after the Second World War and the town's art gallery now stands on the site.[784]

The group of **Congregationalists** who left the Victoria Road chapel in 1877 first rebuilt in **Sanford Street** an iron chapel transported from its original position in Clifton, Bristol. It was on the east side of the street towards the north end, and exceptionally large for an iron church. Gothic, with a clerestory above side aisles, it had a substantial tower to the front containing the door at its base. It had accommodation for 800, but by 1890 it was rusting and umbrellas were said to be sometimes necessary inside the church on rainy days. In 1894 it was replaced by a permanent chapel with accommodation for 550, designed by T B Silcock of Bath. This was of red brick with stone dressings, details showing Arts and Crafts influence, a rose window in a square surround like a clock face, and a tower to the left topped by an open cupola. A Sunday school of 1888 to the rear and left hand side of chapel presented a more conventional appearance and was extended in 1898 by Silcock with Samuel Reay; the Sunday schools were badly damaged or destroyed by fire in 1947 but replaced in 1948 with an assembly hall built to designs of T Burrington of Swindon. The congregation left the chapel for the Central Church in 1972, eventually moving to the Pilgrim Centre in 1990, and it was demolished in 1977 to make way for an office building.[785]

Baptists

Particular Baptists, albeit ones seceding from Newport Street Congregational, chose the Old Town for their first chapel in 1845, and seceders from there in 1882 stayed in the same area. General Baptists, by contrast, under the influence of Baptists from Stratton Green, opened their first chapel in Fleet Street in the New Town and it was they who expanded out into Gorse Hill and Rodbourne.[786]

Providence Particular Baptist Chapel, South Street, set back north of the street, now two houses. This chapel was established by members seceding from the Newport Street Congregational. The original chapel is behind the hipped gable at the east end, dated 1845, with a later porch and two tall but altered windows. Originally seating only 140, it was enlarged in 1872 with a new wing at right angles, there being no space elsewhere, and in 1881 another gallery was added and a Sunday school built. This produced the present appearance, of a three-bay rear block with projecting wings at each end, the structure of squared stone blockwork and the roof of slate. The chapel closed in 1979 and was then converted.[787]

Rehoboth Particular Baptist Chapel, Prospect Hill, at north end of Prospect Hill, in use. Seceders from the Providence chapel built this one in 1882. It is a simple design in brick with ashlar dressings, the gable having a porch with arched doorway, tall arched windows either side and a plaque dated 1882 in the pedimented gable. The doorway was to the side of the porch at one period with the front blocked in and carrying a noticeboard. There are three flat-headed windows in the north wall but the south wall is blank though there seems never to have been any other building immediately adjacent. Excavation work for a new development nearby caused structural damage in 2014 and the chapel had to be extensively strengthened and repaired. The interior is now plain, the pews replaced by chairs during the repair work but the old pulpit retained.[788]

The **General Baptist Chapel** at the junction of **Fleet Street and Bridge Street**, designed by Sir Samuel Morton Peto the railway contractor, opened in 1849 as the first General Baptist in Swindon. Its distinctive Italianate front had a triple-arched doorway below and triple-arched window above, both looking as if they ought to be open loggias in some warmer climate. It had a low roof angle and corner pilasters with a central bell turret and smaller versions of the same at the corners. The sides were of seven bays and the interior had balconies on three sides and a large pulpit in an apse at the north end. A *schoolroom,* to the north at the junction of Bridge

Swindon Fleet Street Baptist – the schoolroom to the rear on Bridge Street still stands.
Photograph courtesy of Local Studies, Swindon Libraries

Street with Henry Street, survives. It was added in 1868 to designs by Thomas Smith Lansdown and consists at the north end of a low building in squared stone block with ashlar dressings. It has two pairs of round-arched windows and a central door to Bridge Street, and the north gable has two more pairs of windows and a circular ventilator above with 'Baptist Schools Anno Domini 1868' inscribed on its surround. Linking the schoolroom to the chapel proper was a further building, initially single storey but later two storeys and with a tower at one corner.

The chapel, initially dependent on that at Stratton Green, became independent in 1855 and was enlarged to seat 520 in 1868, despite which its accommodation was deemed inadequate by 1879. The congregation moved to the new Tabernacle chapel in Regent Circus in 1886 and the chapel had been demolished, bar the schoolroom, by early in the 20th century. The tower in the intermediate section was demolished and the rest altered to become eventually the Albion sports and social club. The schoolroom was empty in 2021 pending possible residential conversion.[789]

Cambria General Baptist Chapel, Cambria Place, * set back south of Cambria Place, Grade 2 listed, now a house. Many Welsh iron-workers came to work in the GWR rolling mills and this chapel was built for them alongside the terraced housing of Cambria Place. It may have been Particular Baptist when it opened in 1866 but by 1882 was dependent upon the Fleet Street General Baptist. It was probably designed by the rolling mill manager, Thomas Ellis, and has a facade characterised as typically Welsh with round-arched door under a slightly protruding pedimented porch and round-arched windows either side; a date plaque for 1866 is above. The front is of squared stone block with ashlar dressings and the three-bay sides are of brick though that to the west was previously slate-hung for weather protection. Inside there was a rear gallery, probably added not long after construction, and a flat boarded ceiling. There was a small rear extension, probably a vestry, late in the century and a schoolroom was added beyond that in 1905. The chapel closed in 1986, became a recording studio for a period and was well converted to a house c1992, the supplementary buildings to the rear being much altered at that time.[790]

Swindon Cambria Place Baptist

General Baptist Chapel, Gorse Hill, 1883 at junction of Ferndale Road and Cricklade Road, in use by Bible Life Fellowship. This chapel was built in 1883 to designs by William Henry Drew following mission work by Fleet Street Baptists. It replaced a short-lived **Tabernacle Baptist** at the corner of **Bright Street and Cricklade Road,** opened in 1878, sold in 1882 but apparently not demolished until the 1980s. In 1904 it in turn was replaced by a larger chapel further south on Cricklade Road (see below) and then became until the early 1950s a GWR Mechanics' Institution reading room before being taken over as the Plessey Social Club for many years and since 2015 by the Bible Life Fellowship. It is of four bays under a conventional pitched slate roof, with various later rear extensions and now scarcely visible because of the two-storey modern extension to the street sides, probably added by Plessey. The front was originally of conventional chapel appearance with a steeply pitched roof to the porch.[791]

Perhaps the most regretted of all Swindon's lost chapels, the vast **Baptist Tabernacle** was opened in 1886 at the south end of **Regent Street** as a larger replacement for that on Fleet Street. It was designed by William Henry Read of Swindon with an impressive giant portico of six Tuscan columns under a pediment in front of two tiers of windows. The front was of stone, the ten-bay sides of brick with stone dressings, and inside were a continuous gallery on three sides, a large bow-fronted pulpit raised on columns and an organ, added in 1911, above and behind in an arched chamber. A schoolroom was built concurrently with the chapel and a second added later. Discussions on the amalgamation of the central nonconformist churches started in the early 1970s and in 1977 agreement was reached that five churches should relocate to a new ecumenical centre, the **Pilgrim Centre** (see below). The Tabernacle closed in July 1977 and was demolished in 1978, though its portico was bought by an individual who tried and failed to obtain permission to re-use it in a private house and subsequently sold it on to the borough council. The Pilgrim Centre was later built on this site.[792]
Photograph on page 40.

The Tabernacle supported missionary work in the poorer districts of the town, including for some years in **Mill Street**, later the west end of Manchester Road, in an initiative started by the Young Persons' Christian Endeavour Society. They started work there in 1899 - perhaps in the cottage previously used by the Wesleyans (see below) and shortly to be demolished to make way for tram lines - and were active until at least 1905.[793]

General Baptist Chapel, Gorse Hill, corner of Beatrice Street and Cricklade Road, in use. This was opened in 1904 as the replacement for the 1883 chapel further north. Designed by George Lansdown of London in red brick, its chief features are the octagonal brick pillars either side of the porch and the continuous clerestory windows on each side. The latter may look industrial but they help create a light interior space, the aisles separated from the main space only by tall wooden pillars. The double-arched Gothic porch entrance sits uncomfortably with the rest of the building which is very much of its time, particularly the five-light window above with its angular tracery. An original Sunday school at right angles to the rear has since been demolished but to the north is a large brick extension dating from 2000.[794]

The Tabernacle Baptists undertook mission work in the Rodbourne area in the early 20th century and in 1907 bought an iron church, formerly used by troops on Salisbury Plain, and erected it as a mission church on the west side of **Rodbourne Road** just north of the railway bridge. It was of substantial length, with three large

bays to the front and four smaller to the rear. Efforts to replace the building with
something better suited to their needs were fruitless until 1964 when, having taken
over the former Primitive Methodist chapel in Cheney Manor Road (see below),
they moved into that. The iron church was demolished, probably soon after, and
has now been replaced by the Iris Redman Gardens development.[795]

Wesleyan Methodists

The second Wesleyan chapel, and the first in the New Town, was built in 1849 on
Bridge Street. It could accommodate 160 people but lasted only until 1858 when
it was pulled down and replaced by a larger one, probably on **Faringdon Road** at
the south west corner of Farnsby Street but perhaps a short distance east of there.
This one, designed in Gothic style by James Wilson of Bath, was much larger with
550 seats but still only lasted a short while, being pulled down in 1869 when the
Wesleyans moved to the GWR 'Barracks'. In 1904, Wesleyan schoolrooms with
a row of shops below were built on the Farnsby Street corner site to designs by
William Bird of Midsomer Norton and these in turn were replaced in the later 20th
century by the present office block.[796]

*Wesleyan Methodist Chapel, 'The Barracks', Faringdon Road,*** Grade 2 listed,
now The Platform children's activity centre. This was the third of the sequence of
Wesleyan chapels in the new town. The building has its origins in a Tudor-style
design by Brunel for a lodging house for single men which was not built because
of a recession. When a building did eventually appear in 1854 it was this much
more forbidding edifice with four-storey towers at either end of the entrance front
facing Emlyn Square and between them five three-storeyed gabled bays, the whole
with cusped and vaguely Gothic windows in sets of two and three lights. Wings
stretched north-east from each tower, creating a U shape with an open courtyard
between them. It was unsuccessful as a lodging house and the GWR eventually
sold it to the Methodists for £1600 as an alternative to another site which they had
agreed on but then decided they needed for their new carriage works.
The conversion in 1869, by Thomas Smith Lansdown of Swindon, created a chapel
with capacity for 1000 people. The Emlyn Square facade was left unchanged, the
ground floor rooms being used for classrooms and vestries, but the wings were
much altered and the courtyard roofed over to create the chapel itself on an axis at
right angles to Faringdon Road: the courtyard roof, hipped at the north east end,
is at right angles to the alignment of the chapel. Gothic windows making much
use of a trefoil shape were added front and back to give a chapel-like appearance
and also let in more light, and the new end wall at the north east also has three tall
Gothic windows. Two square stair towers with octagonal louvres and spires above
were added to the Faringdon Road frontage. Inside, a new ceiling was supported by
two rows of cast iron columns and a gallery for up to 500 Sunday school children
was erected at the Faringdon Road end. The conversion allowed the interior to
be exceptionally wide and light, a clever re-making of a building constructed for
an entirely different purpose: the modern porch aside, it remains equally striking
visually.

      There were further alterations by A G White of Swindon in 1887 and the
Methodists continued to use it until 1959 after which it became the GWR museum

Swindon Barracks Wesleyan, original entrance to the left.

Swindon Barracks Wesleyan, the entrance front created by Lansdown but further altered when it was turned into a railway museum

from 1962, with large glazed openings inserted into the Faringdon Road entrance to allow rolling stock to be taken in and out. The railway museum closed in 2000, moving to a building on the former GWR works site, and it became a children's activity centre from 2010.[797]

Wesleyan Methodist Chapel, Gorse Hill, on Cricklade Road at junction with St Paul's Street, now St Paul's Court flats. The Wesleyans established a presence in the newly developing area of Gorse Hill with a mission hall built in 1871. The chapel was built in front of it in 1883, seating 180; it was enlarged to seat 600 in 1900 and a schoolroom had been added in a separate building to the rear in 1899. In 1964 it was joined by the congregation from the nearby Russell Memorial chapel (see below) which was then demolished. The chapel closed in 1993, was for a time a community centre but by 2018 had been turned into flats. The schoolroom was demolished.

The chapel is tall, in brick with five pairs of tall pointed-arch windows to the sides and a cross-wing at the rear with a rose window at the end. Dormers have been added in the conversion without ill effect and the new glazing in the windows is successful. However, most of the gable facing the road now has protruding render with modern rectangular windows and visible pipework: the previous door and windows are concealed.[798]

Wesleyan Methodist Chapel, Bath Road, ** north of road towards east end, Grade 2 listed, in use. By 1880, when this was built to replace that at The Planks, nonconformists were making their urban chapels not only large to accommodate ever increasing numbers but also assertive to express the confidence of their faith and their place in the town. The Bath Road Wesleyans may have needed to put their schoolrooms in a basement for space reasons but it may be no coincidence that doing so raised the chapel itself further into the air and imposed it even more on the street-scene. It is Gothic, built of rock-faced stone, with steps up to the doorway and traceried windows in two tiers sandwiched between twin octagonal pillars with columned spires. The pillars are joined high up by a balcony below which are two large gargoyles, and behind the balcony, set back from the lower facade, is the

Swindon Bath Road Wesleyan, the simplified interior with rear gallery part walled off

gable head with a further three-part window. The other prominent features are the apsidal stair towers on either side of the facade with lancet windows following the line of the stairs and a continuous clerestory below the roof.

It was designed by Bromilow and Cheers of Liverpool to replace the 1862 Planks chapel, with capacity for 800 and a hall and six schoolrooms in the basement. Renovations were carried out in 1895 by R J Beswick but by its centenary year in 1980 the church needed such extensive repairs that it was under threat of demolition. To save it, the Cirencester architects Eric Cole were employed to make major changes in 1983-4, including demolition of the chancel, a reduction in height of the ceiling and the closing in of the rear gallery to create rooms either side and an open glassed-in space at the centre. Removing the chancel allowed the construction of Epworth Court, a Methodist Housing Association retirement housing block wrapped around three sides of the building. The interior of the chapel is now much simplified as a result but some of the roof trusses are still visible.[799]

Photograph also on page 41.

Wesleyan Methodist Chapel, Percy Street, Even Swindon, north of street towards east end, at the east end of a modern block, in commercial use. Wesleyans expanded into this developing area in 1877 with an iron chapel having seating for 200. In 1894 a new brick chapel by Thomas Smith Lansdown of Swindon was added to the east side and the iron chapel became the Sunday school. The chapel closed c1956 and the iron chapel was demolished and replaced by a commercial block. The 1894 chapel survives, much altered, behind a later white-rendered commercial front. Brick buttresses remain to the rear and the east side, which was of five bays.[800]

Wesleyan Methodists opened a mission hall in **William Street**, in another expanding housing area, in 1887. It was at the junction with Kingshill Road, adjacent to what is now Erin Court, and had a capacity of 400, said in 1904 to be 'hardly enough'. A schoolroom was added to the rear in 1906. The chapel was taken over by **Christian Brethren** in 1951 and there were various alterations and additions before it closed and was demolished in 2006. It has been replaced by a small housing block.[801]

A further mission hall was built by the **Wesleyans** east of the road at the north end of **Princes Street** in 1884, in an area between the old and new towns then infilling with new housing. For several years they had held missions in a cottage at the east end of Mill Street and this was a larger replacement. The mission hall, seating 240 and designed by Orlando Baker, was intended to be followed by a chapel on the same site but this never happened. Instead it was replaced by the Central Mission Hall in 1907 (see below) and a commercial garage was soon erected on the site, to be replaced in its turn by the hotel which now stands there.[802]

The **Wesleyans** built yet another mission hall, on **Cheney Manor Road** – at that date known as Telford Road – in 1902, to designs by Messrs Davies of Swindon. It was accessed off Whitby Grove and unusually had the door in a side wall, perhaps because of the spacious site. The gable end has a triple stepped lancet at the centre between double lancets, and the sides have four bays of double lancets. Now in painted render, it may have been originally brick. There is a small flat-roofed extension. The chapel was sold to Seventh Day Adventists in 1954 and is still used by them.[803]

Methodist Central Halls were a feature of the Forward Movement, seeking a more forceful evangelical style to reach the 'working classes'. They were secular in style, containing not only worship space but also lecture halls and spaces for film shows and concerts as an alternative to public houses and music halls. Swindon's was built in 1907 by William F Bird of Midsomer Norton, on **Clarence Street** immediately north east of what is now the Meca club, a former cinema. It had a distinctive octagonal peaked roof and, on the street, a tall-windowed tower with its own small dome. It had capacity for 1,000 seated on chairs with galleries on three sides. An additional hall, in brick and concrete panels with a flat roof, was built behind facing Princes Street as late as 1956-7, to designs by Cripps & Stewart of Oxford, but both closed in 1973, the congregation joining forces with the Baptists at the Tabernacle before eventually moving to the new Pilgrim Centre. The Central Hall was badly damaged by fire in 1977 and demolished in 1985. The Kingsbridge Point office block now stands on most of the site.[804]

Photograph on page 45.

Primitive Methodists

The first Primitive Methodist chapel was built in 1849 on what later became **Regent Street**. The area has long been fully urban but then was almost in countryside on the southern edge of the New Town, the chapel on its own with no other buildings around. It was of brick, 30 feet square, and held about 150 people. In 1863 a larger chapel with schoolroom was built on the same site and in 1876 this in turn was replaced by a third chapel, also on the same site, with capacity for 600. The 1876 chapel was designed by Orlando Baker of Swindon and was of unusual appearance. It was built of brick with stone dressings on a seven-bay front, the end and middle bays slightly protruding with a parapet above and a pediment above the central bay. The entrance was at the south east end in what was in effect a complicated lean-to, and the stairs to the three-sided gallery were also placed there. An organ and choir stalls above the pulpit occupied the fourth side of the gallery and a basement floor was used as a schoolroom. The chapel was located west of the road where Regent Street bends away from Regent Circus, just north of where the Baptist Tabernacle was later built. The front was altered in 1887 because of road works, and a large Sunday school was built behind in 1895. However, its position in what became a central shopping street was difficult to maintain and it was demolished in 1957 though the Sunday school remained until 1992. The south end of a block of shops now occupies the site.[805]

Primitive Methodist Chapel, Prospect Place, east of road south of South Street, in use by Assemblies of the First Born Church. Primitive Methodists in the Old Town were still meeting in cottages and in the open air for some years after the Regent Street chapel opened, until this one was built in 1870, to designs by Thomas Smith Lansdown of Swindon. It was twice extended to the rear before 1904, at which date it had capacity for 420, and was eventually sold in 1968. The chapel is of brick with stone dressings though the facade is now rendered and the stonework painted. It is attached to the manse, built at the same time, and has an uncomfortable front with two tiers of crowded windows in a variety of round-arched and cusped designs. The porch is set below a scroll, 'Primitive Methodist', there is a horizontal band between the two tiers of windows and a further band below the blind window in the gable head; the gable itself is strangely shouldered at one point. The interior is more comfortable with a three-sided gallery on cast-iron columns, the fronts in metal lattice, and densely packed pews.[806]

The Primitive Methodist chapel in **Clifton Street** was built in 1882, on what was then the western edge of the town and almost equidistant from the Old and New Towns. It was set back from the road but enlarged in 1900 to plans in grand Gothic style by R J Beswick of Swindon so as to fill the whole plot, at which time it had capacity for 360 people. The original chapel, at right angles to the new building, was presumably used as a Sunday school thereafter but a further schoolroom in a separate building, by Cripps and Heard, was added in 1958

Swindon Clifton Street Primitive Methodist, exterior.

Swindon Clifton Street Primitive Methodist dressed for harvest festival. Note the full set of galleries with wrought iron fronts and the lighting by gasoliers. Photographs thanks to Paul Williams, custodian and copyright owner of images from the William Hooper collection

using funds released by the demolition of the Regent Street chapel. The Clifton Street chapel, however, closed not long afterwards and was demolished around 1970. The site is now occupied by Nos. 13 and 14 Clifton Street but the **schoolroom**, in plain brick with gable end to the road on the other side of the cemetery driveway, remains in use as a pre-school.[807]

The Primitive Methodists moved into the expanding area of **Gorse Hill** at much the same time as the Wesleyans, first building a chapel on the north side of **Chapel Street** in 1871 at the point where the public lavatories are now. This soon became too small as the area expanded and it was taken over by the **Salvation Army** (see below). It was replaced in 1890 by a larger chapel with seating for 390 at the corner of **Edinburgh Street and Cricklade Road**, named the **Russell Memorial Church** after an early missioner. This was designed by the builder, Thomas Colborne, but constructed under supervision from R J Beswick. It was in brick with stone dressings, much decorated, with a transverse porch, a prominent shouldered gable, five bays of round-arched windows to the side and a schoolroom at right angles to the rear. It closed in 1964, the congregation joining the nearby former Wesleyan Methodist. It was sold as a warehouse in 1965 but later demolished and replaced by a small block of shops.[808]

Primitive Methodist Chapel, Rodbourne Road, west of road just south of the railway roundabout, in use. As with Gorse Hill, Primitive Methodists established themselves in Even Swindon at much the same time as the Wesleyans. A small chapel was built in 1883 facing Romsey Street; this may have been added to by T S Lansdown in 1885. It was certainly greatly enlarged in 1900-1 to designs by William Drew of Swindon or possibly his son Edward. In brick with a large rose window to the front and six bays to the side, it had at the rear the facade of the old chapel tucked in under the hipped roof of the new and then serving as a schoolroom. A church hall was built immediately to the north in 1957 and it was this which was re-fronted in 2003 to become the new chapel after the increasingly poor condition of the old led to its demolition. The front of the 1957 building is severe with bands of pale brick and a tall central space of window above door; the sides are anonymous.[809]

*Primitive Methodist Chapel, Butterworth Street,** west of street towards south end, now residential. The Primitive Methodists moved promptly into this new housing area, first meeting in a shop until this chapel was opened in 1893. It is of brick, Gothic but standing naturally at the end of the row of terraced houses to which it is attached. The simple facade is enlivened by stone bands and a plaque in an arched surround at the gable head dated 1892. The sides are of four bays and to the rear is the more plain schoolroom extension from c1922. The chapel closed in 2011 and was sympathetically converted into housing in 2012. It is a good example of a small urban chapel being physically part of the local community it serves.[810] *Photograph on page 46.*

Primitive Methodists built their first chapel in **Rodbourne Cheney** in 1894 on the west side of Cheney Manor Road close to the junction with Whitworth Road. When the new chapel a short way south of here was built in 1906 (see below) this became a schoolroom but it cannot have lasted long in this role because by 1922 it had been replaced by infill terraced houses.[811]

Primitive Methodists erected an iron church in **Deacon Street** in 1899, on the east side between the Shelley Street and Dryden Street junctions. It was altered by Read, Osborne and Cook in 1909, perhaps introducing the tall pyramidal-roofed bell-cote, and survived until 1920 but was then closed. There was a succession of further occupants before a new low brick hall was erected on the site, perhaps in the 1980s. Since 2007 this has been occupied by the Redeemed Christian Church of God.[812]

Moredon was a separate village until well into the 20th century and it seems the **Methodists** had a presence there as early as the 1830s, worshipping in a purpose-built chapel from at least 1836. The subsequent history is not clear but they are believed to have bought a brick-built house on the east side of **The Street** in 1902, holding services in an upper room. For some period they may have been **United Methodists** but later became **Primitive**. The house was of conventional appearance with a gable end facing the road, two sash windows above and a window and a door below. They joined with the congregation in the new St Andrew's in 1962 and the house was sold and demolished, forming part of the site of the Maple Court flats.[813]

Primitive Methodist, later Baptist, Chapel, Cheney Manor Road, on west side at north end, in use. This was built in 1906 as a replacement for the 1894 chapel. Designed by W R Osborne of Swindon in brick with ashlar dressings, the facade has a protruding porch with the doorway flanked by pilasters under a broken pediment, a piece of misplaced neo-Classicism. Over this is a three-light window of coloured glass and above that there was the inscription 'Primitive Methodist Church 1906'. The Methodists moved out in 1961 to the new St Andrew's church in Moredon Road and sold this to the Baptists, who altered the inscription by placing boards on top of the originals. The chapel, which is close to buildings either side, has been extended to the rear twice.[814]

Primitive Methodist Chapel, Manchester Road, at junction with Alfred Street, in use as the Shah Jalal mosque. This area, though close to the station, had only become part of the town's eastwards expansion in the 1880s. Methodists were meeting here from the 1890s and in 1902 built this chapel and schoolroom, to designs by R J Beswick. The tall brick front faces Alfred Street and has two tiers of pointed-arch windows and between them an inscription which says 'PM Sunday School 1902': it seems that it was actually built as a 'church school' with the chapel downstairs and the school upstairs. There are six bays of flat-headed windows to the south side and to the north is a lower brick extension, to designs by Cripps and Stewart of Oxford, built in 1960 with money released from the sale of the Regent Street chapel. It closed in 1997 and was reopened as a mosque in 1999.[815]

Despite its proximity to the railway works, the area through which **Ferndale Road** was built remained undeveloped until the early 20th century and it was here that in 1907 a new **Primitive Methodist Chapel** was built, sometimes called the **Centenary Hall** because built in the year of the Primitive Methodist Connexion centenary. It was located south of the road directly opposite Hunter's Grove and was small, of brick with stone dressings to two round-arched windows on the front gable, the schoolroom at right angles to the rear and the porch and doorway in the re-entrant angle. The chapel closed in 1993, was demolished in 1995 and replaced by a pair of houses.[816]

The Brethren

The Brethren's first chapel in the town appears to have been that built in 1869 on **King William Street**, west of the road at its junction with Prospect Place, and used by them until the late 1920s. It has been used by The Assemblies of God since 1938. The gable end is of conventional appearance, though attached to the adjoining terraced houses, and has tall round-arched windows either side of the door with a date plaque for 1869 above. There is a gallery and a modern rear extension.[817]

A small group of Open Brethren came to the town in 1880. After meeting in the open air they acquired a hall in **King Street** which however soon proved too small and in 1883 they transferred to their **Central Hall**, a former auction room on the site of what became the Regent Cinema and is now the Meca club. This meeting collapsed in 1889 when there was a split over doctrinal matters and following this some of the congregation joined with another group, initially meeting in Merton Hall in Merton Street and then when this became too small renting Queenstown School.[818]

In 1899 this group opened their **Regent Hall** in Regent Place. This was designed by William Hooper, one of the leaders of the group, and was on the west side of the Place towards the north end. It was in brick with stone bands, round-arched windows and a stepped gable. There were two doors to the front with two tall windows between, and four bays to the sides. It was eventually demolished in 1972 as part of town centre expansion and the site now forms part of the car park outside the Wyvern Theatre.[819]

Swindon, the Brethren's Regent Hall in a photograph probably taken not long after opening in 1899. Photograph thanks to Paul Williams, custodian and copyright owner of images from the William Hooper collection

A mission hall on **Westcott Place**, under the auspices of the **Open Brethren**, was opened c1903 above a warehouse used for fish brought to Swindon by canal. It was of timber under a lean-to corrugated iron roof, accessed by an open stairway to the side and with a prominent sign 'Prepare to meet thy God' across the front. It closed in 1951, having been condemned by the council, and the congregation took over the **William Street** mission hall from the Methodists. This has since also been demolished (see above under Wesleyan Methodists).[820]

Florence Street Mission Hall, opposite Whiteman Street, in use. This was built as an independent mission in 1903 by Daniel Skinner, a baker, but taken over by the Christian Brethren in 1915, perhaps an offshoot group from those at Regent Hall. It is still used by them. The chapel is of brick with stone dressings, the windows round-arched including a stepped three-light window over the modern porch, and it is dated 1903. The sides are of four bays. Behind is the schoolroom of 1908 and behind that a further modern extension.[821]

The Salvation Army

The Salvation Army were active in the Old Town from around 1880 and in 1881 they were operating from the former Wesleyan Methodist chapel in *The Planks* (see above). By 1898 they had given this up and opened their citadel in *North Street*. This was north of the street and just west of Union Street. They stayed there until c1968 when it was taken over as a Sikh temple until c2002. It was then demolished and replaced by the houses of Acril Court.[822]

They also occupied various premises in the New Town in the 1880s before building their first citadel in Fleet Street in 1891, north of the street and west of John Street. They rebuilt it in 1955 but moved out probably in the 1980s. The frontage, now a help centre for the Universal Church of the Kingdom of God, is a modern shop but set back behind is a long brick-fronted hall with a half-hipped roof, presumably that of 1955. The original facade had a characteristic battlemented top.[823]

By 1898 they had also moved into *Gorse Hill*, occupying the former *Primitive Methodist* chapel in *Chapel Street* (see above). They were there until they moved in 1961 into their present citadel (see below).[824]

Other Denominations

Church of Christ, Broad Street, at junction with Ponting Street, now the Jamia Masjid mosque. This was built in 1901 by a group of railwaymen from the GWR works and was used until the Church of Christ joined the Central Church in 1978. The building is of brick, the front gable having a circular window with string courses and stumpy pilasters. 'Broad Street Chapel' was formerly incised over the two front windows and central doors but a modern porch now obscures the word 'Chapel' and the front is rendered. The main building is four bays deep with short extensions beyond. Inside, there is now a prayer space on both the ground and first floors, the latter possibly using an inserted floor but perhaps more likely using what was previously attic space.[825]

A group of **Unitarian Free Christians** erected a corrugated iron chapel in **Regent Street** in 1861, probably at the corner of what was then Cromwell Street, south east of what is now Canal Walk. It had a segmental curved roof and a porch of the same shape with the inscription 'Free Christian Church 1861' above. With a capacity of 500 it became too big for a dwindling congregation and was closed in 1874, sold to Arkell's brewery and re-erected in St Philip's Road, Upper Stratton as first a barrel store and later an Anglican church.[826]

Photograph on page 37.

It was replaced by a new building in **Rolleston Street**, later **Regent Circus**. The new chapel had a gabled Gothic front. On the east side of the Circus, it proved again to be too big and by 1878 had been taken over by Roman Catholics as the Holy Rood chapel. The Catholics moved out in 1905 to their new church in Groundwell Road and in 1920 the building became the town's first museum until that in turn moved away. The chapel was demolished between the wars and replaced by what is now a restaurant.[827]

A further chapel, which may have been **Free Christian**, was built in 1904 to designs by Ainsworth and Harwood at the south end of **Rolleston Street**, attached to the end of a terrace immediately north of the Baptist chapel,. It may have survived until after the Second World War.[828]

Moravian Church, Dixon Street, south of street towards east end, in use. This was built in 1885 by the Presbyterian Church of England (see below) as a lecture hall but taken over by the Moravians in 1899. The Moravians were a group formed from those employed in the GWR works; they met at first in a hall in Regent Street but then took over this chapel and have been here ever since. Designed by Orlando Baker of Swindon, the church is in red brick Gothic with a substantial porch and above it a three-light stepped window with stone banded decoration over, itself neatly reflected by a miniature copy at the gable head acting as a ventilator. The rear has an apse and to the west an original extension at right angles, presumably a schoolroom, was itself extended both backwards and forwards in similar style in the early 20th century. Set back to the east is a separate hall of corrugated iron, also early 20th century. The interior, with no gallery, retains its original pews.[829]

The Railwaymen's Christian Association built the **Railway Mission** in **Wellington Street** at the junction with Milford Street in 1903. The Association was established

Swindon, the Railway Mission, Wellington Street – decorative timber over corrugated iron. Photograph copyright of Colin Vance

in the 1880s to evangelise the large workforce of the GWR. They met in various halls and were here until at least 1965. The hall was of corrugated iron but with a decorative timber framework cladding giving it a half-timbered look; it was broad with a low roof angle and had two projecting skylights in the ridge. It burned down in 1979 and was replaced by offices.[830]

Swindon Trinity Presbyterian

Trinity Presbyterian Church of England, Victoria Road, * at north end by Groundwell Road, in use by a playgroup. The Presbyterian church in Swindon was established by workers from Scotland and the north of England who first met in the Mechanics' Institute and then in 1885 opened a lecture hall in Dixon Street. By 1898 it was clear that this church was not central enough so they sold it to the Moravians (see above) and built the Trinity Church, opened in 1899. This was designed by William Wallace of London and is a substantial and imposing Gothic brick chapel with dressings in both stone and brick. Above the doorway is a large traceried window, said to be a replica of the great window at Tintern Abbey, and above that the gable has curved shoulders with pilasters. The sides of five bays have paired windows in two tiers with intermediate buttresses and the east end, which has small transepts, is plain but for a high circular window in multiple lights.

The church was in poor repair by 1939, was restored in the 1950s and then in 1978 became for a period a central church for the town before the move in 1990 to the new Pilgrim Centre (see below). Since closure it has been used as a nursery.[831]

The **Catholic Apostolic** Church were meeting in Dixon Street from 1900, probably in the building newly constructed there at that time, next to No.38 and now a set of apartments called Fairview. The church is believed to have closed c1947, whereupon the building was let to the Church of England. The apartments were made in 2008 and are quite possibly based upon the original fabric.[832]

Modern Building

Congregationalists and Baptists

Immanuel Congregational Chapel, Upham Road, Old Walcot, south of road towards west end, in use. The Victoria Road Congregationalists finally opened this replacement chapel in 1939. It was designed by H R Houchin of London in cruciform shape, of brick with shouldered gables and tall rectangular three-light windows. The front gable has flat-roofed porches either side but the almost unrelieved brick creates a dour appearance. The interior has interesting double-angled concrete roof trusses. To the rear is a large block containing Sunday schoolrooms and an assembly hall.[833]

Baptists are believed not to have built any new chapels in the modern period.[834]

Methodists

A **Primitive Methodist Chapel** was built as part of the **Pinehurst Estate** in 1928, designed by W A H Masters of Stanton Fitzwarren. A brick building on the south side of the circle, it had five bays with half timbering in the gable. It thrived for a while after the Second World War as more houses were built but closed in 1969 and by 2017 had been replaced by housing association flats.[835]

Three new Methodist churches were built post-war in expanding areas of the town. Each has architecture of its time, two by the same practice, but one might be considered to be more successful than the other two.

St Andrew's Methodist Church, Moredon Road, * south of road just east of Bourne Road, in use. Built in 1961 following the amalgamation of churches in Rodbourne Cheney, Moredon and Haydon Wick. Designed by W H Cripps of Cripps and Stewart of Oxford, the masses of the main block in buff brick are finely balanced with a big bowed window covering most of the front and a tower to the west side with a pitched roof and a thin metal spire emerging from it. The side windows are large and rectangular; those to the east are at clerestory height above the flat-roofed side entrance porch and those to the west behind the tower are of full height. It was extended in the early 1970s.[836]
Photograph also on page 52.

Methodist Church, Queen's Drive, Walcot, at the corner of Queen's Drive and Whitbourne Avenue, now used by the Saint John Paul 2 Polish Catholic Church. This was built in 1959-60 to designs by W H Cripps of Oxford. The main block

Swindon St Andrew's Methodist

is of conventional shape with a broad open porch below vertical concrete panels holding a large crucifix. The north side has tall rectangular windows but to the south is a tower, tapering, covered with irregular concrete slabs and with an open bell cage above. The interior is more harmonious with plenty of light and a set of three stepped apses at the east end. It closed in 2016 but was then taken over by the Polish Catholic Church.[837]

St Paul's, Covingham (the Dorcan Church), at junction of Kingfisher Drive and St Paul's Drive. Built to serve new housing estates, this was one of the first ecumenical churches in the country, being both Anglican and Methodist. The church met from 1966 in a school but the chapel, to a design by the Brandt, Potter, Hare Partnership, opened in 1971. The exterior appearance is of a rectangular single-storey brick box with a smaller aluminium-sided box on top to create a double height central space. The interior is plain. It is now associated in ecumenical partnership with St Timothy's church in the nearby Liden Centre.[838]

The Brethren

A Gospel Hall in Whitworth Road opened in 1927 immediately north of what is now Pinehurst Circle. It closed in 1947 when it was not possible to renew the lease and the congregation later transferred to the Liddington Street hall.[839]

Pinehurst Gospel Hall, formerly Liddington Street Gospel Hall, north of road at west end, in use. This was built in 1951, primarily by members of the congregation who used materials from the demolished Whitworth Road hall. It is a low building in brick with a flat-roofed porch which used to carry a large advertising sign and the date 1951 but is now plain and pebble-dashed.[840]

Another **Brethren Gospel Hall**, perhaps of the 1970s, is that in the service road to the east of *Goddard Avenue*. This is small, flat-roofed and rendered.[841]

Exclusive Brethren Gospel Hall, Cheney Manor Road, in use as the Swindon Gospel Trust. This is towards the north end of the road, set well back just south of Akers Way. The building, typically anonymous and with a large car park, looks like a small metal-sheathed warehouse and was operational by 2014.[842]

The Salvation Army

In 1961 the Salvation Army moved from the former Primitive Methodist in Chapel Street, Gorse Hill, (see above) into their present citadel, north of the road and a few yards east of its predecessor. It is of two shades of brick, the front section of three bays with tall windows and a low roof angle. Behind are two extensions. It is likely that the entrance was originally in the front facing the road but moved to the side when it was extended.[843]

In c1968 they also moved from North Street to establish their new citadel in the former Anglican church hall on Devizes Road, just south of the junction with Bradford Road, where they remain. This was built in 1913 to designs by Bishop and Fisher in cheerful Gothic with paired windows either side of a buttressed porch, a window over and a part stepped gable all looking quite nonconformist. It is six bays deep with a smaller building, probably original, at right angles to the rear.[844]

Other Denominations

The Assemblies of God Church have been using the former Brethren chapel in King William Street (see above) since 1938 [845]

Bethesda Church, now Light and Life Missions, Malvern Road, north of road towards west end, in use. An offshoot of the Fellowship of Independent Evangelical Churches built this in 1962. It is a large single-storey rendered shed.[846]

Christadelphian Hall, Eastcott Hill, at junction with Warwick Road, in use. Christadelphians started in a room in Temple Street near the Baptist Tabernacle in 1913 but in 1936 built this neat hall in brick, with minimal decoration except for the tiles laid on edge as surrounds to door and windows, very much of their time. It is four bays deep with a small lean-to rear extension.[847]

Christ the Servant Ecumenical Church, Abbey Meads, east of Elstree Way, in use. The group had been active in this new housing area since 1996 and opened this church in 2001. It is in brick, symmetrically cruciform but with complex roof angles.[848]

Elim Foursquare Gospel Alliance, now the Elim Christian Centre, Osborne Street, in use. This group, formed in 1933, set off with the intention of building their temple with no help from any who were not Christians; they also intended to obtain no materials on credit. They succeeded, but though the foundation stone was laid in 1938 the combination of a lack of money and wartime conditions meant that it did not open until 1942. The hall, eight bays long, is of stone block, steel framed and with a front elevation with a stepped parapet in Art Deco style.[849]

Freshbrook Evangelical Church, Worsley Road, at junction with Gainsborough Way, in use. This church, affiliated to the Fellowship of Independent Churches, was opened in 1989 to serve the newly developing Freshbrook area. It is of brick under a hipped roof with a spirelet, a large glazed entrance and linked subsidiary buildings.[850]

Gateway Church, Westlea, in the Trinity Centre. The church has met since 1986 in a large modern block which also contains their other social enterprise activities.[851]

Park Gospel Hall, Park North, Axbridge Close, off Welcombe Avenue, in use. This small brick hall with a flat-roofed extension has been used by this group since 1968.[852]

Penhill Free Church, on Penhill Drive south of junction with Downton Road, later Penhill Gospel Hall, closed in 2020. Congregationalists helped establish services in Penhill from 1954 and in 1959 this plain brick shed was built to designs by Eric Cole and Partners, part financed by Laing's, the estate's developers.[853]

Pilgrim Centre, Regent Street,＊ This 1990 building is on the site of the Baptist Tabernacle church and was built as a central church to replace a series of others. The Tabernacle Baptists, Church of Christ in Broad Street, Sanford Street Congregationalists, Trinity Presbyterians and Central Hall Methodists first came

Swindon, the Pilgrim Centre

together in the Trinity chapel. There was a long legal wrangle with Thamesdown Borough Council, which wished to purchase the site compulsorily, before the case was eventually won and the Centre opened in 1990. Designed by Peter Reynolds of Oxford, the three-storey front has three bays in brick either side of a central glass section with Classical pilasters and pediment and a truncated metal spire above. The worship space, making much use of bare brick walls, is on the first floor under a large skylight.[854]

Swindon Evangelical Church, Devizes Road, * north of junction with Newport Street, in use. A group left the Victoria Street Congregational chapel in 1916 and built this chapel in 1923; a further group left them in 1962 to form the Bethesda church (see above). The church is long, under a corrugated metal roof, and much-extended, but the interest lies in the front, re-faced by R J Beswick and Son in 1935 in a brick neo-Romanesque style which has considerable appeal. Tiles on edge surround the broad doorway and are placed over the two windows, all round-arched. A miniature blind arcade steps its way up the gable. A mission room of unknown denomination was in place at the rear of this site by 1885 and remained as a separate building until at least 1942: its replacement now forms part of the chapel.[855]
Photograph on page 51.

Toothill Church, off Deerhurst Way, in use. This non-denominational church was built c1975 to serve the new estate and is of brick, the main interior square with cross-gables and windows up to the eaves creating a tall and light space.[856]

9. Trowbridge

There was early nonconformist activity in Trowbridge, with a church established by the 1670s, but the difficulties of those early years are reflected in the fact that in 1715 there were said to be only two dissenters' meetings in the town, a Presbyterian and a Baptist. In the course of the 18th century, however, there was a rapid increase in nonconformity and by 1827 it was estimated that three quarters of the town's population were dissenters. The industrial nature of the local economy was one obvious factor, but it was also believed that there were insufficient Anglican churches for the population. The strength of nonconformity resulted in the construction of some imposing town chapels, many of which remain though two of the largest have now been demolished.[858]

Quakers

The **Quakers** were amongst those first active and in the early 18th century four houses were registered for their meetings, but by 1715 there were said to be none in the town and it was believed most had become Baptists. After a very long interval a meeting came here from Westbury in 1944, meeting in the deacons' vestry of the Tabernacle church. In 1952 a group bought a former fish and chip shop in **Shail's Lane** and converted it as a meeting house but by 1970 they had moved to join the Quakers of Bradford on Avon. The Shail's Lane building is believed to have been demolished since.[859]

Presbyterians, Congregationalists and Independents

The **Silver Street Presbyterian, later Congregational, Chapel** was built c1723 by a group which had once been part of the Southwick and Conigre Baptists but had separated from them by the 1680s and initially met in an adapted disused factory. The chapel was set back behind its burial ground on the north side of Silver Street about 40 metres west of the Church Street junction where there is now a large shop. A gallery was added in the 1820s but by late that century numbers were falling and it closed suddenly in 1927 when negotiations to renew the lease failed. It was then successively the Conservative Club and Trowbridge public library before being demolished in 1959. The building had rendered rubble-stone walls and a hipped tiled roof. The substantial round-arched doorway was claimed to have come from Farleigh Hungerford castle, which was indeed being stripped of its fittings at around the time the chapel was built. Highly unusually for a nonconformist chapel, the doorway seems to have been placed off-centre, perhaps because the central position was obstructed by another building for much of its life. There was a cross-window to the left of the doorway and three more symmetrically placed above.[860]

Tabernacle Congregational Chapel, Church Street, ** Grade 2 listed, pending redevelopment in 2021. Here is a remarkable group of buildings but how much it will be possible to appreciate them in future depends entirely on the form of their redevelopment. Their appeal lies not only in the design of the chapel itself and the Sunday schools but also in the way all the buildings on the site combine to create a collegiate atmosphere.

The origins lie in the work of a local woman, Mrs Joanna Turner, who first acquired a cottage as a meeting place, then built a small chapel, then in 1771 built a more substantial one of 40ft by 30ft. There were many changes to this over the years, including addition of a rear and later side galleries, doubling in width and an accumulation of schoolrooms. It was rebuilt on the same site in 1884, its capacity of 730 much the same as that of the previous chapel. In the 1970s the congregation was joined as the United Church by the Methodists from Manvers Street but in 2016 the growing cost of maintenance became too much, the congregation moved out to the Park Club and the whole site was put up for sale.

The 1884 chapel, designed by Paull and Bonella, is handsome in its late Perpendicular style, the west end having two large four-centre arched windows over doors, angled buttresses and a substantial corner tower with an ogee cap; the four bays of side windows in two tiers are mullioned and transomed. The interior is at least as appealing, with galleries on three sides, a turreted organ like a castle gateway above the choir gallery and stone pulpit, and a ceiling which is pitched to the centre but vaulted in plaster over the side galleries.

left: Trowbridge Tabernacle Congregational, from a watercolour by A. C. Fare. Image courtesy of Trowbridge Museum. right: Trowbridge Tabernacle Congregational, the screen and Sunday school facing Church Street making an imposing collegiate entrance but boarded up here awaiting redevelopment in 2021

The schoolrooms add further interest: that of 1842 attached to the chapel has a pyramidal roof and three pairs of very tall lancets, while those of 1883, also by Paull and Bonella, run east, follow the style of the chapel and create the look of a college quadrangle. To note finally are the Gothic screen to Church Street by W J Stent, consisting of an arch with smaller openings either side, and the attached Sunday school by William Smith, both of 1871.[861]

Baptists

*Unitarian (General Baptist) Chapel, Conigre, and Sunday Schools alongside,** the chapel demolished, the schools in use by Bethel Apostolic Church and Grade 2 listed. The Conigre was another early church, certainly of 17th century origin. Various dates are given but it seems most likely that Trowbridge Baptists worshipped originally at Southwick but began to meet in the town after the Act

left: Trowbridge Conigre. Image courtesy of Trowbridge Museum. right: Trowbridge Conigre, the schoolrooms survive and are in use

of Toleration; they were certainly doing so by 1697 and in 1700 built their first chapel. This was substantial, with a three-bay front with two doors and two tiers of windows, the window pattern repeated in the side walls. The double roof was hipped and supported internally by two tall columns from which sprang a ribbed and vaulted plaster ceiling; there were galleries on three sides. It seems the chapel became Unitarian in the 1730s.

By 1856 it was in poor condition and was pulled down and replaced in 1857 by a chapel capable of seating 550 people. New Sunday schools built in 1838 were themselves replaced in 1865 by those still standing. The new chapel had deteriorated badly by the 1970s, largely due to poor quality stone used in its construction, and the congregation moved into one of the schoolrooms in 1972. The church was demolished amidst controversy in 1987/8; the congregation later moved to a bungalow in Seymour Road and the schoolrooms were taken over by the Bethel Apostolic Church from 1993.

The Trowbridge architect William Smith designed both chapel and schoolrooms. The chapel was in Decorated Gothic style, to all appearances a High Victorian Anglican church save for the lack of an altar and a central aisle. It had a long high nave and two side aisles, large five-light windows with circular tracery at either end, and stepped buttresses and pinnacles. Inside were galleries on three sides integrated with the aisle piers, the rear one containing the organ, and a high stone pulpit. The two schoolrooms, also Gothic but on a smaller scale, are identical and each has a doorway with a pair of cusped windows either side and a stepped three-light window above inside a pointed surround; there are buttresses with pinnacles to the front corners. They now face an open car park alongside Back Street but for most of their lives they and the chapel were hemmed in by other buildings.[862]

*Back Street, now Church Street, General Baptist Chapel,*** set back north of Church Street, formerly **Emmanuel Baptist** but now **West Wilts Vineyard Church**. This has one of the most remarkable town chapel interiors in the county. The church was originally formed by members of the Conigre chapel who did not like the preaching there and seceded in 1736 to form what was at first a Particular

Trowbridge Back Street Baptist

The light-filled space of Trowbridge Back Street Baptist: even the vestibules over the gallery stairs are mostly glass

Baptist community. They built a chapel on this site at the end of a garden behind a house in 1754, a vestry was added in 1766 and the chapel was enlarged in both 1784 and c1812. Despite two secessions from its ranks, the congregation continued to grow and the chapel was enlarged again in 1846 and then a further three times by 1890, with further renovations in c1902 and 1920. A schoolroom to the rear was built in 1822, a further schoolroom, for boys, added in 1835 and the original schoolroom replaced by a new building in 1885. So large did it become that in 1890 it was described as the largest Baptist chapel in the west of England after Bristol, Plymouth and Portsmouth: even in 1851, before the later enlargements, it had a capacity of 900.

The doorway, with Tuscan portico, dates from alterations in 1862 and further alterations were made in c1902 when the name Emmanuel was adopted. The ashlar front is mostly of this later date and now has a pedimented shouldered gable and four round-arched stepped three-light windows above, each in a raised segmental-arched surround. Below, the ground floor has been extended forwards either side of the portico and has similar windows though taller. The remarkable interior, brought to this final state only c1900, has ornately pierced cast iron gallery fronts on all four sides, supported on cast iron columns with barley sugar twists; the organ is in a recess above the very broad and elaborately panelled pulpit which is accessed by a double stair. Outside again, the three-bay sides in stone blockwork to the left and rubble-stone to the less-visible right have two tiers of similar windows and to the rear are the schoolrooms, the large one of 1885 by William Smith of Trowbridge creating an impressive interior space with its tall leaded clerestory windows.

The chapel closed in 2008, was used for some years by training providers but became the West Wilts Vineyard Church in 2018.[863]
Photographs also on pages 42, 44 and 46.

Zion Particular Baptist Chapel, Union Street, * Grade 2 listed, in use. This handsome chapel, capable of seating 700, was built in 1816 by people who had seceded from the Back Street Baptist in 1813. After first renting premises on Wicker Hill near the river, they had apparently already started construction of a proper chapel at a site in the Lower Courts when a lawyer passing by told them of this better location and they immediately moved. A baptistery was added in 1825 after they were denied permission to continue baptising in the river and a vestry was built in 1828 as well as a Sunday school to the rear. More schoolrooms were built in 1863 and a further three in 1893, the latter perhaps by W H Stanley.

The chapel front is of ashlar under a

Trowbridge Zion Baptist

hipped slate roof with five round-arched windows, three above separated by a string course from the two below which are either side of a later Classical porch with pilasters; a painted plaque is dated 1816. The sides of three bays of coursed shaped rubble-stone have two tiers of similar windows and to the rear are two ranges of schoolrooms in brick with pitched roofs at right angles to the chapel. The interior, an excellent 'preaching box', was refitted in 1870 and now has galleries with boarded fronts on cast-iron columns on three sides. There are numbered and asymmetrically split pews replacing the former box pews, and a pulpit accessed by stairs both sides.[864]

The **Little Bethel Baptist** congregation was made up of people excluded in 1826 from the Zion chapel following a dispute over the provision of a baptistery. In 1828 they built a chapel at the south end of what became **Castle Street**. It did not flourish, was sold but then re-opened in 1844 and soon had to be enlarged, being almost completely rebuilt in 1850 by William Smith with galleries on three sides, a vestry and a Sunday schoolroom: it was then able to accommodate 300 to 400 people. It closed in the late 1850s, the buildings were sold to the Anglicans in 1863 and converted by the architect T H Wyatt into St Stephen's, a chapel of ease of St James's. The Anglicans added a tower with a spire but this church in turn closed in 1924 and was demolished in 1926.[865]

Bethesda Particular, later General, Baptist Chapel, The Shires, * Grade 2 listed, now in use as a cafe. The facade may look out of place at the centre of the Shires shopping centre but this chapel spent much of its life surrounded by other buildings, mainly the Home woollen mills, so the hemmed-in feel is not too far removed from previous reality. It was opened in 1823 by yet another seceding group,

Trowbridge Bethesda Baptist, now the centre-piece of the Shires shopping centre

this time those who had left Back Street in 1821 during the time of a controversial minister; he joined them at the new church. The congregation had reached 400 by 1829, a Sunday schoolroom was built in 1840 and new galleries were added in 1868. In 1890 it was renovated with the addition of two tiers of galleries on three sides, giving a remarkable capacity for 840 people in a relatively modest space: the chapel was only ever three bays long with two bays beyond for the schoolrooms. It was surrounded by the buildings of the Home Mills and in 1930 the church decided to build a replacement chapel in Gloucester Road. This one was sold to the mill owners, Messrs Salter, and eventually became part of the new Shires centre.

Much of the interior is lost or changed out of recognition but the ashlar facade is an impressive piece of Palladian architecture with three bays of round-arched openings in two tiers, the ground floor rusticated and with a doorway framed by Tuscan columns. The central bay projects slightly, has a pediment against the parapet and, between the floors, still carries the inscription placed there by Messrs Salter, 'Samuel Salter & Co Ltd Estd 1769'.[866]

Bethesda Baptist Church, Gloucester Road, * north end, in use. The Bethesda Baptists moved here in 1931 from the centre of town, to this building designed by W W Snailum of Trowbridge; a Sunday school followed in 1933. With seating for 350, the brick and stone chapel is unsurprisingly smaller than the original and is given a remarkable Renaissance look by the use of round-arched windows below and narrow rectangular attic windows above. This is accentuated by the substantial pilastered porch with its hipped tiled roof onto the five-bay main chapel. The interior is modernised but retains a rear gallery. The schoolroom, at right angles behind amidst other outbuildings, has a Venetian window facing the road.[867] *Photograph on page 51.*

Upper Studley Particular Baptist Chapel, on Frome Road just south of Manor Road, in use. The congregation formed in 1829 and from 1831 met in a converted house opposite the present site. The chapel was built in 1850 as a village station of Back Street, Trowbridge, and a schoolroom was added in 1863. It is small and plain in squared stone block under an eaves slate roof, with rectangular windows and unfortunate modern glazing replacing original sash windows.[868]

Trowbridge Halve Baptist – a back garden chapel accessed through this passage in a terraced house.

Strict Baptist Chapel, The Halve, * behind 30 The Halve, in use. This very small brick chapel with a hipped tiled roof was built in the back garden of an 18th century terraced house which was re-fronted in Victorian times. The house belongs to the Baptists and a passage leads through to the chapel. The members broke away from the Zion Baptist in 1896 because of personal differences and met in a room until they leased this chapel which had been built in 1902 on the space formerly occupied by four tiny weavers' cottages. The chapel, the full width of the plot behind the house, has two flat-headed windows to the rear with the door alongside to the right. There is a further window in the right hand wall and there used to be one above the pulpit. The pulpit and partial panelling are probably original, the replacement pews recently arrived in 2020 from a church in Bristol, and there is some shaping to the exposed principal rafters; otherwise all is plain. The vestry behind, under a lean-to extension to the roof, is from 1951.[869]

General Baptists built a chapel in **Harmony Place**, just off **Dursley Road**, **Lower Studley**, probably in the 1860s and perhaps as an offshoot of Back Street. It was active in the 1870s, with a small congregation, but out of use by the turn of the century. Some of the fabric may remain in 20 Dursley Road. A very short-lived offshoot of the **Silver Street Congregational** was set up in this area at around this time and it is possible that the Baptists used those premises.[870]

The **Pentecostal Trinity Baptist Chapel** in **Westbourne Road** was a small building, probably of timber or corrugated iron, constructed in the back garden of 30 Westbourne Road c1920. It was still active in 1961 but was probably closed and demolished soon after that date.[871]

Wesleyan Methodists

Wesleyan Methodists first preached here in 1754 but, after initial success, found it stony ground and did not return until 1781 when John Knapp, a butcher, rented a 'scribbling shop' to use as a meeting house. The Wesleyans then built a chapel on **Stallard Street** immediately west of the town bridge in 1790. It was prone to flooding and in 1814 a gallery was built to mitigate the worst effects. By 1821 the chapel was too small and though they then considered moving to new premises in the end they enlarged the existing building. In 1836 the congregation moved into their new chapel in Manvers Street and the original chapel was eventually incorporated into the adjacent Innox Mills, later owned by Bowyers. It was built of stone with ashlar quoins and dressings, and on the side facing the street were three bays of pointed-arch windows with Y-tracery at gallery level. A further triple-gabled storey was added, perhaps by 1845, but the building was demolished in 1976.[872]

The **Manvers Street Wesleyan Methodist Chapel**, the successor to that by the town bridge, was conspicuously large, with seating for 800, and demonstrative. The ashlar front had five bays with two tiers of round-arched windows, the three middle bays having a raised pediment with stone scrolls either side. The lower stage was rusticated and had a central doorway with paired Doric columns, and the upper had Corinthian pilasters under an entablature. The sides were of four bays, again in two tiers, and the roof was of slate; the interior had galleries round three sides. It was built on the site of the original scribbling shop and was designed by John Dyer, the husband of Knapp's granddaughter, who was a member of the congregation and also an engineer and inventor: he based his design closely on that of the Wesleyan of 1818 at Bradford on Avon. The chapel was built in 1836, Manvers Street being created as a new road in front of it. It had schoolrooms at basement

Trowbridge Manvers Street Wesleyan. Image courtesy of Wiltshire and Swindon Archives

level but in 1846 a further building with four classrooms and a vestry was added. In 1968 the congregation joined the United Reformed Church congregation at The Tabernacle and the chapel was sold and demolished, to be replaced by the Manvers House offices.[873]

Wesleyan Methodist Chapel, Islington (known as Timbrell Street Wesleyan), almost opposite the garden centre, now a house called Church House. In 1852 teachers from Manvers Street started a Sunday school in a cottage near here and in 1860 a Trowbridge draper presented the church with two cottages which were demolished and this built as a less cramped replacement; it opened in September that year at a cost of £150. The history is obscure but it seems that some time after this date, and certainly by 1889, a group of local Wesleyans started using it as their chapel: they may have been worshipping locally since 1814. It was still used as such in 1939 but Sunday services may have dwindled thereafter, though they were being held again in the postwar period. The Sunday school closed in 1959 but Sunday evening services continued until 1975 when the church was sold to the New Testament Church of God, a group which had been meeting there since c1970. It was converted to a house with an inserted floor after 2003.

This tiny chapel of eccentric design, by William Smith of Trowbridge, was said to accommodate 150 people. Its main roofline is transverse, following those of the buildings either side to which it was originally linked, but the worship space was orientated front to back and it accordingly has gables in those positions. The steep-angled front gable is now rendered though originally it was of rubble-stone with ashlar dressings. It has a Gothic door and adjoining windows with heavy linked drip mouldings, and there is a circular window above with octagonal scalloped edges. The line of the gable continues, inset somewhat, down to ground level in a strange line originally defined by ashlar blocks. The rear gable is of similar size but in rubble-stone with a triple stepped lancet in an ashlar surround, and the roof has bands of fish-scale tiles.[874]

Wesley Road Wesleyan Methodist Chapel, at Newtown junction, in use. Sooner than expand the Manvers Street chapel further to cope with continually increasing demand, the Wesleyans chose to build a chapel in the new suburb of Newtown. It opened in 1872, designed by W J Stent of Warminster in 'Anglo-Italian' style: Wesley Road was built as a new road alongside, paid for by the lord of the manor. The facade in jumbled ashlar has doors either side in gabled porches; to the centre is a low five-light window and above that a tall window of three lights in a round-arched surround. The central section of the facade is stepped forward, there are three further small circular windows and the whole is decked out with miniature columns and capitals to give it indeed a loosely Italianate feel. The six-bay sides have paired round-arched windows and there is a lower rear extension, added in 1900 to contain the organ which stands high within an arch behind the pulpit in the otherwise modernised interior. The chapel had a schoolroom from the start but larger replacements were added in 1881 at right angles to the rear, in style generally similar to the side but not the front of the chapel. The Gregory Hall facing Newtown was added in 1933 to provide further school capacity.[875]

Primitive Methodists

Surprisingly, given the substantial working class population, it seems that **Primitive Methodists** had no significant presence in the town. The only evidence is an 1843 registration for a chapel, apparently made by Primitive Methodists, but there is no indication of where this was or how long it lasted. One possible explanation for their absence may be that most mill owners were strongly Wesleyan and mill workers might have thought it judicious to follow their employers' examples.[876]

Others

A **Sandemanian** church was founded in Trowbridge in 1768, serving poor labourers employed in the clothing industry. It was active in 1806 but it is not known when it closed nor where it was located.[877]

A **Catholic Apostolic** church existed in 1838 but in 1843 its baptismal register was closed and it had gone by 1851. It is not known where it was located.[878]

Meetings of the **Railway Gospel Mission** were first held in a waiting room at the railway station until an iron chapel was built on **Bond Street**, close to the junction with Wesley Road, c 1898. It closed in 1955 and was then demolished and replaced with maisonettes at 29b/c Bond Street.[879]

Exclusive Brethren opened a hall at **12a Prospect Place** c1896, set back behind terraced houses there and accessed via an alleyway. It closed sometime after 1962 and was demolished by the end of the 1960s.[880]

Frome Road Gospel Hall, 11a Frome Road, in use. This was built for the **Open Brethren** in 1924, small and plain in stone block and with a low roof angle, the front altered later. They used it until c1994 and it has been used more recently by the Life Church and now the New Testament Church of God.[881]

Salvation Army Citadel, Castle Street, just north of Market Street, in use. Built in 1930, this is in brick with stone dressings and has echoes of the 'fortress' look so often characteristic of Salvation Army citadels. The door is in a large plain surround with 'The Salvation Army' in applied lettering above and an extended lunette above that. There are tall windows either side and pilasters with alternate bands of stone at the corners; the gable is shouldered both at its base and half way up. The building is relatively deep with extensions to the side and rear and has two prominent roof ventilators. A brick and timber hall previously on this site was built in 1876, used by the Army from 1880 and bought by them in 1888. They used it until it was demolished to make way for the present building.[882]

10. Chapel Architects

Early chapels were simple buildings and not of high status. Their congregations often included tradespeople with relevant skills and these would have been leading members of the communal effort to design and erect the place of worship. Sometimes a single member of the congregation had a particularly influential role, as in the case of Robert Cadby of Bradford on Avon who is thought to have been responsible for the redesign of the Congregational chapel there in 1798.

Builders as designers are found throughout the main period of chapel building. The example of Thomas Hardick has already been quoted in Chapter 3 and another example amongst many is provided by the Reeves family of Bratton. They were builders and engineers but it was Henry Reeves, a member of the family, who designed five Baptist chapels in the county. All were straightforward village chapels but he designed at least three of them without charge. A further late example was the 1903 Wesleyan Methodist at Winsley, designed by another builder, George Brooks. Again this was not done on a commercial basis: he was a leading member of the congregation.

Architects only began to be used more generally from the mid nineteenth century – the list which follows contains very few from before that time – and many of these would not have been formally trained. The line between builder, surveyor and architect remained blurred but as the size and complexity of chapels increased so did the risk of not having a safe, workable and appealing building if the designer lacked competence.

Trained architects were therefore increasingly used, the great majority of them local to the community in question. These were people whose work was known and who would produce designs for reasonable fees affordable from the always constrained funds of the congregation. Of the approximately 70 who designed Wiltshire chapels during the main building period less than 20 came from outside the local area, and most of these were in the county only after 1890.

The choice of an external architect in the later period may have been determined by several considerations. A number of them, like the London firm of Gordon and Gunton – architects' partnerships frequently changed but these two were in partnership from the turn of the century – specialised in chapels and so provided the assurance that they could cope with the practical issues involved in designing a successful space for worship. This, together with their prestige, led to them being awarded the contract for the large and important Monkton Hill Wesleyan Methodist in Chippenham in 1908. Equally, by the turn of the century when the over-riding urge for simplicity had been abandoned, a London firm might be turned to for 'fashionable' design: Gordon and Gunton provided just that in the 1900 Wesleyan in Amesbury and the 1910 Wesleyan in Marlborough, remarkably similar despite their size difference, in brick with middle Gothic window tracery, the combination so distinctively of its time. But such clear reasons for choice of architect are not always apparent: Gordon and Gunton also designed the small Wesleyan at Idmiston, whose white-faced brick presents one of the strangest appearances of any chapel in the county.

There were specialist architects in Wiltshire as well. R J Beswick built and altered a number of chapels in the Swindon area between 1890 and 1902, mostly for the Primitive Methodists. William Smith did likewise in and around Trowbridge for at least 30 years from 1850, though he did plenty of other work also, and Thomas Smith Lansdown did the same around Swindon for a similar period from 1859, including the notable feat of converting the GWR barracks in the town into a Wesleyan chapel.

Most prolific, however, and much the most widespread in his efforts, was William Jervis Stent of Warminster (1815-1887), who built or modified 15 chapels in the county over the 30 years from 1852. A committed Congregationalist, most of his chapels were for that denomination, but he designed for Wesleyans and Baptists as well and also produced numerous secular buildings. One has the sense that, left to his own devices, he might have designed all his chapels in rock-faced stone or flint Gothic, using various Early English and Early French devices in the approved Pugin manner. Most fit this general pattern and the second Mere Congregational, of 1868, and the Calne Free Church of a year earlier are perhaps the pre-eminent examples of this type.

It is hard to tell what caused Stent to diverge from this style – perhaps the insistence of his clients - but diverge he sometimes did. The village chapels at Ebbesbourne Wake and Sutton Veny were modest and barely Gothic; the Wesley Road Methodist in Trowbridge is in ashlar with a strong hint of southern Europe in its Gothic motifs; the re-fronting of the Castle Street Baptist in Calne introduced double-cusped windows of almost Islamic shape; and the late re-fronting of the Brown Street Baptist in Salisbury produced an overpowering dark red brick facade in Lombard style. It would be hard to claim any great originality in Stent's chapel architecture – save possibly for the remarkable whale's jawbone front to the Broad Chalke Congregational - but his contribution to the heritage of Wiltshire's nonconformist chapels is nevertheless significant.

There was plenty of choice for those seeking a national specialist architect. The list below includes a number in this category such as Baines, Bidlake, Curwen, Dinsley, Gordon and Gunton, Tarring and Wilkinson, and Wills. Of these, Curwen, Dinsley, and Gordon and Gunton specialised further, working mainly for the Methodists. Of more local specialists, Beswick, Lansdown, Reeves, Smith and Stent have already been mentioned, with Beswick mainly working for Primitive Methodists, Reeves for Baptists and Stent for Congregationalists. But such specialists by no means dominated: plenty of others received commissions for what was for much of the nineteenth century a substantial volume of work.

As a final comment on architects, it may be noted that the nineteenth century was the great period for 'restoring' and rebuilding Anglican churches, with many architects specialising in that work; but almost none of these touched nonconformist commissions. This may have been residual prejudice against nonconformity but, perhaps more likely, reflected a continuing snobbery, a feeling that such work was beneath them. One who did carry out a nonconformist commission – at Poulshot in 1886 - was Charles Ponting of Marlborough, but he was a prolific architect who carried out a large number of Anglican restorations and other works. The most nationally famous architect in the list, T H Wyatt, did work on one nonconformist chapel, the Little Bethel Baptist in Trowbridge, but only to turn it into an Anglican chapel of ease.

Chapel Architects – An Alphabetical List.[883]

Ainsworth & Harwood, of 18 Regent Circus Swindon. WJ Ainsworth and _ Harwood.
1904 chapel, Rolleston St, Swindon, demolished.

Angell, Thomas, builder and surveyor of Highworth, c1781-1855.
1825 Zion Congregational chapel, High Street, Highworth.

Ansell, William Henry, of London, 1872-1959, designed hospitals and convalescent homes as well as churches and chapels.
1925-6 Wesleyan Methodist chapel, Station Rd, Westbury.

Awdry, Graham, b 1858, of Bristol. Worked with W J Stent in 1882 but joined Foster and Wood in Bristol before 1900.
1886 St Peter's, chapel of ease to St Andrew's Chippenham, later New Testament Church of God.

Baines, George, of London, a prolific designer of nonconformist chapels.[884]
1917 Primitive Methodist chapel, Dew's Road, Salisbury.[885]

Baker, Orlando, of Swindon, 1834-1912. In practice from c1875, emigrated to Hobart 1890.
1876-7 Congregational chapel, Calcutt St, Cricklade.
1876 Primitive Methodist chapel, Regent St, Swindon, demolished.
1878 Wesleyan Methodist chapel, Wroughton, demolished.
1884 Wesleyan Methodist mission hall, Princes St, Swindon, demolished.[886]
1885 Moravian church, Dixon St, Swindon.

Bangma, John, architect and Quaker from Hungerford area.[887]
1986 Conversion of former Congregational school-room to Quaker meeting house, Marlborough.

Barnes, William E, of Letchworth, a Quaker architect, in practice from c1957.
1994, New Quaker meeting house, Sussex Wharf, Devizes.[888]

Bath, Frederick, b 1847, of Salisbury.
1880 Maundrel Hall, Salisbury.[889]

1889 alterations, including new front, to Wesleyan Methodist chapel, St Edmund's Church Street, Salisbury.[890]

Baverstock, William Edwin, of Marlborough, in practice from c1850 to after 1880.
1879 Primitive Methodist chapel, Pewsey.

Beswick, Alfred E, of Swindon, son of RJ Beswick and in partnership with his father as R J Beswick and Son from c1925.
1935 Re-facing Swindon Evangelical Church, Devizes Road, Swindon (R J Beswick and Son).

Beswick, Robert James, of Victoria Rd, Swindon, in practice from c1874-1925.
1886 Baptist Tabernacle chapel, Swindon, demolished. May have assisted W H Read.
1890 Primitive Methodist schoolroom, Lower Stratton, Stratton St Margaret.[891]
1890-1 Primitive Methodist chapel, Gorse Hill, Swindon, (supervised Thomas Colborne), demolished.
1895 alterations to Wesleyan Methodist chapel, Bath Rd, Swindon.
1896 Primitive Methodist chapel, Turnball, Chiseldon.
1900 Primitive Methodist chapel, Clifton Street, Swindon, demolished.
1902 Primitive Methodist chapel and schools, Alfred St, Swindon.

Bidlake, George, of Wolverhampton, architect of Congregational chapels.
1866 plans prepared for Independent chapel, Victoria St, Swindon, demolished. It is not certain if elements of his design were included in the final design by Stent.

Bird, William F, b 1852, of Midsomer Norton, a Methodist.
1904 Wesleyan Methodist Sunday schools and five shops, Faringdon Road, Swindon, demolished.
1907-8 Wesleyan Methodist Central Hall, Clarence Street, Swindon, demolished.

Bothams, Alfred Champney, of Salisbury. B 1861, in practice from 1883.
1894 Coombe Bissett Baptist chapel.[892]
1900 Rebuilding of Bodenham (Odstock) Baptist chapel.[893]

Bothams, A C, and Brown, Bernard Owens, of Salisbury. In partnership from 1927, later also with S S Dixon.
1931-2 Amesbury Wesleyan Methodist schoolroom.[894]
1932 Methodist chapel, Bemerton, Salisbury. (with Dixon).[895]

Brandt, Potter, Hare Partnership. John Brandt, Robert Potter and Richard W Hare, in partnership from 1956.
1971, St Paul's Covingham (the Dorcan Church) ecumenical, Swindon.

Bromilow & Cheers, of Liverpool - _ Bromilow & Harry Arthur Cheers (1853-1916), their partnership a brief one.
1879-80 Wesleyan Methodist chapel, Bath Rd, Swindon.

Bromley, William Harris, of Corsham, builder and architect.
1878 Wesleyan Methodist chapel, Pickwick Rd, Corsham.
1902 alterations, Congregational chapel, Pickwick Rd, Corsham.
1903-4 Wesleyan Methodist chapel, Pickwick Rd, Corsham.

Brooks, George, of Winsley, builder and member of congregation of Winsley Wesleyan Methodist.
1902, Wesleyan Methodist chapel, Winsley.[896]

Brown, Bernard Owens – *see Bothams and Brown*

Burrington, T, of Swindon.
1947-8 Assembly hall at Sanford Street Congregational, Swindon, replacing schoolrooms destroyed by fire, demolished.

Bush, Arthur E. Surveyor and sanitary inspector to Melksham UDC.
1909 Wesleyan Methodist chapel, Broughton Gifford.

Cadby, Robert, Bradford on Avon, moved to Bradford from Bath 1785, trustee and benefactor of Congregational Chapel in 1798 when rebuilt; possibly designed it; built houses in Bradford and did work at the workhouse; died 1815.

Chapman, Joseph, Frome.
1867 Congregational chapel, Chapmanslade.

Colborne, Thomas, builder of Swindon.
1891 Primitive Methodist chapel, Gorse Hill, Swindon carried out to his own designs but under supervision of R J Beswick. Demolished.

Cole, Eric, architects of Cirencester.
1959 Penhill Free Church, Swindon.[897]
1983-4 alterations to Wesleyan Methodist chapel, Bath Rd, Swindon; JC Harbord was job architect.

Cripps, W.H., of Oxford, (Cripps & Stewart).
1932 Wesleyan Methodist chapel, Milton Lilbourne.[898]
1955 extension to former Wesleyan Methodist chapel, Cricklade.[899]
1956-7 additional hall at Central Hall, Swindon.[900]
1958 hall for Primitive Methodist chapel, Clifton St, Swindon.
1959-60, Methodist, Queen's Drive, Walcot, Swindon.[901]
1961 alteration and extension to Primitive Methodist chapel, Manchester Road, Swindon.[902]
1961 St Andrew's Methodist, Moredon Road, Swindon.[903]

Crisp, Henry, of Bristol, c1826-1896.
1857 Downton Particular Baptist chapel, South Lane.[904]

Curwen, Robert, of London, specialising in Wesleyan Methodist chapels.
1885-6 Wesleyan Methodist chapel, Oxford St, Malmesbury.

Davies, _, of Eastcott Hill, Swindon.
1902 Wesleyan Mission Hall, Cheney Manor Road, Swindon.[905]

Dinsley, W. Hugill, of Chorley, Lancs, with an essentially local practice but designed Methodist chapels across the country. Died c1911.
1896 Methodist Reform chapel, Milford St, Salisbury.

Dixon, S S – see Bothams

Drew, William Henry, of Swindon, c1837-1905, started as builder in Highworth c1862.
Drew, Edward, LRIBA, son of the above, born 1867, began practice with his father 1888 and may have been involved in all work from that date.
1883 Primitive Methodist chapel, Ermin St, Stratton St Margaret.
1883 Baptist chapel, Gorse Hill, Swindon.
1894 Conversion of former chapel to Sunday school, Congregational chapel, Calcutt St, Cricklade.
1900-1 Primitive Methodist chapel, Rodbourne Road, Swindon.

Dyer, John, millwright and engineer of Trowbridge, committed Wesleyan, 1779-1856. Invented steam engines c1811-15 and patented rotating fulling machine 1833. He was said to have designed other chapels as well as that below.
1836 Wesleyan Methodist chapel, Manvers St, Trowbridge, demolished.

Ellis, Thomas, Engineer, of Swindon, 1805-69. Welsh manager of Tredegar Iron Works before came to Swindon. Responsible for construction of many buildings in the railway village and may have designed them.
1864-6 General Baptist chapel, Cambria Place, probably designed by him.

Evans, T. L., of London, not a qualified architect.
1816-18 may have designed Wesleyan Methodist chapel, Coppice Hill, Bradford on Avon, part demolished.

Gale, Joseph, of Lacock.
1863 Wesleyan Methodist chapel, The Wharf, Lacock.

George, - Carpenter and architect, probably of Stratton St Margaret.
1861-2 Upper Stratton Baptist chapel, Green Rd, Stratton St Margaret.

Gordon and Gunton, of London. Henry Thomas Gordon in practice from 1879; Josiah Gunton (1861-1930) a partner

Occasionally the architect is also commemorated in a foundation stone, as here for Josiah Gunton in Amesbury Methodist

from 1886 and firm became Gordon and Gunton from 1900. Specialists in nonconformist work, particularly Wesleyan, in early 20th century with Gunton the lead.

1899 Wesleyan Methodist chapel, Amesbury.[906]
1901 Wesleyan Methodist, Idmiston.[907]
1908-9 Wesleyan Methodist chapel, Monkton Hill, Chippenham.
1910 Wesleyan Methodist chapel and schools, New Road, Marlborough.

Hardick, Thomas, of Warminster, 1806-95, a carpenter and builder at various times as well as working for Brunel on the GWR and serving as manager of the Salisbury Gas Company, 1862-95.

1851-2 Baptist chapel, Sheep Street, Devizes.
1856 Baptist chapel, Station Hill, Chippenham.
1858 Schoolroom, Ebenezer Baptist chapel, North Row, Warminster.

Hardick, William, surveyor of Warminster; perhaps son of Thomas Hardick.

1867-8 Baptist chapel, West End, Westbury (or possibly by Thomas Hardick).
1879 alterations to Baptist chapel, Old Broughton Rd, Melksham.
1882 alterations to Ebenezer Baptist chapel, North Row, Warminster. Carried out by W Hardick & Son.

Harding, _, of Fisherton.

1835 enlargement of Wesleyan Methodist chapel, St Edmund's Church Street, Salisbury.[908]

Hart, Mungo, worked in Calne area.

1874-6 Wesleyan Methodist chapel, Silver St, Calne.

Harwood, _ - see Ainsworth and Harwood

Hobbs, Noah, member of North Bradley Baptist congregation.

1874 Yarnbrook (North Bradley) Baptist.[909]

Holloway, Thomas H., d 1918, of Chippenham.

1896 Primitive Methodist chapel, The Causeway, Chippenham.

Hooper, William, 1864-1955, Leading member of Swindon Christian Brethren.

1899 designed Christian Brethren Regent Hall, Regent Place, Swindon; demolished.[910]

Houchin, H. R., of London.

1939 Immanuel Congregational chapel, Upham Road, Walcot, Swindon.[911]

Hudson, _, probably Thomas Hudson of Wincanton who also designed schools between 1894 & 1906.[912]

1896 Primitive Methodist chapel, Hindon.[913]

Isitt, Adkin and Hill, of Bradford, Yorkshire.[914]
1898-9 Wesleyan Methodist chapel, Long Street, Devizes. [915]

Lansdown, George Arthur, of London; perhaps related to T S Lansdown.
1903-4 Gorse Hill Baptist church, Cricklade Rd, Swindon; also schoolroom.

Lansdown, Thomas Smith, of Swindon, 1822-95. In practice first in Malmesbury c1861 and then in Swindon. In partnership with James Rew Shopland (d 1897) from c1870. In later life also a nurseryman and stone quarry proprietor.
1859-60 Primitive Methodist chapel, Brinkworth.
1862 Wesleyan Methodist chapel and schools, The Planks, Old Town, Swindon, demolished.
1867-9 conversion of GWR working-men's barracks, Faringdon Rd, Swindon to Wesleyan Methodist chapel.
1868 Wesleyan Methodist chapel, Play Close, Purton, replaced by larger chapel.
1868 Sunday school, General Baptist chapel, Fleet St, Swindon.
1870 Primitive Methodist chapel, Prospect Place, Swindon, and minister's house.
1873-4 Wesleyan Methodist chapel, North St, Pewsey.
1885 Possible additions to Rodbourne Road Primitive Methodist chapel, Swindon.
1894 new Wesleyan Methodist chapel, Percy St, Rodbourne, Swindon.

Mammen, Eric
1995 porch and other alterations for Wesleyan Methodist chapel, Station Rd, Westbury.

Masters, William Arthur Harvey, of Stanton Fitzwarren, 1876-1928.
1927 Primitive Methodist chapel, The Circle, Pinehurst, Swindon, demolished.

Mullings, Benoni, of Devizes; also spelled Mullens or Mullins.
1868-9 hall and schoolroom, Congregational chapel, Northgate St, Devizes.

Oatley, Sir George Herbert, FRIBA, of Bristol. 1863-1950, partner of Henry Crisp from c1889, then successively with G C Lawrence and R H Brentnall; knighted 1925.
1928 new porch, Congregational Church, Melksham.
1936-38 Sunday School, Forest Methodist Chapel, Woodrow Rd, Melksham.

Osborne, William Robert. Born Corsham 1878. In practice at Regent Circus, Swindon with W H Read as Read and Osborne, but Read died 1901.
1906 Primitive Methodist chapel, Rodbourne Cheney, Swindon; later Baptist.
1907 Primitive Methodist chapel, Broad Hinton.[916]
1909 alterations to Primitive Methodist chapel, Deacon St, Swindon (as Read, Osborne and Cook), demolished.

Paull, Henry John, 1831-88, of Cardiff, Manchester, Burnley and London. Designed Congregational chapels. From c1879 in partnership with A A Bonella.
1882-3 Tabernacle Congregational chapel, Trowbridge, also schools attached to former chapel.

Peto. Sir Samuel Morton, Bt., of Somerleyton Hall, Suffolk, 1809-89. Leading railway contractor, MP 1847-68 and Baptist.
1848-9 Baptist chapel, Fleet St, Swindon, demolished.

Piccaver, J.A. of Northampton.
1900-1 Primitive Methodist chapel, Sheldon Rd, Chippenham.

Pictor, Arthur John, 1861-1938, Bruton and Bath; of the noted family of quarrymen and stonemasons at Box.
1896-7 Wesleyan Methodist chapel, Box.
1905-7 Schoolrooms, Box Wesleyan Methodist chapel.[917]

Pinnegar, James, of Kington Langley, builder.
1835, certainly built, and probably also designed, Union Chapel, Kington Langley.

Pomroy, George, of Wilton.
1875 Primitive Methodist chapel, Kingsbury Square, Wilton; built as Temperance Hall. .[918]

Ponting, Charles Edwin, of Marlborough, 1850-1932. Diocesan architect for Wiltshire and Dorset parts of Salisbury Diocese and for parts of Bristol Diocese; also surveyor to Marlborough College.
1886 Wesleyan Methodist chapel, Poulshot.

Price, Thomas G., of Birmingham.
1906-7 Wesleyan Methodist chapel, Burbage.

Proctor, Philip, of Shaftesbury. Philip Proctor Associates, 2009.
2010 restoration of Quaker Meeting House, Salisbury.

Randell, John Ashley, of Devizes. Died 1898.
1869 Manningford Bohune, Baptist.[919]
1876 Alterations to Congregational chapel, Northgate St, Devizes.
1890 All Cannings, Wesleyan Methodist.

Rawlence & Squarey of Salisbury.[920]
1899 Landford Wood Mission Hall.

Read, William Henry, 1850-1901; of Swindon.
1886 Tabernacle Baptist chapel, Regent St, Swindon, demolished. (May have been assisted by R J Beswick).

Read and Macdonald of London.
1900 Wesleyan Methodist chapel, Littleton Panell (West Lavington).[921]
1909 Alterations to Primitive Methodist chapel, Deacon Street, Swindon (as Read, Osborne and Cook). Demolished.

Reay Samuel Sebastian – see T B Silcock

Reeves, Henry, of Bratton, a member of a family of engineers and committed Baptists.
1882, Baptist chapel, Tilshead (designed without charge).
1884, Baptist mission chapel, Stormore (Dilton Marsh).[922]
1895, Ebenezer Baptist chapel, Littleton Panell.[923]
1899, Baptist chapel, Marden (designed without charge).
1907, Baptist chapel and schoolroom, Great Cheverell (designed without charge).

Reeves, Robert, of Bratton, father of Henry.
1864, Baptist chapel, Steeple Ashton, supervised conversion of house.[924]

Reynolds, Peter, of Oxford.
1990 Pilgrim Centre, Regent Street, Swindon.[925]

Roach, _ , of Charfield, Wotton-under-Edge.
1889 alterations to Baptist chapel, Nettleton.[926]

Roe, William Henry, of Southampton.
1829 Baptist chapel, Brown St, Salisbury, later remodelled by Stent.

Rudman, Walter, of Chippenham, died 1939.
1934 Stratton Green Baptist chapel, Swindon Rd, Stratton St Margaret. The 1937 Sunday school was possibly also by him.

Silcock, Thomas Ball, of Bath. 1854-1924. In practice from c1887, then with Samuel Sebastian Reay from c1897.
1892-3 Renovations to Bearfield Congregational chapel, Bradford on Avon.[927]
1894-5 Congregational chapel, Sanford St, Swindon, demolished [928]
1898 Sunday School at same location, presumably as Silcock & Reay, destroyed by fire 1947.

Smith, William, of Trowbridge, a leading architect locally to whom most of the late 19th century Gothic buildings in Trowbridge are attributable.
1850 Little Bethel Baptist, Trowbridge, demolished.[929]
1857 Unitarian chapel, Conigre, Trowbridge, demolished.
1860 Timbrell Street Methodist, Trowbridge.[930]
1865 Schools at Unitarian chapel, Conigre, Trowbridge (attributed).
1871 Sunday school at Tabernacle Congregational chapel, Trowbridge.[931]
1884 Schools, Emmanuel Baptist chapel, Church St, Trowbridge.
1885 Schoolroom, Lower Westwood Baptist. .[932]
1892 Market Lavington Congregational.[933]

Snailum, Terence W, son of W W Snailum, practice in Bath as Snailum Huggins & Lefevre, later Snailum & Lefevre.
1961 North Bradley Baptist chapel.

Snailum, Walter Wadman, of Trowbridge.
1904 Primitive Methodist chapel, Forest, Melksham.[934]

1908-9 Sunday School, Baptist chapel, Old Broughton Rd, Melksham.
1930-1 Bethesda Baptist chapel, Gloucester Rd, Trowbridge.

Squarey – see Rawlence and Squarey

Stanley, William Henry, of Trowbridge; died 1933 in East Grinstead.
1893 Perhaps designed classrooms, Zion Chapel, Union St, Trowbridge.

Stent, William Jervis of The Close, Warminster, 1815-87. A strong nonconformist specialising in chapel design, and the most prolific chapel architect in Wiltshire.
1853 Congregational chapel, Mere, attributed.[935]
1857 Congregational chapel, Ebbesbourne Wake.
1860-1 Wesleyan Methodist chapel, George St, Warminster.
c1860 re-fronted Congregational chapel, Endless Street, Salisbury; demolished.
c1860 (attributed) Old Congregational, Warminster Road Westbury, alterations.[936]
1862-3 Congregational chapel, Broad Chalke.
1862 classrooms and vestry, New Meeting House, Common Close, Warminster, demolished.
1864 Restoration of Baptist chapel, Castle Street, Calne.[937]
1865-6 Congregational chapel, Victoria St, Swindon, demolished.
1867 Congregational chapel, Westport, Malmesbury.
1867-8 Free Church, Calne.
1868 New Congregational chapel, Mere.
1869-70 Congregational chapel, Sutton Veny; also perhaps school 1869; the chapel demolished.
1871 gate screen, gates, lamps and railings, Tabernacle Congregational chapel, Trowbridge.
1872 Wesleyan Methodist chapel, Wesley St, Newtown, Trowbridge.
1880 Congregational chapel, Holt.
1881-2 Baptist chapel, Brown St, Salisbury, remodelling.

In Memoriam.

WILLIAM JERVIS STENT,
SUPERINTENDENT OF
Common Close Sunday School, Warminster,
Who died in the 50th year of his work,
ON FEB. 14TH, 1887, AGED 72.

In Memoriam card for William Jervis Stent, Wiltshire's most prolific chapel architect. Image courtesy of Warminster Museum

Stocken, Anthony, of Salisbury.
1978, insertion of first floor and other alterations to Congregational chapel, Fisherton Street, Salisbury.[938]

Tarring & Wilkinson, of London. John Tarring was a leading nonconformist architect.
1878-9 Congregational chapel, Fisherton St Salisbury.

Taylor, Julian, of Cherhill.
2003 Allden Room extension to Monkton Hill Methodist, Chippenham.[939]

Wallace, William, of London.
1899 Trinity Presbyterian chapel, Victoria Rd, Swindon.

Watson, S, of Caversham.
1914 Collingbourne Kingston Primitive Methodist.[940]

While, or White, A.G., of Swindon.
1887 alterations to Wesleyan Methodist chapel, Faringdon Rd Swindon.

Wills, John, of Derby, c1845-1906, chapel specialist with a national practice and c200 chapels attributed to him and his two sons.[941]
1880 United Methodist schools, Milford St, Salisbury.

Wilson, Willcox and Wilson of Bath. James Wilson (1816-1900), father of James Buckley Wilson who joined the partnership c1872, architects with an extensive nonconformist practice, especially Wesleyan. Willcox was probably originally a pupil of Wilson senior.
1858 Wesleyan Methodist chapel, Faringdon Rd, Swindon, demolished.[942]
1872 Wesleyan Methodist chapel, High St, Melksham.

Wonnacott, Thomas Robjohn, of Southsea, an early pioneer of concrete construction.
1902 Wesleyan Methodist chapel, Tisbury.[943]

Wyatt, Thomas Henry, of London, 1807-80. Distinguished mid-century architect.
1862-3 Remodelled former Baptist chapel, Castle Street, Trowbridge, as St Stephen's church; demolished.

Wyvern Architects, of Devizes.
1998 New meeting hall, Lower Stratton Methodist.[944]

Young, G L, of Salisbury.
1869 West Grimstead Wesleyan Methodist.[945]

General Sources and Background Reading

General Sources

1851 – information from the 1851 ecclesiastical census.

1864 – 'Returns to Bishop's Visitation Queries, Salisbury Diocese, 1864'. WSAD1/56/7 [Wiltshire Record Society edition forthcoming].

ABC1 and ABC2 – *Architects and Building Craftsmen with work in Wiltshire*, in two volumes compiled by Pamela M Slocombe and others for the Wiltshire Buildings Record, 1996 and 2006.

BoE – Nikolaus Pevsner, *Wiltshire*, 1st edn, 1963 (Penguin: The Buildings of England).

BoE2 – Draft text and notes for the revised edition of *Wiltshire* (The Buildings of England), by kind permission of Julian Orbach.

BoE3 – Julian Orbach, Bridget Cherry & Nikolaus Pevsner, *Wiltshire*, 3rd edn., 2021 (Yale Univ. Press: The Buildings of England).

BNA – British Newspaper Archive (Britishnewspaperarchive.co.uk). Newspaper extracts are given under the name of the relevant journal.

Butler - D.M. Butler, *The Quaker Meeting Houses of Britain*, vol. 2, Friends' Historical Society London 1999.

Doel - William Doel, *Twenty Golden Candlesticks*, 1890 (facsimile edn. Wiltshire County Council and Wiltshire Family History Society 2005).

Grass – Research data on Catholic Apostolic, Brethren and Strict Baptist chapels in Wiltshire, with kind permission of Dr Tim Grass, in personal communication.

Hague - Graham Hague *et al*, *The Unitarian Church, An Architectural Survey*, Unitarian Heritage 1986.

HE – Description of listed building by Historic England, at https://historicengland.org.uk/. HE 'Red Boxes' is an online collection of historic photographs.

Kelly – with date, *Kelly's Directory of Wiltshire* for that year. Wiltshire directories from 1867 to 1915 are available online in Leicester University special collections, along with some other directories.

Lindley - Kenneth Lindley, *Chapels and Meeting Houses*, John Baker, 1969.

MHC – John Chandler (ed.), *Wiltshire Meeting house Certificates and Registrations*, Wiltshire Record Society, vol. 40, 1985.

MyPM – information from the website of 'My Primitive Methodists' https://www.myprimitivemethodists.org.uk, containing mainly extracts from the *Primitive Methodist Magazine*.

Oliver - Robert W Oliver, *The Strict Baptist Chapels of England, vol. 5 Wiltshire and the West'* Fauconberg Press, 1968. Though published in 1968 much of it is an updating of earlier material.

OS – 25" and 6" to one mile Ordnance Survey maps in editions from 1880s through to 1940s. Available online through 'Know Your Place' and the National Library of Scotland. The citing of this as a reference implies use of these maps to ascertain the position and development through time of a particular chapel; they can also be used both to check whether a replacement chapel was built on the same site as its predecessor and whether a present-day building may possibly contain original chapel fabric. The 1840s tithe maps, available on 'Know Your Place', do not indicate chapels by name but their differentiation of domestic from non-domestic buildings can be helpful to the same end.

Stell - Christopher Stell, *Chapels and Meeting Houses in South West England*, HMSO, 1991 (RCHME). One of a notable series produced by Stell for the RCHME, an authoritative listing of nearly all chapels still standing from before the middle of the 19th century.

Stribling - S.B. Stribling, *History of the Wilts and East Somerset Congregational Union 1797-1897*, 1897.

Tonks – William C Tonks, *Victory in the Villages: the history of the Brinkworth Circuit*, Aberdare, 1907.

VCH – *Victoria County History: Wiltshire*. Volumes 4 to 18 available online at British History Online: each has a clearly indicated section on nonconformity so only the volume number is given in references. Volume 3 is an introductory volume on religious history. Parts of forthcoming Volumes 19 and 20 are available in draft (2021) on the website of the Institute for Historical Research, University of London. Five volumes of the VCH remain to be written (2021) in addition to the part-completed volumes 19 and 20, so coverage is not complete countywide, but where available the VCH is usually the most reliable main source for historical information.

WA – List of Wiltshire architects, prepared by Julian Orbach in connection with his revision of the Buildings of England for Wiltshire and available via his website https://julianorbach.weebly.com/.

WBRB - with number: document from the archives of the Wiltshire Buildings Record, collected from many sources over the last 30 years and more.

WCH – Wiltshire Community History pages on the Wiltshire Council website, giving historic information parish by parish; generally reproduces VCH information but also adds usefully to it; particularly useful in parts of the county which have not yet been covered by the VCH.

WRS27 – Mary Ransome (ed.), *Wiltshire Returns to the Bishop's Visitation Queries 1783*, Wiltshire Record Society, vol. 27, 1972.

WSA – with reference number: document from the Wiltshire and Swindon Archives, Chippenham.

Background Reading

In addition to those listed above there are many books and articles which give useful background to nonconformist history and to chapel design. The short list below details those which have proved most useful in researching this book. Books giving information specific to particular places are referenced in the gazetteer.

Binfield, Clyde, *So Down to Prayers, studies in English nonconformity 1780 – 1920*, Dent, 1977.
Chapels Society, The, articles from various newsletters, available online at chapelssociety.org.uk
Council for British Archaeology, *Hallelujah, Recording chapels and meeting houses*, CBA, 1985
Davies, Rupert, E., *Methodism*, Penguin 1963.
Dictionary of Methodism, A, Methodist Publishing House, available online at dmbi.online
Hague, Graham, *et al*, *The Unitarian Church: an Architectural Survey*, Unitarian Heritage, 1986.
Hibbs, John *The Country Chapel*, David & Charles, 1988
Jones, Anthony, *Welsh Chapels*, National Museum of Wales 1984
Lindley, Kenneth, *Chapels and Meeting Houses*, John Baker, 1969
Methodist History, at mymethodisthistory.org.uk

Mingay, G.E., *Rural Life in Victorian England*, Alan Sutton, 1976

Munson, James, *The Nonconformists*, SPCK, 1991

Nonconformist Protestant Chapels, at Buildinghistory.org

Nonconformity, in VCH Explore at victoriacountyhistory.ac.uk/explore

Parker, Derek, and Chandler, John, *Wiltshire Churches, an Illustrated History*, Alan Sutton, 1993.

Report on the Census of religious worship in England and Wales 1851, Available online at archive. org/details/censusgreatbrit00manngoog/page.

Ryrie, Alex, *Protestants: the Radicals who made the Modern World*, William Collins, 2017

Southall, Kenneth H., *Our Quaker Heritage*, Quaker Books, 1984

Thurley, Simon, *The Building of England*, Collins 2013

Who are the Strict Baptists? Available online at sbhs.org.uk.

References

References for chapters 1, 2, 3 and 10 are given in conventional form. Referencing separately each piece of information given in the gazetteers would lead to the text there being over-burdened with numbers so references are instead grouped into a single entry for each chapel mentioned. In addition, and in order not to add to the burden of anyone following up sources, the references quoted in each case are only those which add specific information to the description. Common sources like meeting house certificates, the 1851 ecclesiastical census, the Stell volume and even the Victoria County History are mentioned only when they come into this category and not otherwise.

1. Introduction

1   Quoted numbers of chapels, here and following, are derived from the information in the gazetteers.

2.   Nonconformity in Wiltshire

2   Except where otherwise indicated, information on Wiltshire nonconformity in this chapter comes from VCH3 and information on specific places is as referenced in the gazetteer.

3   The rise and decline of Quakerism in South Wiltshire, Kay S Taylor, Sarum Chronicle 10.

4   MHC

5   Stribling, p34

6   MHC

7   David J Jeremy – The 1798-9 Salisbury Village Preaching Controversy, in Wiltshire Archaeological and Natural History Society Magazine Volume 61.

8   Jeremy – op cit.

9   WRS27

10   VCH10

11   1932 description of Swindon No 1 Primitive Methodist circuit recorded in 'The Souvenir Handbook for the Brinkworth and District Synod, held in Regent Street chapel, Swindon between April 28th and May 4th 1932.'

12   Tonks, p14

13   Tonks, p50

14   Tonks, p24 et seq.

15   William Small - 'Cherished Memories and Associations', acquired 2003 by WSHC and abstracted by Ruth Newman.

16   Stribling, p39

17   Swindon, the legacy of a railway town, John Cattell and Keith Falconer, RCHME 1995, p161

18   Stribling, p53

19   Tonks, p122 et seq

20   Oliver

21   Doel, p62

22   Primitive Methodist Magazine 1830, quoted in MyPM

23   Doel, p162

24   Primitive Methodist Magazine 1859,

quoted in MyPM

25   Wiltshire Times 2/9/1882

26   MHC

27   Tonks, p33

28   Primitive Methodist Magazine 1841, quoted in MyPM

29   Primitive Methodist Magazine 1842, quoted in MyPM

30   Landford, a Wiltshire village in the New Forest, Stephen Ings, Laneford Books, 2005, p100.

31   WSA2695/1

32   Gospelstudies.org.uk quoting an article from the Baptist Quarterly c1925

33   Quoted in boxpeopleandplaces.co.uk, accessed July 2021

34   For Jupe, see for example Mere Papers No 8, Congregationalism in Mere M F Tighe 1998, Friends of church of St Michael the Archangel.

35   Doel, p136

36   Doel, p136

37   Doel, p179

38   The history of nonconformity in Warminster, Henry Mayo Gunn, first published 1853, facsimile edition 2003 by Bedeguar Books on behalf of Warminster and Wylye Valley Society for Local Study, p33.

39   WSA3151/124, p38

40   WSA3909/1, church minutes book.

41   1851, for figures in this and following paragraph

42   WSA2695/1

43   Baptists in Bradford on Avon, Robert W Oliver, Old Baptist Chapel, reprint 2005, p17

44   WSA1614/252

45   Tonks, p122 et seq

46   VCH6

47   VCH7

48   Wiltshire Times 11/4/1896

49   fiec.org.uk, accessed July 2021

50   WSA2485/20

3. Chapel Design

51   Except where otherwise indicated, information on specific places is referenced in the gazetteers.

52   'Welsh Chapels', Anthony Jones. National Museum of Wales 1984, p4.

53   '1880 – 1980, History of Bath Road Methodist Church Swindon by E R Carter' (published by the church, 1981)

54   Quoted in website of Wiltshire Online Parish Clerks, accessed November 2020

55   WSA1614/252

56   Tim Grass in The Chapels Society Newsletter 54, September 2013.

57 Lindley, p34.

58   Hallelujah, Recording chapels and meeting houses, Council for British Archaeology 1985, p9

59   WA

60   Oliver, quoting John Collier in 'The Friendly Companion'

61   'The Origins of Primitive Methodism', Sandy Calder, Boydell Press, 2016.

62   *'Corrugated Iron Buildings', Nick Thomson, Shire Books 2011.*

63   See for example 'The New Affinities of Faith: A Plea for Free Christian Union' by James Martineau, Williams and Norgate, London, 1869.

64   Jones, op cit, p56, quoting Lismer Short.

65   WSA71/5 'Wesleyan Methodism in Trowbridge', by Edward Dyer 1862, p14

66   A Wiltshire Village, Alfred Williams, Duckworth 1912

67   WSA1614/252

68   Tim Grass in The Chapels Society Newsletter 54, September 2013, quoting A N Groves, an early Brethren leader.

69   Photographs in the church

70   Recollections of Gertie Gough recorded in 'Lydiard Life 2000', published locally.

71 Alison Light in The Chapel Society Newsletter 45, September 2010

4. The Villages

72   WRS27.

73 VCH12.

74   VCH12; WSA3916/3/3/1.

75 VCH12.

76   VCH12; WBRB4507; Primitive Methodist Magazine February 1857.

77   Alderbury & Whaddon, A Millenium Mosaic, Alderbury & Whaddon local history research group, 2000; WCH; Salisbury & Winchester Journal,

4/11/1839.

78 WCH; *taking-stock.org.uk/building/ whaddon-holy-family, accessed July 2021; photograph in Salisbury museum archives.*

79 VCH10; HE.

80 VCH10; WA; WBRB905; Wiltshire Times 5/10/1889.

81 VCH15; WBRB10887; old photo courtesy of Angela Armstrong; information from owner.

82 VCH11; OS.

83 VCH13; WBRB16274; Taunton Courier and Western Adviser 8/8/1894.

84 VCH13; OS.

85 VCH18; HE.

86 VCH18; HE; WBRB10957

87 VCH18; Tonks; Ashton Keynes, A Village With No History, Madge Paterson and Ernie Wood 1986.

88 VCH7; 1851; Stell; church website.

89 VCH7; WBRB921.

90 1851; 1864; Kelly 1867.

91 Wiltshire Times 28/9/1877, 5/8/1882, 28/1/1939; personal communication from Effie Gale-Sides, chair of Atworth parish council.

92 VCH12; HE; Stell; WBRB922; WSA1418/40.

93 VCH12; OS.

94 MHC1831; Salisbury Times 14/11/1902; OS; WSA index volume.

95 VCH12; WSA3916/3/4/3.

96 VCH12; OS.

97 VCH12; WSA3916/3/4/4 1939 and 3916/3/4/5.

98 VCH10; OS.

99 VCH17; OS.

100 VCH15; OS.

101 VCH13; HE; WBRB5718.

102 VCH13; WBRB16171.

103 VCH13; OS.

104 MHC1690; Butler; MSS1875 from Wiltshire Museum; Stell.

105 HE; Stell; WBRB12651 & 4657; Wiltshire Times 3/11/1928.

106 Wiltshire Times 25/10/1884; BoE2.

107 The Quakers of Melksham, Harold Fassnidge, Bradford on Avon Friends 1992.

108 1851; VCH7; documents in possession of the owner, Penny Cann.

109 OS; information from parish council

chairman.

110 VCH7; WSA3939/2/1/1.

111 VCH11; 1864.

112 VCH12; Primitive Methodist Magazine 1835; 'Wiltshire online parish clerks' description and photographs accessed July 2021.

113 VCH12; Swindon Advertiser & North Wilts Chronicle 15/9/1885.

114 VCH11; article and photographs on 'Wiltshire online parish clerks' accessed July 2021; short history of the hall by Paul Williams, privately published 2010.

115 VCH11; Stell; information from owner; WBRB11622.

116 VCH8; OS.

117 Stell; Oliver; 1851.

118 Blunsdon Looking Back, Richard S Radway, self-published c1990.

119 Radway, op cit; MyPM quoting 1910 Primitive Methodist Centenary Synod handbook 1910.

120 VCH13; 1851.

121 VCH13; WBRB1396.

122 VCH13; WSA1150/330.

123 BoE2; church website – boxmethodist.org – accessed April 2021; personal communication with Michael Rumsey of Corsham Civic Society; Box, Wiltshire, an Intimate History, Clare Higgins, Downland Press, Frome, 1985; Box Methodist church, 150 years 1834 to 1984, published by the church.

124 Boxmethodist.org; WBRB7827; WCH; notes from Michael Rumsey.

125 As Box Hill.

126 OS; notes from Michael Rumsey.

127 OS; Grass; WCH.

128 OS.

129 WSA 3319/74; information from owner, Richard Adams; WBRB16294; WCH.

130 As Corton Baptist.

131 VCH8; HE; Stell; information from the church minister.

132 1851.

133 VCH8; WCH; Bratton History Association Journal Volume 2, 1991-2, article on nonconformist history by Kathleen White.

134 VCH18; Tonks; WSA1571/71.

135 WRS27; Fassnidge, op cit, p130.

136   Stell; HE; WCH; WBRB7907; BoE2; Bath Chronicle and Weekly Gazette 18/5/1848.
137   VCH17;WSA2225/13.
138   HE; WCH; WSA2783/10; WBRB9695.
139   Stell; OS; WCH.
140   1851; Post Office directory 1855; VCH20 in draft.
141   VCH20 in draft; WBRB8471.
142   MHC1690; WCH.
143   VCH14; Stell; OS; WSA 2755/33.
144   VCH14; HE; WRS27.
145   Swindon Reminiscences, William Morris 1885 (Tabard Press facsimile edition 1970)
146   VCH14; Tonks; Stell; Primitive Methodist Magazine 1829, p287, and 1839; OS.
147   VCH14; Tonks; Stell; Primitive Methodist Magazine May 1860, p305; WA.
148   VCH14; Tonks.
149   VCH14; Tonks.
150   WCH; OS.
151   VCH19 in draft; 1851; OS.
152   VCH13; information from owner and from Michael Powis of Broad Chalke; HE; WBRB9509.
153   VCH13; WA; 1864.
154   VCH13; information from Michael Powis of Broad Chalke; WSA1150/330.
155   VCH12; BoE2; WSA2053/24.
156   WCH; Grass; 1864.
157   VCH9; OS; information from Roger Smith of Wootton Bassett museum.
158   1840s tithe map; OS; VCH9; Tonks. It was the 1842 chapel which was demolished and not that of 1866 as the VCH suggests.
159   VCH14; MyPM.
160   VCH7; WSA1699/104; MHC1690; Fassnidge op cit.
161   VCH7; 1840s tithe map.
162   VCH7; Stell.
163   WCH.
164   VCH7; WCH; WSA3836/6; WBRB3055; Primitive Methodist Magazine 1840.
165   WCH.
166   MHC1724; HE.
167   VCH7; Stell; HE; WSA3151/124.
168   VCH7; WBRB4357; information from Ivor Slocombe.
169   VCH7; WA; Wiltshire & Swindon Historic Environment Record MWI76477.
170   VCH15; HE; Stell; History of Salisbury United Reformed Church, George Abel, published by the church c1978.
171   VCH8; WCH.
172   VCH16
173   VCH16; WSA3299/14; WA.
174   MHC1846.
175   VCH16.
176   VCH17; Stell; HE; Oliver.
177   VCH17; HE; Oliver; WBRB1217; London Gazette 28/3/1980; WSA1458/57.
178   WCH
179   VCH17; photo on Wiltshire online parish clerks website, accessed July 2020; WCH.
180   WBRB6169; MHC1851; Wiltshire Times 15/9/1956 describing 99th anniversary celebrations.
181   VCH17; OS; Primitive Methodist Magazine 1842; WSA3939/2/7/7.
182   Stribling; OS; WBRB7868; Wiltshire Gazette & Herald 1/3/2012 re museum closure.
183   HE; WCH; OS; Church Facebook page accessed July 2021.
184   WCH; OS; 'Castle Combe', E J Cruse, London, Colin Venton 1962.
185   WRS27.
186   OS.
187   VCH8; WSA1418/12; Stribling; WA; The history of nonconformity in Warminster, Henry Mayo Gunn, first published 1853, republished 2003 by Bedeguar Books on behalf of Warminster and Wylye Valley Society for Local Study.
188   VCH8; Stell; Doel; information from owner.
189   VCH14; OS.
190   VCH10; OS.
191   VCH17; OS; information from owner.
192   VCH17; OS; WSA1907/101; Kelly 1867 and 1889.
193   VCH17; OS; 1851.
194   VCH13; OS.
195   VCH13; Salisbury & Winchester

Journal 3/8/1861; WBRB16215.

196 OS; Salisbury Times 3/3/1893 & 13/7/1894; Western Gazette 17/1/1890.

197 VCH16; WCH; OS.

198 VCH20 in draft; OS; 1851; WCH.

199 VCH10; OS.

200 VCH9; North Wilts Herald 15/3/1895; information and photographs from Elaine Jones of Chiseldon Local History Group.

201 VCH9; OS; WSA index volume information. Dr Fred Fuller, writing in Swindon Outlook in 1999, believed the first chapel was south of Turnball but WBR staff assess the brickwork of the rear building on this site as more likely to be of 1809 than 1861.

202 VCH9; WBRB14594; OS; WSA index volume information.

203 VCH9; Handbook of Brinkworth & Swindon District Synod 1910, recorded in MyPM; Primitive Methodist Magazine February 1854; WA; WSA3916/3/5/1.

204 VCH9; North Wilts Herald 7/9/1888; old photographs from Elaine Jones; Souvenir handbook for Brinkworth and District Synod, Swindon 1932.

205 Photograph and information from Elaine Jones.

206 OS; Chitterne, A Wiltshire Village, Sue Robinson, Hobnob Press 2007; WSA2852/21 and 3319/14.

207 VCH15; OS.

208 WRS27; 1851; VCH20 in early draft May 2021; HE; WBRB7815.

209 VCH16; Stell; OS

210 VCH16; OS.

211 VCH16; OS.

212 OS.

213 VCH9; Tonks; OS; WSA2783/21; information from owner on conversion.

214 WCH; Codford, Wool and War in Wiltshire, John Chandler, Phillimore 2007; Stribling; information from Sally Thomson of Codford; Gunn op cit.

215 WCH; HE; The village on the hill, aspects of Colerne history, Colerne History Group 1990; BoE2.

216 WCH; HE; WA; information from Jonathan Tuckey Design; WBRB8450.

217 WCH; OS.

218 WCH; WSA2783/25 and 2783/27.

219 VCH11; 1851; WCH; information from owner;

220 VCH11; Collingbourne Ducis Chapel 1880-1983. Pamela Cogdell, self-published 2008; WBRB6843.

221 VCH16; OS; Collingbourne Kingston, a photographic view, Mary May, Manor Acre 2003;Diss Express, Friday, 26 June 1914;

222 1864.

223 VCH17; OS.

224 VCH19 in draft; OS.

225 WCH; old photograph in Wiltshire online parish clerks; OS; Salisbury Times 2/11/1894.

226 WCH; 1851.

227 VCH8; Doel; church website, whitbournechapel.org.uk, accessed July 2021; Stell.

228 VCH8; HE; WBRB7292.

229 VCH8; WSA1112/9; 1864.

230 VCH14; OS; information from owner.

231 VCH14; OS.

232 VCH14; WBRB8843.

233 VCH8; HE; information from minister, Guy Davies; Doel; Penknap Providence Church - 200th Anniversary booklet, 2010 by Guy Davies, pastor; WBRB15512;The History of the first 50 years of Penknap Providence Chapel, date and author not clear but reproduced on Wiltshire online parish clerks website, accessed July 2021.

234 VCH8; Doel; WBRB4623; church history on stormorechurch.org, accessed October 2020; WSA951/204.

235 VCH8; WBRB9511;WCH; WSA2485/21.

236 VCH13; OS.

237 VCH13; OS; Wiltshire Archaeological and Natural History Magazine 112, 2019, 'A nonconformist minister in 19th century Birdbush, by Sally M Thomson; WSA1202/1 and 1202/8 (pamphlet history); old photograph on Donheadvillagehall.org, accessed May 2021; The Donheads Past and Present, by Michael Coward, David McLean, Rex Sawyer and Christine Speak, Hobnob 2007.

238 VCH13; HE; photograph before conversion on Wiltshire online parish

clerks, accessed June 2021; WBRB7978; Salisbury & Winchester Journal 6/6/1868; Sunday Times 6/4/2008 re sale.

239 VCH13; WCH.

240 VCH11; HE; OS; Stell; WSA2885/23; BoE2.

241 VCH11; WSA2885/24; information from Dr Rosalind Johnson.

242 VCH11; information from Carolyn Birch of Redlynch local history group.

243 VCH11; HE; OS; 1851; information from Dr Rosalind Johnson; Downton, the town that became a village, Elizabeth Hutchinson, Hobnob 2015; Downton: 7000 Years of an English Village, David Waymouth, Downton Millennial Book Fund, 1999.

244 VCH11; OS; information from owner of Chapel Cottage.

245 VCH11; WCH; planning approval details on Wiltshire Council website early 2021.

246 VCH11; 1864; London Gazette 28/3/1980 for cancellation of registration.

247 VCH11; information from Dr Rosalind Johnson; Waymouth op cit; Discovering Downton on Foot, the Downton Society, undated.

248 (Both buildings) VCH15, OS, WA; WSA2806/56; London Gazette 28/3/1980 for cancellation of registration.

249 VCH15; OS; WCH.

250 VCH12; 1864. A VCH suggestion that one of these might have been the later reading room, now East Kennett House, seems unlikely on stylistic grounds.

251 VCH11; WSA3477/9; HE; WBRB12458; Stribling.

252 VCH11; MHC1843; 1851; OS. The VCH has incorrectly assumed that the 1843 registration was for this building, which does not appear on the 1840s tithe map. The 1st edition 25" OS marks it as General Baptist, probably in error.

253 WBRB290; chapel history by current owners at theoldchapel.historians.co.uk, accessed July 2020.

254 Wiltshire Churches, an Illustrated History, Derek Parker and John Chandler, Alan Sutton 1993, p111; OS.

255 VCH16; WSA1464/31; information from owner.

256 OS.

257 VCH13; Stell; WRS27; Stribling; ABC1.

258 VCH8; OS; WSA1112/9; 1851.

259 VCH8; WCH; WBRB14616; WSA3168/99.

260 VCH11; 1864; Kelly 1895.

261 VCH11; information and photographs from owners; Newbury Weekly News 15/10/1896.

262 MHC1821; VCH11.

263 VCH7.

264 VCH10; OS.

265 VCH11; OS.

266 VCH15; OS; WBRB8744; WSA2485/21.

267 OS.

268 VCH11; OS.

269 VCH11; OS.

270 VCH13; OS.

271 WSA1214/89; HE; Stell; BoE2; Stribling; local history website fovanthistory.org, accessed August 2020.

272 VCH16; information and photographs from owner.

273 VCH11; OS; The Congregational Chapel, Marlborough by J W Gale, published by the church 1957, p16.

274 VCH16; Stell; WSA2928/34.

275 VCH16; Primitive Methodist Magazine for 1859, recorded in MyPM; OS.

276 VCH16; OS; WSA3299/15.

277 VCH16; OS and 1840s tithe map.

278 VCH16; WSA1464/25 & 2928/35.

279 WCH; 2003 conservation statement on village website, greatcheverell.org, accessed January 2021.

280 VCH10; WCH.

281 VCH10; WCH; WA; WSA951/204, 1112/87 & 1112/87a; Wiltshire Times 31/8/1907; Wiltshire Gazette & Herald 8/3/2001.

282 VCH10; Kelly 1898 & 1903.

283 VCH8; OS; information and photograph from Diane Norris of Great Hinton.

284 VCH8; information and photograph from the owners, Mr & Mrs Norris.

285   1851; VCH14.

286   VCH14; WBRB9329; Primitive
      Methodist Magazine 1854 and 1860,
      recorded on MyPM; WSA2783/49;
      information from owner.

287   VCH14.

288   VCH15; OS; 1851; photograph from
      Salisbury Museum archives.

289   VCH15; MHC1832; 1864;
      WSA1150/267; Salisbury Times
      14/6/1912

290   WCH; Salisbury & Winchester
      Journal 20/11/1869; WSA4103/8/3.

291   (Both Free United chapels) OS;
      information from owner; WSA index
      volume; 1851.

292   Most comprehensive source of
      information is Historic Chapels Trust
      website, hct.org.uk. Also: Stell; HE;
      BoE2; Wiltshire Times 30/5/1985;
      History of the Parish of Grittleton, Rev J
      E Jackson 1843; Wiltshire Local History
      Forum newsletter No 83 spring 2013,
      article by Patricia Aves, 'Grittleton Strict
      and Particular Baptist Chapel', first
      published in journal of Open University
      History Society.

293   WCH, WSA2098/1; WBRB8356; HE.

294   VCH11; OS.

295   VCH14; WSA1458/62; photograph
      pre-conversion on Wiltshire online
      parish clerks website, accessed June
      2020; Salisbury & Wiltshire Journal
      13/11/1837; London Gazette 28/3/1980
      for cancellation of registration.

296   OS.

297   Information from Rosalind Cowie,
      church member; Wiltshire Independent
      11/10/1849; OS.

298   WSA1614/288; information from
      Swindon Sea Scouts; old photograph in
      Swindon Libraries collection; OS.

299   VCH17.

300   WCH; WBRB9546; WSA1061/1; old
      photo from Salisbury museum archives.

301   Primitive Methodist Magazine
      1863 record of opening, reproduced on
      MyPM; Wiltshire Times 25/5/1895.

302   VCH8, Stribling; 1851; OS;
      WSA951/204; information from Julie
      Shergold of the church. The evidence for
      the 1844 date is weak.

303   WCH; 1851; Post Office directory for
      1855; Salisbury Journal 14/5/1843.

304   VCH9; OS.

305   VCH9; OS; 1851; Kelly 1920 & 1929.

306   VCH9; OS; Oliver.

307   VCH9; WCH photograph; OS.

308   VCH9; Tonks; WCH.

309   VCH7, Oliver, Doel, WBRB3130;
      Grass.

310   VCH7; WSA P2/1855/3 recording
      bequest of money towards a schoolroom
      in 1855; Devizes & Wiltshire Gazette
      19/6/1890; WBRB11776; Wiltshire
      Times 13/3/1989; Wiltshire Times
      14/4/2000.

311   VCH11; OS; Stell; WBRB5193;
      Stribling.

312   VCH11; WCH; Western Gazette
      13/11/1896; recent local information on
      geograph.org.uk.

313   (Both chapels) VCH7; HE;
      WBRB1785; BoE.

314   MHC1700; WCH; Chapels and
      Meeting Houses, Kenneth Lindley,
      John Baker Publishers, London 1969;
      HE; Stell; Wiltshire Archaeological and
      Natural History Magazine 1991 p163/4
      on excavations;Horningsham chapel, the
      story of England's Oldest Free Church,
      by Albert E Banton, published 1952,
      republished 1964.

315   VCH10; OS; 1864.

316   VCH14; WRS27; WSA1699/104 &
      854/44; Fassnidge op cit p134/5.

317   VCH14; HE; information from
      former owner, Tony Westlake.

318   VCH14; information from owner.

319   VCH14; OS; MyPM website, accessed
      October 2020.

320   WCH; Stell; Oliver; VCH3; VCH6;
      information and photographs from
      church members.

321   WSA3381/42; OS; BoE2; History of
      Bourne Valley Methodist church, Melvin
      Curtis, 1999.

322   WCH; WSA3319/15; photos from
      Salisbury museum; Imber then and now,
      Gordon Lewis, self-published 2015.

323   OS; 1851.

324   VCH8; WCH; HE; WBRB2984;
      WSA3168/33; WBR Historic Buildings
      Report B2984, May/June 2021.

325 VCH19 in draft; HE.

326 WCH; WSA1103/72; Kelly – various 1889-1915; Kingston Deverill, a south west Wiltshire village, Julian Wiltshire, Hobnob Press 2016.

327 As Wesleyan Methodist.

328 WCH.

329 WCH; HE; Stell; WSA2755/62.

330 WCH; OS; WBRB7236; WSA2783/37.

331 VCH20 in draft.

332 MHCs1835; information from parish council and village history website, kingtonstmichael.com, accessed July 2021; OS.

333 WCH; OS.

334 MHC1808; OS; WCH; HE; WBRB6908; WSA1647/41 & 3168/44.

335 WCH; WSA3168/41; WBRB710.

336 WSAG3/760/797.

337 WCH; OS; Landford, a Wiltshire village in the New Forest,Stephen Ings, Laneford Books, 2005.

338 WCH; listing proposal from Wiltshire Council – email communication 12/10/2020; Salisbury Journal 19/11/2020 confirms listing.

339 OS.

340 VCH18; OS.

341 OS; Laverstock and Ford: Chapters from Local History, Sarum Studies 6: p 61; email communications with Ruth Newman and Bryan Evans of Laverstock.

342 VCH14; WCH; OS; North Wilts Herald 4/2/1916 & 15/6/1928.

343 VCH14; WSA3083/108 and index volume; MyPM states not converted before 2009.

344 VCH14; OS; 1851.

345 WSA854/44.

346 VCH18; Tonks; OS.

347 VCH9; WSA2293/54; OS.

348 VCH9; OS; MHC1842.

349 VCH7; HE; WSA3211/3; Stell; Doel; WBRB7381.

350 VCH16; OS.

351 VCH10; OS.

352 VCH14; OS.

353 Stribling; WSA2755/51; OS.

354 Stell; HE; Oliver; Gunn op cit; WBRB2653.

355 Stribling.

356 1851; Kelly 1867; OS.

357 WBRB9137; WSA1904/9; Kelly 1867 et seq.; information from owner.

358 WCH; OS; Grass; information from Sheona Beaumont.

359 WCH.

360 WSA3415/14 & 3415/17; VCH15.

361 VCH15; WCH (though the account here of the sequence of buildings appears to be to some degree in error); old photograph on Wiltshire online parish clerks website, accessed June 2020; building record on Wiltshire Historic Environment Record.

362 VCH15; OS.

363 VCH18; Primitive Methodist Magazine August 1852; Brinkworth & Swindon Primitive Methodist Circuit Handbook 1932 reproduced on MyPM, and old photograph on same website, accessed May 2020; Lydiard Life 2000, 'Past and present', published locally, 2000.

364 VCH18; WSA2783/42; OS; Tonks; North Wilts Herald 10/9/1909.

365 VCH18.

366 VCH9; Tonks.

367 VCH9; Tonks; WCH.

368 VCH9; OS; WBRB9330; WSA2293/55; information from Hilary Dunscombe.

369 VCH9; VCH3 (it is suggested in some sources that Isaac Turner designed as well as funded the chapel but there appears to be little evidence for this); HE (whose suggestion that the entrance was originally only from the side seems unconvincing given the asymmetrical positioning of that door and its lack of dressings); Oliver; description on website of Strict Baptist Historical Society, accessed May 2021; old photograph on Wiltshire online parish clerks website, accessed September 2020); Stell.

370 VCH9; Primitive Methodist Magazine 1829, quoted on MyPM website; old photograph on Wiltshire online parish clerks website, accessed September 2020; Tonks.

371 As for the 1828 chapel.

372 VCH9.

373 WCH.

374 WCH; HE; Wiltshire Times

6/12/2013.

375 VCH14; OS; WSA2755/49.

376 VCH14; WBRB7341; North Wilts Herald, various records of services up to 1/4/1932 (there is uncertainty over the closing dates of both Congregational chapels here); information from owner.

377 VCH14; WCH.

378 VCH14; information from owner, Tony Westlake.

379 VCH10; Oliver; WBRB1983; information and old drawing from owner, John Lamb.

380 VCH10; OS; Devizes & Wiltshire Gazette 31/3/1870.

381 VCH10; WSA2852/29 & 951/204; Wiltshire Times 28/10/1899.

382 VCH10; WSA2852/29.

383 VCH10; HE; Stell; information & photographs on Market Lavington Museum website, accessed January 2021;The rise and decline of Quakerism in South Wiltshire, Kay S Taylor, in Sarum Chronicle 10.

384 VCH10; BoE2;information on Market Lavington Museum website, accessed January 2021.

385 VCH10; OS; WSA1458/55;information on Market Lavington Museum website, accessed January 2021.

386 VCH10;information & photographs on Market Lavington Museum website, accessed January 2021.

387 WSA3836/36; 1851.

388 VCH18; OS.

389 VCH7; WCH; WBRB7903; WSA3151/124.

390 VCH7.

391 VCH7; WSA1907/156 & 1907/157; information & photographs on Wilts United Churches website, accessed July 2020.

392 VCH7; WSA3939/2/16/2; OS & 1840s tithe map.

393 VCH7 (incorrectly implying the chapel opened in 1892); Wiltshire Times 2/9/1882 & 4/6/1955.

394 VCH12; OS.

395 VCH15; OS.

396 VCH16; WSA2928/28; information from owner.

397 VCH16; OS.

398 VCH18; Stell; Oliver; photograph in Historic England 'red boxes' website accessed October 2020.

399 VCH18; Tonks; Swindon Advertiser & North Wilts Gazette 23/10/1865; photographs in Historic England 'red boxes' and MyPM websites, both accessed October 2020.

400 VCH7; OS; a mission room at Farleigh Wick is believed to have been Anglican (WCH).

401 VCH11; 1851; Strict Baptist Historical Society website, accessed November 2020.

402 VCH11; WSA4103/4/1 & 2485/20.

403 OS.

404 WCH; Stell; Devizes & Wiltshire Gazette 24/10/1899.

405 OS & 1840s tithe map; Kelly's from 1867 to 1915; 1851.

406 WCH; Oliver; WBRB7346.

407 Kelly 1895.

408 VCH15; old photographs from Angela Armstrong of Bourne Valley Historical Society; old photograph on Wiltshire online parish clerks website, accessed April 2021.

409 VCH8; Doel; OS; photograph on Wiltshire online parish clerks website, accessed February 2020.

410 VCH8; Wiltshire Times 20/1/1961 & 24/11/1961.

411 VCH8; WBRB1263.

412 VCH10.

413 VCH10; Primitive Methodist Magazine, July 1852.

414 Stell; WSA2755/56; OS.

415 WSA2755/56; HE; WBRB4889.

416 VCH14; OS.

417 VCH8; OS.

418 VCH14; WCH; Primitive Methodist Magazine 1843, recorded on MyPM; old photograph from Historic England 'red boxes'.

419 VCH11; WBRB8622; old photograph on Wiltshire online parish clerks website, accessed July 2020; Salisbury Times 19/10/1900; Salisbury & Winchester Journal 20/10/1900.

420 1864; BoE2.

421 VCH12; WCH; information from

Ogbourne St Andrew parish history group supplied by Bruce Fox.

422   VCH12; WCH; 1851; Gale op cit; MHC1842; 1851; Kelly 1867; WSA1464/53; Reading Mercury 23/7/1842; OS & 1840s tithe map. The VCH assertion that this was located where the Primitive Methodist was later built is not backed up by the map evidence. See WSA1464/54 for evidence that this was the chapel later bought by the Wesleyans.

423   VCH12; 1851; MHC1846; 1840s tithe map & OS.

424   VCH12; WCH; Kelly 1867 & Post Office directory 1875; Wiltshire Independent 29/1/1857 & 6/2/1857.

425   VCH12; OS & 1840s tithe map; Kelly, various 1867 to 1915; WSA1464/54. The Wesleyans bought their chapel in 1906 from the Congregational Union, implying that this was the former Independent chapel.

426   VCH12; WCH; information on MyPM website accessed May 2020; MHC1852; OS & 1840s tithe map; Kelly, various 1867 to 1915; WSA1464/54.

427   VCH15; OS.

428   VCH11; OS.

429   VCH16; WCH; OS & 1840s tithe map; WSA2852/33 & 2852/56; A History of Pewsey, Michael J Duckenfield. ELSP, 2005; information from Richard Giles.

430   VCH16; WCH; Oliver; OS & 1840s tithe map; 1851; information from Richard Giles.

431   VCH16; WA; 1851; WSA2928/31 & 2193/22.

432   VCH16; WCH; The Builder, 15/3/1879; Kelly, various from 1889 to 1915; Duckenfield op cit; The Pewsey Vale in Old Photographs, collected by Roger Pope, Alan Sutton 1988.

433   VCH16; WCH; OS; Kelly, various 1889 to 1915; Duckenfield op cit; Pope op cit.

434   WCH; 1864; OS; WSA2485/17 & 2485/18.

435   WCH; Salisbury & Winchester Journal 5/10/1835; OS; Wiltshire Council planning decision February 2013.

436   1851; WCH; OS.

437   VCH7; WSA3939/2/17/1; OS; BoE2.

438   VCH7; WCH; Grass.

439   VCH7; WA; Wiltshire Times 5/6/1886; WSA index volume.

440   VCH12; WSA854/44.

441   VCH12; OS; Kelly 1931; information on MyPM website, accessed March 2021.

442   OS; WBRB11562; Grass; old photograph in Swindon Libraries collection.

443   VCH18; WSA3711/2 & 2755/64; WCH.

444   VCH18; WCH; OS; WSA2783/43.

445   VCH18; WCH; WSA1571/42; Primitive Methodist Magazine 1856 recorded on MyPM website; Tonks.

446   VCH18; Tonks; WSA1571/44; information and old photograph on MyPM website, accessed October 2020.

447   VCH6; OS.

448   VCH12.

449   VCH12; Stell; photograph in Ramsbury Then and now, Barbara Croucher, self-published 1995.

450   VCH12; WSA2988/15.

451   VCH12; WCH; WSA3916/3/6/1; information from owner.

452   VCH12; WSA2928/5.

453   VCH12; Croucher op cit.

454   VCH12; WCH; BoE2; WSA3299/15 and 3916/3/7/3.

455   VCH12; HE; description of opening in Primitive Methodist Magazine 1859 recorded on MyPM website.

456   VCH12; WCH.

457   VCH11; information from Carolyn Birch of Redlynch local history society; OS; 1851; 1864.

458   VCH11; information from Carolyn Birch & Ivor Slocombe; WBRB2057; OS.

459   VCH11; OS.

460   VCH11; information and photograph from Carolyn Birch; WSA1150/516; OS.

461   VCH11; information from Peter Roberts; Salisbury Times & South Wilts Gazette 10/6/1876.

462   1851; information from Peter Roberts; 'The Redlynch Book', 2nd edition, Rosalind Pasmore, for Redlynch and District Local History Society 2009.

463   VCH11; WCH; information on MyPM website, accessed July 2020;

WSA1150/417, 1150/420 & 1150/421.

464 VCH11; information from Carolyn Birch; WBRB10156.

465 VCH11; OS; photographs and description on National Churches Trust website, accessed July 2020.

466 OS.

467 VCH7; WBRB28; WSA3168/46.

468 VCH10; Stell; WSA1322/20.

469 VCH16; OS.

470 VCH14; information from Allie Burchill, administrator of North Wilts Methodist Circuit; Morris op cit.

471 VCH13; HE; Stell.

472 VCH13; Western Gazette 19/10/1877; OS.

473 VCH7; HE; Stell;Seend Methodist Chapel 1775-1975, by H J Griffiths, published by the church 1975; Wiltshire Gazette & Herald 16/3/2020.

474 VCH7; HE; Primitive Methodist Magazine 1841, recorded on MyPM website; WBRB564; WSA3168/71; Gazette & Herald 14/3/2010 records refusal of planning consent for conversion.

475 VCH8; WCH; WBRB3172; WSA1904/10, 1904/13, 1904/17 & 3939/3/19/1; OS & 1840s tithe map.

476 WCH; HE; Newbury Weekly News 19/12/1872; Reading Mercury 16/4/1870 & 5/7/1884; Kelly 1889, 1895 & 1898; OS.

477 WCH; WBRB2069; BoE2.

478 WCH; OS; Kelly 1895 & 1898; Newbury Weekly News 28/6/1894.

479 VCH15; Warminster & Westbury Journal 29/11/1890 & 5/10/1895; Kelly 1895, 1898 & 1903; OS.

480 WCH; Stell; WSA2953/A/1.

481 WCH; Stell; OS; photograph on HE 'red boxes'.

482 OS; information on Strict Baptist Historical Society website, accessed November 2020.

483 WCH; OS.

484 VCH15; OS & 1840s tithe map.

485 VCH15; OS & 1840s tithe map; The Baptist Lights of Shrewton, Alison Light, in The Chapel Society Newsletter 45, September 2010; WSA1112/141 & 3319/101; BoE2; Baptist Intelligencer

21/10/1847, recorded in BoE2;Salisbury and Winchester Journal, 19 December 1846.

486 VCH15; BoE2.

487 VCH15.

488 OS.

489 OS & 1840s tithe map; Kelly, various from 1867 to 1895; Post Office directory for 1855; WSA2293/22; 1851; 'A Wiltshire Village', Alfred Williams, Duckworth 1912.

490 VCH15; OS; information from owner of present house on site.

491 VCH15; WSA1150/267 & 2485/18; Salisbury & Winchester Journal 19/10/1912.

492 VCH7; WCH; OS & 1840s tithe map; 2960/51.

493 VCH7; WBRB11519.

494 VCH8; HE; BoE; Oliver; Doel; WSA486/1; Wiltshire Times 10/10/1980.

495 VCH8; WCH; HE; Doel; information from Roger Newman.

496 VCH8.

497 VCH8; OS; information from Roger Newman.

498 OS.

499 VCH10; OS.

500 VCH14; OS; information from owner of adjacent house; WSA854/44.

501 VCH15.

502 VCH7; HE; WCH; WSA3039/2/20/5.

503 VCH8; HE; OS & 1840s tithe map; WSA1112/90 & 1112/91; 1864; Wiltshire Times 24/9/1864; Sheep Bell and Ploughshare, Marjorie Reeves, Moonraker Press, Bradford-on-Avon 1978.

504 VCH8; OS & 1840s tithe map; 1864; Wiltshire Independent 10/3/1864.

505 VCH15; WSA1150/338B.

506 VCH10; WCH; WSA1270/37; Stert: The Hidden Village, published by the unnamed authors 1999, p42-45.

507 VCH11; OS.

508 OS.

509 OS.

510 WRS27; 'Sutton Benger, from Saxon Times to the Dawn of the 21st century', Kay Taylor, Ex Libris 2000.

511 VCH14.

512 OS.

513   VCH8; WCH; WRS27; photograph on Wiltshire online parish clerks website, accessed February 2021; BoE2; Sutton Veny parish website, accessed February 2021.

514   OS; Kelly, various from 1889 to 1907.

515   VCH8; 1864; OS & 1840s tithe map.

516   VCH13; OS.

517   VCH13; OS. The Band of Hope aimed specifically to evangelise children and keep them from taking to alcohol.

518   VCH8; WSA1150/344; Grass.

519   VCH16; OS.

520   OS; photograph on Wiltshire online parish clerks website, accessed September 2020.

521   VCH15; WBRB9195; WSA3246/17 & 951/204; Wiltshire Times 10/6/1882 & 25/11/1882; village website, accessed September 2020.

522   VCH13; WCH; HE; Stell; WBRB2096; BoE2; HE 'red boxes' photographs.

523   VCH13; WBRB12549; notes of WBR examination of The Old House, 2006; Stribling.

524   VCH13; WCH; HE; WSA1805/2, 1805/36 & 1805/37; WBRB7189.

525   VCH13; Salisbury & Winchester Journal 2/5/1846.

526   VCH13; WCH; BoE2; information from Ken Elcock, church member.

527   OS; Kelly 1898 to 1915; Western Gazette 20/2/1920.

528   VCH9; Tonks; OS.

529   VCH13; MyPM.

530   VCH10; HE; WCH; MHC1837; interior photographs on Alamy.com.

531   VCH10; OS; information from Dr Bill Coker, local resident.

532   VCH10; WCH.

533   OS.

534   VCH8; WSA2852/45; Wiltshire Times 5/6/1920; Kelly 1923, 1927 & 1931.

535   VCH10; OS; information from owner of Chapel House.

536   VCH10; WBRB8736; OS.

537   VCH9; OS & 1840s tithe map.

538   VCH9; WSA1614/361; abstract of 1932 description of Swindon No.1 Primitive Methodist circuit on MyPM

website, accessed May 2020; photograph on Wiltshire online parish clerks website, accessed May 2020.

539   VCH9; Lindley op cit, p32; WSA2293/65.

540   VCH8; OS.

541   WCH; OS; BoE2.

542   VCH19 in early draft; OS.

543   MHC1834; 1851; 1864; OS & 1840s tithe map; Kelly, various from 1867 to 1903; Post Office directory for 1855.

544   VCH7; OS & 1840s tithe map; BoE2; WSA951/204; MHC1839; 1851.

545   VCH7; BoE2; OS; 'Taking Stock' website detailing Catholic churches, accessed July 2021.

546   VCH11; OS; Kelly 1907 et seq. The VCH states that the chapel was Primitive Methodist but uses Kelly's directory for 1907 as its source: this is perhaps more likely to be in error than the OS which marks it as Wesleyan.

547   VCH11; Glass; OS; information from local residents Brian Rayment & Mary Spender.

548   VCH13; information on MyPM website, accessed May 2020; information from owner.

549   VCH13; Kelly 1939.

550   VCH11; Doel.

551   VCH11; WCH; OS; WBRB13236; Wiltshire Times 2/10/1926 & 16/6/1956 (noting 94th anniversary).

552   WCH; WSA4103/1/12; information from Gordon Lewis.

553   WCH; OS; information on MyPM website quoting Primitive Methodist Magazine of 1861, accessed September 2020.

554   VCH10; WSA3299/19 & index volume; WBRB8765; North Wilts Herald 20/5/1938 (noting 97th anniversary).

555   VCH11 (VCH has it under Overton); WSA1464/60 & 1464/62.

556   VCH10; OS.

557   VCH6; OS.

558   VCH7; OS; WSA3319/118; WBRB530; Wiltshire Times 11/4/1896; information from owner of Chapel House.

559   VCH7, which appears to be in error in stating it opened in 1849; WCH; MHC1819.

560 VCH7; HE; WSA1594/29 & 2922/22; information from Gordon Butler, church member.

561 WCH; Stell; MHX1799; WSA3381/42; photographs from Salisbury Museum archives and HE 'red boxes'; History of Bourne Valley Methodist churches, Melvin Curtis, published by the church 1999.

562 WCH; Curtis op cit; Kelly 1927, 1931 and 1939; OS; photograph and information from Angela Armstrong of Bourne Valley History Society.

563 WCH; Curtis op cit; OS; WSA1150/131.

564 VCH12; Tonks.

565 VCH12; OS.

566 VCH15; OS.

567 OS; 1851; MHC1828; information from owner, Tony Bassett.

568 WCH; OS.

569 WCH; WSA1150/264; OS.

570 WCH; WSA1150/261.

571 Kelly 1911 onwards; Salisbury Times 5/2/1892; information on Winterslow village website accessed December 2020; OS.

572 Kelly 1915, 1920 & 1927; OS; Salisbury Times 28/4/1893.

573 VCH10; HE 'red boxes'; information from owner, Stephen Campbell.

574 VCH6; OS.

575 VCH16; WCH; WBRB156; WSA1464/65.

576 VCH7; OS & 1840s tithe map; WSA1907/159 & 3939/2/27/6; 1851; information on the Anglican Catholic church in Wiltshire online parish clerks and Anglican Catholic websites, accessed May 2020.

577 VCH11; BoE2; photograph on HE 'red boxes'; MHC1823; North Wilts Herald 5/11/1878; information from Hilary Dunscombe.

578 VCH11; WSA2879/75; information on MyPM website, accessed July 2020.

579 VCH11; Swindon Advertiser & North Wilts Chronicle 22/11/1879; BoE2; information on MyPM website, accessed July 2020.

580 Information on MyPM website, including synod records from 1910 &

1932, accessed July 2020; OS.

581 Information from Paul Williams.

582 VCH15; WCH; WSA2755/73.

583 WCH; WBRB4934; OS.

584 WCH; Kelly 1895; 1851; information from owner.

585 WCH; OS; information on MyPM website accessed March 2020.

5. The Smaller Towns

586 WCH; church website accessed February 2020.

587 VCH15; BoE2; WSA1150/77 & 1150/79; Salisbury & Winchester Journal 5/10/1835; OS; photographs on Wiltshire online parish clerks website accessed February 2020.

588 VCH15; WSAG1/760/21; History and Description of a South Wiltshire Town – John Chandler & Peter Goodhugh, The Amesbury Society 2012.

589 VCH7; WRS1699/104; WRS8 – Andrews' & Dury's 1773 map of Wiltshire; Memories of Bradford on Avon, Bertram Sidney Niblett, Wiltshire Library and Museum Service 1981, p65; The Quakers of Melksham, Harold Fassnidge, Bradford on Avon Friends 1992; website of Quaker meeting houses heritage project, heritage.quaker.org.uk, accessed May 2020.

590 VCH7; WCH; Quaker meeting houses project op cit.

591 VCH7; WCH; HE; Stell; chapel history, undated, produced by the church; WBRB6786; WSA2544/13; Canon Jones in Wiltshire Archaeological & Natural History Magazine 1859.

592 VCH7; HE; 'Baptists in Bradford on Avon' by Robert W Oliver, Old Baptist Chapel, reprint 2005.

593 VCH7; WCH; HE; WSA3186/28 & 3186/30; WBRB4130; WA; old photographs from Roger Mawby.

594 VCH7; HE; WSA3901/1, 3909/13, 3909/19, 1418/9; WBRB1034.

595 VCH7; HE; WBRB7409; WSA2852/14.

596 VCH7; HE.

597 VCH7; WCH; HE; HE 'red boxes' photographs; Stell; WBRB1081.

598 VCH7; HE; WBRB152; Niblett op cit.

599   Grass.

600   VCH17.

601   VCH17; information on MyPM website, including 1920 history of Calne PM circuit, accessed June 2020; A History of The Borough and Town of Calne, A E W Marsh, 1903, chapter 12.

602   VCH17; HE; Stell; WSA854/15 & 854/44; Butler.

603   VCH17; Stell; BoE2; old photograph and information on Wiltshire online parish clerks website, accessed June 2020; photographs from Jenny & Stanley Woods; 'The History of Calne Baptist Church', George W Dixon, edited Anthony R Cross, published by the church 1995.

604   VCH17; HE; OS; Oliver.

605   VCH17; OS; Marsh op cit p177; information on MyPM website, including 1920 description of Calne PM circuit, accessed June 2020.

606   VCH17; WA; WSA3939/2/6/3; history on church website accessed June 2020.

607   VCH17; BoE; HE; Marsh op cit; church website accessed June 2020.

608   VCH17; OS; Grass; information from Sue Boddington of Calne Heritage Centre.

609   VCH17; Grass.

610   VCH17; OS; Grass.

611   Stell; HE; Butler; BoE2; WBRB7870; chapel website accessed January 2020.

612   WSA1699/104 & 854/44; MSS.808 at Wiltshire Museum; Butler; OS & 1840s tithe map; April 2015 article on the Goldney family on Corsham civic society website accessed January 2020.

613   Stell; HE; WCH; Stribling; BoE2; WBRB7842.

614   1851; OS; information from owner of Chapel House; Post Office directory for 1855 & Kelly, various 1915 to 1931.

615   WCH; HE; Stell; WBRB7843; Wiltshire Independent 4/6/1874; BoE2.

616   WBRB13585; WCH; Wiltshire Times 31/12/1997.

617   WCH; Oliver; WSA1458/7.

618   1851; OS & 1840s tithe map; Bath Chronicle 15/7/1933 records centenary; Wiltshire Times 23/10/1954.

619   'Corsham Methodist Church 1878-1978', Sam Killingback 1978, published by the church; WA; WSA1907/105, 3836/15 & 3836/16; Wiltshire Times 12/10/1878.

620   Primitive Methodist Magazine article, 1856, quoted on MyPM website accessed March2020; 1840s tithe map; WCH.

621   WCH; Grass; 1851; article in 'Precious Seed' magazine 2000, volume 55 issue 4; planning application to Wiltshire Council for conversion, decision August 2015.

622   VCH18; WA; OS; information from Pam Debenham of Cricklade Museum.

623   VCH18; OS; information from Pam Debenham of Cricklade Museum.

624   VCH18; WCH; BoE2; WSA1614/287.

625   VCH18; HE; WBRB9839; WSA2293/22; information from Pam Debenham of Cricklade Museum; Tonks; article from Primitive Methodist Magazine 1856 on MyPM website accessed March 2020.

626   VCH10.

627   VCH10; Butler; Stell; WSA854/44; Dore's map of Devizes, 1759.

628   Butler; Fassnidge op cit p132; BoE2; Quaker meeting houses heritage project on heritage.quaker.org.uk, accessed September 2020.

629   VCH10; OS.

630   VCH10; WCH; Stell; HE; WA; 1851; WSA100/26.

631   VCH10; Stell; Oliver; OS & 1840s tithe map; Dore's map of Devizes, 1759; WBRB5451; WSA1215/17 & 1215/20.

632   VCH10; 1851.

633   VCH10; HE; Oliver; Grass.

634   VCH10; HE; WA; 'Two Hundred Years New, The New Baptist Church, Devizes', John Hurley, published by the church 1996; WBRB78; WSA1270/22, 127024 & 1270/35; The Builder magazine May 1851; information from Christopher Sloane, church member.

635   VCH10; OS.

636   VCH10; WSA1907/113; BoE2; OS.

637   VCH10; OS.

638   VCH10; OS.

639   VCH10; WCH.

640   MHC1788; 1851; HE; WA; Stribling;

WSA3051/15; 'Highworth United Reformed Church, a short history', Elkington 2017, published by the church.

641 WBRB4225; OS; 1851; North Wilts Herald 6/10/1933; information in The National Gazetteer of Great Britain and Ireland, 1868, ed. Nesa Hamilton pub. J.S.Virtue.

642 1851; BoE2; 'Swindon Reminiscences', William Morris 1885 (Tabard Press facsimile edition 1970).

643 Article in Primitive Methodist Magazine October 1851 & extract from 1932 circuit description, both on MyPM website accessed November 2020; OS & 1840s tithe map; information from Christine Suter of Highworth Historical Society.

644 WSA1164/354; BoE2.

645 VCH14; WCH; OS; information on website of Wiltshire Freemasons accessed February 2021; 'Nonconformity in Malmesbury, a brief sketch of the history of the free churches of the town', G L Jenkins, Minister of Silver St Congregational Church, Spinke, Chippenham, 1895.

646 VCH14; WCH; ABC1; WSA1418/23 & 2672/1.

647 VCH14; HE; Oliver; Jenkins op cit.

648 VCH14; WCH; HE; Stell; Jenkins op cit; information from Athelstan Museum.

649 VCh14; WCH; WA; Jenkins op cit.

650 VCH14; WCH; Jenkins op cit; 'Malmesbury's Past, People and Places', Charles Vernon, Malmesbury Civic Trust 2014.

651 VCH14; OS; information on MyPM website accessed February 2021.

652 VCH12.

653 VCH12; Butler; MSS.2009 in Wiltshire Museum; Quaker meeting houses heritage project on heritage. quaker.org.uk, and note on Bangma on same website, accessed September 2020; BoE2.

654 VCH12; HE; Stell; WSA2194/25, 2194/36 & 2194/38; WRS27; 'The Congregational Chapel, Marlborough' by J W Gale, published by the church 1957; Wiltshire Gazette & Herald 22/10/2020;

cinema website accessed July 2021.

655 VCH12; OS.

656 VCH12; HE; BoE2; WSA1464/38.

657 VCH12; OS; 1851.

658 VCH12.

659 VCH12; Grass.

660 VCH12.

661 VCH12.

662 VCH7.

663 VCH7; Butler; Fassnidge op cit; Stell; HE; HE 'red boxes' photograph.

664 VCH7; WCH; HE; WA; WSA1647/29; 'History of the Church' – in frame in church vestibule, by Rev C B Fry, last minister.

665 VCH7; HE; Stell; WA; Oliver;'Broughton Road Baptist Church, Melksham, A Short History,' F W Cooper, Melksham and District Historical Association 1969; WSA3151/128; OS.

666 VCH7; HE; Oliver; history on church website ebenezerchurchmelksham.org, accessed March 2021.

667 VCH7; MHC1840; information from Peter Maslen of Melksham Historical Association; Cooper op cit.

668 VCH7; WRS27; BoE; HE; Stell; WA; WSA1907/16 & 3836/42; OS.

669 VCH7; WCH; OS; Wiltshire Times 29/7/1988; photograph from Peter Maslen.

670 VCH7; OS; old photograph from Peter Maslen.

671 VCH7; WSA3939/2/15/14, 3939/2/15/15 & 3939/2/15/18; Wiltshire Times 26/11/1904.

672 VCH7; WCH; information & photograph from Peter Maslen.

673 Information from chapel website, accessed September 2020.

674 Grass.

675 WCH; HE: 'The Book of Mere', Dr David Longbourne, Halsgrove 2004, p33; 'The story of Mere', (editing committee) Blackmore Press 1958.

676 WCH; Mere Papers No 8, 'Congregationalism in Mere' M F Tighe, Friends of church of St Michael the Archangel 1998; information from Mere Historical Society website, accessed April 2021; Stribling; Longbourne op cit; 'The

story of Mere' op cit.

677 As for first Congregational chapel.

678 As for first Congregational chapel; Western Gazette 21/1/1870; WA.

679 WCH; HE; BoE2; information from Mere Historical Society website, accessed April 2021; Longbourne op cit; information from Salisbury Civic Society website, accessed April 2021.

680 WCH; OS; Grass; Longbourne op cit.

681 WCH; 'The Story of Mere' op cit; HE; OS.

682 VCH9.

683 Information from Clive Carter; WSA2852/44; photographs and information on Wiltshire online parish clerks website accessed September 2020; BoE2; Swindon Advertiser 7/7/2014; OS.

684 Rev Dr Fuller in Stratton Outlook July 1990; information from Clive Carter; OS; information on Wiltshire online parish clerks website accessed September 2020.

685 MHC1839; information from Clive Carter; OS.

686 Information from Clive Carter; OS; ABC2; information from church website accessed September 2020; WSA2941/6, 2941/21 & 2941/23.

687 'Stratton in Camera', Rev Dr Fuller, Redbrick Publishing 1984; information from Clive Carter; WSA3299/48; website of the Chinese Christian Church accessed September 2020.

688 1851; Stell; Red Dr Fuller in Stratton Outlook, May 1998 & July 1999; information and photograph from Clive Carter; OS.

689 Information from Clive Carter; MyPM and Wiltshire online parish clerks websites, accessed September 2020; BoE2.

690 Rev Dr Fuller in Stratton Outlook, March 1992; information from Clive Carter; OS.

691 Rev Dr Fuller in Stratton Outlook, March 1992; information from Clive Carter; MyPM website, information including report of 1910 circuit synod, accessed September 2020; WSA1614/356 & 2293/43.

692 Rev Dr Fuller in Stratton Outlook,

March 1992; information from Clive Carter and Paul Williams; information on Wiltshire online parish clerks website accessed September 2020; information from the owner of 46 Hyde Road; OS.

693 VCH8.

694 VCH8; Stell; HE; 'The history of nonconformity in Warminster', Henry Mayo Gunn, first published 1853, 2003 edition by Bedeguar Books on behalf of Warminster and Wylye Valley Society for Local Study;.

695 VCH8; WCH; Stell; WSA2103/29 & 2103/33; WBRB3517; BoE2; Gunn op cit.

696 VCH8; OS; 'The Changing Face of Warminster', Wilfred Middlebrook, Wylye Valley Society for Local Study, revised edition 2003.

697 VCH8; HE; Stell; BoE2; WBRB720; Gunn op cit.

698 Oliver; OS; Warminster & Westbury Journal 6/10/1906; Kelly, various from 1889 to 1915; information from Andrew Jones of the Strict Baptist Historical Society.

699 VCH8; WBRB7495; photograph on church website, accessed August 2020.

700 VCH8; WBRB1037 & 7495; Gunn op cit; Dorset County Chronicle 14/2/1828; Wiltshire Times 23/11/1979.

701 VCH8; WCH; OS; MHC1842; 1851.

702 Grass.

703 VCH8.

704 VCH8; Butler; WSA854/44; information from Steve Hobbs.

705 VCH8; BoE3; WSA1418/36 & 2028M/1.

706 VCH8; WCH; Stell; HE.

707 VCH8; HE; Stell; Doel; appraisal by Alyson Curtis, April 2019, recorded on WBR website, accessed June 2020; Salisbury Journal 23/8/2012.

708 VCH8; Doel; WA; WSA3147/1 & 3147/2; WBRB3373; history on church website, accessed June 2020.

709 VCH8; OS; information from Rev. Ward Jones.

710 WCH; WA; information from Rev. Ward Jones; history on church website, accessed June 2020.

711 VCH6.

712 VCH6; Butler; OS; information from

Dr Rosalind Johnson; 'Chronology of Wilton', Edward Slow, published Wilton: Edward Slow, and Salisbury: R. R. Edwards, 1903.

713   VCH6; WCH.

714   VCH6; Stell; OS; 'The Book of Wilton', Chris Rousell, Halsgrove 2006.

715   VCH6; WBRB8995; history on church website, accessed April 2020.

716   VCH6; WCH; OS; WSA1150/257 & 1150/259; Rousell op cit.

717   VCH6; OS; Primitive Methodist Magazine 1838, pages 336/7.

718   VCH6; OS; BoE3; Rousell op cit.

719   WCH; HE; BoE2; WSA3381/90.

720   VCH9; WCH; HE; WSA1418/37 & 2673/15; history on church website, accessed November 2020.

721   VCH9; OS; photograph from Roger Smith of Wootton Bassett Museum.

722   VCH9; WCH; photograph from Roger Smith; OS.

723   VCH9; WCH; Tonks; WSA1571/64; history on MyPM website, accessed November 2020; history on church website (rwbmc.co.uk), accessed November 2020; photograph from Roger Smith.

6. Chippenham

724   VCH20 draft text.

725   VCH20 draft text; 'A History of Chippenham from Alfred to Brunel', Richard Baines, Chippenham Civic Society 2009, p133 et seq.

726   VCH20 draft text; WSA2269/44.

727   VCH20 draft text; HE; Stell; 'Chippenham, some notes on its history', J A Chamberlain, Chippenham Charter Trustees 1976, p143; information from Mike Stone.

728   VCH20 draft text; HE; Stell; 'Great is the Faithfulness – 200 years of God's Goodness at Chippenham', G D Buss, Old Baptist Chapel 2004; history on church website, accessed March 2021. Some sources give 1804 as the building date but the registration evidence (MHC1804 and 1810) makes it much more likely that 1810 was the date.

729   VCH20 draft text; OS; information and photograph from Mike Stone; WSA1418/13.

730   VCH20 draft text; HE; WA; WSA1112/139; 'Chippenham Then and Now', Mike Stone, The History Press 2011.

731   VCH20 draft; information from Mike Stone; Devizes & Wiltshire Gazette, 30/10 1890.

732   VCH20 draft text; Stell; HE; Baines op cit p135; OS.

733   VCH20 draft text; OS; BoE2; Chamberlain op cit.

734   VCH20 draft text; HE; WA; WSA1769/68; '100 Not out! Central Methodist Church Chippenham 1909-2009', Mike Sharp, 2009.

735   VCH20 draft text; HE; Butler; Stell; WA; WBTB6284; WSA137/91; information from Mike Stone.

736   VCH20 draft text; OS; Stone op cit.

737   VCH20 draft text; OS; WA.

738   VCH20 draft text; OS; information from Mike Stone.

739   VCH20 draft text; Grass; OS.

740   VCH20 draft text; WCH; 'A Work of God in the Ladyfield area of Chippenham', Ladyfield Evangelical Church, 2009.

741   VCH20 draft text; church website accessed September 2020.

742   WCH; OS; BoE2.

7. Salisbury

743   VCH6.

744   VCH6; Butler; Stell; OS; 'The rise and decline of Quakerism in south Wiltshire', Kay S Taylor, in Sarum Chronicle 10; 'Salisbury Quakers and their meeting houses', Sue Johnson, in Sarum Chronicle 10; 'Supplemental Sarum Chronology, 1881-1900', W A Wheeler, reprinted from Salisbury and Winchester Journal, Brown & Co Salisbury 1901.

745   Butler; WCH; HE; WA; information from Dr Rosalind Johnson; description on Quaker Heritage website, accessed May 2020.

746   VCH6; Stell; OS; WSA1150/194G; MHC1840; 'Ancient & Historical Monuments in the City of Salisbury', RCHME, HMSO 1977; 'History of

Salisbury United Reformed Church',
George Abel, undated but c1978
(MSS360 in Wiltshire Museum); entry
for Salisbury in online Dictionary of
Methodism, accessed May 2020.

747   VCH6; MHC1767 & 1790; Abel op
cit; OS.

748   VCH6; Wheeler op cit; OS.

749   VCH6; WCH; HE; WBRB5233; BoE2;
Wheeler op cit; 'Worthy of the age in
which we live: churches and chapels in
Salisbury', Trevor Cooper, in Ecclesiology
Today 36, December 2006.

750   Abel op cit; OS.

751   VCH6; BoE2; OS; Cooper op cit;
'Sarum Chronology', W A Wheeler,
Brown & Co Salisbury 1889, reprinted
from Salisbury and Winchester Journal.

752   VCH6; OS; Cooper op cit;
information from owner of 12 Mill Road.

753   WCH.

754   VCH6; HE; Stell; BoE2; Salisbury
& Winchester Journal 5/10/1835; HE
'red boxes' photograph; WSA1150/193 &
2485/64; Wheeler op cit (supplemental).
A suggestion in some records that it was
this chapel rather than Brown Street
Baptist which had the 'Egyptian style'
front in its previous form is not backed
up by the evidence of the print on which
this is depicted.

755   VCH6; WSAG23/701/1PC; VCH4;
Salisbury & Winchester Journal
7/5/1859; information from John
Chandler.

756   VCH6; HE; OS; WSA1150/96 &
2485/39; Wheeler op cit (supplemental).

757   VCH6; RCHME op cit; OS;
information from John Chandler.

758   VCH6; WSA1150/296; Cooper op cit;
information from John Chandler.

759   VCH6; WCH; BoE2; WSA1150/296,
1150/297 & 1150/303.

760   VCH6; WCH; OS; WSA1150/309;
Wheeler op cit (supplemental).

761   VCH6; WCH; HE; BoE2;
WBRB9987; photograph from Alan
Clarke of Salisbury Museum; Wheeler op
cit (supplemental).

762   WSA1150/453; OS.

763   VCH6; BoE2; WSA1150/86.

764   VCH6; WCH.

765   VCH6; 1851; RCHME op cit identifies
none of these premises.

766   VCH6; Grass; Cooper op cit; OS;
Kelly, various from 1875 to 1923.

767   VCH6; WCH; Grass; OS.

768   VCH6; OS; Kelly1927 & 1931.

769   Inspection.

770   VCH6; Grass.

771   WCH; BoE2.

772   VCH6; WCH; OS.

773   VCH6; inspection.

774   Referenced under the various
chapels.

775   History on church website, accessed
October 2020; photographs on Salisbury
Health Care History website, accessed
October 2020.

8. Swindon

776   VCH9.

777   VCH9.

778   VCH9; OS; MHC1804; 1851.

779   WSA2421/98; MHC1839; 1851.

780   VCH9.

781   VCH9; OS; WSA1614/251 &
1614/252; ABC2; Kelly 1889; Swindon
Advertiser 25/3/1861; 'Swindon in Old
Photographs volume 2', the Swindon
Society, History Press 1989, p74;
'Swindon Reminiscences', William
Morris 1885 (Tabard Press facsimile
edition 1970). The suggestion in some
sources that the second Planks chapel
was built on a new site next to the Old
Town brewery seems not to be supported
by the map and other evidence.

782   VCH9.

783   VCH9; Butler; Quaker Meeting
Houses Heritage Project website,
accessed January 2021.

784   VCH9; WSA1418/31 & 2421/41;
BoE2; 'A Century of Swindon', Brian
Bridgeman, Sutton, 2000; 'Swindon in
Camera, Peter Sheldon', self-published
1979.

785   VCH9; OS; Kelly 1895; information
from Hilary Dunscombe; information
from Clive Carter; WSA1472/36,
1472/39, 1472/41 & 1472/46; BoE2;
photograph in Swindon Society op cit
volume 4, 1993.

786   VCH9.

787 VCH9; OS; Oliver, 1851; information from Clive Carter.

788 VCH9; Swindon Society op cit volume 3, 1991; OS; Swindon Advertiser 4/4/2016.

789 VCH9; WA; OS; WBRB9115; Swindon Society op cit volume 3; 'Swindon, the legacy of a railway town', John Cattell and Keith Falconer, RCHME 1995; Hilary Dunscombe in 'Swindon Heritage', autumn 2013.

790 VCH9; HE; BoE2; WBRB4982; information from Tom Smith; OS.

791 VCH9; WA; 'Swindon Heritage' winter 2016.

792 VCH9; BoE2; photographs in HE 'red boxes'; information from Hilary Dunscombe; 'The Swindon Baptist Tabernacle, a history', Sheila and David Pope, published by the church 1977.

793 WSA1376/126; OS; Swindon Advertiser 13/1/1905; 'Footprints of Faith' a history of Central Church Swindon, Hilary Dunscombe, published by the Central Church 1988.

794 VCH9; OS; church history recorded on Wiltshire online parish clerks website, accessed January 2021.

795 VCH9; Pope op cit; OS.

796 VCH9; OS; BoE2; Morris op cit; WSA1614/237 & 1614/238; Swindon Society op cit volume 4.

797 VCH9; Cattell & Falconer op cit; HE; WSA1614/245 & 2879/65.

798 VCH9; information from Clive Carter; information on Wiltshire online parish clerks website accessed January 2021.

799 VCH9; HE; BoE2; WSA1614/120; 1880 – 1980, 'History of Bath Road Methodist Church Swindon', E R Carter, published by the church 1981; history on church website accessed January 2021.

800 VCH9; OS; WA.

801 VCH9; OS; WSA1614/266 & 1614/267; information from John Hacker & Paul Williams.

802 VCH9; OS; Dunscombe op cit; North Wilts Herald 13/6/1884; WSA1614/177.

803 WSA1614/256 & 1614/257; OS.

804 VCH9; BoE2; 'Swindon Heritage' summer 2013; article on central halls on Dictionary of Methodism website accessed January 2021; WSA1614/179, 1614/189 & 2293/57; historic aerial photograph in Swindon Advertiser 13/1/2009.

805 VCH9; OS; MHC1849; BoE2; WSA1614/407; information from Clive Carter.

806 VCH9; BoE2; OS.

807 VCH9; OS; BoE2; Fletcher's Directory of Swindon 1967; WSA2293/61; information from Tom Smith.

808 VCH9; OS; WSA1614/348; photograph in Swindon Libraries collection.

809 VCH9; ABC2; BoE2; WSA4045/2/5/2; history and photographs from Rodbourne History website accessed January 2021.

810 VCH9; WSA4043/8/6; 1910 Primitive Methodist synod recorded on MyPM website accessed January 2021; information from Tom Smith.

811 VCH9; OS; 1910 Primitive Methodist synod recorded on MyPM website accessed January 2021.

812 VCH9; OS; website of the Redeemed Christian Church of God accessed January 2021; information from Tom Smith & Katherine Cole.

813 OS; WSA1614/418; 1910 Primitive Methodist synod recorded on MyPM website, with chapel photograph, accessed January 2021.

814 VCH9; OS; BoE2; WSA4045/2/4/1.

815 VCH9; BoE2; WSA3299/40, 3299/41a, 3299/43; information on MyPM website accessed January 2021.

816 VCH9; WSA2518/27; 1910 Primitive Methodist synod recorded on MyPM website accessed January 2021; Bridgeman op cit.

817 Grass; OS; Kelly, various from 1889 to 1931; information from Katherine Cole.

818 Grass; VCH9; OS; history on plymouthbrethren.org accessed January 2021; information from Paul Williams of the Swindon Society; ''These many years' A retrospect of 56 years of the Lord's leading, and a brief survey of the early

days of the Open Brethren in Swindon and District', William Hooper, publisher unknown, 1939.

819   Grass; VCH9; OS; history on plymouthbrethren.org accessed January 2021; information from Paul Williams; Hooper op cit; photograph in Swindon Libraries collection.

820   Information & photographs from John Hacker; information from Paul Williams; OS.

821   VCH9; Grass; OS; information from Paul Williams.

822   VCH9; OS; Wiltshire online parish clerks for Stratton St Margaret accessed February 2021.

823   VCH9; information from Katherine Cole; 'Central Swindon through time', Mark Child, Amberley 2013; information from Clive Carter.

824   VCH9; OS; information from Clive Carter.

825   VCH9; WSA2728/25; WBRB8960; information from Hilary Dunscombe.

826   VCH9; BoE2; OS; photograph in Swindon Library collection; 'Church of the Charlatan', article by Barry Leighton in Swindon Advertiser 20/4/2016.

827   VCH9; BoE2; OS; Leighton op cit.

828   OS; BoE2.

829   VCH9; OS; ABC2.

830   VCH9; photograph in Swindon Library collection; information from Tom Smith.

831   VCH9; WSA2926/13MS; WA; 'Swindon Heritage', winter 2013, article by Hilary Dunscombe; information from Hilary Dunscombe.

832   Grass; North Wilts Herald 24/8/1900; OS.

833   VCH9; WSA2421/80MS & 2421/83.

834   Inspection; modern town plans.

835   VCH9; WSA2293/63 & 2293/64; WA.

836   VCH9; WSA1614/417 & 2785/26.

837   VCH9; WSA2518/42; information about current use from Clive Carter.

838   History on church website accessed February 2021.

839   Information from Paul Williams.

840   Information from Paul Williams.

841   Inspection.

842   Grass; inspection.

843   VCH9; information from Clive Carter.

844   OS; BoE2; information from Clive Carter.

845   See references for that building.

846   VCH9; WSA3127/1.

847   VCH9.

848   Information on church website accessed February 2021.

849   VCH9; information on church website accessed February 2021.

850   BoE2.

851   BoE2.

852   Information on church website accessed February 2021.

853   VCH9; WSA2421/95; information from Paul Williams.

854   BoE2; information from Hilary Dunscombe.

855   VCH9; OS; BoE2; information from Katherine Cole.

856   WSA2879/67; information from church website accessed February 2021.

9. Trowbridge

857   not used

858   VCH7.

859   VCH7; Butler; WCH.

860   VCH7; Stell; OS; WSA1025/1; Wiltshire Times 7/4/1928; history of Farleigh Hungerford castle on English Heritage website, accessed April 2021; photographs from Nikki Ritson of Trowbridge Museum.

861   VCH7; HE; BoE2; WSA 1417/168, 1417/169, 1417/172 & 1417/173; WBRB1403; Wiltshire Times 5/6/2015 & 29/4/2016; development assessment by HPS Archaeological Services on behalf of F W Beresford-Smith & Partners March 2018.

862   VCH7; HE & HE 'red boxes' photographs; Doel; Hague; WBRB1530; WSA1241/39 & 1476/29; Wiltshire Times 15/8/1986 & 1//1988.

863   VCH7; HE; Doel; WSA3297/21.

864   VCH7; HE; Doel; WSA2695/1.

865   VCH7; Doel; OS.

866   VCH7; HE; OS; WBRB2550.

867   VCH7; BoE2; Wiltshire Times 27/3/1931.

868 VCH7; Doel; OS.

869 WCH; OS; information from David Broome of the church; history on church website, accessed April 2021.

870 VCH7; OS; information from Roger Newman; Wiltshire Times 23/9/1876.

871 VCH7; OS; information from Roger Newman; Wiltshire Times 21/10/1922.

872 VCH7; HE; Stell; OS; 'Wesleyan Methodism in Trowbridge', Edward Dyer 1862 (with later entries to 1877), copy at WSA71/5; photograph in 'Trowbridge Through Time', Andrew Jones & Kevin Hartley, Amberley 2009; 'The Bowyers site in Trowbridge', Ken Rogers, Trowbridge Museum 2009.

873 VCH7; Stell; Dyer op cit; WBRB535; HE 'red boxes' photographs; WSA1417/195; Wiltshire Times 28/5/1971.

874 VCH7; Dyer op cit; Trowbridge Advertiser 8/9/1860; WSA1904/30; Kelly 1867 & 1889; Wiltshire Times 6/4/1861, 14/10/1905, 23/3/1935 & 13/3/1948.

875 VCH7; Dyer op cit; OS; WBRB3124; WSA1103/137; Wiltshire Times 17/9/1881 & 14/7/1900.

876 MHC1843; OS; information from Nikki Ritson of Trowbridge Museum.

877 VCH7;'The perfect rule of the Christian religion, Sandemanianism in the 18th century', John Howard Smith, State University of New York 2008, p86;'Michael Faraday, Sandemanian and scientist', Geoffrey Cantor, Macmillan 1991, p107.

878 VCH7; WCH.

879 WCH; OS; information from Roger Newman; Wiltshire Times 13/3/1948.

880 VCH7; WCH; Grass; Kelly 1898, 1903 & 1907; OS; WSAG15/150/138.

881 VCH7; ABC1; OS; Grass; information from Roger Newman. The VCH suggests 1900 for construction date but the 1924 date given by ABC1 is backed up by OS evidence.

882 VCH7; information from Roger Newman; Trowbridge Chronicle 1/9/1888.

10. Chapel Architects

883 All data in the list is derived from ABC1, ABC2 and WA except where otherwise indicated.

884 See for example the website georgebainesarchitect.wordpress.com, accessed July 2021.

885 BoE2.

886 North Wilts Herald 13/6/1884.

887 Butler.

888 WSA2919/26.

889 Kelly 1903.

890 BoE2.

891 WBR – notes by Clive Carter, January 2020.

892 Salisbury Times, 2/11/1894.

893 Salisbury and Winchester Journal, 20/10/1900.

894 WSA1150/79.

895 WSA1150/86.

896 Church History, locally produced.

897 VCH9.

898 WSA2928/28.

899 WSA1614/287.

900 WSA1614/179.

901 VCH9.

902 WSA3299/40.

903 WSA2785/26.

904 BoE2.

905 WSA1614/256.

906 WSA1150/77.

907 BoE2.

908 Salisbury and Winchester Journal 5/10/1835.

909 Western Gazette 13/11/1896.

910 Information from Paul Hooper of the Swindon Society, January 2021.

911 VCH9.

912 Unpublished database of Somerset architects by Julian Orbach.

913 BoE2.

914 BoE2.

915 BoE2.

916 BoE2.

917 BoE2.

918 BoE2.

919 Devizes and Wiltshire Gazette 31/3/1870.

920 BoE2.

921 BoE2.

922 WSA951/204.

923 WSA951/204.

924 'Sheep Bell and Ploughshare', Marjorie Reeves, Moonraker Press, Bradford-on-Avon 1978.

925 BoE2.

926 Devizes and Wiltshire Gazette 24/10/1899.

927 WSA1418/9.

928 VCH9.

929 VCH7.

930 Trowbridge Advertiser 8/9/1860.

931 BoE2.

932 Doel.

933 BoE2.

934 WSA3939/2/15/14.

935 Mere Papers No 8, 'Congregationalism in Mere', M F Tighe 1998, Friends of church of St Michael the Archangel. (But there appears to be no other source for this attribution).

936 BoE2.

937 BoE2.

938 BoE2.

939 '100 not out: the Central Methodist Church, Chippenham 1909-2009', Mike Sharp 2009, published by the church.

940 'Collingbourne Kingston, a photographic view', Mary May, Manor Acre 2003.

941 See for example the online Dictionary of Methodism, accessed July 2021.

942 WSA1614/238.

943 VCH13.

944 Rev. Dr. Fred Fuller, writing in 'Stratton Outlook' May 1998.

945 Salisbury and Winchester Journal 20/11/1869.